Course Student Guide

to accompany

Child Development
Stepping Stones

Fourth Edition

Richard O. Straub

The course ***Child Development: Stepping Stones*** is produced by the Coast Community College District, and KOCE-TV, Channel 50 in cooperation with Worth Publishers.

Distributed by:

Coast Learning Systems
Coastline Community College
11460 Warner Avenue
Fountain Valley, California 92708
phone: 800-547-4748 • fax 714-241-6286
e-mail: CoastLearning@coastline.edu
web site: **www.CoastLearning.org**

Published by Worth Publishers
The Worth Publishers logo is a trademark used herein under license.

Printed in the United States of America

ISBN-10: 1-4292-5244-8
ISBN-13: 978-1-4292-5244-7

Worth Publishers
41 Madison Avenue
New York, NY 10010
www.worthpublishers.com

Contents

Introduction

To the Student

Welcome to ***Child Development: Stepping Stones***. This course has been designed to cover the concepts, vocabulary, and subjects that are typical of an on-campus, college-level child development course. This course presents the development process in three distinct categories or domains—biosocial, cognitive, and psychosocial.

While most children achieve developmental milestones, each child will take his or her own unique path. The twenty-six half-hour video lessons feature an assortment of real-life examples, historical footage, and an array of subject-matter experts. Throughout this course we will emphasize how the development principles you will be learning can be used to improve the quality of your everyday life, as well as those around you.

As with any college-level course, this course has a textbook, a student guide, assignments, and tests. In lieu of classroom lectures, however, you will be watching half-hour video programs. The designers, academic advisors, and producers have created an engaging and comprehensive course that will entertain you as you learn about the fascinating field of child development.

Course Components

Student Guide

The course student guide is an integral part of this course. Think of this guide as your "road map." It gives you a starting point for each lesson, as well as directions and exercises that will help you successfully navigate your way through the course. Reading this guide will provide you with the information that you normally would receive in the classroom if you were taking this course on campus. Each lesson in this course student guide includes the following components:

- **Preview:** An overview of the lesson that informs you of the importance of the subject you are about to study and gives you a brief snapshot of the upcoming video lesson.
- **Prior Knowledge That Will Be Used in This Lesson:** A list of concepts, theories, terms, and other knowledge presented in previous lessons that you should recall in order to prepare for the current lesson.
- **Learning Objectives:** Your instructional goals for the lesson, which will guide your reading, viewing, thinking, and studying. Upon completing each lesson, you should be able to satisfy each of the learning objectives. (Hint: Instructors often develop test questions directly from learning objectives.)

- **Textbook Reading & Video Viewing:** Description of page numbers and sections in the textbook that should be read for each lesson, along with instructions on which video lesson to view and the names of each segment within the video lesson.
- **Practice Questions:** These self-test questions (multiple-choice and true/false questions) help you review and master basic facts and definitions presented in each lesson.
- **Applying Your Knowledge:** These self-test questions (multiple-choice) help you evaluate your understanding of the lesson's broader and conceptual material and its application to real-world situations.
- **Summary:** A summary of the lesson—to be read after reading the textbook and viewing the video lesson—that clarifies key points.
- **Key Terms:** Much of education is learning the meaning of new terms, and concepts. It is important to be able to define each of the key terms and concepts for each lesson.
- **Answer Key:** Answers to the self-test questions are conveniently located at the end of each lesson so that you can get immediate feedback. The answers reference the learning objective the question covers, as well as segments in the video lesson where the information is presented. After completing the self-test questions, be sure to check the Answer Key to make sure you correctly understand the material.
- **Lesson Review:** This chart has been designed to act as a study tool to help you achieve each learning objective. It lists pages in the textbook, segments in the video lesson, and sections in the course student guide where you can find more information on each objective. Use this tool to master concepts and skills that you feel are your weak points.

Textbook

The recommended textbook for this course is *The Developing Person Through Childhood and Adolescence*, ninth edition, by Kathleen Stassen Berger (Worth Publishers, 2012). In much the same way as the course lessons, the textbook is complete with real-life stories—some funny, some dramatic, others quite personal. This textbook allows you to learn about child development by observing and hearing about the lives of real, ordinary people. You will repeatedly discover how the field of child development can enrich the lives of anyone who takes the time to study human change and behavior.

Video Lessons

Each of the video lessons features a real-life situation—a story line that will help you recognize and appreciate how development affects the lives of ordinary people. The award-winning producers and directors at Coast Learning Systems have brought together top professionals from various fields of psychology to help explain different aspects of child development.

Review and Study from the Video Lesson Transcripts

These transcripts, a printed copy of the audio track from each video lesson, are available as PDF files at www.CoastTranscripts.org (user name: development; password: coastkids2). The PDF files may be viewed online or printed for use as an additional study aid. You will need Adobe Reader (which is available free of charge on the Internet) to view these files, and we have provided a link to Adobe Reader on the transcript website.

How to Take a Distance Learning Course

If this is your first experience with a distance learning course, welcome. Distance learning courses are designed for busy people whose schedules do not permit them to take a traditional on-campus college course.

This guide is designed to help you study effectively and learn the material presented in both the textbook and the video lessons. To complete a distance learning course successfully, you will need to schedule sufficient time to watch each lesson, read the textbook, and study the materials outlined in this guide. In conjunction with your instructor, this guide will provide you with:

- directions on how to take this course.
- study recommendations.
- a preview for each lesson.
- a set of learning objectives for each lesson.
- a list of key terms and concepts for each lesson.
- several different types of study activities and self-tests for each lesson.

The course student guide is a complement to the textbook and the video lessons. It is not a substitute. You will not be able to complete this course successfully unless you purchase and read the textbook, watch the video program—and study. By following the instructions in this guide, you should be able to easily master the learning objectives for each lesson.

To complete this course successfully, you will need to:

- contact your instructor to find about any course requirements, time lines, meetings, and scheduled exams.
- purchase a copy of the course textbook.
- read and study the textbook.
- view each video lesson in its entirety.
- understand the key terms and concepts presented in this guide.
- be able to satisfy the learning objectives for each lesson.
- complete the self-tests.
- complete any additional assignments your instructor may require.

Even though you do not have a scheduled class to attend each week, please keep in mind that this is a college-level course. You will not be able to "look at some of the videos" or "just scan the text" and pass this course. It is important that you schedule sufficient time to watch, read, study, and reflect. While taking a distance learning course provides you the convenience of not having to meet at a prearranged time, do not make the mistake of not scheduling enough time to complete the work and study. All learning demands a good measure of self-discipline. Unless you put in the effort, take the time to study, and think about what you are learning, you will not learn.

Try your best to keep up with your work. It is very difficult to catch up if you allow yourself to get a few weeks behind schedule. We strongly recommend that you set aside specific times each week for viewing, reading, and studying. You will do better and will be more likely to succeed if you make a study schedule and stick to that schedule. When you watch the video lessons, try to do so without any interruptions. Each video lesson is approximately thirty minutes long. If you are interrupted during your viewing time, you may miss an important point. If possible, take some time immediately after watching the video program to reflect on what you have just viewed. This is an excellent time to discuss the video lesson with a friend or family member. Remember that your active involvement promotes your success.

It is our goal to give you a good, basic understanding of the field of child development. This course will provide you with all the basic information required for a college-level introductory class in child development.

Minds are like parachutes; they only function when open.

—Thomas R. Dewar

And, don't forget to always check with your instructor. He or she will explain the specific course requirements for your assigned class. We sincerely hope you enjoy your introduction to the discipline of child development.

Study Recommendations

Everyone has his or her own unique learning style. Some people learn best by reading alone the first thing each morning, others by discussing ideas with a group of friends, still others by listening to experts and taking notes. While there is no "best" way to learn, psychologists and educators have identified several things you can do that will help you study and learn more effectively.

One of the advantages of distance learning is that you have many choices in how you learn and study. You can tailor this course to fit your "best" way to learn. Below are several study tips. These are proven methods that will help you learn and retain what you are studying. Please take the time to read through this list. You will discover that by using one or more of these techniques you can significantly improve your ability to learn and remember new information.

Open your mind: One of the major obstacles to learning new information is that new information often differs from what we already "know." For example, if you believe that obesity is caused by depression, it will be difficult for you to learn about new information that reveals that there is no cause-and-effect relationship between obesity and depression. To learn, you need to have an open mind. We are not suggesting you simply believe everything you are told. We want you to think critically about what you are told. However, be cautious and guard against letting old beliefs or opinions stop you from learning anything new.

Reduce interference: One of the major reasons for forgetting information is that new information interferes with other information. When you are studying more than one subject at a time, you are increasing the likelihood of interference occurring. If possible, try to study one thing at a time. If you must take multiple subjects, try to take courses with very different subjects, such as art and psychology or math and history. For example, it would not be a good idea to take Child Development and Introduction to Psychology during the same semester. Of course, visiting with friends, watching television, listening to the radio, or any distraction while you are studying will also interfere with your ability to learn new information. When you engage in these types of activities during or just after studying, you risk letting the information you have just learned interfere with other information. Give yourself time to absorb new information.

Don't cram: You probably already know that staying up all night cramming for an exam the following morning is not a good way to study. The opposite of cramming is, in fact, one of the best ways to study. Spacing out your studying into smaller and more frequent study periods will improve retention. Instead of studying for six hours in one evening, you will learn more and retain more if you study one hour per night for six nights.

Reduce stress: In addition to being bad for your health, stress is bad for learning. Stress and anxiety interfere with learning. You will learn more and enjoy it more if you are relaxed when you study. One of the most effective ways of relaxing that does not interfere with learning is exercise. A good brisk walk or run before you settle in to study is a good prescription for success. Ideally, you would study some, take a break, then get some exercise while you think about what you have just learned. And later, when you are relaxed, return and study some more.

Be a Smart Student: Most top students have one thing in common. They all have excellent study habits. Students who excel have learned, or were fortunate enough to have someone teach them, how to study effectively. There is no magic formula for successful studying. However, there are a few universal guidelines.

Do make a commitment to yourself to learn.

Don't let other people interrupt you when you are studying.

Do make a study schedule and stick to it.

Don't study when you are doing something else, like watching television.

Do create a specific place to study.

Don't study if you are tired, upset, or overly stressed.

Do exercise and relax before you study.

Don't study for extended periods of time without taking a break.

Do give yourself ample time to study.

Don't complain that you have to go study.

Do take a positive approach to learning.

Make the most of your assignments: You will master this material more effectively if you make a commitment to completing all your assignments. The lessons will make more sense to you, and you will learn more, if you follow these instructions:

- Set aside a specific time to view, read, and study each lesson.
- Before you view each video lesson, read the Preview and Learning Objectives outlined in this guide.
- Read the assigned textbook pages for the lesson you are studying.
- View the video lesson.
- Review the Key Terms. Check your understanding of all unfamiliar terms in the glossary notes in the textbook.
- Complete the Practice Questions for each lesson.

Think about what you have learned: You are much more likely to remember new information if you use it. Remember that learning is not a passive activity. Learning is active. As soon as you learn something, try to repeat it to someone or discuss it with a friend. If you will think about what you just learned, you will be much more likely to retain that information. The reason we remember certain information has to do mostly with (1) how important that information is to us, and (2) whether or not we actively use the information. For example, if you suffer from headaches and the textbook or video is discussing various headache remedies, this information will be valuable to you. Because of your personal interest in this subject, you will have little difficulty remembering this information. What do you do, however, when you need to learn some information that is not personally valuable or interesting to you? The best way to remember this type of information is to reinforce it—and the best reinforcer is actively using the information.

Get feedback on what you are studying: Study alone, learn with others. You need feedback to help reinforce learning. Also, feedback helps make sure you correctly understand the information. The study activities and self-tests in this guide are specifically designed to give you feedback and reinforce what you are learning. The more time and practice you devote to learning, the better you will be at remembering that information. When you take a self-test, make sure you immediately check your answers with the answer key. Don't wait and check your answers later. If you miss a question, review that section of the textbook to reinforce the correct understanding of the material.

A good gauge of how well you understand some information is your ability to explain that information to another person. If you are unable to explain some term or concept to a friend, you probably will need to review and study that term or concept further.

Contact your instructor: If you are having an especially difficult time with learning some information, contact your instructor. Your instructor is there to help you. Often a personal explanation will do wonders in helping you clear up a misunderstanding. Your instructor wants to hear from you and wants you to succeed. Don't hesitate to call, write, e-mail, or visit your instructor.

Some students do better with study groups; others do better studying alone. If study groups are helpful to you, let your instructor know of your preference. However, be aware that study groups are not a substitute for studying alone. Study groups often turn into friendly chats and not much actually gets learned. So, remember that study groups are not a substitute for individual effort.

Learn it well: Retention is the key to long-term knowledge. One of the best methods to increase your retention is to overlearn material. It is a common mistake to think that just because you can answer a question or give a brief definition of a term or concept, you really know and will remember that term or concept. Think back about how many things you have already "learned." How much do you really remember? Much of what we learn is quickly forgotten. If you want to really learn some information, learn it in a way that you will not forget it—overlearn it.

Overlearning is simple. After you have learned a fact or new word, spend an additional ten or fifteen minutes actively reviewing that fact or word. You will be amazed how much this will increase your long-term retention.

Enjoy learning: You do not need to suffer to learn. In fact, the opposite is true. You will learn more if you enjoy learning. If you have the attitude that "I hate to study" or "schoolwork is boring," you are doing yourself a real disservice.

You will to progress better and learn more if you adopt a positive attitude about learning and studying. Since you are choosing to learn, you will be well served by also choosing to enjoy the adventure.

We are sure you will enjoy ***Child Development: Stepping Stones.***

Acknowledgments

Several of the individuals responsible for the creation of this course are listed on the copyright page of this book. In addition, appreciation is expressed for these contributions:

Members of the National Advisory Committee

The following gifted scholars, professionals, and teachers helped focus the approach and content of the video lessons, faculty manual, and course student guide to ensure accuracy, academic validity, accessibility, significance, and instructional integrity.

Pauline Abbott, Ed.D., California State University, Fullerton
Mary Belcher, M.A., Orange Coast College
Joyce Bishop, Ph.D., Golden West College
Fredda Blanchard-Fields, Ph.D., Georgia Institute of Technology
Michael Catchpole, Ph.D., R. Psych., North Island College, British Columbia, Canada
Chuansheng Chen, Ph.D., University of California, Irvine
Donald Cusumano, Ph.D., St. Louis Community College
Linda Flickinger, M.A., St. Clair County Community College
Andrea R. Fox, M.D., M.P.H., University of Pittsburgh and VA Pittsburgh Healthcare System
Ellen Greenberger, Ph D., University of California, Irvine
Jutta Heckhausen, Ph.D., University of California, Irvine
Sally Hill, M.A., Bakersfield College
Sandra J. McDonald, M.S., Sierra College
Mary K. Rothbart, Ph.D., University of Oregon
Susan Siaw, Ph.D., California State Polytechnic University, Pomona
Barbara W. K. Yee, Ph.D., University of South Florida
Judy Yip, Ph.D., University of Southern California
Elizabeth Zelinski, Ph.D., University of Southern California

Lead Academic Advisors

Amy Himsel, M.A., University of California, Irvine
Doug Hughey, M.A., Mt. San Antonio College
Jeanne Ivy, M.S., L.P.A., Tyler Community College
Phyllis Lembke, M.A., Coastline Community College
Robert D. Nash, M.S., Ed., Coast Learning Systems

Course Production Team

Vanessa Chambers, Jason Daley, Sharon Dymmel, Liz Ervin, Jim Jackson, Becky Koppenhaver, Alejandro Lopez, Dorothy McCollom, Laurie R. Melby, Salma Montez, Evelyn Moore, Harry Ratner, Greg Rogers, Mike Rust, Wendy Moulton-Tate, Charlie Powell, and the many other talented people who helped make the programs.

Special thanks to Sharon Prevost and the many other able and supportive individuals at Worth Publishers. Also, we appreciate the efforts of Gabrielle Ridley, who helped update this revised fourth edition of the student guide.

The Developing Person

Lesson 1

Introduction:
Theories of Development

Preview

The first lesson of this course introduces the **science of human development**, beginning with the characteristics of development, a description of the scope of the field, and an overview of the major **developmental theories** that have guided research over the past century. A philosopher once said that "nothing is more practical than a good theory," and such has proven to be the case in developmental psychology. Theories help psychologists organize large amounts of information, and focus their research on specific, testable ideas about development.

Several major themes are introduced in this lesson that will be woven throughout the course, including the idea that development is influenced as much by external factors as by internal factors. This theme, framed initially by philosophers many years ago, continues to drive the field today as researchers weigh the relative contributions of biological factors (such as heredity) and environmental factors (such as learning) in development. These complex interactions are often described as the effects of *nature* and *nurture*.

The impact of external factors on development is revealed in the many contexts in which development occurs, especially the context of social relationships. And therein lies a second theme: Each of us as individuals is affected by other individuals (such as family members and friends); groups of individuals (such as the neighbors and fellow community members); and larger systems in the environment (such as ethnicity and culture.) In turn, we affect other people and our environment by our own decisions and actions.

A third theme of the lesson and course is that development is a lifelong process. Although some early theorists believed that our personalities and fates are fully shaped by the end of childhood, developmental psychologists today recognize that people continue to grow and change until the day they die.

As you complete this lesson (and all the lessons in this course), consider your own development. What factors have combined to create the person you are today? Study your immediate family members and note any genetic similarities. Think about your physical growth as a child and recall anything that might have affected that development. Recall your intellectual growth and school experiences. Consider your upbringing at home, your circle of friends, and romantic relationships. How have they influenced you? As you learn more in this lesson about the theories which developmentalists use, consider how these theories might help explain the changes you've experienced over time.

Learning Objectives

Use this information to guide your reading, viewing, thinking, and studying. After successfully completing this lesson, you should be able to:

1. Define the study of human development and discuss some of its major themes.
2. Describe the three major domains of human development and discuss how they interrelate.
3. Describe the many contexts and systems that can affect a person's development, and discuss how they are interrelated.
4. Identify the characteristics of development described by the life-span perspective.
5. Define developmental theory, and describe how theories help explain human behavior and guide researchers who study development.
6. Discuss the major focus of psychoanalytic theory, contrasting the psychosexual development proposed by Freud with the psychosocial development described by Erikson.
7. Discuss the major focus of behaviorism, and explain the basic principles of classical and operant conditioning as well as social learning theory.
8. Discuss the major focus of cognitive theory, summarize Piaget's stages of cognitive development, and describe the information processing perspective.
9. Discuss the basic ideas of Vygotsky and the sociocultural theory of development.
10. Discuss the basic ideas of the universal perspective, including both humanism and evolutionary theory.
11. Summarize the contributions and criticisms of the major developmental theories, and compare the position of the theories regarding three controversies of development.

Textbook Reading & Video Viewing

For the most effective study of this lesson, complete the assignments in the sequence listed below.

Before viewing the video program:

Read Chapter 1, "Introduction," pages 3–21; and Chapter 2, "Theories" pages 35–61.

View the video for Lesson 1, "The Developing Person."

Segment 1: *Contexts and Systems*

Segment 2: *Theories of Development*

Segment 3: *The Life-Span Perspective*

After viewing the video program:

Review all reading assignments for this lesson.

Complete the "Practice Questions" and "Applying Your Knowledge" sections to reinforce your understanding of important terms and concepts and measure your achievement of the Learning Objectives. Check your answers with the feedback given and review when necessary.

Practice Questions I

Multiple-Choice Questions

1. The science of human development is defined as the study of
   a. how and why people change or remain the same over time.
   b. psychosocial influences on aging.
   c. individual differences in learning over the life span.
   d. all of the above.

2. The cognitive domain of development includes
   a. perception.
   b. thinking.
   c. language.
   d. all of the above.

3. Changes in height, weight, and bone thickness are part of the ____________________ domain.
   a. cognitive
   b. biosocial
   c. psychosocial
   d. physical

4. Psychosocial development focuses primarily on personality, emotions, and
   a. intellectual development.
   b. sexual maturation.
   c. relationships with others.
   d. perception.

5. The ecological-systems approach to developmental psychology focuses on the
   a. biochemistry of the body systems.
   b. cognitive domain only.
   c. internal thinking processes.
   d. many environments in which development takes place.

6. Researchers who take a life-span perspective on development focus on
   a. the sources of continuity from the beginning of life to the end.
   b. the sources of discontinuity throughout life.
   c. the "nonlinear" character of human development.
   d. all of the above.
7. The notion that human traits can be molded into different forms and shapes and yet people maintain a certain durability of identity is referred to as
   a. linear change.
   b. plasticity.
   c. a butterfly effect.
   d. eclectic.
8. A developmentalist who is interested in studying the influences of a person's immediate environment on his or her behavior is focusing on which system?
   a. mesosystem
   b. macrosystem
   c. microsystem
   d. exosystem
9. Socioeconomic status (SES) is determined by a combination of variables, including
   a. age, education, and income.
   b. income, ethnicity, and occupation.
   c. income, education, and occupation.
   d. age, ethnicity, and occupation.
10. The purpose of a developmental theory is to
    a. provide a broad and coherent view of the complex influences on human development.
    b. offer guidance for practical issues encountered by parents, teachers, and therapists.
    c. generate testable hypotheses about development.
    d. do all of the above.
11. Which developmental theory emphasizes the influence of unconscious drives and motives on behavior?
    a. psychoanalytic
    b. learning
    c. cognitive
    d. sociocultural

12. Which of the following is the correct order of the psychosexual stages proposed by Freud?
    a. oral stage; anal stage; phallic stage; latency; genital stage
    b. anal stage; oral stage; phallic stage; latency; genital stage
    c. oral stage; anal stage; genital stage; latency; phallic stage
    d. anal stage; oral stage; genital stage; latency; phallic stage
13. Erikson's psychosocial theory of human development describes
    a. eight crises all people are believed to face.
    b. four psychosocial stages and a latency period.
    c. the same number of stages as Freud's, but with different names.
    d. a stage theory that is not psychoanalytic.
14. An American psychologist who explained complex human behaviors in terms of operant conditioning was
    a. Lev Vygotsky.
    b. Ivan Pavlov.
    c. B. F. Skinner.
    d. Jean Piaget.
15. Pavlov's dogs learned to salivate at the sound of a bell because they associated the bell with food. Pavlov's experiment with dogs was an early demonstration of
    a. classical conditioning.
    b. operant conditioning.
    c. positive reinforcement.
    d. social learning.
16. The nature-nurture controversy considers the degree to which traits, characteristics, and behaviors are the result of
    a. early or lifelong learning.
    b. genes or heredity.
    c. heredity or experience.
    d. different historical concepts of childhood.
17. Modeling, an integral part of social learning theory, is so called because it
    a. follows the scientific model of learning.
    b. molds character.
    c. follows the immediate reinforcement model developed by Albert Bandura.
    d. involves people's patterning their behavior after that of others.

18. Which developmental theory suggests that all people have the same basic wants and needs?

    a. sociocultural
    b. cognitive
    c. behaviorism
    d. humanism

19. Vygotsky's theory has been criticized for neglecting

    a. the role of genes in guiding development.
    b. developmental processes that are not primarily biological.
    c. the importance of language in development.
    d. social factors in development.

20. Which is the correct sequence of stages in Piaget's theory of cognitive development?

    a. sensorimotor, preoperational, concrete operational, formal operational
    b. sensorimotor, preoperational, formal operational, concrete operational
    c. preoperational, sensorimotor, concrete operational, formal operational
    d. preoperational, sensorimotor, formal operational, concrete operational

21. According to the ________________ perspective, the human mind is like a sophisticated computer, capable of handling many complicated procedures at once.

    a. universal
    b. robotic
    c. information-processing
    d. social-learning

22. A professor of human development who takes an eclectic approach

    a. does not use any of the theories described in the textbook.
    b. uses parts of several theories rather than sticking to one particular theory.
    c. emphasizes the role of ecosystems.
    d. believes that social learning is the best descriptor of human behavior.

23. The zone of proximal development refers to

    a. the control process by which information is transferred from the sensory register to working memory.
    b. the influence of a pleasurable stimulus on behavior.
    c. the range of skills a child can exercise with assistance but cannot perform independently
    d. the mutual interaction of a person's internal characteristics, the environment, and the person's behavior.

24. Nature is to nurture as
    a. tabula rasa is to blank slate.
    b. Jean Rousseau is to John Locke.
    c. B. F. Skinner is to Ivan Pavlov.
    d. Urie Bronfenbrenner is to Kurt Lewin.

Matching Items

Match each definition or description with its corresponding term.

Terms

25. __________	psychoanalytic theory	30. __________	nurture
26. __________	nature	31. __________	sociocultural theory
27. __________	behaviorism	32. __________	conditioning
28. __________	social learning theory	33. __________	modeling
29. __________	cognitive theory	34. __________	evolutionary theory

Descriptions or Definitions

a. emphasizes the impact of the immediate environment on behavior
b. emphasizes that people learn by observing others
c. environmental influences that affect development
d. a process of learning, as described by Pavlov and Skinner
e. emphasizes the "hidden dramas" that influence behavior
f. emphasizes the cultural context in development
g. emphasizes how our thoughts shape our actions
h. the process whereby a person learns by imitating someone else's behavior
i. emphasizes reproduction and survival as deeply rooted motivators of behavior
j. traits that are inherited

Practice Questions II

Multiple-Choice Questions

1. An individual's context of development refers to his or her
    a. microsystem and mesosystem.
    b. exosystem.
    c. macrosystem.
    d. microsystem, mesosystem, exosystem, and macrosystem.

2. The three domains of developmental psychology are
   a. physical, cognitive, and psychosocial.
   b. physical, biosocial, and cognitive.
   c. biosocial, cognitive, and psychosocial.
   d. biosocial, cognitive, and emotional.
3. Which of the following is true of the three domains of development?
   a. They are important at every age.
   b. They interact in influencing development.
   c. They are more influential in some cultures than in others.
   d. Answers a and b are true.
4. According to the ecological model, the macrosystem would include
   a. the peer group.
   b. the community.
   c. cultural values.
   d. the family.
5. Culture includes all of the following **EXCEPT**
   a. technologies.
   b. customs.
   c. race.
   d. clothes.
6. A cohort is defined as a group of people
   a. of similar national origin.
   b. who share a common language.
   c. born within a few years of each other.
   d. who share the same religion.
7. Which developmental theorist suggested that every child passes through the same fixed stages?
   a. Sigmund Freud
   b. Erik Erikson
   c. Jean Piaget
   d. all of the above

8. Of the following terms, the one that does **NOT** describe a stage of Freud's theory of childhood sexuality is
   a. phallic.
   b. oral.
   c. anal.
   d. sensorimotor.

9. We are more likely to imitate the behavior of others if we particularly admire and identify with them. This suggestion would find expression in
   a. stage theory.
   b. sociocultural theory.
   c. social learning theory.
   d. Pavlov's experiments.

10. According to Erikson, an adult who has difficulty establishing a secure, mutual relationship with a life partner might never have resolved the crisis of
    a. initiative versus guilt
    b. autonomy versus shame
    c. intimacy versus isolation
    d. integrity versus despair

11. Who would be **MOST** likely to agree with the statement, "Anything can be learned"?
    a. Jean Piaget
    b. Lev Vygotsky
    c. John Watson
    d. Erik Erikson

12. Classical conditioning is to ________________ as operant conditioning is to ____________________.
    a. Skinner; Pavlov
    b. Watson; Vygotsky
    c. Pavlov: Skinner
    d. Vygotsky; Watson

13. Learning theorists have found that they can often solve a person's seemingly complex psychological problem by
    a. analyzing the patient.
    b. admitting the existence of the unconscious.
    c. altering the environment.
    d. administering well-designed punishments.

14. The information-processing perspective focuses on all of the following **EXCEPT**
    a. plasticity.
    b. output.
    c. processing.
    d. input.

15. According to Piaget, the stage of cognitive development that generally characterizes preschool children (2 to 6 years old) is the
    a. preoperational stage.
    b. sensorimotor stage.
    c. oral stage.
    d. psychosocial stage.

16. In Piaget's theory, cognitive equilibrium refers to
    a. a state of mental balance.
    b. a kind of imbalance that leads to cognitive growth.
    c. the ultimate stage of cognitive development.
    d. the first stage in the processing of information.

17. You teach your dog to "speak" by giving her a treat each time she does so. This is an example of
    a. classical conditioning.
    b. punishment.
    c. reinforcement.
    d. modeling.

18. According to Piaget, a child who must modify an old idea in order to incorporate a new experience is using the process of
    a. assimilation.
    b. accommodation.
    c. cognitive equilibrium.
    d. guided participation.

19. Which of the following is a common criticism of sociocultural theory?
    a. It places too great an emphasis on unconscious motives and childhood sexuality.
    b. Its mechanistic approach fails to explain many complex human behaviors.
    c. Development is more gradual than its stages imply.
    d. It neglects developmental processes that are not primarily social.

20. A major pioneer of the sociocultural perspective was
    a. Jean Piaget.
    b. Albert Bandura.
    c. Lev Vygotsky.
    d. Ivan Pavlov.

21. The humanist Carl Rogers coined the term ________________________ to refer to accepting and respecting all individuals.
    a. unconditional positive regard
    b. superego
    c. cognitive equilibrium
    d. operant conditioning

22. A pioneer of social learning theory, who studied modeling in children, was
    a. Kurt Lewin.
    b. Ivan Pavlov.
    c. Albert Bandura.
    d. Urie Bronfenbrenner.

True or False Items

Write T (for true) or F (for false) on the line in front of each statement.

23. _____ Behaviorists study what people actually do rather than what they are thinking.

24. _____ Erikson's eight developmental stages are centered not on a body part but on each person's relationship to the social environment.

25. _____ Most developmentalists agree that the nature-nurture controversy has been laid to rest.

26. _____ Few developmental theorists today believe that humans have instincts or abilities that arise from our species' biological heritage.

27. _____ Of the major developmental theories, humanism gives the most emphasis to the interaction of genes and experience in shaping development.

28. _____ Developmental scientists are studying both genetic and environmental factors in their research on ADHD.

29. _____ According to Piaget, a state of cognitive equilibrium must be attained before cognitive growth can occur.

30. _____ In part, cognitive theory examines how an individual's understandings and expectations affect his or her behavior.

31. _____ Behaviorism is the predecessor of the information-processing theory.

32. _____ Most contemporary developmentalists prefer an eclectic perspective on development.

Applying Your Knowledge

1. Dr. Ramirez conducts research on the psychosocial domain of development. She is most likely to be interested in a child's
   a. perceptual abilities.
   b. brain wave patterns.
   c. emotions.
   d. use of language.

2. Jahmal is writing a paper on the role of the social context in development. He would do well to consult the writings of
   a. Jean Piaget.
   b. Sigmund Freud.
   c. Urie Bronfenbrenner.
   d. B. F. Skinner.

3. Dr. Wong looks at human development in terms of the individual's supporting ecosystems. Evidently, Dr. Wong subscribes to the _______________ model.
   a. psychosocial
   b. ecological
   c. biosocial
   d. cognitive

4. Which of the following is unlikely to be influenced by cohort?
   a. eye color
   b. age of entrance to school
   c. parental discipline practices
   d. number of children in family

5. Imelda is quite intelligent throughout her life, but this intellectual capacity takes many forms throughout her life. Of the following, this **BEST** characterizes which characteristic of development?
   a. multidirectional
   b. multicultural
   c. plasticity
   d. multidisciplinary

6. Many songbirds inherit a genetically programmed species song that enhances their ability to mate and establish a territory. The evolution of such a trait is an example of
   a. selective adaptation.
   b. nature vs. nurture.
   c. accommodation.
   d. assimilation.
7. When a pigeon is rewarded for producing a particular response and thus learns to produce that response to obtain rewards, psychologists describe this chain of events as
   a. operant conditioning.
   b. classical conditioning.
   c. modeling.
   d. reflexive actions.
8. A developmentalist that subscribes to the universal perspective would likely be **MOST** interested in which of the following?
   a. the influence of teachers structuring of their students' environments on children's cognitive growth
   b. the ways that spouses influence one another's self-esteem
   c. why all people groups value love and belonging
   d. the impact of socioeconomic status on divorce rate
9. Dr. Cleaver's research focuses on the biological forces that shape each child's characteristic way of reacting to environmental experiences. Evidently, Dr. Cleaver is working from a(n) ____________________ perspective.
   a. psychoanalytic
   b. cognitive
   c. sociocultural
   d. evolutionary
10. Which of the following is the best example of guided participation?
    a. After watching her mother change her baby sister's diaper, four-year-old Brandy changes her doll's diaper.
    b. To help her son learn to pour liquids, Linda engages him in a bathtub game involving pouring water from cups of different sizes.
    c. Seeing his father shaving, three-year-old Jack pretends to shave by rubbing whipped cream on his face.
    d. After reading a recipe in a magazine, Kyle gathers ingredients from the cupboard.

11. A child who calls all furry animals "doggie" will experience cognitive ___________________ when she encounters a hairless breed for the first time. This may cause her to revamp her concept of "dog" in order to ___________________ the new experience.

    a. disequilibrium; accommodate
    b. disequilibrium; assimilate
    c. equilibrium; accommodate
    d. equilibrium; assimilate

12. A confirmed neo-Freudian, Dr. Thomas strongly endorses the views of Erik Erikson. She would be most likely to disagree with Freud regarding the importance of

    a. unconscious forces in development.
    b. irrational forces in personality formation.
    c. early childhood experiences.
    d. sexual urges in development.

13. After watching several older children climbing around a new jungle gym, five-year-old Jennie decides to try it herself. Which of the following best accounts for her behavior?

    a. classical conditioning
    b. modeling
    c. guided participation
    d. reinforcement

14. I am 8 years old, and although I understand some logical principles, I have trouble thinking about hypothetical concepts. According to Piaget, I am in the ______________________ stage of development.

    a. sensorimotor
    b. preoperational
    c. concrete operational
    d. formal operational

15. Eight-year-old Bjorn has just been diagnosed with ADHD. Bjorn's school psychologist explains to his parents that this means some of his brain circuitry functions abnormally leading to a difficulty reading facial expressions and understanding tone which is at the root of much of his troublesome behavior. This school psychologist apparently subscribes to

    a. psychoanalytic theory.
    b. behaviorism.
    c. the life-span perspective.
    d. the information-processing theory.

16. After Ashley's mother lost her job and the family was evicted from their apartment, the junior high school student's grades began to suffer. According to Maslow's theory, this is because

    a. her more basic physiological and safety needs were not being met.
    b. she was experiencing the psychosocial crisis of industry vs. inferiority.
    c. her mother was too preoccupied to reinforce her good studying habits.
    d. she was in a state of cognitive disequilibrium.

17. The school psychologist believes that each child's developmental needs can be understood only by taking into consideration the child's broader social and cultural background. Evidently, the school psychologist is working within the ____________________ perspective.

    a. psychoanalytic
    b. evolutionary
    c. social learning
    d. sociocultural

18. Four-year-old Rashad takes great pride in successfully undertaking new activities. Erikson would probably say that Rashad is capably meeting the psychosocial challenge of

    a. trust vs. mistrust.
    b. initiative vs. guilt.
    c. industry vs. inferiority.
    d. identity vs. role confusion.

19. Dr. Bazzi's developmental research draws upon insights from several theoretical perspectives. Evidently, Dr. Bazzi is working from a(n) ____________________ perspective.

    a. cognitive
    b. learning
    c. eclectic
    d. sociocultural

20. Dr. Ivey believes that development is a lifelong process of gradual and continuous growth, and does not occur in age-related stages. Based on this information, with which of the following theories would Dr. Ivey most likely agree?

    a. Piaget's cognitive theory
    b. Erikson's psychosocial theory
    c. Freud's psychoanalytic theory
    d. Skinner's behaviorism

Key Terms

1. **science of human development:** The science that seeks to understand how and why people of all ages and circumstances change or remain the same over time. (p. 4; video lesson, introduction; objective 1)
2. **theory:** A comprehensive set of ideas. (p. 4; objective 1)
3. **nature:** In development, refers to the traits, capacities, and limitations that each individual inherits genetically from his or her parents at the moment of conception. (p. 6; video lesson, introduction; objectives 1 & 11)
4. **nurture:** In development, includes all the environmental influences that affect the individual. This includes everything from the mother's nutrition while pregnant to the cultural influences in the nation. (p. 6; video lesson, introduction; objectives 1 & 11)
5. **critical period:** A time when a particular type of developmental growth (in body or behavior) must happen for normal development to occur. (p. 8; objective 3)
6. **sensitive period:** A time when a certain type of development is most likely to happen although it may still happen later with more difficulty. For example, early childhood is considered a sensitive period for language learning. (p. 8; objective 3)
7. **plasticity:** The idea that abilities, personality, and other human characteristics can change over time. Plasticity is particularly evident during childhood, but even older adults are not always "set in their ways." (p. 9; objective 4)
8. **difference/deficit error:** The mistaken belief that a deviation from some norm is necessarily inferior to behavior or characteristics that meet the standard. (p. 10; objective 3)
9. **social construction:** An idea that is built on shared perceptions, not on objective reality. Many age-related terms, such as *childhood*, *adolescence*, *yuppie*, and *senior citizen*, are social constructions. (p. 11; objective 4)
10. **socioeconomic status (SES):** A person's position in society as determined by income, occupation, education, and place of residence. (p. 13; objective 3)
11. **dynamic-systems approach:** A view of human development as an ongoing, ever-changing interaction between the physical and emotional being and between the person and every aspect of his or her environment, including the family and society. (p. 15; objective 3)
12. **ecological-systems approach:** The perspective on human development that considers all the influences from the various contexts of development. Later renamed *bioecological theory*. (p. 16; video lesson, segment 1; objective 3)
13. **cohort:** Refers to people born within the same historical period who therefore move through life together, experiencing the same events, new technologies, and cultural shifts at the same ages. (p. 17; objective 3)
14. **biopsychosocial:** A term emphasizing the interaction of the three developmental domains (biosocial, cognitive, and psychosocial). All

development is biopsychosocial, although it is studied piecemeal. (p. 19; objectives 3 & 4)

15. **mirror neurons:** Cells in an observer's brain that are activated by watching an action performed by someone else as they would be if the observer had personally performed that action. (p. 20; objective 4)
16. **developmental theory:** A group of ideas, assumptions, and generalizations that interpret and illuminate the thousands of observations that have been made about human growth. A developmental theory provides a framework for explaining the patterns and problems of development. (pp. 35–36; video lesson, segment 2; objective 5)
17. **norm:** An average, or typical, standard of behavior or accomplishment, such as the norm for age of walking or the norm for greeting a stranger. (p. 37; objective 4)
18. **grand theory:** A view of human development that holds that irrational, unconscious drives and motives, often originating in childhood, underlie human behavior. (p. 39; video lesson, segment 2; objective 6)
19. **behaviorism:** A grand theory of human development that studies observable behavior. Behaviorism is also called *learning theory* because it describes the laws and processes by which behavior is learned. (p. 42; video lesson, segment 2; objective 7)
20. **conditioning:** According to behaviorism, the processes by which responses become linked to particular stimuli and learning takes place. (p. 42; objective 7)
21. **classical conditioning:** The learning process in which a meaningful stimulus (such as the smell of food to a hungry animal) is connected with a neutral stimulus (such as the sound of a tone) that had no special meaning before conditioning. Also known as *respondent conditioning*. (p. 42; video lesson, segment 2; objective 7)
22. **operant conditioning:** The learning process by which a particular action is followed by something desired (which makes the person or animal more likely to repeat the action) or by something unwanted (which makes the action less likely to be repeated). Also known as *instrumental conditioning*. (p. 43; video lesson, segment 2; objective 7)
23. **reinforcement:** The process by which the consequences of a particular behavior strengthen the behavior, making it more likely that the behavior will be repeated. This process is most successful when a behavior is followed by something desired, such as food for a hungry animal or a welcoming smile for a lonely person. (p. 43; objective 7)
24. **social learning theory:** An extension of behaviorism that emphasizes the influence that other people have over a person's behavior. Even without specific reinforcement, every individual learns many things through observation and imitation of other people. Also called *observational learning*. (p. 44; video lesson, segment 2; objective 7)

25. **modeling:** The central process of social learning, by which a person observes the actions of others and then copies them. (p. 44; video lesson, segment 2; objective 7)
26. **self-efficacy:** In social learning theory, the belief of some people that they are able to change themselves and effectively alter the social context. (p. 44; objective 7)
27. **cognitive theory:** A grand theory of human development that focuses on changes in how people think over time. According to this theory, our thoughts shape our attitudes, beliefs, and behaviors. (p. 46; video lesson, segment 2; objective 8)
28. **cognitive equilibrium:** In cognitive theory, a state of mental balance in which people are not confused because they can use their existing thought processes to understand current experiences and ideas. (p. 47; objective 8)
29. **assimilation:** The reinterpretation of new experiences to fit into old ideas. (p. 47; objective 8)
30. **accommodation:** The restructuring of old ideas to include new experiences. (p. 47; objective 8)
31. **information processing:** A perspective that compares human thinking processes, by analogy, to computer analysis of data, including sensory input, connections, stored memories, and output. (p. 48; objective 8)
32. **sociocultural theory:** A newer theory that holds that development results from the dynamic interaction of each person with the surrounding social and cultural forces. (p. 50; objective 9)
33. **apprenticeship in thinking:** Vygotsky's term for how cognition is stimulated and developed in people by more skilled members of society. (p. 50; objective 9)
34. **guided participation:** The process by which people learn from others who guide their experiences and explorations. (p. 50; objective 9)
35. **zone of proximal development:** In sociocultural theory, a metaphorical area, or "zone," surrounding a learner that includes all the skills, knowledge, and concepts that the person is close ("proximal") to acquiring but cannot yet master without help. (pp. 50–51; objective 9)
36. **humanism:** A theory that stresses the potential of all humans for good and the belief that all people have the same basic needs, regardless of culture, gender, or background. (p. 53; objective 10)
37. **selective adaptation:** The process by which living creatures (including people) adjust to their environment. Genes that enhance survival and reproductive ability are selected, over the generations, to become more prevalent. (p. 55; objective 10)
38. **eclectic perspective:** The approach taken by most developmentalists, in which they apply aspects of each of the various theories of development rather than adhering exclusively to one theory. (p. 59; video lesson, segment 3; objectives 1 & 11)

39. **stimulus:** In learning theory, an event or action that triggers a reaction, or response in a person or animal. (video lesson, segment 2; objective 7)
40. **response:** In learning theory, a behavior or reaction in a person or animal that has been elicited by a stimulus. (video lesson, segment 2; objective 7)
41. **life-span perspective:** The view of human development that recognizes that human growth is lifelong and characterized by both continuity (as in personality) and discontinuity (as in the number of brain cells). (video lesson, segment 3; objective 4)

Summary

The **science of human development** is the science that seeks to understand how and why people change with increasing age, and how and why they remain the same.

According to Urie Bronfenbrenner's **ecological-systems approach**, human development is supported by systems at four nested levels: the *microsystem* (immediate social setting), the *mesosystem* (connections among various microsystems), the *exosystem* (the community structures and local educational, medical, employment, and communications systems), and the *macrosystem* (cultural values, political philosophies, economic patterns, and social conditions).

The **life-span perspective** underscores the fact that development is lifelong, *multidirectional*, *multicontextual*, *multicultural*, *multidisciplinary*, and *plastic*. Human development is also *multidimensional* in that it includes many dimensions of many domains. The three major domains of development include the biosocial domain (brain and body as well as changes in them and the social influences that guide them), the cognitive domain (thought processes, perceptual abilities, and language mastery, as well as the educational institutions that encourage them), and the psychosocial domain (emotions, personality, and interpersonal relationships with family, friends, and the wider community).

Developmental theories fall into different categories, including grand theories, minitheories, and emergent theories, but they all provide scientists with formal principles with which to study and explain human development. Theories guide researchers in their work and provide us all with a means of explaining and even predicting human behavior.

Psychoanalytic theory interprets human development in terms of intrinsic drives and motives, many of which are irrational and unconscious. According to Sigmund Freud, development progresses through psychosexual stages; at each stage, sexual interest and pleasure is focused on a particular part of the body.

In his psychosocial theory of human development, Erik Erikson proposed eight developmental stages throughout the life span, each of which is characterized by a particular challenge, or developmental crisis. Erikson emphasized each person's relationship to the social environment and the importance of family and cultural influences in determining how well prepared individuals are to meet these crises.

Proponents of **behaviorism** formulated laws of behavior that operate at every age. As demonstrated by Ivan Pavlov, **classical conditioning** involves learning by association:

the subject comes to associate a neutral **stimulus** with a meaningful one. In **operant conditioning**, proposed by B. F. Skinner, the individual learns that a particular behavior produces a particular consequence. **Social learning theory** emphasizes the ways in which people learn new behaviors by observing and imitating, or **modeling**, the behavior of other people they consider admirable, powerful, or similar.

Cognitive theory focuses on the structure and development of the individual's thought processes and their effect on his or her understanding of the world. Jean Piaget viewed cognitive development as a process that follows a universal sequence of age-related periods. According to Piaget, each person strives for **cognitive equilibrium**—that is, a state of mental balance achieved through the development of mental concepts that explain his or her experiences.

Sociocultural theory seeks to explain individual knowledge, development, and competencies in terms of the guidance, support, and structure provided by the broader cultural context. Lev Vygotsky believed that the development of cognitive competencies results from social interaction between children and more mature members of the society in what has been called an **apprenticeship in thinking**. The basis of this apprenticeship is **guided participation**, in which a skilled tutor engages the learner in joint activities.

The universal perspective—including both humanism and evolutionary theory—is the latest approach to the study of development. It focuses on the similarities rather than the differences among people. Universal theories emphasize the underlying wants, needs, and behaviors shared by all individuals regardless of gender or sociocultural contexts. The humanist Abraham Maslow hypothesized about a hierarchy of basic human needs, while Carl Rogers asserted the intrinsic worth of all human beings who should be met with respect, appreciation, and *unconditional positive regard*. Evolutionary theory is formulated on the basis of Charles Darwin's **selective adaptation**. It is applied to development in terms of hypotheses regarding inherited genetic tendencies that foster survival and reproduction and are thus universal to the human species.

These theories complement one another, as each emphasizes a somewhat different aspect of development and, in itself, are too restricted to account for the diversity of human behavior. Psychoanalytic theory calls attention to the importance of early childhood experiences and "hidden dramas" that influence daily life. Behaviorism highlights the effect of the immediate environment on behavior. Cognitive theory promotes a greater understanding of how intellectual processes and thinking affect our behavior. Sociocultural theory reminds us that development is embedded in a rich and multifaceted cultural context. The universal theories assert our commonalities: **humanism** focuses on our basic wants and needs, while evolutionary theory emphasizes the inherited forces that affect each person—and all humankind—within particular contexts.

Developmentalists agree that, at every point, the interaction between nature and nurture is the crucial influence on any particular aspect of development. Today, most developmentalists have an **eclectic perspective**. Instead of limiting themselves to only one school of thought, they apply insights drawn from various theoretical views.

Answer Key

Practice Questions I

Multiple-Choice Questions

1. a. is the correct answer. (video lesson, introduction; objective 1)

   b. & c. are incorrect. The study of development is concerned with a broader range of phenomena, including biosocial aspects of development, than these answers specify.

2. d. is the correct answer. (objective 2)
3. b. is the correct answer. (objective 2)

   a. is incorrect. This domain is concerned with thought processes.

   c. is incorrect. This domain is concerned with emotions, personality, and interpersonal relationships.

   d. is incorrect. This is not a domain of development.

4. c. is the correct answer. (objective 2)

   a. is incorrect. This falls within the cognitive and biosocial domains.

   b. is incorrect. This falls within the biosocial domain.

   d. is incorrect. This falls within the cognitive domain.

5. d. is the correct answer. This approach sees development as occurring within four interacting levels, or environments. (video lesson, segment 1; objective 3)
6. d. is the correct answer. (video lesson, segment 3; objectives 1 & 4)
7. b. is the correct answer. (objective 4)
8. c. is the correct answer. (video lesson, segment 1; objective 3)

   a. is incorrect. This refers to systems that link one microsystem to another.

   b. is incorrect. This refers to cultural values, political philosophies, economic patterns, and social conditions.

   d. is incorrect. This includes the community structures that affect the functioning of smaller systems.

9. c. is the correct answer. (objective 3)
10. d. is the correct answer. (video lesson, segment 2; objective 5)
11. a. is the correct answer. (video lesson, segment 2; objective 6)

    b. is incorrect. Behaviorism emphasizes the influence of the immediate environment on behavior.

    c. is incorrect. Cognitive theory emphasizes the impact of conscious thought processes on behavior.

    d. is incorrect. Sociocultural theory emphasizes the influence on development of social interaction in a specific cultural context.

12. a. is the correct answer. (objective 6)

13. a. is the correct answer. (video lesson, segment 2; objective 6)

    b. & c. are incorrect. Whereas Freud identified four stages of psychosexual development, Erikson proposed eight psychosocial stages.

    d. is incorrect. Although his theory places greater emphasis on social and cultural forces than Freud's did, Erikson's theory is nevertheless classified as a psychoanalytic theory.

14. c. is the correct answer. (video lesson, segment 2; objective 7)

15. a. is the correct answer. In classical conditioning, a neutral stimulus—in this case, the bell—is associated with a meaningful stimulus—in this case, food. (video lesson, segment 2; objective 7)

    b. is incorrect. In operant conditioning, the consequences of a voluntary response determine the likelihood of its being repeated. Salivation is an involuntary response.

    c. & d. are incorrect. Positive reinforcement and social learning pertain to voluntary, or operant, responses.

16. c. is the correct answer. (video lesson, introduction; objective 11)

    a. is incorrect. These are both examples of nurture.

    b. is incorrect. Both of these refer to nature.

    d. is incorrect. The impact of changing historical concepts of childhood on development is an example of how environmental forces (nurture) shape development.

17. d. is the correct answer. (video lesson, segment 2; objective 7)

    a. & c. are incorrect. These can be true in all types of learning.

    b. is incorrect. This was not discussed as an aspect of developmental theory.

18. d. is the correct answer. (objective 10)

19. a. is the correct answer. (objective 9)

    b. is incorrect. Vygotsky's theory does not emphasize biological processes.

    c. & d. are incorrect. Vygotsky's theory places considerable emphasis on language and social factors.

20. a. is the correct answer. (video lesson, segment 2; objective 8)

21. c. is the correct answer. (objective 8)

22. b. is the correct answer. (objective 11)

23. c. is the correct answer. (objective 9)

    a. is incorrect. This describes attention.

    b. is incorrect. This describes positive reinforcement.

    d. is incorrect. This describes reciprocal determinism.

24. b. is the correct answer. Locke believed that the mind at birth is a *tabula rasa,* or "blank slate" onto which learning (nurture) leaves its mark. Rousseau emphasized the natural (biological) goodness of human beings. (video lesson, introduction; objectives 1 & 11)

Matching Items

25. e (video lesson, segment 2; objective 6)
26. j (video lesson, introduction; objective 11)
27. a (video lesson, segment 2; objective 7)
28. b (video lesson, segment 2; objective 7)
29. g (video lesson, segment 2; objective 8)
30. c (video lesson, introduction; objective 11)
31. f (objective 9)
32. d (video lesson, segment 2; objective 7)
33. h (video lesson, segment 2; objective 7)
34. i (objective 10)

Practice Questions II

Multiple-Choice Questions

1. d. is the correct answer. (objective 3)
2. c. is the correct answer. (objective 2)
3. d. is the correct answer. (objective 2)

   c. is incorrect. Research has not revealed cultural variations in the overall developmental influence of the three domains.
4. c. is the correct answer. (video lesson, segment 1; objective 3)

   a. & d. are incorrect. These are part of the microsystem.

   b. is incorrect. This is part of the exosystem.
5. c. is the correct answer. (objective 3)
6. c. is the correct answer. (objective 3)

   a., b., & d. are incorrect. These are not necessarily attributes of a cohort.
7. d. is the correct answer. (objective 11)
8. d. is the correct answer. This is one of Piaget's stages of cognitive development. (video lesson, segment 2; objective 6)
9. c. is the correct answer. (video lesson, segment 2; objective 7)
10. c. is the correct answer. (objective 6)
11. c. is the correct answer. (objective 7)

    a. is incorrect. Piaget formulated a cognitive theory of development.

    b. is incorrect. Vygotsky formulated a sociocultural theory of development.

    d. is incorrect. Erikson formulated a psychoanalytic theory of development.
12. c. is the correct answer. (video lesson, segment 2; objective 7)
13. c. is the correct answer. (objective 7)

    a. & b. are incorrect. These are psychoanalytic approaches to treating psychological problems.

d. is incorrect. Learning theorists generally do not recommend the use of punishment.

14. a. is the correct answer. Plasticity is the idea that human characteristics can change over time. (objective 8)

15. a. is the correct answer. (video lesson, segment 2; objective 8)

    b. is incorrect. The sensorimotor stage describes development from birth until age 2.

    c. is incorrect. This is a psychoanalytic stage described by Freud.

    d. is incorrect. This is not the name of a stage; "psychosocial" refers to Erikson's stage theory.

16. a. is the correct answer. (objective 8)

    b. is incorrect. This describes disequilibrium.

    c. is incorrect. This is formal operational thinking.

    d. is incorrect. Piaget's theory does not propose stages of information processing.

17. c. is the correct answer. (video lesson, segment 2; objective 7)

    a. is incorrect. Teaching your dog in this way is an example of operant, rather than classical, conditioning.

    b. is incorrect. Punishment decreases the likelihood of a behavior.

    d. is incorrect. Modeling involves learning by imitating others.

18. b. is the correct answer. (objective 8)

    a. is incorrect. Assimilation occurs when new experiences do not clash with existing ideas.

    c. is incorrect. Cognitive equilibrium is mental balance, which occurs when ideas and experiences do not clash.

    d. is incorrect. This is Vygotsky's term for the process by which a mentor engages a child in shared learning activities.

19. d. is the correct answer. (objectives 9 & 11)

    a. is incorrect. This is a common criticism of psychoanalytic theory.

    b. is incorrect. This is a common criticism of behaviorism.

    c. is incorrect. This is a common criticism of psychoanalytic and cognitive theories that describe development as occurring in a sequence of stages.

20. c. is the correct answer. (objective 9)

21. a. is the correct answer. (objective 10)

    b. is incorrect. This is a psychoanalytic term.

    c. is incorrect. This is a term from cognitive theory.

    d. is incorrect. This is a term from behaviorism.

22. c. is the correct answer. (video lesson, segment 2; objective 7)

True or False Items

23. T (video lesson, segment 2; objective 7)
24. T (video lesson, segment 2; objective 6)
25. F Although most developmentalists believe that nature and nurture interact in shaping development, the practical implications of whether nature or nurture plays a greater role in certain abilities keep the controversy alive. (video lesson, introduction; objective 11)
26. F This assumption lies at the heart of evolutionary theory. (objective 10)
27. F This description best fits evolutionary theory. (objective 10)
28. T (objective 11)
29. F On the contrary, disequilibrium often fosters greater growth. (objective 8)
30. T (video lesson, segment 2; objective 8)
31. F Piaget's cognitive theory is the basis of the information-processing framework. (objective 8)
32. T (video lesson, segment 3; objective 11)

Applying Your Knowledge

1. c. is the correct answer. (objective 2)

   a. & d. are incorrect. These pertain to the cognitive domain.

   b. is incorrect. This pertains to the biosocial domain.
2. c. is the correct answer. (video lesson, segment 1; objective 3)

   a. is incorrect. Piaget is notable in the area of cognitive development.

   b. is incorrect. Freud was a pioneer of psychoanalysis.

   d. is incorrect. Skinner is notable in the history of learning theory.
3. b. is the correct answer. (video lesson, segment 1; objective 3)

   a., c., & d. are incorrect. These are the three domains of development.
4. a. is the correct answer. (objective 3)

   b., c., & d. are all likely to be influenced by the historical context
5. c. is the correct answer. (objective 4)
6. a. is the correct answer. (objective 10)

   b. is incorrect. Although related, these terms do not speak directly to the influence of the drives for reproduction and survival in development.

   c. & d. are incorrect. These terms describe the processes by which cognitive concepts incorporate (assimilate) new experiences or are revamped (accommodated) by them.
7. a. is the correct answer. This is an example of operant conditioning because a response recurs due to its consequences. (video lesson, segment 2; objective 7)

   b. & d. are incorrect. In classical conditioning, the individual learns to associate a neutral stimulus with a meaningful stimulus.

c. is incorrect. In modeling, learning occurs through the observation of others, rather than through direct exposure to reinforcing consequences, as in this example.

8. c. is the correct answer. It is the third tier of Maslow's hierarchy of needs. (objective 10)

9. d. is the correct answer. (objective 10)

   a. is incorrect. Psychoanalytic theorists focus on the role of unconscious forces in development.

   b. is incorrect. Cognitive theorists emphasize how the developing person actively seeks to understand experiences.

   c. is incorrect. Sociocultural theorists focus on the social context, as expressed through people, language, and customs.

10. b. is the correct answer. (objective 9)

    a. & c. are incorrect. These are both examples of modeling.

    d. is incorrect. Guided participation involves the coaching of a mentor. In this example, Kyle is simply following written directions.

11. a. is the correct answer. (objective 8)

    b. is incorrect. Because the dog is not furry, the child's concept of dog cannot incorporate (assimilate) the discrepant experience without being revamped.

    c. & d. are incorrect. Equilibrium exists when ideas (such as what a dog is) and experiences (such as seeing a hairless dog) do not clash.

12. d. is the correct answer. This is the most serious disagreement between the theories of Freud and Erikson. (objective 6)

13. b. is the correct answer. Evidently, Jennie has learned by observing the other children at play. (video lesson, segment 2; objective 7)

    a. is incorrect. Classical conditioning is concerned with the association of stimuli, not with complex responses, as in this example.

    c. is incorrect. Guided participation involves the interaction of a mentor and a child.

    d. is incorrect. Reinforcement is a process for getting a response to recur.

14. c. is the correct answer. (video lesson, segment 2; objective 8)

15. d. is the correct answer. When Bjorn experiences something that conflicts with his existing understanding, he experiences disequilibrium. (objective 8)

    a. is incorrect. Conservation is the ability to recognize that objects do not change when their appearances change.

    b. is incorrect. Cognition refers to all mental activities associated with thinking.

    c. is incorrect. If Bjorn's thinking were in equilibrium, all men would be "dad"!

16. a. is the correct answer. (objective 10)

    b. is incorrect. This is from the developmental stages of Erikson's psychoanalytic theory.

    c. is incorrect. Reinforcement is a function of Skinner's operant conditioning.

    d. is incorrect. This is a term from Piaget's cognitive theory.

17. d. is the correct answer. (objective 9)
18. b. is the correct answer. (video lesson, segment 2; objective 6)
    a. is incorrect. According to Erikson, this crisis concerns younger children.
    c. & d. are incorrect. In Erikson's theory, these crises concern older children.
19. c. is the correct answer. (video lesson, segment 3; objective 11)
    a., b., & d. are incorrect. These are three of the many theoretical perspectives upon which someone working from an eclectic perspective might draw.
20. d. is the correct answer. (objective 7)
    a., b., & c. are incorrect. Each of these theories emphasizes that development is a discontinuous process that occurs in stages.

Lesson Review

Lesson 1

Introduction
The Developing Person

Please Note: Use this matrix to guide your study and achieve the learning objectives of this lesson. It will also help you to view the video, which defines and demonstrates important concepts and skills as they relate to everyday life.

Learning Objective	Textbook	Course Student Guide	Video Lesson
1. Define the study of human development and discuss some of its major themes.	pp. 3–4, 6–20, 58–59	Key Terms: 1, 2, 3, 4, 38; Practice Questions I: 1, 6, 24.	Introduction Segment 3: *The Life-Span Perspective*
2. Describe the three major domains of human development and discuss how they interrelate.	pp. 19–21	Practice Questions I: 2, 3, 4; Practice Questions II: 2, 3; Applying Your Knowledge: 1.	
3. Describe the many contexts and systems that can affect a person's development, and discuss how they are interrelated.	pp. 6–18	Key Terms: 5, 6, 8, 10, 11, 12, 13, 14; Practice Questions I: 5, 8, 9; Practice Questions II: 1, 4, 5, 6; Applying Your Knowledge: 2, 3, 4.	Segment 1: *Contexts and System*
4. Identify the characteristics of development described by the life-span perspective.	*	Key Terms: 7, 9, 14, 15, 17, 41; Practice Questions I: 6, 7; Applying Your Knowledge: 5.	Segment 3: *The Life-Span Perspective*
5. Define developmental theory, and describe how theories help explain human behavior and guide researchers who study development.	pp. 35–38	Key Terms: 16; Practice Questions I: 10.	Segment 2: *Theories of Development*
6. Discuss the major focus of psychoanalytic theory, contrasting the psychosexual development proposed by Freud with the psychosocial development described by Erikson.	pp. 39–41	Key Terms: 18; Practice Questions I: 11, 12, 13, 25; Practice Questions II: 8, 10, 24; Applying Your Knowledge: 12, 18.	Segment 2: *Theories of Development*

* The video for this lesson offers excellent coverage of this topic.

Learning Objective	Textbook	Course Student Guide	Video Lesson
7. Discuss the major focus of behaviorism, and explain the basic principles of classical and operant conditioning as well as social learning theory.	pp. 41–44, 46	Key Terms: 19, 20, 21, 22, 23, 24, 25, 26, 39, 40; Practice Questions I: 14, 15, 17, 27, 28, 32, 33; Practice Questions II: 9, 11, 12, 13, 17, 22, 23; Applying Your Knowledge: 7, 13, 20.	Segment 2: *Theories of Development*
8. Discuss the major focus of cognitive theory, summarize Piaget's stages of cognitive development, and describe the information processing perspective.	pp. 46–49	Key Terms: 27, 28, 29, 30, 31; Practice Questions I: 20, 21, 29; Practice Questions II: 14, 15, 16, 18, 29, 30, 31; Applying Your Knowledge: 11, 14, 15.	Segment 2: *Theories of Development*
9. Discuss the basic ideas of Vygotsky and the sociocultural theory of development.	pp. 50–53	Key Terms: 32, 33, 34, 35; Practice Questions I: 19, 23, 31; Practice Questions II: 19, 20; Applying Your Knowledge: 10, 17.	
10. Discuss the basic ideas of the universal perspective including both humanism and evolutionary theory .	pp. 53–58	Key Terms: 36, 37; Practice Questions I: 18, 34; Practice Questions II: 21, 26, 27; Applying Your Knowledge: 6, 8, 9, 16.	
11. Summarize the contributions and criticisms of the major developmental theories, and compare the position of the theories regarding three controversies of development.	pp. 39–59	Key Terms: 3, 4, 38; Practice Questions I: 16, 22, 24, 26, 30; Practice Questions II: 7, 19, 25, 28, 32; Applying Your Knowledge: 19.	Introduction Segment 3: *The Life-Span Perspective*

A Scientific Approach

Lesson 2

Developmental Study as a Science

Preview

Human development is a science that seeks to understand how and why people change over time, and how and why they remain the same. Central to this effort is the set of principles and procedures scientists use to conduct research and produce the most objective results possible. Lesson 2 discusses these principles and procedures, beginning with the **scientific method**. The lesson continues by introducing some of the different research methods and designs that scientists use to gather data and test ideas. Several classic studies in developmental psychology are described in the video. Additionally, each chapter of the textbook features current developmental research designs as informative sidebars. This element is introduced with the presentation of a ground-breaking study of **sudden infant death syndrome (SIDS)**.

The final section of the lesson discusses cautions and challenges in the scientific study of development, notably the ethics of research with humans. To ensure confidentiality and safety, developmentalists who study children are especially concerned that the benefits of research outweigh the risks. Specific protocols have been put in place to promote ethical practice in the field.

As you complete this lesson, recall a scientific study you've heard or read about. What was the purpose of the study? How was it conducted? Who conducted it? Who paid for the study? What methods or procedures did the researchers use to gather their data? What conclusions did the researchers come to? Does anyone dispute these findings? Are you confident in the results of the study? Why or why not?

Prior Knowledge That Will Be Used in This Lesson

- This lesson focuses primarily on research methods, drawing on material from each of the three domains of development. Recall from Lesson 1 that the three domains of development include: (1) the *biosocial* domain, including changes in brain and body and the social influences that guide them, (2) the *cognitive* domain, which includes thought processes, perceptual abilities, and language mastery, as well as the educational institutions that encourage them, and (3) the *psychosocial* domain, including emotions, personality, and interpersonal relationships with family, friends, and the wider community. All three domains are important at every age, and each of the domains is affected by the other two.

Learning Objectives

Use this information to guide your reading, viewing, thinking, and studying. After successfully completing this lesson, you should be able to:

1. List and describe the basic steps of the scientific method, and discuss the challenge researchers face in identifying variables for a particular study.
2. Describe scientific observation and surveys as research methods, noting at least one advantage (or strength) and one disadvantage (or weakness) of each.
3. Define what correlation means in science and offer examples of its use in the study of human development.
4. Describe the components of an experiment, and discuss the main advantage and some limitations of this research method.
5. Describe three basic research designs used by developmental psychologists to study changes over time.
6. Discuss the code of ethics that should be followed by researchers in the field of developmental psychology and the role of an Institutional Review Board (IRB).
7. Describe the difference between quantitative research and qualitative research.

Textbook Reading & Video Viewing

For the most effective study of this lesson, complete the assignments in the sequence listed below.

Before viewing the video program:

Read pages 4–6 and 21–31 in Chapter 1. Also, review Chapter 1, "Introduction," pages 3–4 and "Including All Kinds of People," pages 10–15.

View the video for Lesson 2, "A Scientific Approach."

Segment 1: *The Scientific Method*

Segment 2: *Research Methods*

Segment 3: *Studying Changes over Time*

After viewing the video program:

Review all reading assignments for this lesson.

Complete the "Practice Questions" and "Applying Your Knowledge" sections to reinforce your understanding of important terms and concepts and measure your achievement of the Learning Objectives. Check your answers with the feedback given and review when necessary.

Practice Questions I

Multiple-Choice Questions

1. A hypothesis is a
   a. conclusion.
   b. prediction to be tested.
   c. statistical test.
   d. correlation.

2. One advantage of experiments is that
   a. they can help establish cause and effect.
   b. people behave differently in the artificial environment of the laboratory.
   c. this method is not vulnerable to bias on the part of the researcher.
   d. they can be used to examine any set of variables.

3. In an experiment testing the effects of group size on individual effort in a tug-of-war task, the number of people in each group is the
   a. hypothesis.
   b. independent variable.
   c. dependent variable.
   d. level of significance.

4. Which research method would be most appropriate for investigating the relationship between parents' religious beliefs and their attitudes toward middle school sex education?
   a. experimentation
   b. longitudinal research
   c. naturalistic observation
   d. the survey

5. Developmentalists who carefully observe the behavior of schoolchildren during recess are using a research method known as
   a. the survey.
   b. cross-sectional research.
   c. naturalistic observation.
   d. cross-sequential research.

6. Which of the following characteristics can affect a person's development?
   a. ethnic group
   b. socioeconomic status (SES)
   c. gender
   d. all of the above

7. Harry Harlow found that when monkeys were reared in social isolation, they would seek
   a. contact comfort as much as nourishment.
   b. nourishment over contact comfort.
   c. the company of other monkeys that had been socially isolated.
   d. no food, water, or nourishment of any kind.
8. If shoe size and IQ are negatively correlated, which of the following is true?
   a. People with large feet tend to have high IQs.
   b. People with small feet tend to have high IQs.
   c. People with small feet tend to have low IQs.
   d. IQ is unpredictable based on a person's shoe size.

Matching Items

Match each definition or description with its corresponding term.

Terms

9. __________ code of ethics
10. __________ cohort-sequential research
11. __________ correlation
12. __________ scientific observation
13. __________ variable
14. __________ hypothesis
15. __________ scientific method
16. __________ cross-sectional research
17. __________ longitudinal research
18. __________ Institutional Review Board (IRB)

Definitions or Descriptions

a. a general procedural model that helps researchers remain objective
b. any quantity, characteristic, or action that can take on different values
c. a testable prediction
d. a statistical measure of relationship between two variables
e. a set of moral principles
f research study retesting one group of people at several different times
g. research study comparing people of different ages at the same time
h. research study that follows groups of people of different ages over time
i. a group that ensures established guidelines are followed in research
j. unobtrusively watching and recording of the behavior of a group of research participants

Practice Questions II

Multiple-Choice Questions

1. Professor Cohen predicts that because "baby boomers" grew up in an era that promoted independence and assertiveness, people who are currently in their 50s will respond differently to a political survey than will people who are currently in their 20s and 30s. The professor's prediction regarding political attitudes is an example of a(n)
   a. question.
   b. hypothesis.
   c. independent variable.
   d. dependent variable.

2. A cohort is defined as a group of people
   a. of similar national origin.
   b. who share a common language.
   c. born within a few years of each other.
   d. who share the same religion.

3. In a test of the effects of noise, groups of students performed a proofreading task in a noisy or a quiet room. To what group were students in the noisy room assigned?
   a. experimental
   b. comparison
   c. replication
   d. dependent

4. If developmentalists discovered that poor people are happier than wealthy people are, this would indicate that wealth and happiness are
   a. unrelated.
   b. positively correlated.
   c. negatively correlated.
   d. causally related.

5. In an experiment testing the effects of noise level on mood, mood is the
   a. hypothesis.
   b. independent variable.
   c. dependent variable.
   d. scientific observation.

6. Researchers who wish to study developmental change over time could use which of the following research designs?
   a. cross-sectional
   b. longitudinal
   c. cohort-sequential
   d. all of the above
7. Which of the following research designs does **NOT** belong with the others?
   a. survey
   b. cross-sequential research
   c. longitudinal research
   d. cross-sectional research
8. The procedure designed to ensure that the experimental and comparison groups do not differ prior to the experiment in any way that might affect the experiment's results is called
   a. variable controlling.
   b. random assignment.
   c. representative sampling.
   d. stratification.
9. To test her hypothesis about a correlation between sudden infant death syndrome (SIDS) and sleeping position, scientist Susan Beal convinced a large group of parents to put their newborns to sleep on their backs. In this research design, back sleeping is the ____________________ condition.
   a. experimental
   b. comparison
   c. independent
   d. dependent

Matching Items

Match each definition or description with its corresponding term.

Terms

10. __________ independent variable
11. __________ dependent variable
12. __________ experiment
13. __________ replication
14. __________ experimental group
15. __________ comparison group
16. __________ culture
17. __________ survey

Definitions or Descriptions

a. a system of shared beliefs, norms, behaviors, and expectations
b. the "treatment-absent" condition in an experiment
c. the "treatment-present" condition in an experiment

d. the research strategy in which a representative sample of individuals is questioned
e. to repeat an experiment to check the reliability of its results
f. the variable manipulated in an experiment
g. the method that can establish cause-and-effect relationships
h. the variable measured in an experiment

Applying Your Knowledge

1. In order to study the effects of temperature on mood, Dr. Sanchez had students fill out questionnaires in either very warm or very cool rooms. In this study, the independent variable consisted of the
   a. number of subjects assigned to each group.
   b. students' responses to the questionnaire.
   c. room temperature.
   d. subject matter of the questions.
2. Esteban believes that high doses of caffeine slow a person's reaction time. In order to test his belief, he has five friends each drink three 8-ounce cups of coffee and then measures their reaction time on a learning task. What is wrong with Esteban's research strategy?
   a. No independent variable is specified.
   b. No dependent variable is specified.
   c. There is no control condition.
   d. There is no provision for replication of the findings.
3. When researchers find that the results of a study are statistically significant at the 0.01 level, this means that
   a. they may have been caused purely by chance.
   b. it is unlikely they could be replicated.
   c. it is unlikely they could have occurred by chance.
   d. the sample population was representative of the general population.
4. If height and body weight are positively correlated, which of the following is true?
   a. There is a cause-and-effect relationship between height and weight.
   b. Knowing a person's height allows one to be able to predict his or her weight.
   c. As height increases, weight decreases.
   d. All of the above are true.

5. An example of longitudinal research would be when an investigator compares the performance of

   a. several different age groups on a memory test.

   b. the same group of people, at different ages, on a test of memory.

   c. an experimental group and a comparison group of subjects on a test of memory.

   d. several different age groups on a test of memory as each group is tested repeatedly over a period of years.

6. For her developmental psychology research project, Lakia decides she wants to focus primarily on qualitative data. You advise her to conduct a(n)

   a. survey.

   b. experiment.

   c. cross-sectional study.

   d. naturalistic observation.

7. Professor Levy conducts a study to examine the relation between children's feelings of being controlled by their parents and children's achievement. Following the study, Professor Levy provides each parent with information about his or her children's feelings about being controlled along with advice on how to help their children do well in school. Which aspect of the code of ethics did Professor Levy violate?

   a. Participation must be voluntary.

   b. Participation must be harmless.

   c. Participants must be allowed to stop at any time.

   d. Participation must be confidential.

8. Dr. Weston is comparing research findings for a group of 30 year olds with findings for the same individuals when they were age 20, as well as with findings for other groups who were 30 in 1990. Which research method is she using?

   a. longitudinal research

   b. cross-sectional research

   c. experimental research

   d. cross-sequential research

9. Dr. Albertini wants to describe the ways that couples interact when they are engaging in conflicts. To examine this, she observes several couples in their homes as they go about their typical routines. She records the details of each conflict. Dr. Albertini is conducting which type of research?

   a. longitudinal

   b. qualitative

   c. experimental

   d. quantitative

10. A psychologist studies the play behavior of third-grade children by watching groups during recess at school. Which research technique is being used?

    a. survey
    b. longitudinal research
    c. experimentation
    d. naturalistic observation

Key Terms

1. **scientific method:** A way to answer questions using empirical research and data-based conclusions. (p. 4; video lesson, segment 1; objective 1)
2. **hypothesis:** A specific prediction that can be tested. (p. 4; video lesson, segment 1; objective 1)
3. **empirical:** When something is based on data, on many experiences, on observation, or on experiment; it is not theoretical. (p. 4; objective 1)
4. **replication:** Repeating a study, usually using different participants, perhaps of another age, socioeconomic status (SES), or culture. (p. 5; objective 1)
5. **sudden infant death syndrome (SIDS):** A situation in which a seemingly healthy infant, usually between 2 and 6 months old, suddenly stops breathing and dies unexpectedly while asleep. (p. 5; objective 3)
6. **culture:** A system of shared beliefs, norms, behaviors, and expectations that persist over time and prescribe social behavior and assumptions. (p. 12; objective 1)
7. **ethnic group:** People whose ancestors were born in the same region and who often share a language, culture, and religion. (p. 13; objective 1)
8. **race:** A group of people who are regarded by themselves or by others as distinct from other groups on the basis of physical appearance, typically skin color. Social scientists think race is a misleading concept, as biological differences are not signified by outward appearance. (p. 13; objective 1)
9. **cohort:** People born within the same historical period who therefore move through life together, experiencing the same events, new technologies, and cultural shifts at the same ages. (p. 17; objective 1)
10. **scientific observation:** A method of testing a hypothesis by unobtrusively watching and recording participants' behavior in a systematic and objective manner—in a natural setting, in a laboratory, or in searches of archival data. (p. 21; video lesson, segment 2; objective 2)
11. **independent variable:** In an experiment, the variable that is introduced to see what effect it has on the dependent variable. Also called the *experimental variable*. (p. 23; video lesson, segment 2; objective 4)

    Example: In the study of the effects of a new drug on memory, the drug is the independent variable.

12. **dependent variable:** In an experiment, the variable that may change as a result of whatever new condition or situation the experimenter adds. In other words, the dependent variable depends on the independent variable. (p. 23; video lesson, segment 2; objective 4)

    Hint: The dependent variable is hypothesized to *depend* on the independent variable.

    Example: In the study of the effects of a new drug on memory, the participants' memory is the dependent variable.

13. **survey:** A research method in which information is collected from a large number of people by interviews, written questionnaires, or some other means. (p. 23; video lesson, segment 2; objective 2)

14. **cross-sectional research:** A research design that compares groups of people who differ in age but are similar in other important characteristics. (p. 24; video lesson, segment 3; objective 5)

15. **longitudinal research:** A research design in which the same individuals are followed over time, as their development is repeatedly assessed. (p. 25; video lesson, segment 3; objective 5)

16. **cohort-sequential research:** A research design in which researchers first study several groups of people of different ages (a cross-sectional approach) and then follow those groups over the years (a longitudinal approach). Also called *cross-sequential research* or *time-sequential research*. (p. 27; objective 5)

17. **correlation:** A number between +1.0 and –1.0 that indicates the degree of relationship between two variables, expressed in terms of the likelihood that one variable will (or will not) occur when the other variable does (or does not). A correlation indicates only that two variables are somehow related, not that one variable causes the other to occur. (p. 28; video lesson, segment 2; objective 3)

18. **quantitative research:** Research that provides data that can be expressed with numbers, such as ranks or scales. (p. 29; objective 7)

19. **qualitative research:** Research that considers qualities, not quantities. Narrative accounts and individual variations are often stressed in qualitative research. (p. 29; objective 7)

20. **code of ethics:** A set of moral principles or guidelines that members of a profession or group are expected to follow. (p. 29; video lesson, segment 3; objective 6)

21. **Institutional Review Board (IRB):** A group of individuals within most educational and medical institutions who ensure that research follows established ethical guidelines. Unlike in prior decades, most research in human development cannot begin without IRB approval. (p. 30; objective 6)

22. **experiment:** Type of research method in which an investigator tests a hypothesis in a controlled situation in which the relevant variables are limited and can be manipulated by the experimenter. (video lesson, segment 2; objective 4)

23. **experimental group:** In an experiment, the group in which subjects are exposed to the independent variable being studied. (video lesson, segment 2; objective 4)

24. **comparison group:** In an experiment, the group in which the treatment of interest, or independent variable, is withheld so that comparison to the experimental group can be made. (video lesson, segment 2; objective 4)
25. **attachment:** A lasting emotional bond that an infant forms with a caregiver—a tie that binds them together in space and endures over time. (video lesson, segment 1; objective 1)
26. **Strange Situation:** A laboratory research procedure used to measure an infant's attachment to his or her caregiver. (video lesson, segment 2; objective 2)
27. **variable:** Any quantity, characteristic, or action that can take on different values within a group of individuals or a single individual. (video lesson, segment 2; objective 1)
28. **random assignment:** The procedure of assigning participants to the experimental and control conditions of an experiment by chance in order to minimize preexisting differences between the groups. (video lesson, segment 2; objective 4)

Summary

The **scientific method** consists of five basic steps: (1) formulate a research question, (2) develop a **hypothesis**, (3) test the hypothesis, (4) draw conclusions, and (5) make the findings available. **Replication** of research findings strengthens confidence in the results and leads researchers to more definitive and extensive conclusions.

Scientists often discuss findings in terms of **variables**, those characteristics or actions that may differ between people, from situation to situation, or perhaps even within one person from one moment to the next. Because the variables in research are numerous, it is difficult to determine whether all the relevant ones have been identified in a particular investigation. Most research projects begin with a review of all relevant literature—journal articles that describe previous research on the topic—which can help scientists formulate a research question and identify the important variables to study.

There are many ways to test hypotheses. One method is **scientific observation** of people in their natural environment or in a laboratory setting. Naturalistic observation is limited in that it tells us only if two variables are correlated.

Correlation is a statistical technique used to determine whether two variables are related. In other words, correlation describes the extent to which changes in one variable are associated with changes in another variable. It does not prove what causes these changes. Only **experiments** can reveal cause-and-effect relationships by allowing researchers to observe whether a change in an **independent variable** produces a corresponding change in a **dependent variable**. Experiments are not, however, without their limitations. Because experiments are so carefully designed and controlled, the behavior demonstrated may not mirror behavior in the "real world."

The scientific **survey** asks individuals to report on their own attitudes, feelings, or behaviors by completing questionnaires or structured interviews. This method is especially vulnerable to bias: the phrasing of the questions may affect the responses obtained and people may give answers they think the researcher wants to hear. Similarly, although a case study can be useful in providing an in-depth analysis of one person's experience, it also is not without limitations. Data from this method can be misinterpreted because of the researcher's biases.

While these different research methods are often described separately, they are not mutually exclusive. For example, researchers often use scientific observation during experiments, such as those conducted by Harry Harlow and Mary Ainsworth that were discussed in the video.

To study changes over time, scientists can choose between different research designs. In **cross-sectional research**, groups of people who are different in age but similar in all other important ways are compared on the characteristic that is of interest to the researcher(s). One limitation of cross-sectional research is that it is always possible that some variable other than age differentiates the groups. In **longitudinal research**, the same group of people is studied over a period of time. Longitudinal research is particularly useful in studying developmental trends that occur over a long age span.

Both longitudinal and cross-sectional researchers must bear in mind that research on a single **cohort** may not be valid for people developing in an earlier or later cohort. A cohort is a group of people born within a few years of each other who are exposed to similar historical and societal experiences. In **cohort-sequential research**, several groups of people at different ages (cross-sectional component) are followed over time (longitudinal component).

Although many developmental researchers use **quantitative research** so that they are able to statistically examine their hypotheses, many nuances can be missed by looking at numbers exclusively. Thus, some developmentalists use **qualitative research**, either by itself or as a means of developing hypotheses for quantitative research.

A **code of ethics** is a set of moral principles intended to guide scientific endeavors. An **Institutional Review Board (IRB)** is a federally required group, found in most educational and medical institutions, that oversees research and enforces ethical guidelines. When studying people, scientists take special care to ensure that participation is voluntary and harmless, and that the study's benefits outweigh its costs. Researchers are also obligated to report research findings as accurately and completely as possible.

Answer Key

Practice Questions I

Multiple-Choice Questions

1. b. is the correct answer. (video lesson, segment 1; objective 1)
2. a. is the correct answer. (video lesson, segment 2; objective 4)

   b. is incorrect. This would be a disadvantage to experiments.

   c. is incorrect. No method is entirely invulnerable to bias.

   d. is incorrect. Only variables that can be manipulated can be examined. For instance, one cannot manipulate gender, race, age, or intelligence.

3. b. is the correct answer. (video lesson, segment 2; objective 4)

   a. is incorrect. A possible hypothesis for this experiment would be that the larger the group, the less hard a given individual will pull.

   c. is incorrect. The dependent variable is the measure of individual effort.

   d. is incorrect. Significance level refers to the numerical value specifying the possibility that the results of an experiment could have occurred by chance.

4. d. is the correct answer. (video lesson, segment 2; objective 2)

   a. is incorrect. Experimentation is appropriate when one can manipulate the independent variable; in this example, the researcher cannot manipulate parents' beliefs.

   b. is incorrect. Longitudinal research would be appropriate if the researcher sought to examine the development of these attitudes over a long period of time.

   c. is incorrect. Mere observation would not allow the researcher to determine the attitudes of the subjects.

5. c. is the correct answer. (video lesson, segment 2; objective 2)

   a. is incorrect. In this method, one subject is studied over a period of time.

   b. & d. are incorrect. In these research methods, two or more groups of subjects are studied and compared.

6. d. is the correct answer. (video lesson, segment 2; objective 1)

7. a. is the correct answer. (video lesson, segment 1; objectives 1 & 4)

8. b. is the correct answer. (video lesson, segment 2; objective 3)

   a. & c. are incorrect. These answers would have been correct had the question stated that there is a *positive* correlation between shoe size and IQ.

   d. is incorrect. A zero correlation would indicate that IQ was unpredictable based on shoe size.

Matching Items

9. e (objective 6)
10. h (video lesson, segment 3; objective 5)
11. d (video lesson, segment 2; objective 3)
12. j (video lesson, segment 2; objective 2)
13. b (video lesson, segment 2; objective 1)
14. c (video lesson, segment 1; objective 1)
15. a (video lesson, segment 1; objective 1)
16. g (video lesson, segment 3; objective 5)
17. f (video lesson, segment 3; objective 5)
18. i (objective 6)

Practice Questions II

Multiple-Choice Questions

1. b. is the correct answer. (video lesson, segment 1; objective 1)

   a. is incorrect. The professor is stating a testable prediction, which is a more advanced step of the scientific method than simply asking a question.

   c. & d. are incorrect. Variables are treatments (independent) or behaviors (dependent) in experiments, which this situation clearly is not.

2. c. is the correct answer. (video lesson, segment 3; objective 5)

   a., b., & d. are incorrect. These are attributes of an ethnic group.

3. a. is the correct answer. The experimental group is the one in which the variable or treatment—in this case, noise, is present. (video lesson, segment 2; objective 4)

   b. is incorrect. Students in the quiet room would be in the comparison condition.

   c. is incorrect. There is no such group in an experiment.

   d. is incorrect. The word *dependent* refers to a kind of variable in experiments; groups are either experimental or comparison.

4. c. is the correct answer. (video lesson, segment 2; objective 3)

   a. is incorrect. This research suggests that wealth and happiness are related.

   b. is incorrect. This answer would be correct if wealthy people were found to be happier than poor people.

   d. is incorrect. Correlation does not imply causation.

5. c. is the correct answer. (video lesson, segment 2; objective 4)

   a. is incorrect. Hypotheses make specific, testable predictions.

   b. is incorrect. Noise level is the independent variable.

   d. is incorrect. Scientific observation is a research method in which subjects are watched, while their behavior is recorded unobtrusively.

6. d. is the correct answer. All three types enable researchers to study developmental change over time and all three have advantages and drawbacks. (video lesson, segment 2; objective 5)

   a., b., & c. are incorrect because only by directly controlling the variables of interest can a researcher uncover cause-and-effect relationships.

7. a. is the correct answer. Case studies only study a single individual; the remaining three designs examine development using many participants. (video lesson, segment 2; objectives 2 & 5)

8. b. is the correct answer. If enough participants are used in an experiment and they are randomly assigned to the two groups, any differences that emerge between the groups should stem from the experiment itself. (video lesson, segment 2; objective 4)

   a., c., & d. are incorrect. None of these terms describes precautions taken in setting up groups for experiments.

9. a. is the correct answer. Back sleeping is the experimental condition being tested. (video lesson, segment 2; objectives 3 & 4)

   b. is incorrect. The comparison (control) condition in this research design is stomach sleeping as this was the European and American custom at the time.

   c. & d. are incorrect. These words refer to a kind of variable in experiments; conditions are either experimental or comparison/control.

Matching Items

10. f (video lesson, segment 2; objective 4)
11. h (video lesson, segment 2; objective 4)
12. g (video lesson, segment 2; objective 4)
13. e (objective 1)
14. c (video lesson, segment 2; objective 4)
15. b (video lesson, segment 2; objective 4)
16. a (objective 1)
17. d (video lesson, segment 2; objective 2)

Applying Your Knowledge

1. c. is the correct answer. (video lesson, segment 2; objective 4)
2. c. is the correct answer. In order to determine the effects of caffeine on reaction time, Esteban needs to measure reaction time in a control, or comparison, group that does not receive caffeine. (video lesson, segment 2; objective 4)

   a. is incorrect. Caffeine is the independent variable.

   b. is incorrect. Reaction time is the dependent variable.

   d. is incorrect. Whether or not Esteban's experiment can be replicated is determined by the precision with which he reports his procedures, which is not an aspect of research strategy.
3. c. is the correct answer. (objective 4)
4. b. is the correct answer. (video lesson, segment 2; objective 3)

   a. is incorrect. Correlation does not imply causation.

   c. is incorrect. If height and body weight are positively correlated, an increase in one is associated with an increase in the other.
5. b. is the correct answer. (video lesson, segment 3; objective 5)

   a. is incorrect. This is an example of cross-sectional research.

   c. is incorrect. This is an example of an experiment.

   d. is incorrect. This is an example of cross-sequential research.
6. d. is the correct answer. (objectives 2 & 7)

   a., b., & c. are incorrect. These research methods generally yield quantitative, rather than qualitative, data.
7. d. is the correct answer. Providing the parents information about individual children's responses is considered breaking confidentiality. (objective 6)

8. d. is the correct answer. (objective 5)

   a. & c. are incorrect. In these research methods, only one group of subjects is studied.

   b. is incorrect. Dr. Weston's design includes comparison of groups of people of different ages over time.

9. b. is the correct answer. (objective 7)

   a. is incorrect. This type of research design examines changes over extended periods of time.

   c. is incorrect. This type of research manipulates a variable. This research did not involve any manipulation.

   d. is incorrect. This type of research uses data that can be expressed in numbers.

10. d. is the correct answer. (video lesson, segment 2; objective 2)

Lesson Review

Lesson 2

Developmental Study as a Science

Please Note: Use this matrix to guide your study and achieve the learning objectives of this lesson. It will also help you to view the video, which defines and demonstrates important concepts and skills as they relate to everyday life.

Learning Objective	Textbook	Course Student Guide	Video Lesson
1. List and describe the basic steps of the scientific method, and discuss the challenge researchers face in identifying variables for a particular study.	pp. 4–6, 10–20	Key Terms: 1, 2, 3, 4, 6, 7, 8, 9, 25, 27; Practice Questions I: 1, 6, 7, 13, 14, 15; Practice Questions II: 1, 13.	Segment 1: *The Scientific Method* Segment 2: *Research Methods*
2. Describe scientific observation and surveys as research methods, noting at least one advantage (or strength) and one disadvantage (or weakness) of each.	pp. 21–24	Key Terms: 10, 13, 26; Practice Questions I: 4, 5, 12; Practice Questions II: 7, 16, 17; Applying Your Knowledge: 6, 10.	Segment 2: *Research Methods*
3. Define what correlation means in science and offer examples of its use in the study of human development.	pp. 5–6, 28–29	Key Terms: 5, 17; Practice Questions I: 8, 11; Practice Questions II: 4, 9; Applying Your Knowledge: 4.	Segment 2: *Research Methods*
4. Describe the components of an experiment, and discuss the main advantage and some limitations of this research method.	pp. 22–23	Key Terms: 11, 12, 22, 23, 24, 28; Practice Questions I: 2, 3, 7; Practice Questions II: 3, 5, 8, 9, 10, 11, 12, 14, 15; Applying Your Knowledge: 1, 2, 3.	Segment 1: *The Scientific Method* Segment 2: *Research Methods*
5. Describe three basic research designs used by developmental psychologists to study changes over time.	pp. 24–27	Key Terms: 14, 15, 16; Practice Questions I: 10, 16, 17; Practice Questions II: 2, 6, 7; Applying Your Knowledge: 5, 8.	Segment 2: *Research Methods* Segment 3: *Studying Changes over Time*
6. Discuss the code of ethics that should be followed by researchers in the field of developmental psychology and the role of an Institutional Review Board (IRB).	pp. 29–31	Key Terms: 20, 21; Practice Questions I: 9, 18; Applying Your Knowledge: 7.	Segment 3: *Studying Changes over Time*
7. Describe the difference between quantitative research and qualitative research.	p. 29	Key Terms: 18, 19; Applying Your Knowledge: 6, 9.	

Nature and Nurture: The Dance of Life

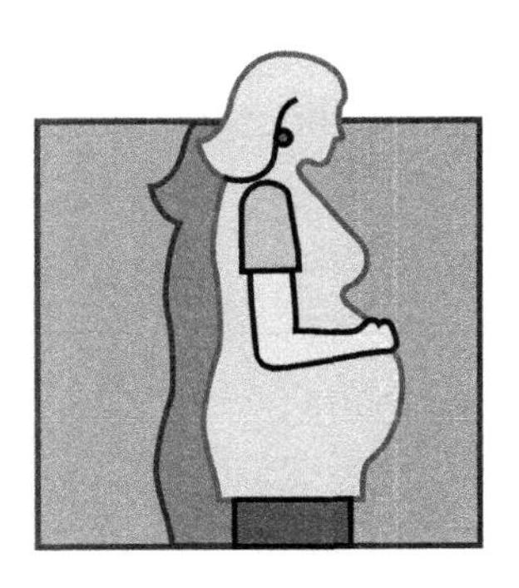

Lesson 3

The Beginnings:
Heredity and Environment

Preview

Much is determined at the moment of *conception*, when a sperm and ovum unite to initiate the developmental processes that will culminate in the birth of a new human being. The genetic legacies of the mother and father influence virtually everything about the developing person—including physical traits, such as gender and appearance, as well as intellectual and personality characteristics. And yet, each person is also shaped by powerful external factors, such as nutrition, parental guidance, health care, schooling, peer groups, and so on.

This lesson describes the fusion of the female's ovum and the male's sperm and the biological mechanisms by which chromosomes and genes are transmitted to the developing person. But, although development is strongly influenced by **heredity** (genes), its ultimate course depends on interaction with a person's **environment** (the outside factors that affect how those genes are expressed). In other words, we are all the product of an ongoing interaction between *nature* and *nurture*.

This lesson also discusses the benefits of **genetic counseling** for prospective parents who are at risk of giving birth to children with genetic disorders. Prenatal diagnosis of genetic disorders has been greatly facilitated by recent advances in medical technology, allowing prospective parents to make more informed decisions about the risks of childbearing.

As you complete this lesson, consider your own heredity and environment. (If possible, you may want to interview your immediate relatives to discuss your family's background.) For example, in what ways are you like your mother and father? In what ways are you different? How are you similar to your aunts, uncles, and grandparents? Now, recall the different environmental factors or contexts that may have influenced your development—your parents, your siblings, your school experiences, your religion, your neighborhood, your friends and peers, your socioeconomic status (SES), cultural values, etc. Consider how these external influences may have interacted with your basic genetic makeup to "mold" you into the person you are today.

Prior Knowledge That Will Be Used in This Lesson

- This lesson focuses primarily on the *biosocial domain* of development (introduced in Lesson 1). The biosocial domain includes all the growth and change that occurs in a person's body as well as the genetic, nutritional, and health factors that affect that growth and change. But keep in mind, although the division of human development into three domains makes it easier to study, development is a holistic, interactive process—changes in one domain often produce changes in another. Development reflects an interaction between all three domains.

Learning Objectives

Use this information to guide your reading, viewing, thinking, and studying. After successfully completing this lesson, you should be able to:

1. Define gamete, describe conception, and discuss early development of the zygote, including the processes of duplication, division, and differentiation.
2. Define gene, chromosome, human genome, and allele, describe how genetic instructions are transmitted from parents to their children, and explain how sex is determined.
3. Discuss the reasons for genetic continuity and diversity, and distinguish between monozygotic and dizygotic twins.
4. Describe the common treatment methods and ethical considerations of infertility.
5. Differentiate genotype from phenotype, explain the polygenic and multifactorial nature of human traits, and define the Human Genome Project.
6. Describe additive and nonadditive patterns of gene interaction, including the dominant-recessive pattern, X-linked inheritance, copy number variations, and parental imprinting, and give examples of some traits that result from each type of interaction.
7. Define epigenetics and explain how scientists use twin studies to attempt to distinguish the effects of genes (nature) and environment (nurture) on human development.
8. Describe the ways in which genetic and nongenetic influences interact, especially with reference to schizophrenia, alcoholism, and visual acuity.
9. Identify some of the most common chromosomal abnormalities and genetic disorders, describe the use of prenatal tests, gene therapy, and genetic counseling, and discuss some of the dilemmas and ethical questions that can result from these interventions.

Textbook Reading & Video Viewing

For the most effective study of this lesson, complete the assignments in the sequence listed below.

Before viewing the video program:

Read Chapter 3, "Heredity and Environment," pages 63–91.

View the video for Lesson 3, "Nature and Nurture: The Dance of Life."

Segment 1: *The Beginning of Development*

Segment 2: *The Twin Perspective*

Segment 3: *From Genotype to Phenotype*

Segment 4: *Genetic and Chromosomal Abnormalities*

After viewing the video program:

Review all reading assignments for this lesson.

Complete the "Practice Questions" and "Applying Your Knowledge" sections to reinforce your understanding of important terms and concepts and measure your achievement of the Learning Objectives. Check your answers with the feedback given and review when necessary.

Practice Questions I

Multiple-Choice Questions

1. When a sperm and an ovum merge, a one-celled ________________ is formed.
   a. zygote
   b. reproductive cell
   c. gamete
   d. monozygote

2. Genes are discrete segments that provide the biochemical instructions for specific
   a. zygotes.
   b. chromosomes.
   c. proteins.
   d. personality traits.

3. A pair of genes with identical letters in their codes are
   a. monozygotic.
   b. homozygous.
   c. additive.
   d. heterozygous.

4. Since the twenty-third pair of chromosomes in females is XX, each ovum carries an
   a. XX zygote.
   b. X zygote.
   c. XY zygote.
   d. X chromosome.

5. When a zygote splits, the two identical, independent clusters that develop become
   a. dizygotic twins.
   b. monozygotic twins.
   c. fraternal twins.
   d. trizygotic twins.
6. In scientific research, the best way to separate the effects of genes and the environment is to study
   a. dizygotic twins.
   b. adopted children and their siblings.
   c. adopted children and their adoptive parents.
   d. monozygotic twins raised in different environments.
7. Most of the known genetic disorders are
   a. dominant.
   b. recessive.
   c. seriously disabling.
   d. sex-linked.
8. When we say that a characteristic is multifactorial, we mean that
   a. many genes are involved.
   b. many chromosomes are involved.
   c. many genetic and environmental factors are involved.
   d. the characteristic is polygenic.
9. Genes are segments of molecules of
   a. genotype.
   b. deoxyribonucleic acid (DNA).
   c. karyotype.
   d. phenotype.
10. During in vitro fertilization (IVF),
    a. a zygote is produced outside of a woman's body, then surgically implanted in her uterus.
    b. donor sperm are used for intrauterine insemination.
    c. a woman takes drugs to cause ovulation, then conceives without further medical assistance.
    d. a zygote is produced within a woman's body, surgically removed, then developed in a glass laboratory dish.

11. A chromosomal abnormality that affects males only involves a(n)

    a. XO chromosomal pattern.
    b. XXX chromosomal pattern.
    c. YY chromosomal pattern.
    d. XXY chromosomal pattern.

12. Almost all human traits are

    a. dominant
    b. unifactorial
    c. polygenic
    d. recessive

13. Babies born with trisomy-21 (Down syndrome) are often

    a. born to older parents.
    b. unusually aggressive.
    c. abnormally tall by adolescence.
    d. blind.

14. To say that a trait is polygenic means that

    a. many genes make it more likely that the individual will inherit the trait.
    b. it is affected by many genes.
    c. the trait is multifactorial.
    d. most people carry genes for the trait.

15. Some genetic diseases are recessive, so the child cannot inherit the condition unless both parents

    a. have the same dominant gene.
    b. carry the same recessive gene.
    c. have XO chromosomes.
    d. have the disease.

Matching Items

Match each definition or description with its corresponding term.

Terms

16. __________ gametes
17. __________ chromosome
18. __________ genotype
19. __________ phenotype
20. __________ monozygotic twins
21. __________ dizygotic twins
22. __________ epigenetics
23. __________ fragile X syndrome
24. __________ carrier
25. __________ stem cells
26. __________ allele
27. __________ XX
28. __________ XY

Definitions or Descriptions

a. chromosome pair inherited by genetic females
b. identical twins
c. sperm and ovum
d. cells that can produce any other type of cell
e. a person who has a recessive gene in his or her genotype that is not expressed in the phenotype
f. fraternal twins
g. the interaction of environmental forces, genes, and genetic expression
h. a DNA molecule
i. the behavioral or physical expression of genetic potential
j. a chromosomal abnormality
k. alternate versions of a gene
l. chromosome pair inherited by genetic males
m. a person's entire genetic inheritance

Practice Questions II

Multiple-Choice Questions

1. Assisted reproductive technology (ART) includes
   a. artificial insemination.
   b. in vitro fertilization.
   c. surrogate pregnancies.
   d. all of the above.

2. Research studies of monozygotic twins who were raised apart suggest that
   a. virtually every human trait is affected by both genes and environment.
   b. only a few psychological traits, such as emotional reactivity, are affected by genes.
   c. most traits are determined by environmental influences.
   d. most traits are determined by genes.

3. Males with fragile X syndrome are
   a. feminine in appearance.
   b. less severely affected than females.
   c. frequently retarded.
   d. unusually tall and aggressive.

4. Disorders that are ______________________ are most likely to pass undetected from generation to generation.

   a. dominant

   b. sex-linked

   c. recessive

   d. lethal

5. The incidences of sickle-cell anemia, phenylketonuria, thalassemia, and Tay-Sachs disease indicate that

   a. these disorders are more common today than 50 years ago.

   b. these disorders are less common today than 50 years ago.

   c. certain genetic disorders are more common in certain ethnic groups.

   d. certain genetic disorders are more common in males than in females.

6. Dizygotic twins result when

   a. a single egg is fertilized by a sperm and then splits.

   b. a single egg is fertilized by two different sperm.

   c. two eggs are fertilized by two different sperm.

   d. either a single egg is fertilized by one sperm or two eggs are fertilized by two different sperm.

7. Molecules of DNA that in humans are organized into twenty-three complementary pairs are called

   a. zygotes.

   b. genes.

   c. chromosomes.

   d. ova.

8. Shortly after the zygote is formed, it begins the processes of duplication and division. Each resulting new cell has

   a. the same number of chromosomes as was contained in the zygote.

   b. half the number of chromosomes as was contained in the zygote.

   c. twice, then four times, then eight times the number of chromosomes as was contained in the zygote.

   d. half the number of chromosomes except those that determine sex.

9. In a male, the 23rd pair of chromosomes (XY) are _______________ because the two genes that make up the pair are different.

   a. fragile

   b. homozygous

   c. heterozygous

   d. stem cells

10. When the male cells in the testes and the female cells in the ovaries divide to produce gametes, the process differs from that in the production of all other cells. As a result of the different process, the gametes have

    a. one rather than both members of each chromosome pair.
    b. twenty-three chromosome pairs.
    c. X but not Y chromosomes.
    d. chromosomes from both parents.

11. Within hours of conception, the zygote begins all of the following processes **EXCEPT**

    a. differentiation.
    b. division.
    c. deletion.
    d. duplication.

12. Genotype is to phenotype as ____________________ is to ____________________.

    a. genetic potential; physical expression
    b. physical expression; genetic potential
    c. sperm; ovum
    d. gamete; zygote

13. The genes that influence height and skin color interact according to the ______________________ pattern.

    a. dominant-recessive
    b. X-linked
    c. additive
    d. nonadditive

14. X-linked recessive genes explain why some traits seem to be passed from

    a. father to son.
    b. father to daughter.
    c. mother to daughter.
    d. mother to son.

15. Research on nearsightedness and alcoholism has provided evidence of the importance of ______________________ on visual acuity and the importance of ______________________ on alcoholism.

    a. family characteristics; genetic factors alone
    b. outdoor play; psychological characteristics
    c. culture and cohort factors; family characteristics
    d. personality characteristics; culture and cohort factors

True or False Items

Write T (for true) or F (for false) on the line in front of each statement.

16. _____ Most human characteristics are multifactorial, caused by the interaction of genetic and environmental factors.
17. _____ According to the Berger textbook, about 5 to 10 percent of all zygotes have more or fewer than 46 chromosomes.
18. _____ Research suggests that susceptibility to alcoholism is at least partly the result of genetic inheritance.
19. _____ Two X-shaped chromosomes in the 23rd pair mean the zygote is a female.
20. _____ Only a very few human traits are polygenic.
21. _____ The zygote contains all the biologically inherited information—the genes and chromosomes—that a person will have during his or her life.
22. _____ A couple should probably seek genetic counseling if several earlier pregnancies ended in spontaneous abortion.
23. _____ Copy number variations correlate with almost every disease and condition.
24. _____ Two people who have the same phenotype may have a different genotype for a trait such as eye color.
25. _____ When cells divide to produce reproductive cells (gametes), each sperm or ovum receives only twenty-three chromosomes, half as many as the original cell.
26. ______ A developmentalist studying epigenetics would likely be interested in why identical twins are not identical in their development of schizophrenia.

Applying Your Knowledge

1. The international effort to map the complete human genetic code revealed that
   a. the total number of human genes is far greater than the 100,000 previously estimated.
   b. almost all genes present in the human genome are present in other creatures as well.
   c. differences among the human races constitute 15 to 20 percent of genetic variation.
   d. all of these are true.

2. Before their first child was born, Jack and Diane decided that they should be karyotyped, which means that

   a. their chromosomes were photographed.

   b. a genetic counselor filled out a complete history of genetic diseases in their families.

   c. they each took a fertility test.

   d. they selected the sex of their child.

3. Celia and Gregor have four children. Gregor has Trait X, but Celia does not. Trait X is known to be recessive. Half of Celia's children were born with Trait X. Celia is

   a. a carrier of Trait X.

   b. a genotype for Trait X.

   c. polygenic for Trait X.

   d. probably going to develop Trait X later in life.

4. Some men are color-blind because they inherit a particular recessive gene from their mother. That recessive gene is carried on the

   a. X chromosome.

   b. XX chromosome pair.

   c. Y chromosome.

   d. X or Y chromosome.

5. If your mother is much taller than your father, it is most likely that your height will be

   a. about the same as your mother's, because the X chromosome determines height.

   b. about the same as your father's, because the Y chromosome determines height.

   c. somewhere between your mother's and father's heights because of additive heredity.

   d. greater than both your mother's and father's because of your grandfather's dominant gene.

6. If a monozygotic twin develops schizophrenia, the likelihood of the other twin developing schizophrenia is much higher than would be true with dizygotic twins. This suggests that

   a. schizophrenia is caused by genes.

   b. schizophrenia is influenced by genes.

   c. environment is unimportant in the development of schizophrenia.

   d. monozygotic twins are especially vulnerable to schizophrenia.

7. A person's skin turns yellow-orange as a result of a carrot-juice diet regimen. This is an example of

   a. an interaction between heredity and environment.

   b. an alteration in genotype.

   c. polygenic inheritance.

   d. a chromosomal abnormality.

8. Heredity appears to make some people highly susceptible to alcoholism. A child who inherits the relevant genes is susceptible to alcoholism
   a. under most circumstances.
   b. only if alcoholism is the dominant gene.
   c. if the environment supports it.
   d. if he or she is raised by biological rather than adoptive parents.

9. If a man carries the recessive gene for Tay-Sachs disease and his wife does not, the chances of their having a child with Tay-Sachs disease is
   a. one in four.
   b. fifty-fifty.
   c. zero.
   d. dependent upon the wife's ethnic background.

10. One of the best ways to distinguish the relative influence of genetic and environmental factors on behavior is to compare children who have
    a. the same genes and environments.
    b. different genes and environments.
    c. different genes and similar environments.
    d. the same genes but different environments.

11. When identical twins have been reared apart, researchers have generally found
    a. strong behavioral and psychological similarities.
    b. strong behavioral, but not necessarily psychological, similarities.
    c. striking behavioral and psychological differences.
    d. that it is impossible to predict how such twins will develop.

12. Susan and Bryan, who both have a history of schizophrenia in their families, are concerned that the child they hope to have will inherit a genetic predisposition to schizophrenia. Based on information presented in the textbook, what advice should you offer them?
    a. "Stop worrying; schizophrenia is only weakly genetic."
    b. "It is almost certain that your child will become schizophrenic."
    c. "Influences other than biology, such as family emotionality and undernutrition, play a critical role in determining whether schizophrenia is expressed."
    d. "Wait to have children until you are both middle aged, in order to see if the two of you become schizophrenic."

13. Sixteen-year-old Karson experiences some mental slowness and hearing and heart problems, yet he is able to care for himself and is unusually sweet-tempered. Of the following, the most likely cause of Karson's condition is

    a. hemophilia.
    b. Alzheimer's disease.
    c. Klinefelter syndrome.
    d. Down syndrome.

14. Genetically, Billy's potential height is 6' 0". Because he did not receive a balanced diet, however, he grew to only 5' 9". Billy's actual height is

    a. a recessive gene.
    b. a dominant gene.
    c. part of his genotype.
    d. part of his phenotype.

15. Ann has Prader-Willi syndrome as a result of a deletion inherited from her father's chromosome 15. If the deletion had been from her mother's chromosome 15, she would have Angelman syndrome instead. The reason for this difference is

    a. heritability.
    b. fragile X syndrome.
    c. parental imprinting.
    d. epigenetics.

Key Terms

1. **deoxyribonucleic acid (DNA):** The chemical composition of the molecules that contain the genes, which are the chemical instructions for cells to manufacture various proteins. (p. 64; video lesson, segment 1; objective 2)
2. **chromosome:** One of the 46 molecules of DNA (in 23 pairs) that virtually each cell of the human body contains and that, together, contain all the genes. Other species have more or fewer chromosomes. (p. 64; video lesson, segment 1; objective 2)
3. **gene:** A small section of a chromosome; the basic unit for the transmission of heredity. A gene consists of a string of chemicals that provide instructions for the cell to manufacture certain proteins. (p. 64; video lesson, segment 1; objective 2)
4. **allele:** A variation that makes a gene different in some way from other genes for the same characteristics. Many genes never vary; others have several possible alleles. (p. 64; objective 2)
5. **genome:** The entire set of all the genes that are instructions to make human an individual member of a certain species. (p. 65; objective 2)

6. **gamete:** A reproductive cell; that is, a sperm or ovum that can produce a new individual if it combines with a gamete from the other sex to make a zygote. (p. 66; objective 1)
7. **zygote:** The single cell formed from the union of two gametes, a sperm and an ovum. (p. 66; video program, segment 2; objective 1)
8. **genotype:** An organism's entire genetic inheritance, or genetic potential. (p. 66; video lesson, segment 3; objective 5)
9. **homozygous:** Referring to two genes of one pair that are exactly the same in every letter of their code. Most gene pairs are homozygous. (p. 66; objective 2)
10. **heterozygous:** Referring to two genes of one pair that differ in some way. Typically one allele has only a few base pairs that differ from the other member of the pair. (p. 66; objective 2)
11. **twenty-third pair:** The chromosome pair that, in humans, determines sex. The other 22 pairs are autosomes—inherited equally by males and females. (p. 67; objective 2)
12. **XX:** A twenty-third chromosomal pair consisting of two X-shaped chromosomes (one from the mother and one from the father). XX zygotes become females. (p. 67; objective 2)
13. **XY:** A twenty-third chromosomal pair consisting of one X-shaped chromosome from the mother and one Y-shaped chromosome from the father. XY zygotes become males. (p. 67; objective 2)
14. **stem cells:** Cells from which any other specialized type of cell can form. (p. 69; objective 1)
15. **monozygotic (MZ) twins:** Twins who originate from one zygote that splits apart very early in development. Also called *identical twins*. Other monozygotic multiple births (such as triplets and quadruplets) can occur as well. (p. 70; video lesson, segment 2; objective 3)

    Memory aid: *Mono* means "one"; monozygotic twins develop from one fertilized ovum.
16. **dizygotic (DZ) twins:** Twins who are formed when two separate ova are fertilized by two separate sperm at roughly the same time. Also called *fraternal twins*. (p. 70; video lesson, segment 2; objective 3)

    Memory aid: A fraternity is a group of two (*di*) or more nonidentical individuals.
17. **assisted reproductive technology (ART):** The general term for the techniques used to help infertile couples conceive and sustain a pregnancy. (p. 71; objective 4)
18. **in vitro fertilization (IVF):** Fertilization that takes place outside a woman's body (as in a glass laboratory dish). The procedure involves mixing sperm with ova that have been surgically removed from the woman's ovary. If a zygote is produced, it is inserted into a woman's uterus, where it may implant and develop into a baby. (p. 71; objective 4)

19. **phenotype:** The observable characteristics of a person, including appearance, personality, intelligence, and all other traits. (p. 73; video lesson, segment 3; objective 5)
20. **polygenic:** Referring to a trait that is influenced by many genes. (p. 73; objective 5)
21. **multifactorial:** Referring to a trait that is affected by many factors, both genetic and environmental, that enhance, halt, shape, or alter the expression of genes, resulting in a phenotype that may differ markedly from the genotype. (p. 73; objective 5)

    Memory aid: The roots of the words polygenic and multifactorial give their meaning: *poly* means "many" and *genic* means "of the genes"; *multi* means "several" and *factorial* clearly refers to factors.
22. **epigenetic:** Referring to environmental factors that affect genes and genetic expression—enhancing, halting, shaping, or altering the expression of genes and resulting in a phenotype that may differ markedly from the genotype. (p. 74; objective 7)
23. **Human Genome Project:** The international effort to map the complete genetic code that was virtually completed in 2001, though analysis is ongoing. (p. 75; objective 5)
24. **dominant-recessive pattern:** The interaction of a heterozygous pair of alleles in such a way that the phenotype reflects one allele (the dominant gene) more than the other (the recessive gene). (p. 76; objective 6)
25. **carrier:** A person whose genotype includes a gene that is not expressed in the phenotype. The carried gene occurs in half of the carrier's gametes and thus is passed on to half of the carrier's children. If such a gene is inherited from both parents, the characteristic appears in the phenotype. (p. 76; objective 8)
26. **X-linked:** A gene carried on the X chromosome. If a male inherits an X-linked recessive trait from his mother, he expresses that trait because the Y from his father has no counteracting gene. Females are more likely to be carriers of X-linked traits but are less likely to express them. (p. 76; objective 6)
27. **copy number variations:** Genes with various repeats or deletions of base pairs. (p. 77; objective 6)
28. **heritability:** A statistic that indicates what percentage of the variation in a particular trait within a particular population, in a particular context and era, can be traced to genes. (p. 80; objectives 2 & 7)
29. **Down syndrome:** A condition in which a person has 47 chromosomes instead of the usual 46, with 3 rather than 2 chromosomes at the 21st site. People with Down syndrome typically have distinctive characteristics, including unusual facial features, heart abnormalities, and language difficulties. Also called *trisomy-21*. (p. 82; objective 9)
30. **fragile X syndrome:** A genetic disorder in which part of the X chromosome seems to be attached to the rest of it by a very thin string of molecules. The cause is a single gene that has more than 200 repetitions of one triplet. (p. 83; objective 9)

31. **genetic counseling:** Consultation and testing by trained experts that enable individuals to learn about their genetic heritage, including harmful conditions that they might pass along to any children they may conceive. (p. 88; video lesson, segment 4; objective 9)

32. **phenylketonuria (PKU):** A genetic disorder in which a child's body is unable to metabolize an amino acid called phenylalanine. Unless the infant immediately begins a special diet, the resulting buildup of phenylalanine in body fluids causes brain damage, progressive mental retardation, and other symptoms. (p. 89; objective 9)

33. **heredity:** The transmission of traits and predispositions from parent to child through the genes. (video lesson, introduction; objectives 2 & 7)

34. **environment:** When social scientists discuss the effects of the environment on genes, they are referring to everything—from the impact of the immediate cell environment to the multitude of factors in the outside world, such as nutrition, climate, family interactions, and the cultural context—that are not part of a person's genetic inheritance. (video lesson, segment 1; objective 7)

35. **amniocentesis:** A prenatal diagnostic procedure in which a sample of amniotic fluid is withdrawn by syringe and tested to determine if the developing fetus is healthy. (video lesson, segment 4; objective 9)

36. **gene therapy:** The altering of an organism's genetic instructions through the insertion and addition of normal genes by way of a blood transfusion, bone marrow transplant, or direct insertion into a cluster of cells. (video lesson, segment 4; objective 9)

37. **dominant gene:** When alleles interact according to the dominant-recessive pattern, the resulting phenotype reveals the influence of the dominant gene more than the other allele. (video lesson, segment 3; objective 6)

38. **recessive gene:** When alleles interact according to the dominant-recessive pattern, the resulting phenotype reveals the influence of one allele more than the other allele, called the recessive gene. (video lesson, segment 3; objective 6)

Summary

Conception occurs when the male **gamete** (or sperm) penetrates the membrane of the female gamete (the ovum); the sperm and egg then fuse, and their genetic material combines in the one-celled **zygote**. Within hours, the zygote initiates human development through the processes of duplication, division, and differentiation. Each body cell created from these processes carries an exact copy of the zygote's genetic instructions.

Genes, the basic units of heredity, are discrete segments of a **chromosome**, and each chromosome is one molecule of **DNA (deoxyribonucleic acid)**. Every human body cell, except the sperm and ovum, has 23 pairs of chromosomes (one chromosome in each pair from each parent). In contrast, the sperm and ovum contain only 23 single chromosomes each. The **twenty-third pair** of chromosomes, which determines sex, is designated **XY** in the male and **XX** in the female. The critical factor in the determination of the zygote's sex is which sperm reaches the ovum first, a Y sperm, creating a boy, or an X sperm, creating a girl.

Approximately once in every 270 pregnancies a single zygote splits into two separate identical cells that develop into genetically identical, or **monozygotic twins**, who have the potential for developing the same physical appearance and psychological characteristics and the same vulnerability to specific diseases. Fraternal or **dizygotic twins** occur about once in every sixty births. Dizygotic twins begin life as two separate zygotes and share no more genes than any other siblings (about 50 percent). The number of multiple births has doubled in many nations because of the increased use of fertility drugs, **in vitro fertilization (IVF)**, and other **assisted reproductive technologies (ART)**.

Most human traits are **polygenic**—that is, affected by many genes—and **multifactorial**—that is, influenced by many factors, including factors in the environment. **Genotype** refers to the sum total of all the genes a person inherits. **Phenotype** refers to the characteristics that are expressed. Thus, people may carry genes that are not expressed.

The various genes underlying height and skin color, for example, interact in an additive pattern: the phenotype in question reflects the sum of all the genes involved. Less commonly, genes interact in a nonadditive fashion. Genes that have a controlling influence over weaker, **recessive genes** are called **dominant genes**. Hundreds of physical characteristics follow this dominant-recessive pattern (a nonadditive pattern). **X-linked** genes are carried on the X chromosome. If an X-linked gene is recessive, then the trait will be more likely to be expressed in males, as they do not have a second X to carry a corresponding dominant **allele**.

As you learned in the video, scientists use twin research to help distinguish between genetic and environmental influences. For example, for any given characteristic, if monozygotic twins are much more alike than dizygotic twins, it seems likely that genes play a significant role in the appearance of that trait. The best way to separate the effects of genes and environment is to study identical twins who were separated at birth and raised in different families.

Epigenetic theory emphasizes the interaction between genes and the environment. "Epi-" refers to the various environmental factors that affect the expression of each person's genetic instructions. These include facilitating factors, such as nourishing food and freedom to play, as well as potentially disruptive factors such as injury, temperature, or crowding. "Genetic" refers both to the genes that make each person unique and to the genes humans share with all other humans. We may debate how much any given trait is result of genes and how much is the result of experience. But, experts agree that every aspect of our development is a product of both nature and nurture, not one or the other.

Scientists are particularly interested in how genetic influences and nongenetic influences interact. Some experts summarize the association between genes and environment is this way: Genes represent an individual's potential, and the environment influences how and whether the gene is expressed. Schizophrenia, alcoholism, and nearsightedness provide interesting examples of the influence of family environment, personality, culture, and cohort.

An estimated half of all zygotes have too few or too many chromosomes. Most are lost through miscarriage, also called spontaneous abortion. Once in every 200 births, however, a baby is born with a chromosomal abnormality that leads to a recognizable syndrome.

Although most known genetic disorders are dominant, recessive and multifactorial disorders claim many more victims. Among the more common recessive genetic disorders are cystic fibrosis, thalassemia, and sickle-cell anemia. For most of human history, couples at risk for having a child with a genetic problem did not know it. **Genetic counseling** and prenatal testing are means by which couples can learn more about their genes and make informed decisions about childbearing. Couples who have a high probability of producing a baby with a serious genetic condition have several alternatives—from avoiding pregnancy to adoption to considering abortion. In cases where the consequences of a disease are variable, the decision making is often more difficult.

Answer Key

Practice Questions I

Multiple-Choice Questions

1. a. is the correct answer. (video lesson, segment 2; objective 1)

   b. & c. are incorrect. The reproductive cells (sperm and ova), which are also called gametes, are individual entities.

   d. is incorrect. Monozygote refers to one member of a pair of identical twins.

2. c. is the correct answer. (video lesson, segment 1; objective 2)

   a. is incorrect. The zygote is the first cell of the developing person.

   b. is incorrect. Chromosomes are molecules of DNA that carry genes.

   d. is incorrect. Genes do not code for specific personalities.

3. b. is the correct answer. (objective 2)

4. d. is the correct answer. When the ova are formed, one member of each chromosome pair splits off; because in females both are X chromosomes, each ovum must carry an X chromosome. (objective 2)

   a., b., & c. are incorrect. The zygote refers to the merged sperm and ovum that is the first new cell of the developing individual.

5. b. is the correct answer. Mono means “one.” Thus, monozygotic twins develop from one zygote. (video lesson, segment 2; objective 3)

   a. & c. are incorrect. Dizygotic, or fraternal, twins develop from two (di) zygotes.

   d. is incorrect. A trizygotic birth would result in triplets (tri), rather than twins.

6. d. is the correct answer. In this situation, one factor (genetic similarity) is held constant while the other factor (environment) is varied. Therefore, any similarity in traits is strong evidence of genetic inheritance. (video lesson, segment 2; objective 7)

7. a. is the correct answer. (objective 9)

   b., c. & d. are incorrect. Most dominant disorders are neither seriously disabling, nor sex-linked.

8. c. is the correct answer. (objective 5)

   a., b., & d. are incorrect. Polygenic means "many genes"; the "many factors" indicated by "multifactorial" are not limited to either genetic or environmental ones.

9. b. is the correct answer. (video lesson, segment 1; objective 2)

   a. is incorrect. Genotype is a person's genetic potential.

   c. is incorrect. A karyotype is a picture of a person's chromosomes.

   d. is incorrect. Phenotype is the observable characteristics of a person.

10. a. is the correct answer (objective 4)

11. d. is the correct answer. An XXY pattern results in Klinefelter syndrome. (objective 9)

    a. & b. are incorrect. These chromosomal abnormalities affect females, indicated by the lack of a Y chromosome.

    c. is incorrect. There is no such abnormality, as every surviving human being has at least one X chromosome.

12. c. is the correct answer. (objective 5)

    a. & d. are incorrect. Genes that operate with a dominant-recessive pattern are less common than other types of genes.

    b. is incorrect. On the contrary, most human traits are *multi*factorial.

13. a. is the correct answer. (objective 9)

14. b. is the correct answer. (objective 5)

15. b. is the correct answer. (video lesson, segment 4; objectives 6 & 9)

    a. & d. are incorrect. In order for an offspring to inherit a recessive condition, the parents need only be carriers of the recessive gene in their genotypes; they need not actually have the disease or a dominant gene for the disease.

    c. is incorrect. This abnormality involves the sex chromosomes, not genes.

Matching Items

16. c (objective 1)
17. h (video lesson, segment 1; objective 2)
18. m (video lesson, segment 3; objective 5)
19. i (video lesson, segment 3; objective 5)
20. b (video lesson, segment 2; objective 3)
21. f (video lesson, segment 2; objective 3)
22. g (objective 7)
23. j (objective 9)

24. e (objectives 5 & 8)
25. d (objective 1)
26. k (objective 2)
27. a (objective 2)
28. l (objective 2)

Practice Questions II

Multiple-Choice Questions

1. d. is the correct answer. (objective 4)
2. a. is the correct answer. (video lesson, segment 2; objective 7)
3. c. is the correct answer. (objective 9)

   a. is incorrect. Physical appearance is usually normal in this syndrome.

   b. is incorrect. Males are more frequently and more severely affected.

   d. is incorrect. This is true of the XYY chromosomal abnormality, but not the fragile X syndrome.
4. c. is the correct answer. A recessive gene is not expressed in the phenotype. (objectives 6 & 9)

   a. is incorrect. Dominant genes are expressed in the phenotype, and thus would not go undetected.

   b. is incorrect. Most disorders are not sex-linked.

   d. is incorrect. Lethal disorders would certainly not go undetected.
5. c. is the correct answer. Sickle-cell anemia is more common among African Americans; phenylketonuria, among those of Norwegian and Irish ancestry; thalassemia, among Americans of Greek, Italian, Thai, and East Indian ancestry; and Tay-Sachs, among Jews as well as certain French-Canadians. (objective 9)

   a. & b. are incorrect. The textbook does not present evidence indicating that the incidence of these disorders has changed.

   d. is incorrect. These disorders are not sex-linked.
6. c. is the correct answer. (video lesson, segment 2; objective 3)

   a. is incorrect. This would result in monozygotic twins.

   b. is incorrect. Only one sperm can fertilize an ovum.

   d. is incorrect. A single egg fertilized by one sperm would produce a single offspring or monozygotic twins.
7. c. is the correct answer. (video lesson, segment 1; objective 2)

   a. is incorrect. Zygotes are fertilized ova.

   b. is incorrect. Genes are the smaller units of heredity that are organized into sequences on chromosomes.

   d. is incorrect. Ova are female reproductive cells.
8. a. is the correct answer. (video lesson, segment 1; objective 1)
9. c. is the correct answer. (objective 2)

10. a. is the correct answer. (objectives 1 & 2)

    b. & d. are incorrect. These are true of all body cells except the gametes.

    c. is incorrect. Gametes have either X or Y chromosomes.

11. c. is the correct answer. (objective 1)
12. a. is the correct answer. Genotype refers to the sum total of all the genes a person inherits; phenotype refers to the actual expression of the individual's characteristics. (video lesson, segment 3; objective 5)
13. c. is the correct answer. (objective 6)
14. d. is the correct answer. X-linked genes are located only on the X chromosome, and males inherit their single X chromosome from their mother. (objective 6)
15. b. is the correct answer. (objective 8)

True or False Items

16. T (objective 5)
17. T (objective 9)
18. T (objective 8)
19. T (objective 1)
20. F Most traits are polygenic. (objective 5)
21. T (objective 1)
22. T (video lesson, segment 4; objective 9)
23. T (objectives 6 & 9)
24. T (video lesson, segment 3; objectives 5, 6, & 9)
25. T (objective 1)
26. T (objective 7)

Applying Your Knowledge

1. b. is the correct answer. (objective 5)

   a. is incorrect. In fact, the total number of human genes is about 25,000.

   c. is incorrect. Differences among the groups constitute only 3 to 5 percent.

2. a. is the correct answer. (objectives 2 & 10)
3. a. is the correct answer. (objective 8)

   b. is incorrect. Genotype refers to an organism's genetic potential.

   c. is incorrect. Polygenic refers to traits, not to individuals.

   d. is incorrect. There is no indication of this, as her children were born with the trait.

4. a. is the correct answer. (objective 6)

   b. is incorrect. The male genotype is XY, not XX.

   c. & d. are incorrect. The mother contributes only an X chromosome.

5. c. is the correct answer. (objective 6)

6. b. is the correct answer. Since monozygotic twins are genetically identical, while dizygotic twins share only 50 percent of their genes, greater similarity of traits between monozygotic twins suggests that genes are an important influence. (video lesson, segment 2; objectives 3, 6 & 7)

   a. & c. are incorrect. Even though schizophrenia has a strong genetic component, it is not the case that if one twin has schizophrenia the other also automatically does. Therefore, the environment, too, is an important influence.

   d. is incorrect. This does not necessarily follow.

7. a. is the correct answer. The environmental factor influenced the skin color in a way that was genetically possible. (video lesson, introduction; objective 8)

8. c. is the correct answer. (objective 8)

   a. is incorrect. Alcoholism is multifactorial, with environmental factors playing an important role.

   b. is incorrect. Alcoholism is polygenic and is does not have a dominant-recessive pattern of inheritance.

   d. is incorrect. In fact, the environment of the biological parents (who also have the genes for alcoholism) is probably more likely to support the development of alcoholism.

9. c. is the correct answer. Tay-Sachs is a recessive gene disorder; therefore, in order for a child to inherit this disease, he or she must receive the recessive gene from both parents. (objective 9)

10. d. is the correct answer. To separate the influences of genes and environment, one of the two must be held constant. (video lesson, segment 2; objective 7)

    a., b., & c. are incorrect. These situations would not allow a researcher to separate the contributions of heredity and environment.

11. a. is the correct answer. (objective 7)

12. c. is the correct answer. (objective 8)

    a. is incorrect. Some people's inherited biochemistry makes them more susceptible to schizophrenia.

    b. is incorrect. Despite a strong genetic influence, the environment plays a critical role in the expression of schizophrenia.

    d. is incorrect. Not only is this advice unreasonable, but it might increase the likelihood of chromosomal abnormalities in the parents' sperm and ova.

13. d. is the correct answer. (objective 9)

14. d. is the correct answer. (objective 5)

    a. & b. are incorrect. Genes are discrete segments of a chromosome.

    c. is incorrect. Genotype refers to genetic potential.

15. c. is the correct answer. (objective 6)

    a. is incorrect. This is a statistic having to do with genetic variation.

    b. is incorrect. It is an entirely different syndrome from the two mentioned.

    d. is incorrect. Ann has the syndrome regardless of environmental effects.

Lesson Review

Lesson 3

The Beginnings
Heredity and Environment

Please Note: Use this matrix to guide your study and achieve the learning objectives of this lesson. It will also help you to view the video, which defines and demonstrates important concepts and skills as they relate to everyday life.

Learning Objective	**Textbook**	**Course Student Guide**	**Video Lesson**
1. Define gamete, describe conception, and discuss early development of the zygote, including the processes of duplication, division, and differentiation.	pp. 66–70	Key Terms: 6, 7, 14; Practice Questions I: 1, 16, 25; Practice Questions II: 8, 10, 11, 19, 21, 25.	Segment 1: *The Beginning of Development* Segment 2: *The Twin Perspective*
2. Define gene, chromosome, human genome, and allele, describe how genetic instructions are transmitted from parents to their children, and explain how sex is determined.	pp. 64–66	Key Terms: 1, 2, 3, 4, 5, 9, 10, 11, 12, 13, 28, 33; Practice Questions I: 2, 3, 4, 9, 17, 26, 27, 28; Practice Questions II: 7, 9, 10; Applying Your Knowledge: 2.	Introduction Segment 1: *The Beginning of Development* Segment 2: *The Twin Perspective*
3. Discuss the reasons for genetic continuity and diversity, and distinguish between monozygotic and dizygotic twins.	pp. 70–71	Key Terms: 15, 16; Practice Questions I: 5, 20, 21; Practice Questions II: 6; Applying Your Knowledge: 6.	Segment 2: *The Twin Perspective*
4. Describe the common treatment methods and ethical considerations of infertility.	pp. 71–73	Key Terms: 17, 18; Practice Questions I: 10; Practice Questions II: 1	
5. Differentiate genotype from phenotype, explain the polygenic and multifactorial nature of human traits, and define the Human Genome Project.	pp. 73–75, 78–81	Key Terms: 8, 19, 20, 21, 23; Practice Questions I: 8, 12, 14, 18, 19, 24; Practice Questions II: 12, 16, 20, 24; Applying Your Knowledge: 1, 14.	Segment 3: *From Genotype to Phenotype*

Learning Objective	Textbook	Course Student Guide	Video Lesson
6. Describe additive and nonadditive patterns of gene interaction, including the dominant-recessive pattern, X-linked inheritance, copy number variations, and parental imprinting, and give examples of some traits that result from each type of interaction.	pp. 75–78	Key Terms: 24, 26, 27, 37, 38; Practice Questions I: 15; Practice Questions II: 4, 13, 14, 23, 24; Applying Your Knowledge: 4, 5, 6, 15.	Segment 2: *The Twin Perspective* Segment 3: *From Genotype to Phenotype* Segment 4: *Genetic and Chromosomal Abnormalities*
7. Define epigenetics and explain how scientists use twin studies to attempt to distinguish the effects of genes (nature) and environment (nurture) on human development.	p. 74	Key Terms: 22, 28, 33, 34; Practice Questions I: 6, 22; Practice Questions II: 2, 26; Applying Your Knowledge: 6, 10, 11.	Introduction Segment 1: *The Beginning of Development* Segment 2: *The Twin Perspective*
8. Describe the ways in which genetic and nongenetic influences interact, especially with reference to schizophrenia, alcoholism, and visual acuity.	pp. 78-81, 86–87	Key Terms: 25; Practice Questions I: 24; Practice Questions II: 15, 18; Applying Your Knowledge: 3, 7, 8, 12.	Introduction
9. Identify some of the most common chromosomal abnormalities and genetic disorders, describe the use of prenatal tests, gene therapy, and genetic counseling, and discuss some of the dilemmas and ethical questions that can result from these interventions.	pp. 82–89	Key Terms: 29, 30, 31, 32, 35, 36; Practice Questions I: 7, 11, 13, 15, 23; Practice Questions II: 3, 4, 5, 17, 22, 23, 24; Applying Your Knowledge: 2, 9, 13.	Segment 3: *From Genotype to Phenotype* Segment 4: *Genetic and Chromosomal Abnormalities*

The Wondrous Journey

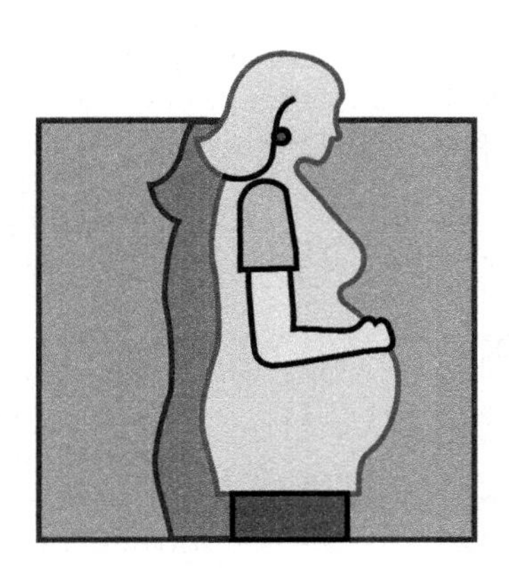

Lesson 4

The Beginnings: Prenatal Development and Birth

Preview

Anticipating the birth of a child is one of life's most enriching experiences. As the video for this lesson begins, we meet Sandra and Darrin in the anxious moments just before Sandra gives birth. The personal experiences of this young family throughout Sandra's pregnancy and delivery form the backdrop for the lesson's exploration of prenatal development and birth.

The period of prenatal development is a time of incredibly rapid growth during which the emerging person develops from a single cell into a fully functioning individual. This lesson describes that development, along with some of the problems that can occur—including prenatal exposure to disease, drugs, and other hazards—and the factors that moderate the risks of that exposure.

A person's birth marks the most radical transition of the entire life span. No longer sheltered from the outside world, the newborn becomes a separate human being who begins life almost completely dependent upon its caregivers. This lesson also examines the process of birth, its possible variations and problems, and **postpartum depression** and the **parent–newborn bonding** process.

As you complete this video, recall your experiences with pregnancy or those of someone you know. (You may want to interview that person during your study of this lesson.) What did the mother look and feel like during the early, middle and final stages of this pregnancy? What sort of prenatal care did she receive? What did she do to stay healthy? For example, what did she eat and how did she exercise? Did she smoke, drink alcohol, or take any medications during the pregnancy? Was the baby born close to the "due date"? What was the birthing experience like? Where did the mother have the baby, in what type of facility? Did she have any surgical procedures performed? If so, which ones? Were there any complications during birth? If so, what were they and how were the mother and baby treated? Did the mother and father both get to hold and bond with the baby in the first few hours after birth? Did the mother experience any depression in the days and weeks after birth? If so, how was she treated?

Prior Knowledge That Will Be Used in This Lesson

- This lesson begins with the development of the zygote after conception. Remember from Lesson 3 that conception occurs when the male's sperm and female's ovum unite. The resulting cell, called a zygote, then develops through a process of duplication and division.
- This lesson will also return to the epigenetic theory introduced in Lesson 3. Recall the basic tenet of this theory is that our development is shaped not only by our genetics or by the environment in which we live, but rather by the interaction between the two. Nature *and* nurture make us who we are. This is just as true for prenatal development (before birth) as it is for postnatal development (after birth).

Learning Objectives

Use this information to guide your reading, viewing, thinking, and studying. After successfully completing this lesson, you should be able to:

1. Describe the significant developments of the germinal period.
2. Describe the significant developments of the embryonic period.
3. Describe the significant developments of the fetal period, noting the importance of the age of viability.
4. Define teratogens, behavioral teratogens, and teratology and describe the factors that determine whether a particular teratogen will be harmful.
5. Outline the effects of at least three specific teratogens on the developing embryo or fetus, and describe protective steps that can be taken to moderate the risk of exposure.
6. Distinguish among low-birthweight (LBW), preterm birth, and small-for-gestational-age (SGA) infants, and identify the causes of low-birthweight.
7. Describe the normal process of birth, specifying the events of each stage.
8. Describe the tests used to assess the newborn's condition at birth.
9. Describe the variations available during the birthing process, and discuss the pros and cons of medical intervention and other variations.
10. Explain the causes of cerebral palsy, and discuss the special needs and care of high-risk infants.
11. Describe the importance of the father in the lives of the fetus and the expectant mother, describe postpartum depression, and explain the concept of parent-infant bonding and the current view of most developmentalists regarding early bonding in humans.

Textbook Reading & Video Viewing

For the most effective study of this lesson, complete the assignments in the sequence listed below.

Before viewing the video program:

Read Chapter 4, "Prenatal Development and Birth," pages 93–123, and review Table 3.2 on pages 84–85 in Chapter 3.

View the video for Lesson 4, "The Wondrous Journey."

Segment 1: The First Trimester

Segment 2: Risk Reduction

Segment 3: The Second Trimester

Segment 4: The Third Trimester

After viewing the video program:

Review all reading assignments for this lesson.

Complete the "Practice Questions" and "Applying Your Knowledge" sections to reinforce your understanding of important terms and concepts and measure your achievement of the Learning Objectives. Check your answers with the feedback given and review when necessary.

Practice Questions I

Multiple-Choice Questions

1. The first two weeks after conception are called the
   a. embryonic period.
   b. critical period.
   c. fetal period.
   d. germinal period.

2. Implantation occurs during the
   a. embryonic period.
   b. germinal period.
   c. ovarian period.
   d. fetal period.

3. To say that a teratogen has a "threshold effect" means that it is
   a. virtually harmless until exposure reaches a certain level.
   b. harmful only to low-birthweight infants.
   c. harmful to certain developing organs during periods when these organs are developing most rapidly.
   d. harmful only if the pregnant woman's weight does not increase by a certain minimum amount during her pregnancy.

4. By the eighth week after conception, the embryo has almost all the basic body parts **EXCEPT** the
   a. skeleton.
   b. elbows and knees.
   c. sex organs.
   d. fingers and toes.
5. The most critical factor in attaining the age of viability is development of the
   a. placenta.
   b. eyes.
   c. brain.
   d. skeleton.
6. Neural tube defects, such as spina bifida, have been linked to a maternal gene that prevents normal utilization of _______________ from an expectant mother's diet.
   a. vitamin A
   b. zinc
   c. guanine
   d. folic acid
7. The Brazelton Neonatal Behavioral Assessment Scale (NBAS)
   a. records infant behaviors such as the palmar grasping reflex.
   b. can be administered in place of the Apgar scale.
   c. was designed to assess risk in preterm infants.
   d. is the European equivalent to the Apgar scale commonly used in the United States.
8. A teratogen
   a. cannot cross the placenta during the embryonic period.
   b. is usually inherited from the mother.
   c. can be counteracted by good nutrition most of the time.
   d. may be a virus, drug, chemical, radiation, or environmental pollutants.
9. Among the characteristics of babies born with fetal alcohol syndrome are
   a. hyperactivity and slow learning.
   b. addiction to alcohol and methadone.
   c. deformed arms and legs.
   d. blindness.

10. The birth process begins
    a. when the fetus moves into the right position.
    b. when the uterus begins to contract at regular intervals to push the fetus out.
    c. about eight hours (in the case of firstborns) after the uterus begins to contract at regular intervals.
    d. when the baby's head appears at the opening of the vagina.

11. The Apgar scale is administered
    a. only if the newborn is in obvious distress.
    b. once, just after birth.
    c. usually twice, 1 minute and 5 minutes after birth.
    d. every two minutes for several hours.

12. The average newborn weighs about
    a. 5 pounds.
    b. 6 pounds.
    c. 7.5 pounds.
    d. 8.5 pounds.

13. Low-birthweight babies born near the due date but weighing substantially less than they should
    a. are classified as preterm.
    b. are called small for gestational age.
    c. usually have no sex organs.
    d. are generally not considered high-risk.

14. Approximately 1 out of every 4 low-birthweight births worldwide is caused by maternal use of
    a. alcohol.
    b. tobacco.
    c. crack cocaine.
    d. household chemicals.

15. The idea that immediate skin-to-skin contact between a mother and her newborn was crucial for the development of a parent-infant bond arose from ______________________ and has ______________________ supported by research.
    a. observations in the delivery room; been
    b. data on adopted infants; been
    c. animal studies; not been
    d. studies of disturbed mother-newborn pairs; not been

Matching Items

Match each definition or description with its corresponding term.

Terms

16. __________ embryonic period
17. __________ fetal period
18. __________ placenta
19. __________ preterm
20. __________ teratogens
21. __________ false positive
22. __________ critical period
23. __________ neural tube
24. __________ fetal alcohol syndrome
25. __________ germinal period
26. __________ couvade

Definitions or Descriptions

a. term for the period during which a developing organ or other body part is most susceptible to damage
b. common ones are tobacco and alcohol
c. the age when viability is attained
d. the precursor of the central nervous system
e. characterized by abnormal facial characteristics, behavior problems, and mental retardation
f. an incorrect result on a laboratory test that shows something is true when it is not
g. the life-giving organ that nourishes the embryo and fetus
h. when implantation occurs
i. the prenatal period when all major body structures begin to form
j. a baby born three or more weeks early
k. symptoms of pregnancy and birth experienced by the father

Practice Questions II

Multiple-Choice Questions

1. During which period are behavioral teratogens safe?
   a. germinal period
   b. embryonic period
   c. fetal period
   d. none of the above periods

2. In order, the correct sequence of prenatal stages of development is
   a. embryonic; germinal; fetal.
   b. germinal; fetal; embryonic.
   c. germinal; embryonic; fetal.
   d. ovarian; fetal; embryonic.

3. Tetracycline, retinoic acid, and lithium

   a. can be harmful to the human fetus.

   b. have been proven safe for pregnant women after the embryonic period.

   c. will prevent spontaneous abortions.

   d. are safe when used before the fetal period.

4. Pregnant women should take care to avoid which of the following?

   a. caffeine

   b. calcium

   c. bug spray

   d. folic acid

5. The most realistic way for pregnant women to reduce the risk of birth defects in their unborn children is to avoid unnecessary drugs and

   a. have a diagnostic X-ray or ultrasound.

   b. improve their genetic predispositions.

   c. seek early and regular prenatal care.

   d. take extra vitamin and mineral supplements.

6. Among the characteristics rated on the Apgar scale are

   a. shape of the newborn's head and nose.

   b. presence of body hair.

   c. interactive behaviors.

   d. muscle tone and color.

7. Cerebral palsy was once believed to be caused solely by ____________________; it is now understood to be influenced by ____________________.

   a. birth complications; genetic vulnerability, teratogens, and anoxia

   b. genetic vulnerability and teratogens; birth complications

   c. teratogens and anoxia; heredity.

   d. birth complications and anoxia; heredity

8. Most U.S. births now take place

   a. in birthing centers.

   b. at home.

   c. in high-tech operating rooms.

   d. in hospital labor rooms.

9. Which of the following is true of kangaroo care?
   a. It is beneficial for the parents as well as the infant.
   b. It involves carrying an infant in a carrier or sling for many hours each day.
   c. There is no evidence to support any potential benefits.
   d. It can only be used with full-term infants.

10. The minimum Apgar score necessary to indicate that a newborn is in normal health is
   a. 5.
   b. 6.
   c. 7.
   d. 10.

11. In the United States, low birthweight
   a. is nearly always caused by tobacco use.
   b. rates are decreasing.
   c. is caused by many factors that tend to occur together.
   d. is a problem only for poor and young mothers.

12. The critical period for physical structure and form is
   a. the period of the zygote.
   b. the embryonic period.
   c. the third trimester only.
   d. the entire pregnancy.

True or False Items

Write T (for true) or F (for false) on the line in front of each statement.

13. _____ Beginning at about 28 weeks, the fetus can hear the mother's voice.

14. _____ Eight weeks after conception, the embryo has formed almost all the basic organs.

15. _____ In general, behavioral teratogens have the greatest effect during the embryonic period.

16. _____ The effects of cigarette smoking during pregnancy remain highly controversial.

17. _____ The Apgar scale is used to measure vital signs such as heart rate, breathing, and reflexes.

18. _____ Newborns usually cry on their own, moments after birth.

19. _____ Research shows that immediate mother-newborn contact at birth is necessary for the normal emotional development of the child.

20. _____ Preterm and low-birthweight babies are at risk of experiencing difficulties starting in infancy and continuing through adulthood.

21. _____ Prenatal tests can result in both "false positives" and "false negatives."

22. _____ On average, babies are born approximately 12 hours after the onset of active labor for first births and 7 hours for subsequent births.

Applying Your Knowledge

1. Babies whose mothers took psychoactive drugs during pregnancy are at an increased risk of
   a. structural problems.
   b. behavioral problems.
   c. both a and b.
   d. neither a nor b.

2. I am about 1 inch long and 1 gram in weight. I have all of the basic organs (except sex organs) and the features of a human being. What am I?
   a. a zygote
   b. an embryo
   c. a fetus
   d. an indifferent gonad

3. Karen and Brad report to their neighbors that, 5 weeks after conception, an ultrasound of their child-to-be revealed female sex organs. The neighbors are skeptical of their statement because
   a. ultrasounds are never administered before the ninth week.
   b. ultrasounds only reveal the presence or absence of male sex organs.
   c. the fetus does not begin to develop female sex organs until about the ninth week.
   d. it is impossible to determine that a woman is pregnant until six weeks after conception.

4. Five-year-old Benjamin can't sit quietly and concentrate on a task for more than a minute. Dr. Simmons, who is a teratologist, suspects that Benjamin may have been exposed to _______________ during prenatal development.
   a. human immunodeficiency virus
   b. a behavioral teratogen
   c. rubella
   d. lead

5. Sylvia and Stan, who are of British descent, are hoping to have a child. Doctor Caruthers asks for a complete nutritional history and is particularly concerned when she discovers that Sylvia may have a deficiency of folic acid in her diet. Doctor Caruthers is probably worried about the risk of ______________ in the couple's offspring.

   a. FAS

   b. brain damage

   c. neural-tube defects

   d. malformed limbs

6. Three-year-old Kenny was born underweight and premature. Today, he is small for his age. His doctor suspects that

   a. Kenny is a victim of fetal alcohol syndrome.

   b. Kenny suffers from spina bifida.

   c. Kenny's mother smoked heavily during her pregnancy.

   d. Kenny's mother used heroin during her pregnancy.

7. Trina is pregnant with dizygotic twins, one male and one female. Unfortunately, she has unknowingly exposed her developing embryos to a behavioral teratogen. Which of the following is true?

   a. Since exposure was early in the pregnancy, effects are unlikely for both twins.

   b. Both twins are at the same risk of developing problems.

   c. The female twin is at a higher risk of developing problems than is the male twin.

   d. The male twin is at a higher risk of developing problems than is the female twin.

8. Fetal alcohol syndrome is common in newborns whose mothers were heavy drinkers during pregnancy, whereas newborns whose mothers were moderate drinkers may suffer fetal alcohol effects. This finding shows that to assess and understand risk we must know

   a. the kind of alcoholic beverage (for example, beer, wine, or whiskey).

   b. the level of exposure to the teratogen.

   c. whether the substance really is teratogenic.

   d. the timing of exposure to the teratogen.

9. Which of the following infants would be the **MOST** worrisome to doctors?

   a. a full-term infant who is SGA

   b. a preterm infant who is LBW

   c. Neither of the above would be worrisome.

   d. Both of the above would be equally worrisome.

10. Which of the following newborns would be **MOST** likely to have problems in body structure and functioning?

    a. Anton, whose Apgar score is 6.

    b. Debora, whose Apgar score is 7.

    c. Sheila, whose Apgar score is 3.

    d. Simon, whose Apgar score is 5.

11. At birth, Clarence was classified as small for gestational age. It is likely that he

    a. was born in a rural hospital.

    b. suffered several months of prenatal malnutrition.

    c. was born in a large city hospital.

    d. comes from a family with a history of such births.

12. Francine has a two-week-old infant, and she is finding the care of her baby to be burdensome. She often has thoughts of neglecting her infant, and she sometimes has thoughts of hurting her infant. Francine

    a. needs to be committed to a mental institution.

    b. clearly has a high-risk infant.

    c. is suffering from postpartum depression.

    d. will likely never develop a parent-infant bond.

13. An infant born 266 days after conception, weighing 4 pounds, would be designated as which of the following?

    a. a preterm infant

    b. a low-birthweight infant

    c. a small-for-gestational-age infant

    d. both b and c

14. An infant who is born at 34 weeks weighing 6 pounds would be considered to be

    a. preterm.

    b. low birthweight.

    c. small for gestational age.

    d. both a and b.

15. The five characteristics evaluated by the Apgar scale are

    a. heart rate, length, weight, muscle tone, and color.

    b. orientation, muscle tone, reflexes, interaction, and responses to stress.

    c. reflexes, breathing, muscle tone, heart rate, and color.

    d. pupillary response, heart rate, reflex irritability, alertness, and breathing.

Key Terms

1. **germinal period:** The first two weeks of prenatal development after conception, characterized by rapid cell division and the beginning of cell differentiation. (p. 94; video lesson, segment 1; objective 1)

   Memory aid: A germ cell is one from which a new organism can develop. The germinal period is the first stage in the development of the new organism.

2. **embryonic period:** The stage of prenatal development from approximately the third through the eighth week after conception, during which the basic forms of all body structures, including internal organs, develop. (p. 94; video lesson, segment 1; objective 2)

3. **fetal period:** The stage of prenatal development from the ninth week after conception until birth, during which the fetus gains about 7 pounds (more than 3,000 grams) and organs become more mature, gradually able to function on their own. (p. 94; video lesson, segment 1; objective 3)

4. **implantation:** The process, beginning about 10 days after conception, in which the developing organism burrows into the placenta that lines the uterus, where it can be nourished and protected as it continues to develop. (p. 94; video lesson, segment 1; objective 1)

5. **embryo:** A developing organism between three and eight weeks following conception. (p. 94; video lesson, segment 1; objective 2)

6. **fetus:** A developing organism from the ninth week following conception until birth. (p. 96; video lesson, segment 1; objective 3)

7. **ultrasound:** An image of an unborn fetus (or an internal organ produced by using high-frequency sound waves (sonogram). (p. 96; objective 6)

8. **age of viability:** The time, about twenty-two weeks after conception, when the fetus has at least some slight chance of survival outside the uterus if specialized medical care is available. (p. 97; video lesson, segment 3; objective 3)

9. **Apgar scale:** A quick assessment of a newborn's health. The baby's color, heart rate, reflexes, muscle tone, and respiratory effort are given a score of 0, 1, or 2 twice—at one minute and five minutes after birth—and each time the total of all five scores is compared with the maximum score of 10 (rarely attained). (p. 100; video lesson, segment 4; objective 8)

10. **cesarean section (c-section):** A surgical birth, in which incisions through the mother's abdomen and uterus allow the fetus to be removed quickly, instead of being delivered through the vagina. (p. 101; objective 9)

11. **doula:** A woman who helps with the birth process. Traditionally in Latin America, a doula was the only professional who attended childbirth. Now doulas are likely to arrive at the woman's home during early labor and later work alongside a hospital's staff. (p. 104; objective 9)

12. **teratogens:** Agents and conditions, including viruses, drugs, and chemicals, that can impair prenatal development and result in birth defects or even death. (p. 106; video lesson, segment 2; objective 4)

13. **behavioral teratogens:** Agents and conditions that can harm the prenatal brain, impairing the future child's intellectual and emotional functioning. (p. 106; objective 4)
14. **threshold effect:** In prenatal development, when a teratogen is relatively harmless in small doses but becomes harmful once exposure reaches a certain level (the threshold). (p. 108; video lesson, segment 2; objective 4)
15. **fetal alcohol syndrome (FAS):** A cluster of birth defects, including abnormal facial characteristics, slow physical growth, and retarded mental development, that may occur in the fetus of a woman who drinks alcohol while pregnant. (p. 108; objective 5)
16. **false positive:** The result of a laboratory test that reports something as true when in fact it is not true. This can occur for pregnancy tests, when a woman might not be pregnant even though the test says she is, or during pregnancy when a problem is reported that actually does not exist. (p. 113; objective 5)
17. **low birthweight (LBW):** Newborns who weigh less than 2.5 kilograms (5.5 pounds) are considered to be low birthweight (LBW). Such infants are at risk for many immediate and long-term problems. (p. 114; video lesson, segment 3; objective 6)
18. **very low birthweight (VLBW):** A body weight at birth of less than 3 pounds, 5 ounces (1,500 grams). (p. 114; video lesson, segment 3; objective 6)
19. **extremely low birthweight (ELBW):** A body weight at birth of less than 2 pounds, 3 ounces (1,000 grams). (p. 114; video lesson, segment 3; objective 6)
20. **preterm:** A birth that occurs 3 or more weeks before the full 38 weeks of the typical pregnancy—that is, at 35 or fewer weeks after conception. (p. 114; objective 6)
21. **small for gestational age (SGA):** A term for a baby whose birthweight is significantly lower than expected, given the time since conception. For example, a 5-pound (2,265-gram) newborn is considered SGA if born on time but not SGA if born two months early. (p. 114; objective 6)
22. **cerebral palsy:** A disorder that results from damage to the brain's motor centers. People with cerebral palsy have difficulty with muscle control, so their speech and/ or body movements are impaired. (p. 116; objective 10)
23. **anoxia:** A temporary lack of fetal oxygen during the birth process that, if prolonged, can cause brain damage or even death. (p. 116; video lesson, segment 4; objective 10)
24. **Brazelton Neonatal Behavioral Assessment Scale (NBAS):** A test often administered to newborns that measures responsiveness and records 46 behaviors, including 20 reflexes. (p. 117; objective 8)
25. **reflex:** An unlearned, involuntary action or movement in response to a stimulus. A reflex occurs without conscious thought. (p. 117; objective 8)
26. **couvade:** Symptoms of pregnancy and birth experienced by fathers. (p. 119; objective 11)

27. **parental alliance:** Cooperation between a mother and a father based on their mutual commitment to their children. In a parental alliance, the parents support each other in their shared parental roles. (p. 120; objective 11)
28. **postpartum depression:** A new mother's feelings of inadequacy and sadness in the days and weeks after giving birth. (p. 120; objective 11)
29. **parent–infant bond:** The strong, loving connection that forms as parents hold, examine, and feed their newborn. (p. 120; video lesson, segment 4; objective 11)
30. **kangaroo care:** A form of newborn care in which mothers (and sometimes fathers) rest their babies on their naked chests, like kangaroo mothers that carry their immature newborns in a pouch on their abdomen. (p. 121; objective 10)
31. **interaction effect:** Occurs when one teratogen intensifies the harmful effects of another. (video lesson, segment 2; objective 4)
32. **placenta:** The organ that connects the mother's circulatory system with that of her growing embryo, providing nourishment to the developing organism and removing wastes. (video lesson, segment 1; objective 1)
33. **amniotic fluid:** A clear, slightly yellowish liquid that surrounds the unborn child (fetus) during pregnancy, protecting and cushioning its development. (video lesson, segment 1; objectives 2 & 3)
34. **critical period:** During prenatal development, the time when a particular organ or other body part of the fetus is particularly vulnerable to the effects of teratogens. (video lesson, segment 2; objective 4)
35. **spina bifida:** A birth defect that results from the failure of the spine to close properly during the first month of pregnancy. Research has shown that poor maternal utilization of folic acid (a common B vitamin) increases the risk of neural tube defects such as spina bifida. (video lesson, segment 2; objectives 4 & 5)

Summary

The first two weeks of prenatal development are called the **germinal period**. Within hours after conception, the one-celled zygote begins the process of cell division and growth as it travels down the fallopian tube. The **embryonic period** begins as the organism begins differentiating into three layers of tissue that will become the various body systems. At the end of the first month, the cardiovascular system is functioning; the eyes, ears, nose, mouth, and arm and leg buds start to form; and the embryo is about one-fifth of an inch (just 6 millimeters) long. By the end of the second month, the developing organism weighs about 1 gram, is 1 inch long, and has all the basic organs (except the sex organs) and features of a human being. During the third month, the **fetal period** begins, and the sex organs begin to take shape.

The crucial factor in the fetus's attaining the **age of viability**, beginning at about 22 to 24 weeks, is neurological maturation, which is essential to the regulation of the basic body functions of breathing, sucking, and sleeping. By 28 weeks, the typical fetus weighs about 1,300 grams (3 pounds) and has a greater than 50 percent chance of survival outside the womb.

Teratology is a science of risk analysis, which attempts to evaluate what factors can make prenatal harm more (or less) likely to occur. Three crucial factors that determine whether a specific teratogen will cause harm, and of what nature, are the timing of exposure, the amount of exposure, and the developing organism's genetic vulnerability to damage from the substance. Although each body structure has its own **critical period** during which it is most susceptible to teratogenic damage, for **behavioral teratogens** that affect the brain and nervous system, the entire prenatal period is critical. Teratogens can also include conditions, such as maternal malnutrition and extreme levels of stress. Some **teratogens** have a cumulative effect on the developing individual. For other teratogens, there is a **threshold effect**; that is, the substance is virtually harmless until exposure reaches a certain frequency or dosage. However, the **interaction effect** of teratogens taken together may make them more harmful at lower dosage levels than they would be individually.

A major, preventable health hazard for the fetus is **low birthweight**, defined as birthweight that is less than 2,500 grams (5.5 pounds). Babies who weigh less than 3 pounds, 5 ounces (1,500 grams) are classified as **very low birthweight**, whereas those who weigh less than 2 pounds, 3 ounces (1,000 grams) are classified as **extremely low birthweight**. Infants who are born more than three weeks early are called **preterm**. Others, born close to the due date but weighing less than most full-term neonates, are called **small for gestational age (SGA)**.

The normal birth begins at about the 266th day after conception, when the fetus's brain signals the release of hormones that trigger uterine contractions in the mother. Labor usually lasts eight to twelve hours in first births and four to seven hours in subsequent births, but this can vary greatly. The **Apgar scale** is used to assign a score between 0 and 2 to the neonate's heart rate, breathing, muscle tone, color, and reflexes at one minute after birth and again at five minutes. A score of 7 or better indicates the newborn is not in danger; below 7, that the infant needs help in establishing normal breathing; and below 4, that the baby is in critical condition and needs immediate medical attention. Very few newborns score an immediate perfect 10, but most readily adjust to life outside the womb. The **Brazelton Neonatal Behavioral Assessment Scale (NBAS)** is another assessment typically administered within the first day or two after birth during which 46 of the newborn's behaviors (including 20 **reflexes**) are recorded.

The quality of the birth experience depends on many factors, including the mother's preparation for birth, the support provided by others, and the nature and degree of medical intervention. Birth complications are much more likely if a fetus is at risk because of low weight, preterm birth, genetic abnormality, teratogenic exposure, or because the mother is unusually young, old, small, or in poor health. **Cerebral palsy**, for example, which was once thought to be solely caused by birth procedures (such as excessive analgesia or misapplied forceps) is now known to result from a combination of factors, including genetic vulnerability, exposure to teratogens, and **anoxia** (lack of oxygen) during birth. Parents now have many options available to them when they are deciding how and where they would like to give birth. Indeed, **doulas** are becoming much more common in the United States.

Low birthweight and preterm infants are at an increased risk of many developmental difficulties. **Kangaroo care,** in which mothers (and sometimes fathers) hold their LBW infants in skin-to-skin contact, has been shown to have benefits for both parent and baby. These benefits have been seen in healthy newborns, as well.

The popular term **parent–infant bond** is used to emphasize the tangible as well as intangible attachment between parent and child in the early moments after birth. In many animals, early contact between mother and infant can be crucial to bonding. Most developmentalists now believe that the importance of early contact between a human mother and child has been overly popularized and that the events right after birth are just one episode in a long-term process of bonding and development.

Fathers have been acknowledged to play a critical role in prenatal development, by encouraging pregnant women to make healthy choices and by helping to reduce stress, in the delivery process, during which their presence has been shown to reduce complications, and in life following birth. Many fathers even experience symptoms of pregnancy and childbirth called **couvade**. A **parental alliance** is crucial, and the father's support can assist a woman suffering from **postpartum depression**.

Answer Key

Practice Questions I

Multiple-Choice Questions

1. d. is the correct answer. (video lesson, segment 1; objective 1)

   a. is incorrect. The embryonic period from the third through the eighth week after conception.

   b. is incorrect. This term refers to the time when a particular organ or other body part of the developing organism is particularly at risk for damage from teratogens.

   c. is incorrect. The fetal period is from the ninth week until birth.
2. b. is the correct answer. (video lesson, segment 1; objective 1)
3. a. is the correct answer. (video lesson, segment 2; objectives 4 & 5)

   b., c., & d. are incorrect. Although low birthweight (b), critical periods of organ development (c), and maternal malnutrition (d) are all hazardous to the developing person during prenatal development, none is an example of a threshold effect.
4. c. is the correct answer. The sex organs do not begin to take shape until the fetal period. (objective 2)
5. c. is the correct answer. (video lesson, segment 3; objective 3)
6. d. is the correct answer. (video lesson, segment 2; objectives 4 & 5)
7. a. is the correct answer. (objective 8)
8. d. is the correct answer. (video lesson, segment 2; objective 4)

   a. is incorrect. In general, teratogens can cross the placenta at any time.

   b. is incorrect. Teratogens are agents in the environment, not heritable genes (although susceptibility to individual teratogens has a genetic component).

c. is incorrect. Although nutrition is an important factor in healthy prenatal development, nutrition alone cannot counteract the harmful effects of most teratogens.

9. a. is the correct answer. (objective 5)
10. b. is the correct answer. (video lesson, segment 4; objective 7)
11. c. is the correct answer. (video lesson, segment 4; objective 8)
12. c. is the correct answer. (objective 3)
13. b. is the correct answer. (objective 6)
14. b. is the correct answer. (objectives 5 & 6)
15. c. is the correct answer. (objective 11)

Matching Items

16. i (video lesson, segment 1; objective 2)
17. c (video lesson, segment 1; objective 3)
18. g (video lesson, segment 1; objective 1)
19. j (objective 6)
20. b (video lesson, segment 2; objective 4)
21. f (objective 5)
22. a (video lesson, segment 2; objective 4)
23. d (objective 2)
24. e (objective 5)
25. h (video lesson, segment 1; objective 1)
26. k (objective 11)

Practice Questions II

Multiple-Choice Questions

1. d. is the correct answer. (objective 5)
2. c. is the correct answer. (video lesson, segment 1; objectives 1, 2, & 3)
3. a. is the correct answer. (objective 5)
4. c. is the correct answer. (objective 5)

   a. is incorrect. Caffeine is considered safe in moderate doses.

   b. & d. are incorrect. These are necessary for healthy prenatal development.
5. c. is the correct answer. (video lesson, segment 2; objective 5)
6. d. is the correct answer. (video lesson, segment 4; objective 8)
7. a. is the correct answer. (objective 8)
8. d. is the correct answer. (objective 9)

   a. is incorrect. About 5 percent of U.S. births take place in birthing centers that are not in a hospital.

   b. is incorrect. Less than 1 percent of U.S. births occur at home.

   c. is incorrect. Although, most labor rooms have high-tech operating rooms nearby in case of emergency.

9. a. is the correct answer. (objective 10)

   b. is incorrect. Infants are held skin-to-skin between the mother's breasts or on the father's chest for an hour per day.

   c. is incorrect. A number of studies have indicated its benefits.

   d. is incorrect. It is used with low-birthweight babies, who tend to also be preterm.

10. c. is the correct answer. (video lesson, segment 4; objective 8)

11. c. is the correct answer. (objective 6)

    a. is incorrect. Many factors, including drug use, malnutrition, and maternal illness, are common causes of low birthweight.

    b. & d. are incorrect. In fact, the rates are increasing, in large part as a result of the high incidence of multiple births resulting from assisted reproductive technology.

12. b. is the correct answer. (objective 4)

True or False Items

13. T (objective 3)
14. T (video lesson, segment 1; objective 2)
15. F Behavioral teratogens can affect the fetus at any time during the prenatal period. (video lesson, segment 2; objective 4)
16. F There is no controversy about the damaging effects of smoking during pregnancy; tobacco is a dangerous teratogen. (video lesson, segments 2 & 3; objectives 5 & 6)
17. T (video lesson, segment 4; objective 8)
18. T (objective 8)
19. F Though highly desirable, mother-newborn contact at birth is not necessary for the child's normal development or for a good parent-child relationship. (video lesson, segment 4; objective 11)
20. T (objective 10)
21. T (objective 5)
22. T (objective 7)

Applying Your Knowledge

1. c. is the correct answer. (objective 5)

2. b. is the correct answer. (video lesson, segment 1; objective 2)

   a. is incorrect. The zygote is the fertilized ovum.

   c. is incorrect. The developing organism is designated a fetus starting at the ninth week.

   d. is incorrect. The indifferent gonad is the mass of cells that will eventually develop into female or male sex organs.

3. c. is the correct answer. (objective 3)

4. b. is the correct answer. (objectives 4 & 5)

   a. is incorrect. This is the virus that causes AIDS.

   c. is incorrect. Rubella may cause blindness, deafness, and brain damage.

   d. is incorrect. The textbook does not discuss the effects of exposure to lead.

5. c. is the correct answer. (video lesson, segment 2; objectives 4 & 5)
6. c. is the correct answer. (video lesson, segments 2 & 3; objectives 5 & 6)
7. d. is the correct answer. (objective 4)

   a. is incorrect. Behavioral teratogens are dangerous throughout the entire prenatal period.

   b. and c. are incorrect. Males are more genetically vulnerable than are females, and this is especially true in regard to behavioral teratogens.

8. b. is the correct answer. (objective 4)
9. a. is the correct answer. (objective 6)
10. c. is the correct answer. If a neonate's Apgar score is below 4, the infant is in critical condition and needs immediate medical attention. (video lesson, segment 4; objective 8)
11. b. is the correct answer. (objective 6)

    a., c., & d. are incorrect. Prenatal malnutrition and maternal tobacco use are the most common causes of a small-for-dates neonate.

12. c. is the correct answer. (objective 11)
13. d. is the correct answer. (objective 6)

    a. is incorrect. At 266 days, this infant is full term.

14. a. is the correct answer. (objective 6)

    b. is incorrect. Low birthweight is defined as weighing less than 5.5 pounds.

    c. & d. are incorrect. Although an infant can be both preterm and small for gestational age, this baby's weight is within the normal range of healthy babies.

15. c. is the correct answer. (video lesson, segment 4; objective 8)

Lesson Review

Lesson 4

The Beginnings
Prenatal Development and Birth

Please Note: Use this matrix to guide your study and achieve the learning objectives of this lesson. It will also help you to view the video, which defines and demonstrates important concepts and skills as they relate to everyday life.

Learning Objective	Textbook	Course Student Guide	Video Lesson
1. Describe the significant developments of the germinal period.	p. 94	Key Terms: 1, 4, 32; Practice Questions I: 1, 2, 18, 25; Practice Questions II: 2.	Segment 1: *The First Trimester*
2. Describe the significant developments of the embryonic period.	pp. 94–95	Key Terms: 2, 5, 33; Practice Questions I: 4, 16, 23; Practice Questions II: 2, 14; Applying Your Knowledge: 2.	Segment 1: *The First Trimester*
3. Describe the significant developments of the fetal period, noting the importance of the age of viability.	pp. 96–98	Key Terms: 3, 6, 8, 33; Practice Questions I: 5, 12, 17; Practice Questions II: 2, 13; Applying Your Knowledge: 3.	Segment 1: *The First Trimester* Segment 3: *The Second Trimester*
4. Define teratogens and behavioral teratogens, and describe the factors that determine whether a particular teratogen will be harmful.	pp. 106–113	Key Terms: 12, 13, 14, 31, 34, 35; Practice Questions I: 3, 6, 8, 20, 22; Practice Questions II: 12, 15; Applying Your Knowledge: 4, 5, 7, 8.	Segment 2: *Risk Reduction*
5. Outline the effects of at least three specific teratogens on the developing embryo or fetus, and describe protective steps that can be taken to moderate the risk of exposure.	pp. 110–113	Key Terms: 15, 16, 35; Practice Questions I: 3, 6, 9, 14, 21, 24; Practice Questions II: 1, 3, 4, 5, 16, 21; Applying Your Knowledge: 1, 4, 5, 6.	Segment 2: Risk Reduction Segment 3: *The Second Trimester*

Learning Objective	Textbook	Course Student Guide	Video Lesson
6. Distinguish among low-birthweight (LBW), preterm birth, and small-for-gestational-age (SGA) infants, and identify the causes of low birthweight.	pp. 114–116	Key Terms: 7, 17, 18, 19, 20, 21; Practice Questions I: 13, 14, 19; Practice Questions II: 11, 16; Applying Your Knowledge: 6, 9, 11, 13, 14.	Segment 2: Risk Reduction Segment 3: *The Second Trimester*
7. Describe the normal process of birth, specifying the events of each stage.	p. 99	Practice Questions I: 10; Practice Questions II: 22.	Segment 4: *The Third Trimester*
8. Describe the tests used to assess the newborn's condition at birth.	pp. 100, 117–118	Key Terms: 9, 24, 25; Practice Questions I: 7, 11; Practice Questions II: 6, 10, 17, 18; Applying Your Knowledge: 10, 15.	Segment 4: *The Third Trimester*
9. Describe the variations available during the birthing process, and discuss the pros and cons of medical intervention and other variations.	pp. 101–105	Key Terms: 10, 11; Practice Questions II: 8.	
10. Explain the causes of cerebral palsy, and discuss the special needs and care of high-risk infants.	pp. 116–117, 121	Key Terms: 22, 23, 30; Practice Questions II: 7, 9, 20.	Segment 4: *The Third Trimester*
11. Describe the importance of the father in the lives of the fetus and the expectant mother, describe postpartum depression, and explain the concept of parent-infant bonding and the current view of most developmentalists regarding early bonding in humans.	pp. 118–121	Key Terms: 26, 27, 28, 29; Practice Questions I: 15, 26; Practice Questions II: 19; Applying Your Knowledge: 12.	Segment 4: *The Third Trimester*

A Delicate Grasp

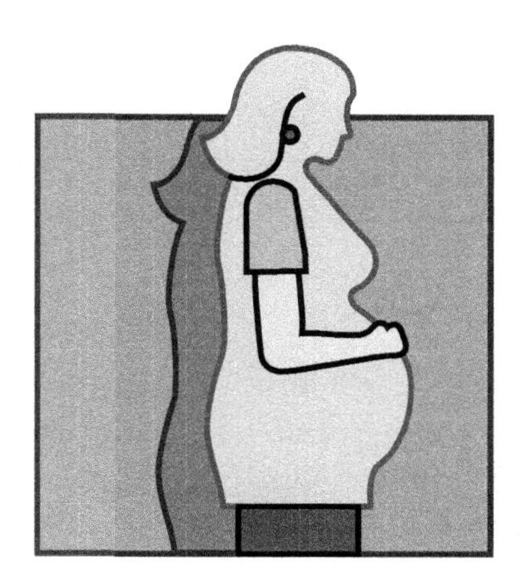

Lesson 5

The Beginnings:
Special Topic

Preview

Each of the major units in this course ("The Beginnings," "The First Two Years," "The Play Years," "The School Years," and "Adolescence") will end with a special topic and/or summary lesson. Lesson 5, the first of these special topic lessons, follows the stories of three couples who are struggling to have a child. Although each of their stories is unique, they share a common theme of hope—to be loving parents. Today, there are many options available for **infertile** couples, including alternate means of conception, alternative means of bringing the developing infant to term, and adoption.

Prior Knowledge That Will Be Used in This Lesson

- This lesson returns to the subject of infertility that was introduced in Lesson 3. Recall that a couple is considered "infertile" if they cannot conceive after a year of trying. Techniques for helping infertile couples will also be discussed, including **in vitro fertilization**.
- This lesson will also discuss the conditions of preterm birth and low birthweight introduced in Lesson 4. Recall that an infant is preterm if it is born at least 3 weeks earlier than the normal full term of 38 weeks. These infants are often of low birthweight, which is defined as 5.5 pounds (2,500 grams) or less. The average normal birthweight is 7.5 pounds (3,400 grams).

Learning Objectives

Use this information to guide your reading, viewing, thinking, and studying. After successfully completing this lesson, you should be able to

1. List the odds of a zygote growing to become a living newborn baby and describe several reasons for this survival rate.
2. Define infertile and describe various options for infertile couples including artificial insemination, in vitro fertilization, and gestational surrogacy.

3. Discuss the potential problems of low-birthweight and preterm newborns.
4. Discuss several factors that determine whether a specific teratogen will be harmful and how a mother-to-be can avoid these harmful effects.
5. Explain several alternative methods of conception, and relate several personal and ethical questions raised by these methods.

Textbook Reading & Video Viewing

For the most effective study of this lesson, complete the assignments in the sequence listed below.

Before viewing the video program:

Review pages 71–73 ("Assisted Reproduction"), pages 94–95 ("Germinal: The First 14 Days," "Embryo: From the Third Through the Eighth Week," Table 4.2 "Vulnerability During Prenatal Development"), pages 96–99 ("Fetus: From the Ninth Week Until Birth"), pages 106–113 ("Risk Analysis," "Applying the Research"), and pages 114–116 ("Low Birthweight"). (Note: Because of the overlapping content of Lessons 3, 4, and 5, the short reading assignment for this lesson is drawn from the two earlier lessons.)

View the video for Lesson 5, "A Delicate Grasp."

Segment 1: *Overcoming Infertility*

Segment 2: *The Ties That Bind*

Segment 3: *The Surrogate Mom*

After viewing the video program:

Review all reading assignments for this lesson.

Complete the "Practice Questions" section to reinforce your understanding of important terms and concepts and measure your achievement of the Learning Objectives. Check your answers with the feedback given and review when necessary.

Practice Questions

Multiple-Choice Questions

1. To say that a teratogen has a "threshold effect" means that it is
   a. virtually harmless until exposure reaches a certain level.
   b. harmful only to low-birthweight infants.
   c. harmful to certain developing organs during periods when these organs are developing most rapidly.
   d. harmful only if the pregnant woman's weight does not increase by a certain minimum amount during her pregnancy.

2. The most critical factor in attaining the age of viability is development of the
   a. placenta.
   b. eyes.
   c. brain.
   d. skeleton.

3. A teratogen
   a. cannot cross the placenta during the embryonic period.
   b. is usually inherited from the mother.
   c. can be counteracted by good nutrition most of the time.
   d. may be a virus, a drug, a chemical, radiation, or environmental pollutants.

4. Low-birthweight babies born near the due date but weighing substantially less than they should
   a. are classified as preterm.
   b. are called small for gestational age.
   c. usually have no sex organs.
   d. show many signs of immaturity.

5. Approximately 1 out of every 4 low-birthweight births worldwide is caused by maternal use of
   a. alcohol.
   b. tobacco.
   c. crack cocaine.
   d. household chemicals.

6. During which period are behavioral teratogens safe?
   a. germinal period
   b. embryonic period
   c. fetal period
   d. none of the above periods

7. In the United States, low birthweight
   a. is nearly always caused by tobacco use.
   b. rates are decreasing.
   c. is caused by many factors that tend to occur together.
   d. is a problem only for poor and young mothers.

8. Three-year-old Kenny was born underweight and premature. Today, he is small for his age. His doctor suspects that

   a. Kenny is a victim of fetal alcohol syndrome.
   b. Kenny suffers from fetal alcohol effects.
   c. Kenny's mother smoked heavily during her pregnancy.
   d. Kenny's mother used cocaine during her pregnancy.

9. Trina is pregnant with dizygotic twins, one male and one female. Unfortunately, she has unknowingly exposed her developing embryos to a behavioral teratogen. Which of the following is true?

   a. Since exposure was early in the pregnancy, effects are unlikely for both twins.
   b. Both twins are at the same risk of developing problems.
   c. The female twin is at a higher risk of developing problems than is the male twin.
   d. The male twin is at a higher risk of developing problems than is the female twin.

10. An infant born 266 days after conception and weighing 4 pounds would be designated as which of the following?

    a. preterm
    b. low birthweight
    c. small for gestational age
    d. both b and c

11. An infant who is born at 34 weeks weighing 6 pounds would be considered to be

    a. preterm.
    b. low birthweight.
    c. small for gestational age.
    d. very low birthweight.

12. The procedure in which an egg is fertilized by sperm in the laboratory is called

    a. artificial insemination.
    b. in vitro fertilization.
    c. gestational surrogacy.
    d. in vivo fertilization.

13. The age of viability

    a. has remained stable at a minimum of 22 weeks past conception.
    b. varies across cultures and ethnicities.
    c. currently ranges between 25 and 30 weeks of pregnancy.
    d. decreased dramatically as a result of medical advances in the twentieth century.

14. Infertility affects what percentage of the general population?
    a. less than 2 percent
    b. 2 to 30 percent
    c. 5 to 15 percent
    d. 25 to 30 percent

15. Most cases of infertility are caused by problems related to
    a. the male partner.
    b. the female partner.
    c. a ratio of 20/80 male to female factors.
    d. males and females contribute equally to infertility problems.

Matching Items

Match each definition or description with its corresponding term.

Terms

16. __________ in vitro fertilization
17. __________ age of viability
18. __________ artificial insemination
19. __________ preterm birth
20. __________ teratology
21. __________ low birthweight
22. __________ small for gestational age
23. __________ infertile
24. __________ assisted reproductive technology
25. __________ gestational surrogacy
26. __________ behavioral teratogen

Definitions or Descriptions

a. the scientific study of birth defects
b. when the fetus has a chance to survive outside the womb with medical help
c. a baby born 3 or more weeks early
d. egg and sperm are united in the laboratory
e. being unable to conceive after one year of trying
f. a woman carries another couple's embryo to term
g. a general term for the various techniques designed to help couples conceive
h. the preparation and placement of a semen sample inside a woman's uterus
i. a baby who weighs less than 5.5 pounds
j. a term applied to newborns who weigh substantially less than they should at their age
k. a toxin that tends to harm the prenatal brain and affect intellectual functioning

Key Terms

1. **infertile:** A couple is said to be infertile when they have been unable to conceive after at least one year of trying. (video lesson, segment 1; objective 2)
2. **assisted reproductive technology (ART):** The general term for the techniques used to help infertile couples conceive and sustain a pregnancy. (p. 71; objectives 2 & 5)
3. **in vitro fertilization (IVF):** Fertilization that takes place outside a woman's body (as in a glass laboratory dish). The procedure involves mixing sperm with ova that have been surgically removed from the woman's ovary. If a zygote is produced, it is inserted into a woman's uterus, where it may implant and develop into a baby. (p. 71; video lesson, segment 1; objectives 2 & 5)
4. **age of viability:** The time, between 22 and 24 weeks after conception, when the fetus has at least some slight chance of survival outside the uterus if specialized medical care is available. (p. 97; video lesson, segment 3; objective 1)
5. **teratogens:** Agents and conditions, including viruses, drugs, and chemicals, that can impair prenatal development and result in birth defects or even death. (p. 106; video lesson, segment 3; objective 4)
6. **behavioral teratogens:** Agents and conditions that can harm the prenatal brain, impairing the future child's intellectual and emotional functioning. (p. 106; objective 4)
7. **low birthweight (LBW):** Newborns who weigh less than 2,500 grams (5.5 pounds) are called low-birthweight (LBW) infants. Such infants are at risk for many immediate and long-term problems. (p. 114; video lesson, segment 2; objective 3)
8. **preterm birth:** A birth that occurs 3 or more weeks before the full 38 weeks of the typical pregnancy—that is, at 35 or fewer weeks after conception. (p. 114; video lesson, segment 2; objective 3)
9. **small for gestational age (SGA):** A term for a baby whose birthweight is significantly lower than expected, given the time since conception. For example, a 5-pound (2,265-gram) newborn is considered SGA if born on time but not SGA if born two months early. (p. 114; objective 3)
10. **artificial insemination:** The preparation and placement of a semen sample inside a woman's uterus. (video lesson, segment 1; objectives 2 & 5)
11. **gestational surrogacy:** An arrangement between the intended parents of the child and a woman who agrees to carry the embryo(s) made from the egg(s) and sperm of the intended parents. The child(ren) of gestational surrogacy is/are the genetic child(ren) of the intended parents, and the surrogate carries the embryo/fetus to term in the role of "host" uterus. In this form of surrogacy, the surrogate may also be called the "gestational mother." (video lesson, segment 3; objectives 2 & 5)

Summary

Starting a family, for most couples, is a process that ends happily with the birth of a healthy child. Yet, for some couples who are **infertile** (unable to conceive despite a year of trying), the road is not so smooth. Infertility affects approximately 2 to 30 percent of the general population, with women and men contributing equally to the inability to conceive. One reason that infertility is more common in recent years is that many couples are waiting longer to have their first child.

The remedies for infertility include the use of medication to induce ovulation in women; **artificial insemination**, in which a sample of semen is collected from the male partner and inserted into the woman's uterus; and **in vitro fertilization (IVF)**, in which eggs are fertilized with sperm in the laboratory and the resulting zygote is inserted into the woman's uterus. For couples who are unable to conceive even with this **assisted reproductive technology (ART)**, **surrogacy** and adoption are often viable options.

Even after conception has occurred and prenatal development has begun, a healthy birth is not guaranteed. Miscarriages occur in about 15 percent of pregnancies (especially among older women), toxins called **teratogens** may interrupt or disrupt the development of the growing fetus, and the newborn may be born early and/or underweight.

The crucial factor in the fetus's attaining the **age of viability**, beginning from 22 to 24 weeks of pregnancy, is neurological maturation, which is essential to the regulation of the basic body functions of breathing, sucking, and sleeping. By 28 weeks, the typical fetus weighs about 1,300 grams (3 pounds) and has a greater than 50 percent chance of survival.

Teratology is a science of risk analysis, which attempts to evaluate what factors can make prenatal harm more, or less, likely to occur. Three crucial factors that determine whether a specific teratogen will cause harm, and of what nature, are the timing of exposure, the amount of exposure, and the developing organism's genetic vulnerability to damage from the substance.

A major, preventable health hazard for the fetus is **low birthweight**, defined as birthweight that is less than 2,500 grams (5.5 pounds). Babies that weigh less than 3 pounds, 5 ounces (1,500 grams) are classified as very low birthweight, while those that weigh less than 2 pounds, 3 ounces (1,000 grams) are classified as extremely low birthweight. Low-birthweight infants who are born more than three weeks early are called **preterm**. Others, born close to the due date but weighing less than most full-term neonates, are called **small for gestational age** (SGA).

Answer Key

Practice Questions

Multiple-Choice Questions

1. a. is the correct answer. (objective 4)

   b., c., & d. are incorrect. Although low birthweight (b), critical periods of organ development (c), and maternal malnutrition (d) are all hazardous to the developing person during prenatal development, none is an example of a threshold effect.

2. c. is the correct answer. (objective 1)

3. d. is the correct answer. (video lesson, segment 3; objective 4)

   a. is incorrect. In general, teratogens can cross the placenta at any time.

   b. is incorrect. Teratogens are agents in the environment, not heritable genes (although susceptibility to individual teratogens has a genetic component).

   c. is incorrect. Although nutrition is an important factor in healthy prenatal development, the textbook does not suggest that nutrition alone can usually counteract the harmful effects of teratogens.

4. b. is the correct answer. (objective 3)

5. b. is the correct answer. (objectives 3 & 4)

6. d. is the correct answer. (objective 4)

7. c. is the correct answer. (objectives 3 & 4)

   a. is incorrect. Many factors, including drug use, malnutrition, and maternal illness, are common causes of low birthweight.

   b. & d. are incorrect. In fact, the rates are increasing, in large part as a result of the high incidence of multiple births resulting from assisted reproductive technology.

8. c. is the correct answer. (objective 3)

9. d. is the correct answer. (objective 4)

   a. is incorrect. Behavioral teratogens are dangerous throughout the entire prenatal period.

   b. and c. are incorrect. Males are more genetically vulnerable than are females, and this is especially true in regard to behavioral teratogens.

10. d. is the correct answer. (video lesson, segment 2; objective 3)

    a. & c. are incorrect. At 266 days, this infant is full term.

11. a. is the correct answer. (video lesson, segment 2; objective 3)

    b. & d. are is incorrect. Low birthweight is defined as weighing less than 5.5 pounds.

    c. is incorrect. Although an infant can be both preterm and small for gestational age, this baby's weight is within the normal range of healthy babies.

12. b. is the correct answer. (video lesson, segments 1 & 3; objectives 2 & 5)

13. d. is the correct answer. (objective 1)
14. b. is the correct answer. (video lesson, segment 1; objective 2)
15. d. is the correct answer. (video lesson, segment 1; objective 2)

Matching Items

16. d (video lesson, segments 1 & 3; objectives 2 & 5)
17. b (video lesson, segment 3; objective 1)
18. h (video lesson, segment 1; objectives 2 & 5)
19. c (video lesson, segment 3; objective 3)
20. a (video lesson, segment 3; objective 4)
21. i (video lesson, segment 3; objective 3)
22. j (objective 3)
23. e (video lesson, segment 1; objective 2)
24. g (objectives 2 & 5)
25. f (video lesson, segment 3; objectives 2 & 5)
26. k (objective 4)

Lesson Review

Lesson 5

The Beginnings
Special Topic

Please Note: Use this matrix to guide your study and achieve the learning objectives of this lesson. It will also help you to view the video, which defines and demonstrates important concepts and skills as they relate to everyday life.

Learning Objective	Textbook	Course Student Guide	Video Lesson
1. List the odds of a zygote growing to become a living newborn baby and describe several reasons for this survival rate.	pp. 94–98, 102	Key Terms: 4; Practice Questions: 2, 13, 17.	Segment 3: *The Surrogate Mom*
2. Define infertile and describe various options for infertile couples including artificial insemination, in vitro fertilization, and gestational surrogacy.	pp. 71–73	Key Terms: 1, 2, 3, 10, 11; Practice Questions: 12, 14, 15, 16, 18, 23, 24, 25.	Segment 1: *Overcoming Infertility* Segment 3: *The Surrogate Mom*
3. Discuss the potential problems of low-birthweight and preterm newborns.	pp. 97–98, 114–116	Key Terms: 7, 8, 9; Practice Questions: 4, 5, 7, 8, 10, 11, 19, 21, 22.	Segment 2: *The Ties That Bind*
4. Discuss several factors that determine whether a specific teratogen will be harmful and how a mother-to-be can avoid these harmful effects.	pp. 106–113	Key Terms: 5, 6; Practice Questions: 1, 3, 5, 6, 7, 9, 20, 26.	Segment 3: *The Surrogate Mom*
5. Explain several alternative methods of conception, and relate several personal and ethical questions raised by these methods.	pp. 71–73	Key Terms: 2, 3, 10, 11; Practice Questions: 12, 16, 18, 24, 25.	Segment 1: *Overcoming Infertility* Segment 3: *The Surrogate Mom*

Grow, Baby, Grow!

Lesson 6

The First Two Years: Biosocial Development

Preview

This is the first of a five-lesson unit that describes the developing person from birth through age two in terms of biosocial, cognitive, and psychosocial development. This unit also includes *Summary* and *Special Topic* lessons. The biosocial domain is the part of human development that includes all the growth and changes that occur in a person's body. It also includes the social, cultural, and environmental factors that affect biological development, such as nutrition and health care.

The lesson begins with observations on the overall growth of infants, including their size and shape. A discussion of brain growth follows, including how a child's experiences can affect this development. At birth, the brain contains more than 100 billion nerve cells, or **neurons**, but the nerve fibers that interconnect them are incomplete. During the first few years of a child's life, extensive growth occurs in these neural pathways, enabling new capabilities in each domain of development.

The lesson then turns to the baby's developing senses, along with research on infant **sensation** and **perception**. This is followed by a look at how babies move and control their bodies and the ages at which the average infant advances in ability. Preventative medicine is discussed next, including the importance of **immunization**. The final section covers proper nutrition during the first two years and the consequences of severe **malnutrition**.

As you complete this lesson, consider a baby you know. What is the height and weight of this child and how does that compare to other babies of the same age? Note the child's ability to sense and perceive the world. Study reactions to outside stimuli and the way he or she moves arms, legs, fingers and toes. Talk to the baby's parents about the health care this child has received. Have they taken the baby to see a doctor? Which immunizations has the child received? Finally, discuss the mother and father's choices regarding nutrition. Did the mother breast-feed? If so, for how long? What is the child's diet now?

Prior Knowledge That Will Be Used in This Lesson

- This is the first lesson to focus on a single "domain" of development (biosocial). Remember, although the division of human development into three domains makes it easier to study, development occurs holistically not in separate pieces. Virtually all aspects of human development reflect all three domains.
- This lesson will also return to the concept of *epigenetics* from Lesson 3. Recall that all development stems from the interaction between our genes and the influences of our environment.
- Recall from Lesson 4 that *reflexes* are newborns' automatic responses to experiences. While they initially function for survival, reflexes are the foundation of reciprocal social interactions and motor skills and are thus building blocks of biosocial development.

Learning Objectives

Use this information to guide your reading, viewing, thinking, and studying. After successfully completing this lesson, you should be able to:

1. Describe the size and proportions of an infant's body, and discuss how babies change during the first two years and how their bodies compare with those of adults.
2. Describe the sleep patterns of children during the first two years, and discuss the influence of parental caregiving on these patterns.
3. Describe a typical brain cell and discuss ways in which the brain changes or matures during infancy.
4. Discuss the influence of experience on brain development.
5. Distinguish between sensation and perception, and describe the extent and development of an infant's perceptual abilities using hearing or vision as an example.
6. Describe the basic reflexes of the newborn and distinguish between gross motor skills and fine motor skills.
7. Describe the basic pattern of motor-skill development during the first two years and discuss variations in the timing of motor-skill acquisition.
8. Discuss the roles that preventative medicine and immunization have played in improving the survival of young children.
9. Describe the nutritional needs of infants and toddlers, noting the benefits of mother's milk.
10. Describe protein-calorie malnutrition, identify the causes and effects of this condition, and discuss methods of prevention.

Textbook Reading & Video Viewing

For the most effective study of this lesson, complete the assignments in the sequence listed below.

Before viewing the video program:

Read Chapter 5, "The First Two Years: Biosocial Development," pages 127–159.
Review the discussion of reflexes in Chapter 4, pages 117–118.

View the video for Lesson 6, "Grow, Baby, Grow!"

Segment 1: *Physical Growth and Health*

Segment 2: *Brain Growth and Development*

Segment 3: *Basic Reflexes and Motor Skills*

Segment 4: *Infant Nutrition*

After viewing the video program:

Review all reading assignments for this lesson.

Complete the "Practice Questions" and "Applying Your Knowledge" sections to reinforce your understanding of important terms and concepts and measure your achievement of the Learning Objectives. Check your answers with the feedback given and review when necessary.

Practice Questions I

Multiple-Choice Questions

1. The average North American newborn
   a. weighs approximately 6 pounds.
   b. weighs approximately 7 pounds.
   c. is "overweight" because of the diet of the mother.
   d. weighs 10 percent less than what is desirable.

2. Compared to the first year, growth during the second year
   a. proceeds at a slower rate.
   b. continues at about the same rate.
   c. includes more insulating fat.
   d. includes more bone and muscle.

3. The major motor skill likely to be mastered by 95 percent of infants before the age of 6 months is
   a. sitting with support and with head steady.
   b. sitting without support.
   c. turning the head in search of a nipple.
   d. grabbing an object with thumb and forefinger.

4. Norms among nations suggest that the earliest walkers in the world are infants from
   a. Western Europe.
   b. the United States.
   c. Africa.
   d. Eastern Europe.
5. Head-sparing is the phenomenon in which
   a. the brain continues to grow even though the body stops growing as a result of malnutrition.
   b. the proportions of the infant's body often seem "top heavy."
   c. axons develop more rapidly than dendrites.
   d. dendrites develop more rapidly than axons.
6. Dreaming is characteristic of
   a. slow-wave sleep.
   b. transitional sleep.
   c. REM sleep.
   d. quiet sleep.
7. Proportionally, the head of the infant is about __________________ of total body length; the head of an adult is about __________________ of total body length.
   a. one-fourth; one-third
   b. one-eighth; one-fourth
   c. one-fourth; one-eighth
   d. one-third; one-fourth
8. Brain functions that require basic common experiences—such as babies' having things to see and people to feed them—are called
   a. experience-dependent.
   b. experience-expectant.
   c. pruning functions.
   d. transient exuberance.
9. Compared with formula-fed infants, breast-fed infants tend to have
   a. greater weight gain.
   b. fewer allergies and digestive upsets.
   c. less frequent feedings during the first few months.
   d. more social approval.

10. Marasmus and kwashiorkor are caused by
    a. bloating.
    b. protein-calorie deficiency.
    c. living in a developing country.
    d. poor family food habits.
11. The infant's first body movements are
    a. fine motor skills.
    b. gross motor skills.
    c. reflexes.
    d. pincer skills.
12. Which of the following is said to have had the greatest impact on human mortality reduction and population growth?
    a. improvements in infant nutrition
    b. oral rehydration therapy
    c. medical advances in newborn care
    d. childhood immunization
13. Kara is an infant whose left eye has very poor vision and thus somewhat limited stimulation. Her brain will use whatever experiences are available to develop the brain, a phenomenon known as
    a. transient exuberance.
    b. self-righting.
    c. pruning.
    d. head-sparing.
14. Which of the following is true of motor-skill development in healthy infants?
    a. It follows the same basic sequence the world over.
    b. It occurs at different rates from individual to individual.
    c. It follows norms that vary from one ethnic group to another.
    d. All of the above are true.
15. Most of the nerve cells that a human brain will ever possess are present
    a. at conception.
    b. about 1 month following conception.
    c. at birth.
    d. at age 5 or 6.

Matching Items

Match each definition or description with its corresponding term.

Terms

16. __________ neurons
17. __________ dendrites
18. __________ kwashiorkor
19. __________ marasmus
20. __________ gross motor skill
21. __________ fine motor skill
22. __________ reflex
23. __________ sucking reflex
24. __________ protein-calorie malnutrition
25. __________ transient exuberance
26. __________ prefrontal cortex
27. __________ metabolism
28. __________ self-righting
29. __________ wasting

Definitions or Descriptions

a. the inborn drive to remedy a developmental deficit

b. protein deficiency during the first year in which growth stops and body tissues waste away

c. picking up an object

d. the most common serious nutrition problem of infancy

e. protein deficiency during toddlerhood

f. newborns suck anything that touches their lips

g. nerve fibers that allow communication among neurons

h. declining physiological response to a familiar stimulus

i. running or jumping

j. the process in which axons are coated with an insulating sheath

k. an involuntary response

l. the phenomenal increase in neural connections over the first 2 years

m. nerve cells

n. area of the brain that specializes in anticipation, planning, and impulse control

o. the physical and chemical processes that sustain life

p. extremely low weight due to severe malnutrition

Practice Questions II

Multiple-Choice Questions

1. Dendrite is to axon as neural __________ is to neural __________.
   a. input; output
   b. output; input
   c. myelin; synapse
   d. synapse; myelin
2. A reflex is best defined as a(n)
   a. fine motor skill.
   b. motor ability mastered at a specific age.
   c. involuntary physical response to a given stimulus.
   d. gross motor skill.
3. A norm is
   a. a standard, or average, that is derived for a specific group or population.
   b. a point on a ranking scale of 0 to 100.
   c. a milestone of development that all children reach at approximately the same age.
   d. all of the above.
4. Most babies can reach for, grasp, and hold onto an object by about the ____________ month.
   a. second
   b. sixth
   c. ninth
   d. fourteenth
5. During the first weeks of life, babies seem to focus reasonably well on
   a. little in their environment.
   b. objects at a distance of 4 to 30 inches.
   c. objects at a distance of 1 to 3 inches.
   d. objects several feet away.
6. Which sleep stage increases markedly at about 3 or 4 months?
   a. REM
   b. Transitional
   c. Fast-wave
   d. Slow-wave

7. An advantage of breast milk over formula is that it
   a. is always sterile and at body temperature.
   b. contains traces of medications ingested by the mother.
   c. can be given without involving the father.
   d. contains more protein and vitamin D than does formula.

8. The primary cause of malnutrition in developing countries is
   a. formula feeding.
   b. inadequate food supply.
   c. disease.
   d. early cessation of breast-feeding.

9. Transient exuberance and pruning demonstrate that
   a. the pace of acquisition of motor skills varies markedly from child to child.
   b. newborns sleep more than older children because their immature nervous systems cannot handle the higher, waking level of sensory stimulation.
   c. the specifics of brain structure and growth depend partly on the infant's experience.
   d. good nutrition is essential to healthy biosocial development.

10. Climbing is to using a crayon as ___________ is to ___________.
    a. fine motor skill; gross motor skill
    b. gross motor skill; fine motor skill
    c. reflex; fine motor skill
    d. reflex; gross motor skill

11. Some infant reflexes
    a. are essential to life.
    b. disappear in the months after birth.
    c. provide the foundation for later motor skills.
    d. do all of the above.

12. Professor Atlas learns that children are able to learn a particular skill better when they are between the ages of 5 and 6 than when they are either younger or older. Professor Atlas would call the year between ages 5 and 6 a(n) ___________ period for this skill.
    a. critical
    b. exuberant
    c. plastic
    d. sensitive

13. Neurotransmitters are chemical messengers that diffuse across the
    a. axon.
    b. myelin sheath.
    c. dendrite.
    d. synaptic gap.

14. Reflexes are ____________ responses, whereas gross motor skills and fine motor skills __________________.
    a. involuntary; require active participation
    b. voluntary; are involuntary
    c. slow-to-develop; require extensive practice
    d. permanent; are temporary

True or False Items

Write T (for true) or F (for false) on the line in front of each statement.

15. _____ Much of the weight increase in the first few months of life is fat.
16. _____ Reflexive hiccups, sneezes, and thrashing are signs that the infant's reflexes are not functioning properly.
17. _____ Infants of all ethnic backgrounds develop the same motor skills at approximately the same age.
18. _____ The typical two-year-old is almost one-fifth its adult weight and one-half its adult height.
19. _____ Vision is better developed than hearing in most newborns.
20. _____ Today, most infants in the United States are still being breast-fed at six months of age.
21. _____ Certain basic sensory experiences seem necessary to ensure full brain development in the human infant.
22. _____ Current research indicates that the risks of immunizations are far less than the risks of the diseases themselves.
23. _____ The infant's first motor skills are actually reflexes.
24. _____ Infants typically grow about one inch per month during the first year.
25. _____ Over the first two years, the infant's metabolic activity decreases steadily.
26. _____ Stunting is when a child's head is extremely small as a result of chronic malnutrition.

Applying Your Knowledge

1. Newborns cry, shiver, and tuck their legs close to their bodies. This set of reflexes helps them

   a. ensure proper muscle tone.

   b. learn how to signal distress.

   c. maintain constant body temperature.

   d. communicate serious hunger pangs.

2. Research studies of the more than 100,000 Romanian children orphaned and severely deprived in infancy reported all **EXCEPT** which of the following?

   a. Self-righting was apparent, especially in height and weight.

   b. The children had smaller heads.

   c. During early childhood, many still showed signs of emotional damage.

   d. All of the children placed in healthy adoptive homes eventually completely recovered.

3. Mrs. Bartholomew opens the door to her infant's room to be sure everything is all right. She notices that her son's eyes are flickering behind closed lids. The infant is in which stage of sleep?

   a. quiet sleep

   b. REM sleep

   c. transitional sleep

   d. one somewhere between b and c

4. The average child is at what percentile?

   a. between the 25th and 75th percentiles

   b. the 50th percentile

   c. between the 40th and 60th percentiles

   d. the 100th percentile

5. According to developmental research, which of the following is the **BEST** advice to give parents who are concerned about their children's sleep habits?

   a. "Go to your baby and rock him or her back to sleep whenever he or she stirs in the middle of the night."

   b. "Let the baby determine the sleep schedule and then don't let anything interfere with it."

   c. "Do not allow co-sleeping."

   d. All of the above are good pieces of advice for parents.

6. Michael stares blankly at whatever he sees and is able to discriminate subtle sound differences. Michael most likely

   a. is a preterm infant.

   b. has brain damage in the visual processing areas of the cortex.

   c. is a newborn.

   d. is slow-to-mature.

7. A baby turns her head and starts to suck when her receiving blanket is brushed against her cheek. The baby is displaying the

   a. sucking reflex.

   b. rooting reflex.

   c. Babinski reflex.

   d. Moro reflex.

8. Sensation is to perception as __________ is to __________.

   a. hearing; seeing

   b. detecting a stimulus; making sense of a stimulus

   c. making sense of a stimulus; detecting a stimulus

   d. tasting; smelling

9. Amalya, a three-month-old infant, is particularly sensitive to which of the following sounds?

   a. low-pitched sounds

   b. human voices

   c. bells

   d. recurring noises, such as metronomes, vacuum cleaners, and the sound of rain

10. To say that most developmentalists are multidisciplinary and believe in plasticity means that they believe personality, intellect, and emotions

    a. change throughout life as a result of biological maturation.

    b. change throughout life for a combination of reasons.

    c. remain very stable throughout life.

    d. more strongly reveal the impact of genes as people get older.

11. Like all newborns, Serena is able to

    a. turn her head toward the source of a sound.

    b. see objects more than 30 inches from her face quite clearly.

    c. focus both eyes on one thing.

    d. do all of the above.

12. Three-week-old Nathan should have the **LEAST** difficulty focusing on the sight of
    a. stuffed animals on a bookshelf across the room from his crib.
    b. his mother's face as she holds him in her arms.
    c. the checkerboard pattern in the wallpaper covering the ceiling of his room.
    d. the family dog as it dashes into the nursery.

13. Geneva has been malnourished throughout childhood. It is likely that she will be
    a. smaller and shorter than her genetic potential would dictate.
    b. slow in intellectual development.
    c. less resistant to disease.
    d. all of the above.

Key Terms

1. **head-sparing:** A biological mechanism that protects the brain when malnutrition affects body growth. The brain is the last part of the body to be damaged by malnutrition. (p. 129; objective 1)
2. **percentile:** A point on a ranking scale of 0 to 100. The 50th percentile is the midpoint; half the people in the population being studied rank higher and half rank lower. (p. 129; objective 1)
3. **REM sleep:** Rapid eye movement sleep is a stage of sleep characterized by flickering eyes behind closed eyelids, dreaming, and rapid brain waves. (p. 130; objective 2)
4. **co-sleeping:** A custom in which parents and their children (usually infants) sleep together in the same room. (p. 131; objective 4)
5. **neuron:** The nerve cell that is the main component of the central nervous system, especially the brain. (p. 132; video lesson, segment 2; objective 3)
6. **cortex:** The outer layers of the brain in humans and other mammals. Most thinking, feeling, and sensing involve the cortex.

   Memory aid: Cortex in Latin means "bark." As bark covers a tree, the cortex is the "bark of the brain." (p. 133; objective 3)
7. **prefrontal cortex:** The area of cortex at the front of the brain that specializes in anticipation, planning, and impulse control. (p. 133; objective 4)
8. **axon:** A fiber that extends from a neuron and transmits electrochemical impulses from that neuron to the dendrites of other neurons. (p. 133; video lesson, segment 2; objective 3)
9. **dendrite:** A nerve fiber extension that receives the impulses transmitted from other neurons via their axons. (p. 133; video lesson, segment 2; objective 3)
10. **synapse:** The point at which the axon of a sending neuron meets the dendrites of a receiving neuron. (p. 133; objective 3)

11. **transient exuberance:** The dramatic, temporary increase in neural connections that occurs in an infant's brain over the first 2 years of life. (p. 134; video lesson, segment 2; objective 3)
12. **pruning:** When applied to brain development, the process by which unused connections in the brain atrophy and die. (p. 134; objective 3)
13. **experience-expectant brain functions:** Those brain functions that require basic common experiences which an infant can be expected to have (such as having things to see and hear) in order to grow. (p. 135; objective 4)
14. **experience-dependent brain functions:** Those brain functions that depend on particular, and variable, experiences (such as experiencing language) in order to grow. As such, these may or may not develop in a particular infant. (p. 135; objective 4)
15. **shaken-baby syndrome:** A life-threatening injury that occurs when an infant is forcefully shaken back and forth, a motion that ruptures blood vessels in the brain and breaks neural connections. (p. 139; objective 4)
16. **self-righting:** The inborn drive to remedy a developmental deficit; literally, to return to sitting or standing upright, after being tipped over. People of all ages have self-righting impulses, for emotional as well as physical imbalance. (p. 141; objective 4)
17. **sensation:** The response of a sensory system (eyes, ears, skin, tongue, nose) when it detects a stimulus. (p. 142; objective 5)
18. **perception:** The mental processing of sensory information when the brain interprets a sensation. Perception occurs in the cortex. (p. 142; objective 5)
19. **binocular vision:** The ability to focus the two eyes in a coordinated manner in order to see one image. This ability is absent at birth. (p. 143; objective 5)

    Memory aid: *Bi-* indicates "two"; *ocular* means something pertaining to the eye. Binocular vision is vision for "two eyes."
20. **motor skills:** The learned abilities to move some part of the body, in actions ranging from a large leap to a flicker of the eyelid. (The word *motor* here refers to movement of muscles.) (p. 145; video lesson, segment 3; objective 6)
21. **gross motor skills:** Physical abilities that demand large body movements, such as climbing, jumping, or running. (The word *gross* here means "big.") (p. 146; video lesson, segment 3; objective 6)
22. **fine motor skills:** Physical abilities involving small body movements, especially of the hands and fingers, such as drawing and picking up a coin. (The word *fine* here means "small.") (p. 146; video lesson, segment 3; objective 6)
23. **immunization:** The process of protecting a person against a disease, via antibodies. Immunization can happen naturally, when someone survives a disease, or medically, usually via a small dose of the virus that stimulates the production of antibodies and thus renders a person immune. Also called *vaccination*. (p. 149; objective 8)

24. **protein-calorie malnutrition:** A condition in which a person does not consume sufficient food of any kind. This deprivation can result in several illnesses, severe weight loss, and even death. (p. 154; objective 11)
25. **stunting:** The failure of children to grow to a normal height for their age as a result of severe and chronic malnutrition. (p. 154; objective 11)
26. **wasting:** The tendency for children to be severely underweight for their age as a result of malnutrition. (p. 154; objective 11)
27. **marasmus:** A disease caused by severe protein-calorie deficiency during the first year of life. Growth stops, body tissues waste away, and the infant eventually dies. (p. 156; objective 11)
28. **kwashiorkor:** A disease of chronic malnutrition during childhood, in which a protein deficiency makes the child more vulnerable to other diseases, such as measles, diarrhea, and influenza. (p. 156; objective 11)
29. **metabolism:** The physical and chemical processes in the body that promote growth and sustain life. (video lesson, segment 2; objective 3)
30. **enriched environment:** An environment that provides the developing child with a highly nurturing and stimulating atmosphere in which to grow and learn. (video lesson, segment 2; objective 4)
31. **sucking reflex:** The involuntary tendency of newborns to suck anything that touches their lips. This reflex fosters feeding. (video lesson, segment 3; objective 6)
32. **rooting reflex:** This involuntary tendency, which helps babies find a nipple, causes them to turn their heads and start to suck when something brushes against their cheek. (video lesson, segment 3; objective 6)
33. **breathing reflex:** An involuntary physical response that ensures that the infant has an adequate supply of oxygen and discharges carbon dioxide. (video lesson, segment 3; objective 6)
34. **pincer grasp:** A type of fine motor coordination in which the thumb and forefinger are used together to hold an object. (video lesson, segment 3; objective 6)
35. **undernutrition:** A nutritional problem in which a child is noticeably underweight or short in stature compared to the norms. (video lesson, segment 4; objective 10)
36. **failure to thrive:** A type of undernutrition that involves a child who lives in an adequately nourished community but is not exhibiting normal childhood weight gain. (video lesson, segment 4; objectives 1, 9, & 10)
37. **reflexes:** Involuntary physical responses to specific stimuli. A reflex occurs without conscious thought. (p. 117; video lesson, segment 3; objective 6)

Summary

Biosocial development during the first two years is so rapid that infants often seem to change before their parents' very eyes. The newborn seems top-heavy in body proportions, with its head being one-fourth of total body length (in comparison to one-eighth of body length as an adult). By age two, the average toddler's body weight is about one-fifth adult weight and body length has increased to about one-half adult height.

Brain development is also rapid during infancy. By age two, the brain has attained about 75 percent of its adult weight, and there has been a fivefold increase in the density of **dendrite** networks in the **cortex**. Although some brain development is maturational, experience is also essential. Some experiences are necessary for normal brain development (**experience-expectant** brain development), and some experiences are unique to each individual (**experience-dependant** brain development).

The newborn's motor ability is limited to **reflexes**, including those that maintain adequate oxygen, body temperature, and nourishment. By 6 months, most babies can reach, grab, and hold onto dangling objects. The average child can walk with assistance at 9 months, stand momentarily at 10 months, and take steps unassisted at 12 months. Although all healthy infants develop the same **motor skills** in the same sequence, the age at which these skills are acquired varies greatly from infant to infant. Variations in the acquisition of motor skills can be attributed in part to inherited factors, such as activity level, rate of physical maturation, and body type. Environmental factors, such as medical care, nutrition, and patterns of infant care, are also influential. Note that the video for this lesson draws a distinction between reflexes, which are involuntary responses to stimuli, and motor skills, which require voluntary participation.

At birth, both **sensation** and **perception** are apparent. Vision is the least well developed of the senses. Newborns can focus better on objects that are between 4 and 30 inches away. By 6 months, visual acuity approaches 20/20, and infants can use both eyes to track moving objects well. In contrast, hearing is comparatively acute in the newborn. Newborns can differentiate their mother's voice from those of other women; by 1 month, they can perceive differences between very similar sounds.

For its nutritional benefits, breast milk is the ideal food for most babies. It is always sterile and at body temperature, contains more essential vitamins and iron than cow's milk, is more digestible, and provides the infant with the mother's immunity to disease. The primary cause of **protein-calorie malnutrition** in developing countries is early cessation of breast-feeding. Severe deficiency can cause **marasmus** in infants and **kwashiorkor** in toddlers.

Answer Key

Practice Questions I

Multiple-Choice Questions

1. b. is the correct answer. (objective 1)
2. a. is the correct answer. (objective 1)
3. a. is the correct answer. (objective 7)

   b. is incorrect. The age norm for this skill is 7.8 months.

   c. is incorrect. This is a reflex, rather than an acquired motor skill.

   d. is incorrect. This skill is acquired between 9 and 14 months.
4. c. is the correct answer. (objective 7)
5. a. is the correct answer. (objectives 1 & 10)
6. c. is the correct answer. (objective 2)
7. c. is the correct answer. (video lesson, segment 1; objective 1)
8. b. is the correct answer. (objective 4)

   a. is incorrect. Experience-dependent functions depend on particular, and variable experiences in order to grow.

   c. is incorrect. Pruning refers to the process by which some neurons wither because experience does not activate them.

   d. is incorrect. This refers to the great increase in the number of neurons, dendrites, and synapses that occurs in an infant's brain over the first 2 years of life.
9. b. is the correct answer. Breast milk is more digestible than cow's milk or formula. (pp. 154–156; video lesson, segment 4; objective 9)

   a., c., & d. are incorrect. Breast- and bottle-fed babies do not differ in these attributes.
10. b. is the correct answer. (objective 10)
11. c. is the correct answer. (video lesson, segment 3; objective 6)

    a., b., & d. are incorrect. These motor skills do not emerge until somewhat later; reflexes are present at birth.
12. d. is the correct answer. (objective 8)
13. b. is the correct answer. (objective 4)
14. d. is the correct answer. (objective 7)
15. c. is the correct answer. (objective 3)

Matching Items

16. m (video lesson, segment 2; objective 3)
17. g (video lesson, segment 2; objective 3)
18. e (objective 10)
19. b (objective 10)
20. i (video lesson, segment 3; objective 6)

21. c (video lesson, segment 3; objective 6)
22. k (video lesson, segment 3; objective 6)
23. f (video lesson, segment 3; objective 6)
24. d (objective 10)
25. l (video lesson, segment 2; objective 3)
26. n (objective 4)
27. o (video lesson, segment 2; objective 3)
28. a (objective 4)

Practice Questions II

Multiple-Choice Questions

1. a. is the correct answer. (video lesson, segment 2; objective 3)
2. c. is the correct answer. (video lesson, segment 3; objective 6)

   a., b., & d. are incorrect. Each of these refers to voluntary responses that are acquired only after a certain amount of practice; reflexes are involuntary responses that are present at birth and require no practice.
3. a. is the correct answer. (objective 1)
4. b. is the correct answer. (objective 7)
5. b. is the correct answer. (objective 5)

   a. is incorrect. Although focusing ability seems to be limited to a certain range, babies do focus on many objects in this range.

   c. is incorrect. This is not within the range at which babies can focus.

   d. is incorrect. Babies have very poor distance vision.
6. d. is the correct answer. (objective 2)
7. a. is the correct answer. (video lesson, segment 4; objective 9)

   b. is incorrect. If anything, this is a potential disadvantage of breast milk over formula.

   c. is incorrect. So can formula.

   d. is incorrect. Breast milk contains more iron, vitamin C, and vitamin A than cow's milk; it does not contain more protein and vitamin D, however.
8. b. is the correct answer. (objective 10)
9. c. is the correct answer. (objective 4)
10. b. is the correct answer. (video lesson, segment 3; objective 6)

    c. & d. are incorrect. Reflexes are involuntary responses; climbing and using a crayon are both voluntary responses.
11. d. is the correct answer. (video lesson, segment 3; objective 6)
12. d. is the correct answer. (objective 4)
13. d. is the correct answer. (objective 3)

14. a. is the correct answer. (video lesson, segment 3; objective 6)

    b. & c. are incorrect. Reflexes are involuntary responses (therefore not b) that are present at birth (therefore not c).

    d. Some reflexes disappear with age.

True or False Items

15. T Boys are both slightly heavier and taller than girls at 2 years. (objective 1)
16. F Hiccups, sneezes, and thrashing are common during the first few days, and they are entirely normal reflexes. (objective 6)
17. F Although all healthy infants develop the same motor skills in the same sequence, the age at which these skills are acquired can vary greatly from infant to infant. (objective 7)
18. T (objective 1)
19. F Vision is relatively poorly developed at birth, whereas hearing is well developed. (objective 5)
20. F Only one third of infants are still being breast-fed at 6 months of age. (objective 9)
21. T (video lesson, segment 2; objective 4)
22. T (objective 8)
23. T (objective 6)
24. T (video lesson, segment 1; objective 1)
25. F Metabolic activity increases, partly as a result of the dramatic growth occurring in the brain. (video lesson, segment 2; objective 3)
26. F Stunting refers to a child being short for his or her age as a result of malnutrition (objective 10)

Applying Your Knowledge

1. c. is the correct answer. (objective 6)
2. d. is the correct answer. Although all of the children improved, persistent deficits remained in many of them. (objective 4)
3. b. is the correct answer. (objective 2)

    a. is incorrect. Relatively slow and regular breathing and relaxed muscles characterize this state.

    c. is incorrect. This state is characterized by being half awake while dozing.

4. b. is the correct answer. (objective 1)
5. b. is the correct answer. (objective 2)
6. c. is the correct answer. (objective 5)
7. b. is the correct answer. (video lesson, segment 3; objective 6)

    a. is incorrect. This is the reflexive sucking of newborns in response to anything that touches their lips.

    c. is incorrect. This is the response that infants make when their feet are stroked.

d. is incorrect. In this response to startling noises, newborns fling their arms outward and then bring them together on their chests as if to hold on to something.

8. b. is the correct answer. (objective 5)

   a. & d. are incorrect. Sensation and perception operate in all of these sensory modalities.

9. b. is the correct answer. (objective 5)

10. b. is the correct answer. (objective 4)

11. a. is the correct answer. (objective 5)

    b. is incorrect. Objects at this distance are out of focus for newborns.

    c. is incorrect. This ability does not emerge until about 14 weeks of age.

12. b. is the correct answer. This is true because, at birth, focusing is best for objects between 4 and 30 inches away. (objective 5)

    a., c., & d. are incorrect. Newborns have very poor distance vision; each of these situations involves a distance greater than the optimal focus range.

13. d. is the correct answer. (video lesson, segment 4; objective 10)

Lesson Review

Lesson 6

The First Two Years
Biosocial Development

Please Note: Use this matrix to guide your study and achieve the learning objectives of this lesson. It will also help you to view the video, which defines and demonstrates important concepts and skills as they relate to everyday life.

Learning Objective	Textbook	Course Student Guide	Video Lesson
1. Describe the size and proportions of an infant's body, and discuss how babies change during the first two years and how their bodies compare with those of adults.	pp. 128–129	Key Terms: 1, 2, 36; Practice Questions I: 1, 2, 5, 7; Practice Questions II: 3, 15, 18, 24; Applying Your Knowledge: 4.	Segment 1: *Physical Growth and Health* Segment 4: *Infant Nutrition*
2. Describe the sleep patterns of children during the first two years, and discuss the influence of parental caregiving on these patterns.	pp. 130–132	Key Terms: 3; Practice Questions I: 6; Practice Questions II: 6; Applying Your Knowledge: 3, 5.	
3. Describe a typical brain cell and discuss ways in which the brain changes or matures during infancy.	pp. 132–135	Key Terms: 5, 6, 8, 9, 10, 11, 29; Practice Questions I: 15, 16, 17, 25, 27; Practice Questions II: 1, 13, 25.	Segment 2: *Brain Growth and Development*
4. Discuss the influence of experience on brain development.	pp. 135–141	Key Terms: 4, 7, 13, 14, 15, 16, 30; Practice Questions I: 8, 13, 26, 28; Practice Questions II: 9, 12, 21; Applying Your Knowledge: 2, 10.	Segment 2: *Brain Growth and Development*
5. Distinguish between sensation and perception, and describe the extent and development of an infant's perceptual abilities using hearing or vision as an example.	pp. 141–145	Key Terms: 17, 18, 19; Practice Questions II: 5, 19; Applying Your Knowledge: 6, 8, 9, 11, 12.	

Learning Objective	Textbook	Course Student Guide	Video Lesson
6. Describe the basic reflexes of the newborn and distinguish between gross motor skills and fine motor skills.	pp. 117–118, 145–148	Key Terms: 20, 21, 22, 31, 32, 33, 34, 37; Practice Questions I: 11, 20, 21, 22, 23; Practice Questions II: 2, 10, 11, 14, 16, 23; Applying Your Knowledge: 1, 7.	Segment 3: *Basic Reflexes and Motor Skills*
7. Describe the basic pattern of motor-skill development during the first two years and discuss variations in the timing of motor-skill acquisition.	pp. 145–148	Practice Questions I: 3, 4, 14; Practice Questions II: 4, 17.	
8. Discuss the roles that preventative medicine and immunization have played in improving the survival of young children.	pp. 148–151	Key Terms: 23; Practice Questions I: 12; Practice Questions II: 22.	
9. Describe the nutritional needs of infants and toddlers, noting the benefits of mother's milk.	pp. 151–154	Key Terms: 36; Practice Questions I: 9; Practice Questions II: 7, 20.	Segment 4: *Infant Nutrition*
10. Describe protein-calorie malnutrition, identify the causes and effects of this condition, and discuss methods of prevention.	pp. 154–157	Key Terms: 24, 25, 26, 27, 28, 35, 36; Practice Questions I: 5, 10, 18, 19, 24; Practice Questions II: 8,; Applying Your Knowledge: 13.	Segment 4: *Infant Nutrition*

The Little Scientist

Lesson 7

The First Two Years: Cognitive Development

Preview

Lesson 7 is the first of the lessons to focus on the domain of *cognition,* by which we mean the mental processes involved in thinking. The lesson focuses on the various ways in which infant cognitive development is revealed: through perception (which, as you'll recall from Lesson 6, refers to the mental processing of sensory information), memory, and language development.

The video for this lesson, "The Little Scientist," outlines Jean Piaget's theory of **sensorimotor intelligence**, which maintains that infants think exclusively with their senses and motor skills. Piaget's six stages of sensorimotor intelligence are examined.

The lesson also gives a description of infant perception and the influential theory of **affordances**. Central to this theory is the idea that infants gain cognitive understanding of their world through affordances, that is, opportunities to perceive and interact with the objects and environments around them. The lesson also describes research on infant memory, including how infants' memories are both fragile and enduring.

Finally, the lesson turns to the most remarkable cognitive achievement of the first two years, the acquisition of language. Beginning with a description of the infant's first attempts at language, the video and chapter follow the sequence of events that leads to the child's ability to utter two-word sentences. The lesson concludes with an examination of language learning as teamwork involving babies and adults, who, in a sense, teach each other the unique human process of verbal communication.

As you complete this lesson, think about a baby you know (and/or interview the child's parents, if time allows). Would you describe this child as a smart baby? How does this infant express his or her intelligence? Observe how this child reacts to new stimuli and assimilates new information. Study the child's usual environment. What objects, people and situations does the child typically encounter that could afford him or her the opportunity to learn? What kinds of things can this baby remember, and under what circumstances? How far has this child's language advanced relative to other babies of the same age? What were his or her first vocalizations and/or first words? Speculate on how one could encourage language development in this child.

Prior Knowledge That Will Be Used in This Lesson

- The textbook and video will return to Piaget's theory of cognitive development (Lesson 1) with a discussion of sensorimotor intelligence. (Recall that Piaget's theory specifies four major periods):
    1. **Sensorimotor (birth to 2 years) ← The First Two Years**
    2. Preoperational (2 to 6 years)
    3. Concrete Operational (7 to 11 years)
    4. Formal Operational (12 years through adulthood)
- You may wish to review the theories of B. F. Skinner and Lev Vygotsky (Lesson 1). They will come up again as the textbook and video lesson discuss how babies acquire language and what caregivers can do to help.
- In the section on perception, the textbook will refer to the importance of brain growth and development (Lesson 6). You may wish to review terms such as cortex, axons, dendrites, and myelination.
- Recall information processing theory from Lesson 1. As an extension and alternative to Piaget's approach to cognitive development, this perspective looks at each step of the human thinking process, from input to output, in terms analogous to the processes of a sophisticated computer.

Learning Objectives

Use this information to guide your reading, viewing, thinking, and studying. After successfully completing this lesson, you should be able to:

1. Identify and describe Piaget's stages of sensorimotor intelligence, and give examples of the behavior associated with each stage.
2. Explain what object permanence is, how it is tested in infancy, and what these tests reveal.
3. Explain what habituation and fMRI research has revealed about cognitive development in infancy.
4. Describe the information processing model of cognition.
5. Explain the Gibsons' contextual view of perception, and relate it to the idea of affordances, giving examples of affordances perceived by infants.
6. Explain how the infant's focus on movement and change enhances sensory and perceptual skills and thus overall cognitive growth.
7. Discuss research findings on infant memory.
8. Describe language development during the first two years, and identify its major hallmarks.
9. Explain the importance of child-directed speech (motherese), and identify its main features.

10. Summarize the different theories that explain early language learning, and discuss how each theory might help caregivers encourage their child's language development.

Textbook Reading & Video Viewing

For the most effective study of this lesson, complete the assignments in the sequence listed below.

Before viewing the video program:

Read Chapter 6, "The First Two Years: Cognitive Development," pages 161–189.

View the video for Lesson 7, "The Little Scientist."

Segment 1: *Sensorimotor Intelligence*

Segment 2: *Language Development*

After viewing the video program:

Review all reading assignments for this lesson.

Complete the "Practice Questions" and "Applying Your Knowledge" sections to reinforce your understanding of important terms and concepts and measure your achievement of the Learning Objectives. Check your answers with the feedback given and review when necessary.

Practice Questions I

Multiple-Choice Questions

1. In general terms, the Gibsons' concept of affordances emphasizes the idea that the individual perceives an object in terms of its
   a. economic importance.
   b. physical qualities.
   c. function or use to the individual.
   d. role in the larger culture or environment.

2. According to Piaget, when a baby repeats an action that has just triggered a pleasing response from his or her caregiver, a stage __________ behavior has occurred.
   a. one
   b. two
   c. three
   d. six

3. Sensorimotor intelligence begins with a baby's first
   a. attempt to crawl.
   b. reflex actions.
   c. auditory perception.
   d. adaptation of a reflex.

4. Developmentalists now agree that very young infants can remember if all of the following are true **EXCEPT**
   a. motivation is high.
   b. special measures aid memory retrieval.
   c. sufficient time following the event is provided for neural connections to form.
   d. experimental conditions are similar to real life.
5. Piaget and the Gibsons would most likely agree that
   a. perception is largely automatic.
   b. language development is biologically predisposed in children.
   c. learning and perception are active cognitive processes.
   d. it is unwise to "push" children too hard academically.
6. By the end of the first year, infants usually learn how to
   a. accomplish simple goals.
   b. manipulate various symbols.
   c. construct mental combinations.
   d. pretend.
7. When an infant begins to understand that objects exist even when they are out of sight, she or he has begun to understand the concept of object
   a. displacement.
   b. importance.
   c. permanence.
   d. location.
8. Today, most cognitive psychologists view language acquisition as
   a. primarily the result of imitation of adult speech.
   b. a behavior that is determined primarily by biological maturation.
   c. a behavior determined entirely by learning.
   d. determined by both biological maturation and learning.
9. Which of the following is true of language development across cultures?
   a. Children attain language according to ethnically specific timetables.
   b. Children attain language at about the same age in the same sequence across a wide variety of cultures.
   c. Children attain language according to culturally specific timetables.
   d. Children attain language at about the same age but in a different sequence in different cultures.

10. The average baby speaks a few words at about

    a. 6 months.
    b. 9 months.
    c. 12 months.
    d. 24 months.

11. A single word used by toddlers to express a complete thought is

    a. a holophrase.
    b. baby talk.
    c. an affordance.
    d. babbling.

12. Compared with children's rate of speech development, their comprehension of language develops

    a. more slowly.
    b. at about the same pace.
    c. more rapidly.
    d. more rapidly in certain cultures than it does in other cultures.

13. A distinctive form of language, with a particular pitch, structure, and other elements, that adults use in talking to infants is called

    a. a holophrase.
    b. the LAD.
    c. child-directed speech.
    d. conversation.

14. Recent research using fMRI has demonstrated preverbal infants have which of the following at an earlier age than predicted by Piaget?

    a. goals
    b. mental combinations
    c. memories
    d. all of the above

15. The imaging technique that measures changes in activity anywhere in the brain is called

    a. ERP.
    b. EEG.
    c. fMRI.
    d. a CAT scan.

16. A toddler who taps on the computer's keyboard after observing her mother sending e-mail is demonstrating

  a. assimilation.
  b. accommodation.
  c. deferred imitation.
  d. dynamic perception.

Matching Items

Match each definition or description with its corresponding term.

Terms

17. __________	affordances	23. __________	holophrase
18. __________	object permanence	24. __________	child-directed speech
19. __________	visual cliff	25. __________	dynamic perception
20. __________	adaptation	26. __________	reduplicative babbling
21. __________	sensorimotor intelligence	27. __________	implicit memory
22. __________	babbling	28. __________	explicit memory

Definitions or Descriptions

a. high-pitched, simplified, repetitive adult speech
b. repetitive utterance of certain syllables
c. perception that focuses on movement and change
d. the realization that something that is out of sight continues to exist
e. opportunities for interaction that an object or place offers
f. a device for studying depth perception
g. a single word used to express a complete thought
h. cognitive process by which information is taken in and responded to
i. thinking using the senses and motor skills
j. a type of babbling in which a baby puts two syllables together and repeats them over and over
k. memory for events that can be recognized but not necessarily recalled
l. memory that is available for immediate recall

Practice Questions II

Multiple-Choice Questions

1. Stage five (12 to 18 months) of sensorimotor intelligence is best described as

  a. first acquired adaptations.
  b. the period of the "little scientist."
  c. procedures for making interesting sights last.
  d. new means through symbolization.

2. Which of the following is **NOT** evidence of dynamic perception during infancy?
   a. Babies prefer to look at things in motion.
   b. Babies form simple expectations of the path that a moving object will follow.
   c. Babies use movement cues to discern the boundaries of objects.
   d. Babies quickly grasp that even though objects look different when seen from different viewpoints, they are the same objects.
3. Recent research suggests that the concept of object permanence
   a. fades after a few months.
   b. is a skill some children never acquire.
   c. occurs earlier and more gradually than Piaget recognized.
   d. involves pretending as well as mental combinations.
4. According to the Gibsons, an affordance is
   a. an opportunity perceived by a baby.
   b. a quality that resides in toys and other objects.
   c. an ability that emerges at about 12 months.
   d. evidence of manual dexterity in the infant.
5. For Noam Chomsky, the "language acquisition device" refers to
   a. the human predisposition to acquire language.
   b. the portion of the human brain that processes speech.
   c. the vocabulary of the language the child is exposed to.
   d. all of the above.
6. The first stage of sensorimotor intelligence lasts until
   a. infants can anticipate events that will fulfill their needs.
   b. infants begin to adapt their reflexes to the environment.
   c. object permanence has been achieved.
   d. infants are capable of thinking about past and future events.
7. As an advocate of the social-pragmatic theory, Professor Robinson believes that
   a. infants communicate in every way they can because they are social beings.
   b. biological maturation is a dominant force in language development.
   c. infants' language abilities mirror those of their primary caregivers.
   d. language develops in many ways for many reasons.
8. Piaget was incorrect in his belief that infants under 8 months do not have any
   a. comprehension of object permanence.
   b. intelligence.
   c. goal-directed behavior.
   d. all of the above.

9. The purposeful actions that begin to develop in sensorimotor stage four are called
   a. reflexes.
   b. affordances.
   c. goal-directed behaviors.
   d. mental combinations.

10. What is the correct sequence of language development in babies?
    a. crying, babbling, cooing, first word
    b. crying, cooing, babbling, first word
    c. crying, babbling, first word, cooing
    d. crying, cooing, first word, babbling

11. Which of the following is true of deaf babies' babbling?
    a. Deaf babies do not babble.
    b. Compared with hearing babies, deaf babies are more likely to make babbling sounds.
    c. Deaf babies begin to babble vocally at about the same age as do hearing babies.
    d. Deaf babies begin to babble manually at about the same age as hearing babies begin to babble vocally.

12. According to Skinner, children acquire language
    a. as a result of an inborn ability to use the basic structure of language.
    b. through reinforcement and conditioning.
    c. mostly because of biological maturation.
    d. in a fixed sequence of predictable stages.

Matching Items

Match each definition or description with its corresponding term.

Terms

13. __________	goal-directed behavior	19. __________	people preference
14. __________	deferred imitation	20. __________	habituation
15. __________	holophrase	21. __________	primary circular reaction
16. __________	intonation	22. __________	LAD
17. __________	little scientist	23. __________	semantics
18. __________	naming explosion	24. __________	baby talk

Definitions or Descriptions

a. the ability to witness, remember, and later copy a behavior that has been witnessed
b. a dynamic increase in an infant's vocabulary that begins at about 18 months of age
c. a single word that expressed an entire thought
d. the process of getting used to an object or event through repeated exposure
e. babies' innate attraction to humans

f. a hypothetical device that facilitates language development
g. also called "motherese"
h. Piaget's term for the stage-five toddler
i. purposeful actions
j. feedback loop that involves the infant's own body
k. the cadence, tone, or emphasis of speech
l. the underlying meaning of words

Applying Your Knowledge

1. A nine-month-old repeatedly reaches for his five-year-old sister's doll and puts it in his mouth, even though he has been told "no" many times. This is an example of
   a. pretend play.
   b. habituation.
   c. deferred imitation.
   d. goal-directed behavior.
2. Eighteen-month-old Troy puts a collar on his stuffed dog, and then pretends to take it for a walk. Troy's behavior is indicative of which stage of the sensorimotor intelligence period?
   a. stage 3
   b. stage 4
   c. stage 5
   d. stage 6
3. According to Skinner's theory, an infant who learns to delight his father by saying "da-da" is probably benefiting from
   a. social reinforcers, such as smiles and hugs.
   b. modeling.
   c. learning by imitation.
   d. an innate ability to use language.
4. A child's use of the word "Milk" to mean "Can I have milk?" or "I want milk," or "That's my milk," is an example of
   a. a holophrase.
   b. babbling.
   c. child-directed speech.
   d. deferred imitation.

5. About nine months after speaking his or her first words, the typical child will
   a. have a vocabulary of between 50 and 100 words.
   b. begin to speak in holophrases.
   c. put words together to form rudimentary sentences.
   d. do all of the above.

6. A twenty-month-old girl who is able to try out various actions mentally without having to actually perform them is learning to solve simple problems by using
   a. dynamic perception.
   b. object permanence.
   c. intermodal perception.
   d. mental combinations.

7. A baby who repeatedly waves her arms once she sees that this triggers a smile in her mother is demonstrating an ability that is characteristic of which stage of sensorimotor development?
   a. Stage 1
   b. Stage 2
   c. Stage 3
   d. Stage 4

8. According to the concept of dynamic perception, which of the following will be **MOST** interesting to a six-month-old infant?
   a. a cup
   b. a book
   c. a spider
   d. a key

9. A baby who realizes that a rubber duck that has fallen out of the tub must be somewhere on the floor has achieved
   a. object permanence.
   b. goal-directed behavior.
   c. mental combinations.
   d. implicit memory.

10. As soon as her babysitter arrives, twenty-one-month-old Christine holds onto her mother's legs and says, "bye-bye?" in a questioning manner. Christine's utterance can be classified as
   a. babbling.
   b. an affordance.
   c. a holophrase.
   d. subject-predicate order.

11. The six-month-old infant's continual repetition of sound combinations such as "ba-ba-ba" is called

    a. cooing.
    b. reduplicative babbling.
    c. a holophrase.
    d. habituation.

12. Which of the following is an example of a holophrase?

    a. saying "bye-bye" to indicate that he or she wants to go outside
    b. pointing to a cat and saying "doggie"
    c. repeating certain syllables, such as "ma-ma"
    d. reversing word order, such as "want it, paper"

13. Fifteen-month-old Joshua is into everything. He loves to pull things out of his mother's purse and his father's wallet and either throw them across the room or drop them haphazardly on the floor. He loves to open cabinets and dump the recyclables. Joshua is demonstrating

    a. secondary circular reactions.
    b. the stage of the little scientist.
    c. mental combinations.
    d. object permanence.

14 Like most Korean toddlers, Ok Cha has acquired a greater number of __________ in her vocabulary than her North American counterparts, who tend to acquire more __________.

    a. verbs; nouns
    b. nouns; verbs
    c. adjectives; verbs
    d. adjectives; nouns

Key Terms

1. **sensorimotor intelligence:** Piaget's term for the way infants think—by using their senses and motor skills—during the first period of cognitive development. (p. 162; video lesson, segment 1; objective 1)
2. **primary circular reactions:** The first of three types of feedback loops in sensorimotor intelligence, this one involving the infant's own body. The infant senses motion, sucking, noise, and other stimuli and tries to understand them. (p. 162; objective 1)
3. **secondary circular reactions:** The second of three types of feedback loops in sensorimotor intelligence, this one involving people and objects. Infants respond to other people, to toys, and to any other object they can touch or move. (p. 163; objective 1)

4. **object permanence:** The realization that objects (including people) still exist when they can no longer be seen, touched, or heard. (p. 164; video lesson, segment 1; objective 2)
5. **tertiary circular reactions:** The third of three types of feedback loops in sensorimotor intelligence, this one involving active exploration and experimentation. Infants explore a range of new activities, varying their responses as a way of learning about the world. (p. 165; objective 1)
6. **"little scientist":** The stage-five toddler (age 12 to 18 months) who experiments without anticipating the results, using trial and error in active and creative exploration. (p. 166; video lesson, segment 1; objective 1)
7. **deferred imitation:** A sequence in which an infant first perceives something done by someone else and then performs the same action hours or even days later. (p. 166; video lesson, segment 1; objective 4)
8. **habituation:** The process of becoming accustomed to an object or event through repeated exposure to it, and thus becoming less interested in it. (p. 167; objective 3)
9. **fMRI:** Functional magnetic resonance imaging, a measuring technique in which the brain's electrical excitement indicates activation anywhere in the brain; fMRI helps researchers locate neurological responses to stimuli. (p. 167; objective 4)
10. **information-processing theory:** A perspective that compares human thinking processes, by analogy, to computer analysis of data, including sensory input, connections, stored memories, and output. (p. 169; objective 4)
11. **affordance:** An opportunity for perception and interaction that is offered by a person, place, or object in the environment. (p. 169; objective 5)
12. **visual cliff:** An experimental apparatus that gives the illusion of a sudden drop-off between one horizontal surface and another. (p. 170; objective 5)
13. **dynamic perception:** A universal principle of infant perception, specifically an innate attraction to other humans, evident in visual, auditory, and other preferences. (p. 170; objective 6)
14. **people preference:** The innate attraction that babies have to other humans. (p. 171; objective 6)
15. **reminder session:** A perceptual experience that helps a person recollect an idea, a thing, or an experience. (p. 173; objective 4)
16. **implicit memory:** Unconscious or automatic memory that is usually stored via habits, emotional responses, routine procedures, and various sensations. (p. 174; objective 4)
17. **explicit memory:** Memory that is easy to retrieve on demand (as in a specific test). Most explicit memory involves consciously learned words, data, and concepts. (p. 174; objective 4)
18. **child-directed speech:** The high-pitched, simplified, repetitive speech that adults use with infants and young children. Also called ***baby talk***, or ***motherese***. (p. 177; objective 9)

19. **babbling:** An infant's repetition of certain syllables, such as "ma-ma" or "ba-ba-ba," that begins between 6 and 9 months of age. (p. 177; video lesson, segment 2; objective 8)
20. **holophrase:** A characteristic of infant speech in which a single word is used to convey a complete thought. (p. 177; objective 8)
21. **naming explosion:** The dramatic increase in the infant's vocabulary, especially in the number of nouns, that begins at about 18 months of age. (p. 179; objective 8)
22. **grammar:** All the methods—word order, verb forms, and so on—that languages use to communicate meaning, apart from the words themselves. (p. 181; objective 8)
23. **language acquisition device (LAD):** Chomsky's term for a hypothesized mental structure that enables humans to learn language, including the basic aspects of grammar, vocabulary, and intonation. (p. 185; video lesson, segment 2; objective 10)
24. **baby talk (motherese):** Now referred to as child-directed speech, this is a form of speech used by adults when talking to infants. Its hallmark is exaggerated expressiveness; it employs more questions, commands, and repetitions and fewer past tenses, pronouns, and complex sentences; it uses simpler vocabulary and grammar; it has a higher pitch and more low-to-high fluctuations. (video lesson, segment 2; objective 9)
25. **language structure:** One of the keys to effective communication that babies must learn—that is, the particular words and rules of the infant's native tongue. Within the first two years of life, language structure begins to take shape. (video lesson, segment 2; objective 8)
26. **reduplicative babbling:** A form of speech in which babies, at about seven to nine months, string together two syllables and repeat them over and over. (video lesson, segment 2; objective 8)
27. **semantics:** The set of rules by which we derive meaning from the spoken sounds in a given language; also, the study of the meaning of words. (video lesson, segment 2; objective 8)
28. **intonation:** The cadence, tone, or emphasis of a given utterance. Babies learn a great deal about intonation, including how to adjust the intonation of their sounds to change the meaning of an utterance. (video lesson, segment 2; objective 8)
29. **language function:** Early communication skills, like crying, laughing, body movements, gestures, and facial expressions, can all have specific meaning. These early communication skills serve the primary role of language function: that is, to understand and be understood by others. (video lesson, segment 2; objective 8)

Summary

During the first two years of life, cognitive development proceeds at a phenomenal pace as the infant is transformed from a baby who can know its world only through a limited set of basic reflexes into a toddler capable of imitating others, anticipating and remembering events, and pretending. According to Jean Piaget—often called the "father of cognitive development"—infants learn about their environment by using their senses and motor skills (**sensorimotor intelligence**). They begin by using and then adapting their reflexes (Stages 1 and 2); soon thereafter they become aware of their own and others' actions and reactions, and this awareness guides their thinking (Stage 3). By the end of the first year, they are able to set and achieve simple goals (Stage 4). During the second year, toddlers discover new ways to achieve their goals, first by actively experimenting with objects and actions (Stage 5) and then by manipulating mental images of objects and behaviors (Stage 6). Most significant among the advances of infancy is the development of language. By age 2, the average toddler has a relatively large vocabulary and is able to converse effectively with others.

Although standard Piagetian tasks suggest that infants do not search for hidden objects until about 8 months of age, studies using the **habituation** technique demonstrate that infants as young as 3.5–4.5 months have a basic understanding of **object permanence** long before they can demonstrate this on a hidden-object task. Infants as young as 3 months are capable of anticipating what will occur next in a sequence of events they have observed repeatedly. By 9 months, infants can show **deferred imitation** of a model whose actions they had observed a day earlier.

Information-processing theory is interested in infants' understanding of **affordances**, or opportunities for perception and interaction. Infants' memory develops greatly over the first two years of life, from being able to remember under only very particular circumstances at a few months of life to being able to remember sequences of events in toddlerhood.

Infants are well equipped to learn language from birth, partly because of innate readiness and partly because of their auditory experiences during the final prenatal months. All children follow the same sequence of accomplishments in early language development, although their timing may vary considerably. At every stage of development—including the preverbal stage when infants use cries, cooing, **babbling**, and gestures to communicate—children understand much more than they are capable of expressing.

Toddlers differ in their vocabulary growth: some learn mainly naming words, while others learn a higher proportion of words that facilitate social interaction. The first words, used as one-word sentences, occur by about 1 year, and the first two-word sentence occurs at about 21 months.

Three theories of language learning exist have been proposed. Learning theorists argue that language must be taught and is learned through association and reinforcement. Chomsky and his followers believe that the human brain has a **language acquisition device** (**LAD**) that enables children to derive the rules of grammar quickly and effectively. The social-pragmatic theory focuses on language as communicative. A hybrid theory has attempted to merge the three theories into a single unifying theory.

Answer Key

Practice Questions I

Multiple-Choice Questions

1. c. is the correct answer. (objective 5)
2. c. is the correct answer. (video lesson, segment 1; objective 1)
3. b. is the correct answer. This was Piaget's most basic contribution to the study of infant cognition—that intelligence is revealed in behavior at every age. (video lesson, segment 1; objective 1)
4. c. is the correct answer. (objective 7)
5. c. is the correct answer. (objectives 1 & 5)

   b. is incorrect. This is Chomsky's position.

   d. is incorrect. This issue was not discussed in the textbook.
6. a. is the correct answer. (video lesson, segment 1; objective 1)

   b. & c. are incorrect. These abilities are not acquired until children are much older.

   d. is incorrect. Pretending is associated with stage six (18 to 24 months).
7. c. is the correct answer. (video lesson, segment 1; objective 2)
8. d. is the correct answer. This is a synthesis of the theories of Skinner and Chomsky. (video lesson, segment 2; objective 10)
9. b. is the correct answer. (video lesson, segment 2; objective 8)

   a., c., & d. are incorrect. Children the world over follow the same sequence and approximately the same timetable for early language development.
10. c. is the correct answer. (video lesson, segment 2; objective 8)
11. a. is the correct answer. (objective 8)

    b. is incorrect. Baby talk is the speech adults use with infants.

    c. is incorrect. An affordance is an opportunity for perception and interaction.

    d. is incorrect. Babbling is the extended repetition of particular sounds.
12. c. is the correct answer. At every age, children understand more speech than they can produce. (objective 8)
13. c. is the correct answer. (video lesson, segment 2; objective 9)

    a. is incorrect. A holophrase is a single word uttered by a toddler to express a complete thought.

    b. is incorrect. According to Noam Chomsky, the LAD, or language acquisition device, is an innate ability in humans to acquire language.

    d. is incorrect. These characteristic differences in pitch and structure are precisely what distinguish baby talk from regular conversation.
14. d. is the correct answer. (objective 3)
15. c. is the correct answer. (objective 3)

16. c. is the answer (video lesson, segment 1; objective 7)

    a. & b. are incorrect. In Piaget's theory, these refer to processes by which mental concepts incorporate new experiences (assimilation) or are modified in response to new experiences (accommodation).

    d. is incorrect. Dynamic perception is perception that is primed to focus on movement and change.

Matching Items

17. e (objective 5)
18. d (video lesson, segment 1; objective 2)
19. f (objective 6)
20. h (objective 1)
21. i (video lesson, segment 1; objective 1)
22. b (video lesson, segment 2; objective 8)
23. g (objective 8)
24. a (objective 9)
25. c (objective 5)
26. j (video lesson, segment 2; objective 8)
27. k (objective 7)
28. l (objective 7)

Practice Questions II

Multiple-Choice Questions

1. b. is the correct answer. (video lesson, segment 1; objective 1)

   a. & c. These are stages two and three.

   d. is incorrect. This is not one of Piaget's stages of sensorimotor intelligence.
2. d. is the correct answer. This is an example of perceptual constancy. (objective 6)
3. c. is the correct answer. (video lesson, segment 1; objective 2)
4. a. is the correct answer. (objective 5)

   b. is incorrect. Affordances are perceived by children; they don't reside in objects.

   c. & d. are incorrect. Infants perceive affordances at an earlier age and long before their manual dexterity enables them to actually act on an affordance.
5. a. is the correct answer. Chomsky believed this device is innate. (video lesson, segment 2; objective 10)
6. b. is the correct answer. (video lesson, segment 1; objective 1)

   a. & c. are incorrect. Both of these occur later than stage one.

   d. is incorrect. This is a hallmark of stage six.
7. a. is the correct answer. (objective 10)
8. a. is the correct answer. (video lesson, segment 1; objective 2)

9. c. is the correct answer. (video lesson, segment 1; objective 1)

   a. is incorrect. Reflexes are involuntary (and therefore unintentional) responses.

   b. is incorrect. Affordances are perceived opportunities for interaction with objects.

   d. is incorrect. Mental combinations are actions that are carried out mentally, rather than behaviorally. Moreover, mental combinations do not develop until a later age, during sensorimotor stage six.

10. b. is the correct answer. (video lesson, segment 2; objective 8)

11. d. is the correct answer. (objective 8)

    a. is incorrect. Deaf babies do babble, both vocally and manually.

    b. is incorrect. Deaf babies make fewer babbling sounds.

    c. is incorrect. Deaf babies begin to babble vocally several months later than hearing babies do.

12. b. is the correct answer. (video lesson, segment 2; objective 10)

    a., c., & d. are incorrect. These views on language acquisition describe the theory offered by Noam Chomsky.

Matching Items

13. i (video lesson, segment 1; objective 1)
14. a (video lesson, segment 1; objective 4)
15. c (objective 8)
16. k (video lesson, segment 2; objective 8)
17. h (video lesson, segment 1; objective 1)
18. b (objective 8)
19. e (objective 6)
20. d (objective 3)
21. j (objective 1)
22. f (video lesson, segment 2; objective 8)
23. l (video lesson, segment 2; objective 10)
24. g (video lesson, segment 2; objective 9)

Applying Your Knowledge

1. d. is the correct answer. The baby is clearly behaving purposefully, the hallmark of goal-directed behavior. (objective 1)

   a. is incorrect. There is nothing imaginary in the child's behavior.

   b. is incorrect. Habituation occurs when an individual's response to a stimulus decreases as a result of repeated exposure.

   c. is incorrect. Delayed imitation is the ability to imitate actions seen in the past. It is unlikely that the baby's sister is playing with her doll in this way.

2. d. is the correct answer. Stage 6 involves considering before doing, as Troy did by placing the collar on the dog in order to take him for a walk. (objective 1)

3. a. is the correct answer. The father's expression of delight is clearly a reinforcer in that it has increased the likelihood of the infant's vocalization. (video lesson, segment 2; objective 10)

   b. & c. are incorrect. Modeling, or learning by imitation, would be implicated if the father attempted to increase the infant's vocalizations by repeatedly saying "da-da" himself, in the infant's presence.

   d. is incorrect. This is Chomsky's viewpoint; Skinner maintained that language is acquired through learning.

4. a. is the correct answer. The child is using a single word to express a complete thought. (objective 8)

   b. is incorrect. Babbling is the repetitious uttering of certain syllables, such as "ma-ma," or "da-da."

   c. is incorrect. Child-directed speech is the characteristic manner in which adults change the structure and pitch of their speech when conversing with infants.

   d. is incorrect. Deferred imitation is repeating a behavior some time after observing someone else enact the behavior.

5. c. is the correct answer. (video lesson, segment 2; objective 8)

   a. is incorrect. At 21 months of age, most children have much larger vocabularies.

   b. is incorrect. Speaking in holophrases is typical of younger children.

6. d. is the correct answer. (video lesson, segment 1; objective 1)

   a. is incorrect. Dynamic perception is perception primed to focus on movement and change.

   b. is incorrect. Object permanence is the awareness that objects do not cease to exist when they are out of sight.

   c. is incorrect. Intermodal perception is the ability to associate information from one sensory modality with information from another.

7. c. is the correct answer. (video lesson, segment 1; objective 1)

8. c. is the correct answer. Dynamic perception is primed to focus on movement and change. (objective 6)

9. a. is the correct answer. Before object permanence is attained, an object that disappears from sight ceases to exist for the infant. (video lesson, segment 1; objective 2)

   b. is incorrect. Goal-directed behavior is purposeful action.

   c. is incorrect. Mental combinations are actions that are carried out mentally.

   d. is incorrect. Implicit memory includes memory for routines and memories that cannot be recalled on demand.

10. c. is the correct answer. Christine was communicating a whole thought—"Are you going bye-bye?"—with a single word. (objective 8)

    a. is incorrect. Because Christine is expressing a complete thought, her speech is much more than babbling.

b. is incorrect. An affordance is an opportunity for perception or interaction.

d. is incorrect. The ability to understand subject-predicate order emerges later, when children begin forming two-word sentences.

11. b. is the correct answer. (video lesson, segment 2; objective 8)

    a. is incorrect. Cooing is the pleasant-sounding utterances of the infant at about 2 month

    c. is incorrect. The holophrase occurs later and refers to the toddler's use of a single word to express a complete thought.

    d. is incorrect. Habituation is a decrease in response due to repeated presentation of a stimulus.

12. a. is the correct answer. (objective 8)
13. b. is the correct answer. (objective 1)
14. a. is the correct answer. (objective 8)

Lesson Review

Lesson 7

The First Two Years
Cognitive Development

Please Note: Use this matrix to guide your study and achieve the learning objectives of this lesson. It will also help you to view the video, which defines and demonstrates important concepts and skills as they relate to everyday life.

Learning Objective	**Textbook**	**Course Student Guide**	**Video Lesson**
1. Identify and describe Piaget's stages of sensorimotor intelligence, and give examples of the behavior associated with each stage.	pp. 161–166	Key Terms: 1, 2, 3, 5, 6; Practice Questions I: 2, 3, 5, 6, 20, 21; Practice Questions II: 1, 6, 9, 13, 17, 21; Applying Your Knowledge: 1, 2, 6, 7, 13.	Segment 1: *Sensorimotor Intelligence*
2. Explain what *object permanence* is, how it is tested in infancy, and what these tests reveal.	pp. 164–165	Key Terms: 4; Practice Questions I: 7, 18; Practice Questions II: 3, 8; Applying Your Knowledge: 9.	Segment 1: *Sensorimotor Intelligence*
3. Explain what habituation and fMRI research has revealed about cognitive development in infancy.	pp. 166–168	Key Terms: 8; Practice Questions I: 14, 15; Practice Questions II: 20.	
4. Describe the information processing model of cognition.	p. 169	Key Terms: 7, 9, 10, 15, 16, 17; Practice Questions II: 14.	Segment 1: *Sensorimotor Intelligence*
5. Explain the Gibsons' contextual view of perception, and relate it to the idea of *affordances*, giving examples of affordances perceived by infants.	pp. 169–170	Key Terms: 11, 12; Practice Questions I: 1, 5, 17, 25; Practice Questions II: 4.	

Learning Objective	**Textbook**	**Course Student Guide**	**Video Lesson**
6. Explain how the infant's focus on movement and change enhances sensory and perceptual skills and thus overall cognitive growth.	pp. 170–172	Key Terms: 13, 14; Practice Questions I: 19; Practice Questions II: 2, 19; Applying Your Knowledge: 8.	
7. Discuss research findings on infant memory.	pp. 172–175	Practice Questions I: 4, 16, 27, 28.	Segment 1: *Sensorimotor Intelligence*
8. Describe language development during the first two years, and identify its major hallmarks.	pp. 175–182	Key Terms: 19, 20, 21, 22, 25, 26, 27, 28, 29; Practice Questions I: 9, 10, 11, 12, 22, 23, 26; Practice Questions II: 10, 11, 15, 16, 18, 22; Applying Your Knowledge: 4, 5, 10, 11, 12, 14.	Segment 2: *Language Development*
9. Explain the importance of child-directed speech (motherese), and identify its main features.	pp. 176–177, 179	Key Terms: 18, 24; Practice Questions I: 13, 24; Practice Questions II: 24.	Segment 2: *Language Development*
10. Summarize the different theories that explain early language learning, and discuss how each theory might help caregivers encourage their child's language development.	pp. 182–187	Key Terms: 23; Practice Questions I: 8; Practice Questions II: 5, 7, 12, 23; Applying Your Knowledge: 3.	Segment 2: *Language Development*

Getting to Know You

Lesson 8

The First Two Years: Psychosocial Development

Preview

Lesson 8 explores the psychosocial life of the developing person during the first two years. It begins with a description of the infant's emerging emotions and how they reflect increasing cognitive abilities. Newborns are innately predisposed to sociability, and they are capable of expressing distress, sadness, contentment, and many other emotions, as well as responding to the emotions of other people.

This lesson also explores the social context in which a baby's emotions develop. By referencing their caregivers' signals, infants learn when and how to express their emotions. As **self-awareness** develops, many new emotions emerge, including embarrassment, shame, guilt, and pride. Parents who communicate effectively with their children are more responsive and tend to have children who are more skilled in communicating with others.

This lesson also presents the five major theories—psychoanalytic theory, behaviorism, cognitive theory, sociocultural theory, and the universal perspective—that help us understand the infant's psychosocial development. Important research on the nature and origins of **temperament**, which informs virtually every characteristic of the individual's developing personality, is also considered. Babies are not born with fully developed personalities. Instead, they come equipped with a basic set of temperamental tendencies in emotional expressiveness, activity level, and attention that, through their interactions with caregivers and others and the strong influence of their cultural contexts, are molded to form personality.

The final section of the lesson examines emotions and relationships from the perspective of parent–infant interaction. Videotaped studies of parents and infants, combined with laboratory studies, have greatly expanded our understanding of psychosocial development. In the video lesson, experts explain how the intricate patterns of parent–child interaction, called **synchrony**, help infants learn to express and read emotions and promote **attachment** to caregivers. Developmental psychologist Mary Ainsworth describes an experimental procedure she developed to measure the quality of attachment. The concept of **social referencing** is also discussed. The lesson concludes with a discussion of the characteristics of high-quality **nonparental child care** and the impact of early day care on psychosocial development.

As you complete this lesson, consider an infant or toddler you know (and interview the child's parents if time allows). How would you describe the emotional development of this baby relative to others of the same age? What emotions have you noticed and in what situations? Describe the temperament of this child. For example, is this baby generally adventurous or cautious, easy going or fussy, active or sedentary? Does the child seem more attached to mom or dad at this stage? Does this emotional bond seem healthy and secure? What behavior leads you to believe that? Does this child attend day care? If so, describe the facility and the type of care provided. Would you say this is a "high-quality" facility? Why or why not?

Prior Knowledge That Will Be Used in This Lesson

- This lesson will return to the developmental theories of Sigmund Freud and Erik Erikson (from Lesson 1) to help explain psychosocial development during the early years.
- Recall (from Lesson 1) that Freud's theory specifies five major stages of *psychosexual development,* during which the sensual satisfaction associated with the mouth, anus, or genitals is linked to the major developmental needs and challenges that are associated with that stage. This lesson focuses on the first two stages:
    1. **Oral Stage (birth to 1 year) ← The First Two Years**
    2. **Anal Stage (1 to 3 years) ← The First Two Years**
    3. Phallic Stage (3 to 6 years)
    4. Latency Stage (7 to 11 years)
    5. Genital Stage (adolescence through adulthood)
- Recall (from Lesson 1) that Erik Erikson's theory specifies eight stages of *psychosocial development,* each of which is characterized by a particular challenge, or *developmental crisis,* that is central to that stage of life and must be resolved. This lesson focuses on the first two stages:
    1. **Trust versus Mistrust (birth to 1 year) ← The First Two Years**
    2. **Autonomy versus Shame and Doubt ← The First Two Years (1 to 3 years)**
    3. Initiative versus Guilt (3 to 6 years)
    4. Industry versus Inferiority (7 to 11 years)
    5. Identify versus Role Confusion (adolescence)
    6. Intimacy versus Isolation (adulthood)
    7. Generativity versus Stagnation (adulthood)
    8. Integrity versus Despair (adulthood)
- The four other major developmental theories (from Lesson 1) will be also used to help explain psychosocial development during the early years. Recall that:
    1. Behaviorism focuses on patterns of association and reinforcement in shaping the individual.
    2. Cognitive theory emphasizes individuals' thoughts and understanding of the world.

3. Sociocultural theory seeks to explain development as the result of the interaction between developing individuals and their surrounding culture.
4. The universal perspective focuses on what is common to all people: our basic needs for growth and well-being and the urgency of species survival.

Learning Objectives

Use this information to guide your reading, viewing, thinking, and studying. After successfully completing this lesson, you should be able to:

1. Describe the basic emotions expressed by infants during the first days and months and the developments that take place during the first year of life.
2. Describe the main developments in the emotional life of the child during the second year of life.
3. Discuss the links between an infant's emerging self-awareness and his or her continuing emotional development, and describe these links in relationship to brain maturation, synesthesia, social impulses, and stress.
4. Discuss how Freud's psychosexual stages and Erikson's psychosocial stages can be used to explain psychosocial development during the first two years.
5. Discuss how behaviorism and cognitive theory can be used to explain psychosocial development during the first two years.
6. Define and describe the concept of temperament, discuss its development as an interaction of nature and nurture, and explain the significance of research on temperament for parents and caregivers.
7. Describe how sociocultural theory informs our understanding of psychosocial development in the first two years, describing the concepts of ethnotheory, personal theories, and proximal and distal parenting. Cite examples of cultural differences in early psychosocial development and offer explanations for their effects.
8. Describe the synchrony of parent–infant interaction during the first year, and discuss the significance for the developing person, noting how the development of social bonds is central to the universal perspective.
9. Define attachment, explain how it is measured and how it is influenced by context, and discuss the predictors and consequences of secure and insecure attachment.
10. Discuss the concept of social referencing, including its development and role in shaping later emotions.
11. Discuss contemporary views on the role of the father in infant psychosocial development.
12. Discuss the potential effects of nonmaternal care on a baby's development, and identify the factors that define high-quality day care.

Textbook Reading & Video Viewing

For the most effective study of this lesson, complete the assignments in the sequence listed below.

Before viewing the video program:

Read Chapter 7, "The First Two Years: Psychosocial Development," pages 191–221.

View the video for Lesson 8, "Getting to Know You."

Segment 1: *Development through Crises*

Segment 2: *Attachment*

Segment 3: *Attachment and Day Care*

After viewing the video program:

Review all reading assignments for this lesson.

Complete the "Practice Questions" and "Applying Your Knowledge" sections to reinforce your understanding of important terms and concepts and measure your achievement of the Learning Objectives. Check your answers with the feedback given and review when necessary.

Practice Questions I

Multiple-Choice Questions

1. Newborns have two identifiable emotions:
   a. shame and distress.
   b. distress and contentment.
   c. anger and joy
   d. pride and guilt
2. Which of the following is customarily used to assess synchrony?
   a. the Strange Situation
   b. the habituation technique
   c. the still-face technique
   d. social referencing
3. An infant's fear of being left by the mother or other caregiver, called __________, peaks between __________ months.
   a. separation anxiety; 9 and 14
   b. stranger wariness; 6 and 8
   c. separation anxiety; 6 and 8
   d. stranger wariness; 9 and 14

4. Social referencing refers to
   a. parenting skills that change over time.
   b. changes in community values regarding, for example, the acceptability of using physical punishment with small children.
   c. the support network for new parents provided by extended family members.
   d. the infant response of looking to trusted adults for emotional cues in uncertain situations.
5. The "Big Five" temperament dimensions are
   a. emotional stability, openness, introversion, sociability, and locus of control.
   b. neuroticism, extroversion, openness, emotional stability, and sensitivity.
   c. agreeableness, conscientiousness, neuroticism, openness, and extroversion.
   d. neuroticism, gregariousness, extroversion, impulsiveness, and sensitivity.
6. The concept of a working model is most consistent with
   a. psychoanalytic theory.
   b. behaviorism.
   c. cognitive theory.
   d. sociocultural theory.
7. Freud's oral stage corresponds to Erikson's crisis of
   a. oral fixation versus anal fixation.
   b. trust versus mistrust.
   c. autonomy versus shame and doubt.
   d. secure versus insecure attachment.
8. Erikson proposes that the development of a sense of trust in early infancy depends on the quality of the
   a. infant's food.
   b. child's genetic inheritance.
   c. relationship with caregiver.
   d. introduction to toilet training.
9. The increasing tendency of older infants to express frustration and anger is closely linked to new developments in their cognitive abilities, especially those related to
   a. goal-directed actions.
   b. social referencing.
   c. self-awareness.
   d. stranger wariness.

10. "Easy," "slow to warm up," and "difficult" are descriptions of different

    a. forms of attachment.
    b. temperamental styles.
    c. types of parenting.
    d. toddler responses to the Strange Situation.

11. Which of the following is true of toddlers' interactions with their fathers?

    a. Toddlers rarely use social referencing with their fathers.
    b. Toddlers often seek their fathers' approval rather than their mothers' approval when they want to explore.
    c. The social information provided by fathers is less encouraging than that provided by mothers.
    d. Fathers' parenting tends to be more distal and less proximal than that of mothers.

12. Synchrony is a term that describes

    a. the carefully coordinated interaction between parent and infant.
    b. a mismatch of the temperaments of parent and infant.
    c. a research technique involving videotapes.
    d. the concurrent evolution of different species.

13. The emotional tie that develops between an infant and his or her primary caregiver is called

    a. self-awareness.
    b. synchrony.
    c. affiliation.
    d. attachment.

14. An important component of secure attachment is the promotion of

    a. self-awareness.
    b. comfort and confidence.
    c. dependency.
    d. all of the above.

15. Which of the following theories is particularly interested in parent–child social interactions and the context of social bonds?

    a. psychoanalytic theory
    b. cognitive theory
    c. humanism
    d. sociocultural theory

True or False Items

Write T (for true) or F (for false) on the line in front of each statement.

16. _____ Western parents' ethnotheory values independence.
17. _____ A major difference between a six-month-old and a twelve-month-old is that emotions become less discriminating.
18. _____ An 11-month-old baby is likely to display both stranger wariness and separation anxiety.
19. _____ Motivation, cognition, and parents' responses to infants' and toddlers' emotions affect later emotional expression.
20. _____ A securely attached toddler is most likely to stay close to his or her mother even in a familiar environment.
21. _____ Current research shows that the majority of infants in day care are insecurely attached.
22. _____ Fear of specific things, as opposed to reflexive fear, emerges in the later part of the second year.
23. _____ Temperamental traits originate in the genes and the environment influences their expression.
24. _____ Self-awareness enables toddlers to experience emotions about and direct them toward other people.
25. _____ Achieving a goodness of fit appears to be particularly important for easy children.
26. _____ Children who are not securely attached display at least three different patterns of attachment behavior.
27. _____ Developmental psychologists express the greatest concerns about the early mental health of children who display insecure-resistant attachment.
28. _____ Studies show that the influence of nonparental child care can be both positive and negative.
29. _____ Personal theories influence parental attitudes and behavior.

Practice Questions II

Multiple-Choice Questions

1. Infant–caregiver interactions that are marked by inconsistency are usually classified as
   a. disorganized.
   b. insecure-avoidant.
   c. insecure-resistant.
   d. none of the above.

2. Freud's anal stage corresponds to Erikson's crisis of
   a. autonomy versus shame and doubt.
   b. trust versus mistrust.
   c. orality versus anality.
   d. identity versus role confusion.
3. Not until the sense of self begins to emerge do babies realize that they are seeing their own faces in the mirror. This realization usually occurs
   a. shortly before 3 months.
   b. at about 6 months.
   c. between 15 and 24 months.
   d. after 24 months.
4. Eight-month-old Kevin is irregular in his sleeping and eating schedules, unhappy much of the day, and hard to distract. These characteristics are indicative of having a(n)
   a. slow-to-warm-up temperament.
   b. difficult temperament.
   c. disorganized attachment.
   d. insecure-avoidant attachment.
5. Emotions such as shame, guilt, embarrassment, and pride emerge at the same time that
   a. the social smile appears.
   b. aspects of the infant's temperament can first be discerned.
   c. self-awareness begins to emerge.
   d. parents initiate toilet training.
6. According to cognitive theory, family experiences are important to psychosocial development because they
   a. are used to develop a working model.
   b. get burned into the brain as patterns.
   c. are in line with the culture's ethnotheory.
   d. get buried in the unconscious.
7. In the second six months, stranger wariness is a
   a. result of insecure attachment.
   b. result of social isolation.
   c. normal emotional response.
   d. setback in emotional development.

8. A key to synchrony is
   a. information.
   b. intensity.
   c. memory.
   d. responsiveness.

9. Compared to children who are insecurely attached, those who are securely attached are
   a. more independent.
   b. more academically skilled.
   c. more sociable.
   d. characterized by all of the above.

10. The later consequences of secure and insecure attachment for children are
    a. subject to change due to the child's current rearing circumstances.
    b. irreversible, regardless of the child's current rearing circumstances.
    c. more significant in girls than in boys.
    d. more significant in boys than in girls.

11. The attachment pattern marked by anxiety and uncertainty is
    a. insecure-avoidant.
    b. insecure-resistant/ambivalent.
    c. disorganized.
    d. Type B.

12. Compared with mothers, fathers are more likely to
    a. engage in noisy, boisterous play.
    b. encourage intellectual development in their children.
    c. encourage social development in their children.
    d. read to their toddlers.

13. Which of the following most accurately summarizes the relationship between early attachment and later social relationships?
    a. Attachment in infancy determines whether a child will grow to be sociable.
    b. Attachment relationships are sometimes, though rarely, altered as children grow older.
    c. There is, at best, only a weak correlation between early attachment and later social relationships.
    d. Early attachment biases, but does not inevitably determine, later social relationships.

14. Which of the following does **NOT** increase the likelihood of an insecure attachment?
    a. The parents are highly stressed.
    b. The parents are controlling.
    c. The child's temperament is "difficult."
    d. The parents still have beliefs, thoughts, and memories regarding their attachments with their own parents.

Matching Items

Match each theorist, term, or concept with its corresponding description or definition.

Theorists, Terms, or Concepts

15. _______ temperament
16. _______ Erik Erikson
17. _______ the Strange Situation
18. _______ synchrony
19. _______ trust versus mistrust
20. _______ Sigmund Freud
21. _______ social referencing
22. _______ autonomy versus shame and doubt
23. _______ self-awareness
24. _______ Mary Ainsworth
25. _______ proximity-seeking behaviors
26. _______ contact-maintaining behaviors

Descriptions or Definitions

a. looking to caregivers for emotional cues
b. the crisis of infancy
c. the crisis of toddlerhood
d. approaching, following, and climbing
e. theorist who described psychosexual stages of development
f. researcher who devised a laboratory procedure for studying attachment
g. laboratory procedure for studying attachment
h. the relatively consistent, basic dispositions inherent in a person
i. clinging and resisting being put down
j. coordinated interaction between parent and infant
k. theorist who described psychosocial stages of development
l. a person's sense of being distinct from others

Applying Your Knowledge

1. In laboratory tests of attachment, when the mother returns to the playroom after a short absence, a securely attached infant is most likely to
    a. cry and protest the mother's return.
    b. climb into the mother's lap, then leave to resume play.
    c. climb into the mother's lap and stay there.
    d. continue playing without acknowledging the mother.

2. After a scary fall, eighteen-month-old Jaime looks to his mother to see if he should cry or laugh. Jaime's behavior is an example of

   a. proximity-seeking behavior.
   b. social referencing.
   c. insecure attachment.
   d. the crisis of trust versus mistrust.

3. Which of the following is typical behavior of a securely attached infant?

   a. The infant turns to the caregiver when distressed.
   b. The infant protests when the caregiver leaves a room.
   c. The infant may cry when strangers appear.
   d. All of the above are typical of a secure attachment.

4. If you had to predict a newborn baby's temperament "type" solely on the basis of probability, which classification would be the most likely?

   a. easy
   b. slow to warm up
   c. difficult
   d. There is not enough information to make a prediction.

5. Six-month-old Javier is participating with his father in an experiment using the still-face technique. Of the following, which is Javier's most likely response to his father's still face?

   a. Javier will not notice his father's still face because he is too young.
   b. Javier will notice his father's still face but will be unconcerned because infants do not generally have synchrony with their fathers.
   c. Javier will try to make his father laugh by giggling and waving his arms.
   d. Javier will cry and suck his fingers.

6. Which of the following is **NOT** an essential characteristic of high-quality day care?

   a. Teachers must explicitly instruct children in language and sensorimotor skills.
   b. Caregivers must be professional and well-trained.
   c. Caregivers must be warm and responsive.
   d. There must be a low caregiver-to-infant ratio.

7. Arshad's mother left him alone in the room for a few minutes. When she returned, Arshad seemed indifferent to her presence. According to Mary Ainsworth's research with children in the Strange Situation, Arshad is probably

   a. a normal, independent infant.
   b. an abused child.
   c. insecurely attached.
   d. securely attached.

8. Eight-month-old Claire's mother often teases her and doesn't respond to her when she falls and hurts herself, even laughing instead sometimes. She changes her mood suddenly and often holds Claire at arm's length, talking to her very sharply. Sometimes she holds Claire as if she were not alive. Claire is **MOST** likely to develop which attachment type?

   a. secure
   b. insecure-resistant
   c. insecure-avoidant
   d. disorganized

9. Bart's parents live in a culture that focuses on the importance of children's compliance and thus they go to great lengths to teach Bart to comply with the demands of authority figures. Nadia's parents live in a culture that focuses on individual choices and freedom and thus they allow Nadia to make her own decisions about a variety of behaviors. It appears that Bart's and Nadia's parents differ in their

   a. attachment.
   b. temperaments.
   c. ethnotheories.
   d. synchrony.

10. Rachael and Lev, who are first-time parents, are concerned because their two-month-old baby is difficult to care for and hard to soothe. They are worried that they are doing something wrong. You inform them that their child is probably that way because

    a. they are reinforcing the child's tantrum behaviors.
    b. they are not meeting some biological need of the child's.
    c. of his or her inherited temperament.
    d. at two months of age all children are difficult to care for and hard to soothe.

11. Two-year-old Anita and her mother visit a day-care center. Seeing an interesting toy, Anita runs a few steps toward it, then stops and looks back to see if her mother is coming. Anita's behavior illustrates

    a. the crisis of autonomy versus shame and doubt.
    b. synchrony.
    c. dyssynchrony.
    d. social referencing.

12. Felix eats, chews, and talks excessively in quest of pleasures that were denied in infancy. Freud would probably say that Felix is

    a. anally expulsive.
    b. anally retentive.
    c. fixated in the oral stage.
    d. experiencing the crisis of trust versus mistrust.

13. A researcher at the child development center places a dot on an infant's nose and watches to see if the infant reacts to her image in a mirror by touching her nose. Evidently, the researcher is testing the child's

    a. attachment.
    b. temperament.
    c. self-awareness.
    d. social referencing.

14. Four-month-old Aaron and his thirteen-month-old sister Carla are left in the care of a babysitter. As their parents are leaving, it is to be expected that

    a. Aaron will become extremely upset, while Carla will calmly accept her parents' departure.
    b. Carla will become more upset over her parents' departure than will Aaron.
    c. Aaron and Carla will both become quite upset as their parents leave.
    d. Neither Aaron nor Carla will become very upset as their parents leave.

15. You have been asked to give a presentation on "Mother–Infant Attachment" to a group of expectant mothers. Basing your presentation on the research of Mary Ainsworth, you conclude your talk by stating that mother–infant attachment depends mostly on

    a. an infant's innate temperament.
    b. the amount of time mothers spend with their infants.
    c. sensitive and responsive caregiving in the early months.
    d. whether the mother herself was securely attached as an infant.

16. While vacationing in Mexico, Barbara (a Caucasian grandmother from Oregon) was dismayed to see so many local parents "spoiling" their children with offers of toys and sweets in return for compliance. She thought the children should be firmly told what to do and punished for their misbehavior. These differences in childrearing opinions and behaviors are best attributed to

    a. the adults' differing ethnotheories.
    b. the adults' differing personal theories.
    c. the adults' differing cultural contexts.
    d. all of the above.

Key Terms

1. **social smile:** A smile evoked by a human face, normally evident in infants about six weeks after birth. (p. 192; objective 1)
2. **stranger wariness:** An infant's expression of concern—a quiet stare, clinging to a familiar person, or sadness—when a stranger appears. (p. 193; objective 1)
3. **separation anxiety:** An infant's distress when a familiar caregiver leaves, most obvious between 9 and 14 months. (p. 193; objective 1)

4. **self-awareness:** A person's realization that he or she is a distinct individual, whose body, mind, and actions are separate from those of other people. (p. 194; objective 3)
5. **temperament:** Inborn differences between one person and another in emotions, activity, and self-regulation. Temperament is epigenetic, originating in genes but affected by child-rearing practices. (p. 196; objective 6)
6. **goodness of fit:** A similarity of temperament and values that produces a smooth interaction between an individual and his or her social context, including family, school, and community. (p. 198; objective 6)
7. **Big Five:** The five basic clusters of personality traits that remain quite stable throughout life: openness, conscientiousness, extroversion, agreeableness, and neuroticism. (p. 198; objective 6)
8. **trust versus mistrust:** Erikson's first psychosocial crisis. Infants learn basic trust if their basic needs (for food, comfort, attention, and so on) are met. (p. 199; objective 5)
9. **autonomy versus shame and doubt:** Erikson's second crisis of psychosocial development. Toddlers either succeed or fail in gaining a sense of self-rule over their own actions and bodies. (p. 199; objective 5)
10. **social learning:** Learning that is accomplished by observing others. (p. 200; objective 11)
11. **working model:** In cognitive theory, a set of assumptions that the individual uses to organize perceptions and experiences. For example, a person might assume that other people are always trustworthy and be surprised when this working model of human behavior is proven inadequate. (p. 200; objective 4)
12. **ethnotheory:** A theory that underlies the values and practices of a culture but is not usually apparent to the people within the culture. (p. 201; objective 7)
13. **proximal parenting:** Caregiving practices that involve being physically close to a baby, with frequent holding and touching. (p. 202; objective 11)
14. **distal parenting:** Caregiving practices that involve remaining distant from a baby, providing toys, food, and face-to-face communication with minimal holding and touching. (p. 202; objective 7)
15. **synchrony:** A coordinated, rapid, and smooth exchange of responses between a caregiver and an infant. (p. 205; objective 8)
16. **still-face technique:** An experimental practice in which an adult keeps his or her face unmoving and expressionless in face-to-face interaction with an infant. (p. 206; objectives 8 & 9)
17. **attachment:** According to Ainsworth, an affectional tie that an infant forms with a caregiver—a tie that binds them together in space and endures over time. (p. 207; objective 9)
18. **secure attachment:** A relationship (type B) in which an infant obtains both comfort and confidence from the presence of his or her caregiver. (p. 208; video lesson, segment 2; objective 9)

19. **insecure-avoidant attachment:** A pattern of attachment (type A) in which an infant avoids connection with the caregiver, as when the infant seems not to care about the caregiver's presence, departure, or return. (p. 208; video lesson, segment 2; objective 9)
20. **insecure-resistant/ambivalent attachment:** A pattern of attachment (type C) in which anxiety and uncertainty are evident, as when an infant becomes very upset at separation from the caregiver and both resists and seeks contact on reunion. (p. 208; video lesson, segment 2; objective 9)
21. **disorganized attachment:** A type of attachment (type D) that is marked by an infant's inconsistent reactions to the caregiver's departure and return. (p. 208; video lesson, segment 2; objective 9)
22. **Strange Situation:** A laboratory procedure for measuring attachment by evoking infants' reactions to stress in eight episodes of three minutes each. (p. 209; objective 9)
23. **social referencing:** Seeking information about how to react to an unfamiliar or ambiguous object or event by observing someone else's expressions and reactions. That other person becomes a social reference. (p. 212; objective 10)
24. **family day care:** Child care that occurs in the home of someone to whom the child is not related and who usually cares for several children of various ages. (p. 215; objective 12)
25. **center day care:** Child care that occurs in a place especially designed for the purpose, where several paid adults care for many children. Usually the children are grouped by age, the day-care center is licensed, and providers are trained and certified in child development. (p. 215; objective 12)
26. **proximity-seeking behaviors:** Following, approaching, and other proximity-seeking behaviors are intended to place an individual close to another person to whom he or she is attached. (video lesson, segment 2; objective 9)
27. **contact-maintaining behaviors:** Clinging, resisting being put down, and other contact-maintaining behaviors are intended to keep a person near another person to whom he or she is attached. (video lesson, segment 2; objective 9)
28. **insecure attachment:** A pattern of attachment characterized by the infant's fear, anger, or seeming indifference toward the caregiver. (video lesson, segment 2; objective 9)
29. **nonmaternal/nonparental child care:** Nonmaternal child care means care provided by anyone but the mother, which can include the father or other relatives. Nonparental child care means care provided by anyone except the mother or father. As the child's age increases, this care is more likely to take the form of an organized and structured program conducted outside the home. (video lesson, segment 3; objective 12)

Summary

Contemporary developmentalists have revised a number of the traditional views of psychosocial development. It was once believed, for example, that infants did not have any real emotions. Researchers now know, however, that in the very first days and weeks of life, infants express and sense many emotions, including fear, anger, happiness, and surprise. Over the first two years, emotions change from a basic set of reactions to complex, self-conscious responses as infants become increasingly independent.

In the traditional view of personality development, the infant was seen as a passive recipient of the personality created almost entirely by the actions of his or her primary caregivers. Yet it is now apparent that many aspects of **temperament** are present in infants at birth and that active caregiver-infant interaction within a secure and nurturing environment is a central factor in the child's psychosocial development. The concept of **goodness of fit** draws attention to the notion of the fit between a child's temperament and the parents' actions.

During infancy, increasing independence, which Sigmund Freud explains in terms of the oral and anal stages, mark psychosocial development at this age. Erik Erikson explains it in terms of "**trust versus mistrust**" and "**autonomy versus shame and doubt**."

Like psychoanalytic theory, behaviorism emphasizes the role of the parent in molding infants' emotions and personalities. Cognitive theory, however, suggests that early psychosocial development is shaped by infants' own **working model**, which includes their assumptions about what they can expect from other people.

Sociocultural theory extends the thinking about individuals' psychosocial development to note the impact of social and cultural factors on parent–child interactions. These interactions are influenced by the parents' *personal theories* and the particular **ethnotheory** present in that culture.

Key factors in infants' psychosocial development are **synchrony**—the moment-by-moment interaction between an infant and his or her parent, and **attachment**—the affectional tie between infants and their primary caregivers. In infants the world over, attachment develops at about 7 months, when babies first become aware that other people stay in existence even when they're out of sight. **Secure attachment** helps ensure that the relatively helpless infant receives the adult care he or she needs in order to survive, and sets the stage for the child's increasingly independent exploration of the world. By age 2, the toddler has a distinct personality that is the product of the social context and the innate temperament of the young infant.

Nonparental child care, when it is of high quality, appears to have positive effects on cognitive development and no negative effects on the quality of parent–child attachment. It is the quality of care that infants receive at home that is especially relevant to attachment, rather than the number of hours spent in nonparental care.

Special Note: We will cover the father–child relationship (pp. 212–213) in more detail in Lesson 10, "Fatherhood."

Answer Key

Practice Questions I

Multiple-Choice Questions

1. b. is the correct answer. (objective 1)

   a., c., & d. are incorrect. These emotions emerge later in infancy, at about the same time as self-awareness emerges.

2. c. is the correct answer. (objective 8)

   a. is incorrect. The Strange Situation is used to measure attachment.

   b. is incorrect. Habituation, which was discussed in the previous chapter, is used to measure an infant's perceptual and cognitive abilities.

   d. is incorrect. Social referencing is not a research technique; it is the phenomenon in which infants look to trusted caregivers for emotional cues in uncertain situations.

3. a. is the correct answer. (objectives 1 & 2)

4. d. is the correct answer. (video lesson, segment 2; objective 10)

5. c. is the correct answer. (objective 6)

6. c. is the correct answer. (objective 2)

7. b. is the correct answer. (objective 4)

   a. & d. are incorrect. These are not crises in Erikson's theory.

   c. is incorrect. According to Erikson, this is the crisis of toddlerhood, which corresponds to Freud's anal stage.

8. c. is the correct answer. (video lesson, segment 1; objective 5)

9. a. is the correct answer. Anger increases with age because toddlers are able to anticipate events and realize that other people's actions sometimes block their own efforts. (objective 1)

10. b. is the correct answer. (video lesson, segment 1; objective 6)

    a. is incorrect. "Secure" and "insecure" are different forms of attachment.

    c. is incorrect. These are not used to describe different types of parenting.

    d. is incorrect. The Strange Situation is a test of attachment, rather than of temperament.

11. b. is the correct answer. (objectives 10 & 11)

    a. is incorrect. In fact, toddlers readily reference their fathers.

    c. is incorrect. In fact, social information provided by fathers is more encouraging.

    d. is incorrect. In fact, fathers are more proximal.

12. a. is the correct answer. (video lesson, segment 2; objective 8)

13. d. is the correct answer. (video lesson, segment 2; objective 9)

    a. is incorrect. Self-awareness refers to the infant's developing sense of "me and mine."

    b. is incorrect. Synchrony describes the coordinated interaction between infant and caregiver.

    c. is incorrect. Affiliation describes the tendency of people at any age to seek the companionship of others.

14. b. is the correct answer. (video lesson, segment 2; objective 9)

    a. is incorrect. The textbook does not link self-awareness to secure attachment.

    c. is incorrect. On the contrary, secure attachment promotes independence in infants and children.

15. c. is the correct answer. (objective 8)

True or False Items

16. T (objective 7)
17. F Emotions become less frequent and more discriminating. (objective 2)
18. T (objective 1)
19. T (objective 2)
20. F A securely attached toddler is most likely to explore the environment, the mother's presence being enough to give him or her the courage to do so. (video lesson, segment 2; objective 9)
21. F Many researchers believe that high-quality day care is not likely to harm the child. In fact, it is thought to be beneficial to the development of cognitive and social skills. (video lesson, segment 3; objective 12)
22. F Stranger wariness and separation anxiety emerge in the second part of the first year. (objective 1)
23. T (objective 6)
24. T (objective 3)
25. F In fact, positive children may tend to do well in most situations, but difficult children are more affected by a mother's responsiveness. (objective 6)
26. T (video lesson, segment 2; objective 9)
27. F Experts express the greatest concerns about children who display disorganized attachment. (video lesson, segment 2; objective 9)
28. T (video lesson, segment 3; objective 12)
29. T (objective 7)

Practice Questions II

Multiple-Choice Questions

1. a. is the correct answer. (objective 7)
2. a. is the correct answer. (objectives 4 & 5)
3. c. is the correct answer. (objective 3)
4. b. is the correct answer. (objective 6)
5. c. is the correct answer. (objective 3)

   a. & b. are incorrect. The social smile and temperamental characteristics emerge well before the first signs of self-awareness.

   d. is incorrect. Contemporary developmentalists link these emotions to self-awareness, rather than any specific environmental event such as toilet training.
6. a. is the correct answer. (objective 5)

   b. is incorrect. This is suggested by behaviorism.

   c. is incorrect. This is suggested by sociocultural theory.

   d. is incorrect. This is suggested by psychoanalytic theory.
7. c. is the correct answer. (objective 1)
8. d. is the correct answer. (objective 8)

9. d. is the correct answer. (video lesson, segment 2; objective 9)
10. a. is the correct answer. (video lesson, segment 2; objective 9)

    c. & d. are incorrect. The textbook does not suggest that the consequences of secure and insecure attachment differ in boys and girls.
11. b. is the correct answer. (objective 7)

    a. is incorrect. Insecure-avoidant attachment is marked by behaviors that indicate an infant is uninterested in a caregiver's presence or departure.

    c. is incorrect. Disorganized attachment is marked only by the inconsistency of infant–caregiver behaviors.

    d. is incorrect. Type B, or secure attachment, is marked by behaviors that indicate an infant is using a caregiver as a secure base from which to explore the environment.
12. a. is the correct answer. (objective 11)
13. d. is the correct answer. (video lesson, segment 2; objective 9)
14. d. is the correct answer. In fact, a working model of a secure attachment to parents' own parents increases the likelihood of a secure attachment. (objective 9)

Matching Items

15. h (video lesson, segment 1; objective 6)
16. k (video lesson, segment 1; objective 4)
17. g (video lesson, segment 2; objective 9)
18. j (video lesson, segment 2; objective 8)
19. b (video lesson, segment 1; objective 5)
20. e (objective 4)
21. a (video lesson, segment 2; objective 10)
22. c (video lesson, segment 1; objective 5)
23. l (objective 3)
24. f (video lesson, segment 2; objective 9)
25. d (video lesson, segment 2; objective 9)
26. i (video lesson, segment 2; objective 9)

Applying Your Knowledge

1. b. is the correct answer. (video lesson, segment 2; objective 8)

    a., c., & d. are incorrect. These responses are more typical of insecurely attached infants.
2. b. is the correct answer. (video lesson, segment 2; objective 9)
3. d. is the correct answer. (video lesson, segment 2; objective 9)
4. a. is the correct answer. About 40 percent of young infants can be described as "easy." (objective 6)

    b. is incorrect. About 15 percent of infants are described as "slow to warm up."

    c. is incorrect. About 10 percent of infants are described as "difficult."

5. d. is the correct answer. (objective 8)

   a. & b. are incorrect. Six-month-olds do notice and get upset by still-faced fathers.

   c. is incorrect. This is not a typical response.

6. a. is the correct answer. (objective 12)
7. c. is the correct answer. (video lesson, segment 2; objective 9)

   a. & d. are incorrect. When their mothers return following an absence, securely attached infants usually reestablish social contact (with a smile or by climbing into their laps) and then resume playing.

   b. is incorrect. There is no evidence in this example that Arshad is an abused child. In fact, abusive behaviors are particularly associated with a disorganized attachment.

8. d. is the correct answer. (objective 9)
9. c. is the correct answer. (objective 7)
10. c. is the correct answer. (objective 9)

    a. & b. are incorrect. There is no evidence in the question that the parents are reinforcing tantrum behavior or failing to meet some biological need of the child's.

    d. is incorrect. On the contrary, about 40 percent of infants are "easy" in temperamental style.

11. d. is the correct answer. (video lesson, segment 2; objective 10)

    a. is incorrect. According to Erikson, this is the crisis of toddlerhood.

    b. is incorrect. This describes a moment of coordinated and mutually responsive interaction between a parent and an infant.

    c. is incorrect. Dyssynchrony occurs when the coordinated pace and timing of a synchronous interaction are temporarily lost.

12. c. is the correct answer. (objective 4)

    a. & b. are incorrect. In Freud's theory, a person who is fixated in the anal stage exhibits messiness and disorganization or compulsive neatness.

    d. is incorrect. Erikson, rather than Freud, proposed crises of development.

13. c. is the correct answer. (objective 3)
14. b. is the correct answer. The fear of being left by a caregiver (separation anxiety) emerges at about 8 or 9 months, and peaks at about 14 months. For this reason, four-month-old Aaron can be expected to become less upset than his older sister. (objective 2)
15. c. is the correct answer. (video lesson, segment 2; objective 8)
16. d. is the correct answer. (objective 7)

Lesson Review

Lesson 8

The First Two Years
Psychosocial Development

Please Note: Use this matrix to guide your study and achieve the learning objectives of this lesson. It will also help you to view the video, which defines and demonstrates important concepts and skills as they relate to everyday life.

Learning Objective	**Textbook**	**Course Student Guide**	**Video Lesson**
1. Describe the basic emotions expressed by infants during the first days and months and the developments that take place during the first year of life.	pp. 192–193	Key Terms: 1, 2, 3; Practice Questions I: 1, 3, 9, 18, 22; Practice Questions II: 7.	
2. Describe the main developments in the emotional life of the child during the second year of life.	p. 193	Practice Questions I: 3, 6, 17, 19; Applying Your Knowledge: 14.	
3. Discuss the links between an infant's emerging self-awareness and his or her continuing emotional development, and describe these links in relationship to brain maturation, synesthesia, social impulses, and stress.	pp. 194–196	Key Terms: 4; Practice Questions I: 24; Practice Questions II: 3, 5, 23; Applying Your Knowledge: 13.	
4. Discuss how Freud's psychosexual stages and Erikson's psychosocial stages can be used to explain psychosocial development during the first two years.	p. 199	Key Terms: 11; Practice Questions I: 7; Practice Questions II: 2, 16, 20; Applying Your Knowledge: 4, 12.	Segment 1: *Development through Crises*
5. Describe how behaviorism and cognitive theory can be used to explain psychosocial development during the first two years.	pp. 200–201	Key Terms: 8, 9; Practice Questions I: 8; Practice Questions II: 2, 6, 19, 22.	Segment 1: *Development through Crises*
6. Define and describe the concept of temperament, discuss its development as an interaction of nature and nurture, and explain the significance of research on temperament for parents and caregivers.	pp. 196–198	Key Terms: 5, 6, 7; Practice Questions I: 5, 10, 23, 25; Practice Questions II: 4, 15; Applying Your Knowledge: 4.	Segment 1: *Development through Crises*

Learning Objective	Textbook	Course Student Guide	Video Lesson
7. Describe how sociocultural theory informs our understanding of psychosocial development in the first two years, describing the concepts of ethnotheory, personal theories, and proximal and distal parenting. Cite examples of cultural differences in early psychosocial development and offer explanations for their effects.	pp. 201–204	Key Terms: 12, 14; Practice Questions I: 16; Practice Questions II: 1, 11, 29; Applying Your Knowledge: 9, 16.	
8. Describe the synchrony of parent–infant interaction during the first year, and discuss its significance for the developing person, noting how the development of social bonds is central to the universal perspective.	pp. 205–207	Key Terms: 15, 16; Practice Questions I: 2, 12, 15; Practice Questions II: 8, 18; Applying Your Knowledge: 1, 5, 15.	Segment 2: *Attachment*
9. Define attachment, explain how it is measured and how it is influenced by context, and discuss the predictors and consequences of secure and insecure attachment.	pp. 207–212	Key Terms: 16, 17, 18, 19, 20, 21, 22, 26, 27, 28; Practice Questions I: 13, 14, 20, 26, 27; Practice Questions II: 9, 10, 13, 14, 17, 24, 25, 26; Applying Your Knowledge: 2, 3, 7, 8, 10.	Segment 2: *Attachment*
10. Discuss the concept of social referencing, including its development and role in shaping later emotions.	p. 212	Key Terms: 23; Practice Questions I: 4, 11; Practice Questions II: 21; Applying Your Knowledge: 11.	Segment 2: *Attachment*
11. Discuss contemporary views on the role of the father in infant psychosocial development.	pp. 212–213	Key Terms: 10, 13; Practice Questions I: 11 Practice Questions II: 12.	Segment 2: *Attachment*
12. Discuss potential effects of nonmaternal care on a baby's development, and identify the factors that define high-quality day care.	pp. 213–218	Key Terms: 24, 25, 29; Practice Questions I: 21, 28; Applying Your Knowledge: 6.	Segment 3: *Attachment and Day Care*

Off to a Good Start

Lesson 9

The First Two Years: Summary

Preview

Each of the major developmental units in this course ("The First Two Years," "The Play Years," "The School Years," and "Adolescence") will end with a summary lesson. Lesson 9, which is the first of these summary lessons, summarizes biosocial, cognitive, and psychosocial development in the first two years.

During the first two years of life, children are on a journey from a state of dependence on their caregivers to a growing independence. This journey is reflected separately in each of the three domains of development, as well as in interactions among the domains. This lesson underscores the fact that every family provides a unique environment for the developing child—an environment shaped by family members' culture, affluence, size, and patterns of interaction. Parents can help ensure their children's healthy development by providing a stable routine, filled with stimulating learning opportunities and interactions that promote the formation of strong healthy bodies, cognitive growth, and trusting relationships.

Prior Knowledge That Will Be Used in This Lesson

- Biosocial development during the first two years (Lesson 6) will be referred to as we discuss the development of motor skills.
- Cognitive development during the first two years (Lesson 7) will be referred to as we examine language development, including the benefits of growing up in a bilingual home.
- Psychosocial development during the first two years (Lesson 8) will be referred to as we cover the nature and influence of temperament and attachment bonds between children and their caregivers.

Learning Objectives

Use this information to guide your reading, viewing, thinking, and studying. After successfully completing this lesson, you should be able to:

1. Give examples of the basic pattern of motor-skill development, and discuss variations in biosocial development during the first two years.
2. Summarize key aspects of cognitive development during the first two years, especially language development during this time.
3. Discuss psychosocial development during the first two years, focusing on the concepts of temperament and attachment and their influence on the developing child.
4. Discuss Erik Erikson's first two stages of psychosocial development, and offer examples of how caregivers can encourage trust and autonomy in their children.
5. Offer examples of how a child's development in any one domain (biosocial, cognitive, or psychosocial) can affect development in a different domain.

Textbook Reading & Video Viewing

For the most effective study of this lesson, complete the assignments in the sequence listed below.

Before viewing the video program:

Read Chapter 5, "Summary: The First Two Years: Biosocial Development," page 158; Chapter 6, "Summary: The First Two Years: Cognitive Development," page 188; and Chapter 7, "Summary: The First Two Years: Psychosocial Development," page 219, and "The Developing Person So Far: The First Two Years," page 221.

View the video for Lesson 9, "Off to a Good Start."

Segment 1: *Ryan*

Segment 2: *Omari*

Segment 3: *Luke*

Segment 4: *Ryan, Omari, and Luke*

Video Viewing Tips

This video lesson will feature three children—Ryan (16 months), Omari (18 months), and Luke (2.5 years). In their typical daily routines, you will see living examples of some concepts you've learned in the last three lessons. As you view the video, it will help you to watch for particular issues and situations.

For example, note differences between the families in this program (size, socioeconomic status, and so on), and consider how this might affect their developing children. You'll see how dependent these children are on their caregivers, but notice also how they are attempting to assert more independence in thinking and acting for themselves. Watch what their parents are doing to allow them room to grow and explore, while still providing guidance and safety.

Also consider where these children are in their gross and fine motor skill development and how that might affect development in the other domains (cognitive and psychosocial).

Pay close attention to any cultural differences and consider how these factors might affect these children. Also take note of the individual variations between the children themselves, for example, any differences in temperament and personality that might affect how they interact with their world.

Finally, pay particular attention to the parent child-interactions in this video lesson. Try to discern any signs of secure or insecure attachment. Note how involved the parents are in their children's lives, how they model behavior they would like to see in their children, and speculate on how all this might ultimately affect development. Before you watch this lesson, it may help you to review the vocabulary in the Key Terms section below.

After viewing the video program:

Review all reading assignments for this lesson.

Complete the "Practice Questions" and "Applying Your Knowledge" sections to reinforce your understanding of important terms and concepts and measure your achievement of the Learning Objectives. Check your answers with the feedback given and review when necessary.

Practice Questions

Multiple-Choice Questions

1. Compared to the first year, growth during the second year
   a. proceeds at a slower rate.
   b. continues at about the same rate.
   c. includes more insulating fat.
   d. includes more bone and muscle.

2. The infant's first body movements are
   a. fine motor skills.
   b. gross motor skills.
   c. reflexes.
   d. pincer skills.

3. Some infant reflexes
   a. are essential to life.
   b. disappear in the months after birth.
   c. provide the foundation for later motor skills.
   d. do all of the above.

4. Which of the following is true of motor-skill development in healthy infants?
   a. It follows the same basic sequence the world over.
   b. It occurs at different rates from individual to individual.
   c. It follows norms that vary from one ethnic group to another.
   d. All of the above are true.
5. Most of the nerve cells that a human brain will ever possess are present
   a. at conception.
   b. about 1 month following conception.
   c. at birth.
   d. at age 5 or 6.
6. Climbing is to using a crayon as _____________ is to ___________.
   a. fine motor skill; gross motor skill
   b. gross motor skill; fine motor skill
   c. reflex; fine motor skill
   d. reflex; gross motor skill
7. Today, most cognitive psychologists view language acquisition as
   a. primarily the result of imitation of adult speech.
   b. a behavior that is determined primarily by biological maturation.
   c. a behavior determined entirely by learning.
   d. determined by both biological maturation and learning.
8. Which of the following is true of language development across cultures?
   a. Children attain language according to ethnically-specific timetables.
   b. Children attain language at about the same age in the same sequence across a wide variety of cultures.
   c. Children attain language according to culturally-specific timetables.
   d. Children attain language at about the same age but in a different sequence in different cultures.
9. The average baby speaks a few words at about
   a. 6 months.
   b. 9 months.
   c. 12 months.
   d. 24 months.

10. What is the correct sequence of language development in babies?

    a. crying, babbling, cooing, first word
    b. crying, cooing, babbling, first word
    c. crying, babbling, first word, cooing
    d. crying, cooing, first word, babbling

11. Social referencing refers to

    a. parenting skills that change over time.
    b. changes in community values regarding, for example, the acceptability of using physical punishment with small children.
    c. the support network for new parents provided by extended family members.
    d. the infant response of looking to trusted adults for emotional cues in uncertain situations.

12. Erikson proposes that the development of a sense of trust in early infancy depends on the quality of the

    a. infant's food.
    b. child's genetic inheritance.
    c. relationship with caregiver.
    d. introduction of toilet training.

13. The increasing tendency of toddlers to express frustration and anger is most closely linked to new developments in their cognitive abilities, especially those related to

    a. goal-directed actions.
    b. social referencing.
    c. self-awareness.
    d. stranger wariness.

14. The emotional tie that develops between an infant and his or her primary caregiver is called

    a. self-awareness.
    b. synchrony.
    c. affiliation.
    d. attachment.

15. An important component of secure attachment is the promotion of

    a. self-awareness.
    b. comfort and confidence.
    c. dependency.
    d. all of the above.

16. Which of the following most accurately summarizes the relationship between early attachment and later social relationships?
    a. Attachment in infancy determines whether a child will grow to be sociable.
    b. Attachment relationships are sometimes, though rarely, altered as children grow older.
    c. There is, at best, only a weak correlation between early attachment and later social relationships.
    d. Early attachment biases, but does not inevitably determine, later social relationships.
17. Which of the following is typical behavior of a securely attached infant?
    a. The infant turns to the caregiver when distressed.
    b. The infant protests when the caregiver leaves a room.
    c. The infant may cry when strangers appear.
    d. All of the above are typical of a secure attachment.
18. Regarding the importance of a stable family environment, developmental psychologists have discovered that
    a. predictable daily routines help children feel secure.
    b. stability in the home environment is less important than the overall stimulating quality of the child's experiences.
    c. predictable routines are more important for insecurely attached children.
    d. predictable routines are more important for children who are temperamentally "slow-to-warm-up."

True or False Items

Write T (for true) or F (for false) on the line in front of each statement.

19. ____ Regarding parent–infant interaction during the first two years, most developmentalists believe that quality is more important than quantity.
20. ____ Through guided participation in activities such as feeding, parents help their children achieve independence.
21. ____ Although most babies eventually reach the same developmental milestones, they don't always do it in the same way or at the same time.
22. ____ Crying babies who soothe themselves are displaying a healthy step on the way to greater independence.
23. ____ Children who are not securely attached display at least three different patterns of attachment behavior.
24. ____ A major difference between a six-month-old and a twelve-month-old is that emotions become less discriminating.

25. ____ Temperamental traits originate in the genes and the environment influences their expression.

26. ____ A securely attached toddler is most likely to stay close to his or her mother even in a familiar environment.

27. ____ Cognitive development in bilingual children tends to be somewhat slower than that in children who learn a single language.

Questions for Reflection

1. **Students who are not parents:** Of all the changes that occur between birth and age 2, which is the most remarkable to you? Why? Do you believe that someone's personality is well set by the time he or she goes to school?

   Students who are parents: Did any of the episodes in this program provide insight into the development of your own child or children? Explain.

2. If you were growing at the rate of an infant, how much would you weigh one year from today? What would your height be one year from today?

3. Below is a list of achievements in the life of a normal baby girl. However, these achievements are not presented in the correct order. To demonstrate your understanding of Piaget's stages of sensorimotor intelligence, number the events in the proper sequence from 1 to 6 using the blanks provided.

   ___ (a) The baby cries when she sees her mother putting on her coat.

   ___ (b) The baby laughs when she is tickled and shakes her arm with pleasure when a rattle is put into her hand.

   ___ (c) The baby sucks the nipple and anything else that comes near her mouth.

   ___ (d) The baby experiments with her spoon, banging first the dish, then the high chair, and finally throwing the spoon on the floor.

   ___ (e) The baby refuses the pacifier and shows her displeasure by crying.

   ___ (f) The baby imitates a temper tantrum she has observed in an older child.

Key Terms

1. **attachment:** According to Ainsworth, an affectional tie that an infant forms with a caregiver—a tie that binds them together in space and endures over time. (p. 207; video lesson, segments 1 & 3; objective 3)
2. **temperament:** Inborn differences between one person and another in emotions, activity, and self-regulation. Temperament is epigenetic, originating in genes but affected by child-rearing practices. (p. 196; objective 3)
3. **motor skills:** The learned abilities to move some part of the body, in actions ranging from a large leap to a flicker of the eyelid. (The word *motor* here refers to movement of muscles.) (p. 145; video lesson, introduction; objective 1)

4. **gross motor skills:** Physical abilities that demand large body movements, such as climbing, jumping, or running. (The word *gross* here means "big.") (p. 146; video lesson, segment 2; objective 1)
5. **fine motor skills:** Physical abilities involving small body movements, especially of the hands and fingers, such as drawing and picking up a coin. (The word *fine* here means "small.") (p. 146; video lesson, segment 2; objective 1)
6. **self-awareness:** A person's realization that he or she is a distinct individual, whose body, mind, and actions are separate from those of other people. (p. 194; video lesson, segment 2; objective 3)
7. **secure attachment:** A relationship (type B) in which an infant obtains both comfort and confidence from the presence of his or her caregiver. (p. 208; video lesson, segment 3; objective 3)
8. **trust versus mistrust:** Erikson's first psychosocial crisis. Infants learn basic trust if their basic needs (for food, comfort, attention, and so on) are met. (p. 199; objective 4)
9. **autonomy versus shame and doubt:** Erikson's second crisis of psychosocial development. Toddlers either succeed or fail in gaining a sense of self-rule over their own actions and bodies. (p. 199; objective 4)
10. **babbling:** An infant's repetition of certain syllables, such as "ma-ma" or "ba-ba-ba," that begins between 6 and 9 months of age. (p. 177; objective 2)
11. **reflexes:** Involuntary physical responses to specific stimuli. A reflex occurs without conscious thought. (p. 117; objective 1)
12. **sensorimotor intelligence:** Piaget's term for the way infants think—by using their senses and motor skills—during the first period of cognitive development. (p. 162; objective 2)
13. **stranger wariness:** An infant's expression of concern—a quiet stare, clinging to a familiar person, or sadness—when a stranger appears. (p. 193; objective 3)
14. **separation anxiety:** An infant's distress when a familiar caregiver leaves, most obvious between 9 and 14 months. (p. 193; objective 3)
15. **neuron:** The nerve cell that is the main component of the central nervous system. (p. 132; objective 1)
16. **social referencing:** Seeking information about how to react to an unfamiliar or ambiguous object or event by observing someone else's expressions and reactions. That other person becomes a social reference. (p. 212; objective 3)
17. **language acquisition device (LAD):** Chomsky's term for a hypothesized mental structure that enables humans to learn language, including the basic aspects of grammar, vocabulary, and intonation. (p. 185; objective 2)
18. **insecure attachment:** A pattern of attachment characterized by the infant's fear, anger, or seeming indifference toward the caregiver. (pp. 208–209; objective 3)

Summary

The pace of growth in each of the three domains of development during the first two years is remarkable. During these years, children reach half their adult height, develop cognitive abilities that startle their caregivers (and developmentalists), learn to express almost every human emotion, demonstrate distinct personalities, and move from a state of almost complete dependence on others to one of growing independence.

In the biosocial domain, over the first two years body weight quadruples and the brain triples in weight. As new connections between neurons are formed, the growing maturity of the brain enables the development of gross and fine motor skills that give babies the mobility they need to explore their world, leading to a greater number of learning opportunities which may stimulate growth in the cognitive domain. As they explore their environments, infants' active curiosity and developing sensory and perceptual abilities enable them to progress from knowing the world only through their immediate experiences to being able to "experiment" through the use of mental images and other developing cognitive skills.

Language development is another remarkable cognitive achievement during the first two years, as babies progress from simple cries, cooing, and babbling to speaking in short sentences. Cultural factors influence language development extensively. Bilingual children may have a cognitive advantage because they are exposed to a variety of linguistic and multicultural experiences, which creates a richer, more stimulating environment.

Infants' developing abilities to communicate enable them to become increasingly active participants in their social interactions with caregivers. They also become more sophisticated in expressing emotions, which change from simple reactions to the more complex, self-conscious responses that are a healthy sign of their increasing independence. By age 2, toddlers have formed distinct personalities.

Temperament refers to relatively consistent inborn dispositions that underlie and affect a person's response to people, situations, and events. Temperament is epigenetic: It begins in the child's genetic inheritance and is affected by many prenatal experiences, especially those relating to the nutrition and health of the mother. Later, the social context and the individual's experiences have an effect on temperament. Most infants can be described as possessing one of three relatively stable temperaments: easy, slow to warm up, and difficult.

Answer Key

Practice Questions

Multiple-Choice Questions

1. a. is the correct answer. (objective 1)
2. c. is the correct answer. (objective 1)

   a., b., & d. are incorrect. These motor skills do not emerge until somewhat later; reflexes are present at birth.
3. d. is the correct answer. (objective 1)

4. d. is the correct answer. (objective 1)
5. c. is the correct answer. (objective 1)
6. b. is the correct answer. (video lesson, segment 2; objective 1)

   c. & d. are incorrect. Reflexes are involuntary responses; climbing and using a crayon are both voluntary responses.
7. d. is the correct answer. This is a synthesis of the theories of Skinner and Chomsky. (video lesson, segment 2; objective 2)
8. b. is the correct answer. (p.; video lesson, segment 2; objective 2)

   a., c., & d. are incorrect. Children the world over follow the same sequence and approximately the same timetable for early language development.
9. c. is the correct answer. (objective 2)
10. b. is the correct answer. (objective 2)
11. d. is the correct answer. (objective 3)
12. c. is the correct answer. (video lesson, segments 1 & 3; objective 4)
13. a. is the correct answer. Anger increases with age because toddlers are able to anticipate events and realize that other people's actions sometimes block their own efforts. (video lesson, segment 3; objective 3)
14. d. is the correct answer. (video lesson, segments 1 & 3; objective 3)

    a. is incorrect. Self-awareness refers to the infant's developing sense of "me and mine."

    b. is incorrect. Synchrony describes the coordinated interaction between infant and caregiver.

    c. is incorrect. Affiliation describes the tendency of people at any age to seek the companionship of others.
15. b. is the correct answer. (video lesson, segments 1 & 3; objective 3)

    a. is incorrect. The textbook does not link self-awareness to secure attachment.

    c. is incorrect. On the contrary, secure attachment promotes independence in infants and children.
16. d. is the correct answer. (video lesson, segments 1 & 3; objective 3)
17. d. is the correct answer. (video lesson, segments 1 & 3; objective 3)
18. a. is the correct answer. (video lesson, segment 1; objective 3)

    b. is incorrect. Both stability and stimulation are important features of a health environment for child development.

    c. & d. are incorrect. The video lesson did not discuss the relationships among children's temperaments, attachments, and the importance of predictable environmental routines.

True or False Items

19. F Quality and quantity are equally important. (video lesson, segment 3; objective 3)
20. T (video lesson, segment 1; objectives 1 & 2)

21. T (video lesson, segment 1; objective 1)
22. T (video lesson, segment 1; objective 3)
23. T Insecure-avoidant, insecure-resistant, and disorganized patterns have been identified. (objective 3)
24. F Emotions become less frequent and more discriminating. (objective 3)
25. T (objective 3)
26. F A securely attached toddler is most likely to explore the environment, the mother's presence being enough to give him or her the courage to do so. (video lesson, segments 1 & 3; objective 3)
27. F Bilingual children often benefit from the multiple perspectives provided by their rich linguistic environments. (video lesson, segment 2; objective 2)

Questions for Reflection

1. There is no single correct answer to this question. This question is intended to help you make meaningful connections with your personal experiences.
2. There is no single correct answer to this question. This question is intended to help you make meaningful connections with your personal experiences.
3. The proper sequence is c, e, b, d, a, f. (objective 2)

Lesson Review

Lesson 9

The First Two Years
Summary

Please Note: Use this matrix to guide your study and achieve the learning objectives of this lesson. It will also help you to view the video, which defines and demonstrates important concepts and skills as they relate to everyday life.

Learning Objective	Textbook	Course Student Guide	Video Lesson
1. Give examples of the basic pattern of motor-skill development, and discuss variations in biosocial development during the first two years.	pp. 127–159	Key Terms: 3, 4, 5, 11, 15; Practice Questions: 1, 2, 3, 4, 5, 6, 20, 21;	all segments
2. Summarize key aspects of cognitive development during the first two years, especially language development during this time.	pp. 161–189	Key Terms: 10, 12, 17; Practice Questions: 7, 8, 9, 10, 20, 27.	all segments
3. Discuss psychosocial development during the first two years, focusing on the concepts of temperament and attachment and their influence on the developing child.	pp. 191–221	Key Terms: 1, 2, 6, 7, 13, 14, 16, 18; Practice Questions: 11, 13, 14, 15, 16, 17, 18, 19, 22, 23, 24, 25, 26.	all segments
4. Discuss Erik Erikson's first two stages of psychosocial development, and offer examples of how caregivers can encourage trust and autonomy in their children.	p. 199	Key Terms: 8, 9; Practice Questions: 12.	all segments
5. Offer examples of how a child's development in any one domain (biosocial, cognitive, or psychosocial) can affect development in a different domain.	*		all segments

* The video for this lesson offers excellent coverage of these topics.

Fatherhood

Lesson 10

The First Two Years:
Special Topic

Preview

Traditional views of child development focused almost entirely on mothers, in part because fathers were often removed from most caregiving activities. Today, however, with more and more mothers working outside the home, fathers are taking an increasingly active role in household chores and caregiving duties for their children. This trend, which is apparent throughout the world, is applauded by virtually all developmental psychologists and educators. These experts agree that fathers have a significant role in influencing their children's cognitive, social, and emotional development. This lesson touches on several aspects of this role, including the powerful influence fathers have as role models for their children.

The lesson also explores fatherhood and attachment. Although historically, we have often thought only of mothers when discussing bonding and attachment, fathers form secure attachments with their children that are comparable to the bond between children and their mothers. These attachments are vividly revealed during playtime, especially the rough-and-tumble play that fathers often engage in with their children. However, despite the fact that fathers can and increasingly do master caregiving, women around the world still spend far more time at child care than men do, especially in the child's first few months. The video lesson concludes by exploring how couples can work together to support each other in sharing parenting and other childcare responsibilities.

As you study this lesson, think about your own upbringing. What unique roles did your mother and father play in your care and development? If you have children yourself, what role have you played in their care and development? If you anticipate having children someday, what hopes do you have for the roles that you and your spouse will play in their care and upbringing?

Prior Knowledge That Will Be Used in This Lesson

- Social learning theory, the idea that people can learn by observing and imitating others (from Lesson 1), will be referred to as we discuss the impact that fathers have as role models on their children.

- Attachment, the emotional bond between children and their caregivers (from Lesson 8), will be referred to as the lesson looks at the nature and development of attachment bonds between children and their mothers as compared to that of their fathers. Recall that attachments can be classified as either "secure" or "insecure."

Learning Objectives

Use this information to guide your reading, viewing, thinking, and studying. After successfully completing this lesson, you should be able to:

1. Discuss social learning theory as an extension of learning theory, focusing specifically on fathers as role models for their children.
2. Summarize how culture influences a father's role in the family, and how this in turn can affect a child's development.
3. Discuss contemporary views on the role of the father in infant psychosocial development, focusing on the development of attachment.
4. Discuss how some mothers may interfere with the developing relationship between father and child, and list some things couples can do to effectively share parenting roles.

Textbook Reading & Video Viewing

For the most effective study of this lesson, complete the assignments in the sequence listed below.

Before viewing the video program:

Review Chapter 2, "Theories of Development," pages 43–44 ("Social Learning"); Chapter 7, "The First Two Years: Psychosocial Development," pages 212–213 ("Fathers as Social Partners," and "Comparing Fathers and Mothers").

View the video for Lesson 10, "Fatherhood."

Segment 1: *Fatherhood Across Cultures*

Segment 2: *Attachment and Dad*

Segment 3: *Bonding with Dad*

Segment 4: *And Baby Makes Three*

After viewing the video program:

Review all reading assignments for this lesson.

Complete the "Practice Questions" section to reinforce your understanding of important terms and concepts and measure your achievement of the Learning Objectives. Check your answers with the feedback given and review when necessary.

Practice Questions

Multiple-Choice Questions

1. Social learning is sometimes called modeling because it
   a. follows the scientific model of learning.
   b. molds character.
   c. follows the immediate reinforcement model developed by Bandura.
   d. involves people's patterning their behavior after that of others.

2. Compared to *their* fathers, modern-day fathers
   a. are more actively involved in the care of their children.
   b. are less actively involved in the care of their children.
   c. have about the same level of involvement in the care of their children.
   d. are much less predictable in their level of involvement in child care.

3. Fathers have a significant influence on their children's
   a. cognitive development.
   b. social development.
   c. emotional development.
   d. development in every domain.

4. The stereotypical "Ozzie and Harriet family" in which fathers were the breadwinners and mothers were the caregivers
   a. has been an accurate depiction of the American family since the late 1900s.
   b. has been on the rise since the late 1990s.
   c. probably never existed.
   d. is more typical of certain ethnic groups than others.

5. According to experts in the video lesson, which of the following was the major factor in the shift in fathers' caregiving responsibility?
   a. The rising cost of child care.
   b. The steady increase in the number of women working outside the home.
   c. The economic recession of the 1960s and 1970s.
   d. The steadily increasing divorce rate.

6. The number of women working outside their homes began to sharply increase in the ___________ with the advent of the ________________.
   a. 1950s; Korean War
   b. 1960s; Civil Rights Act
   c. 1960s and 1970s; Women's movement
   d. 1980s; School Lunch Act

7. An important way that fathers interact with infants is
   a. through physical play.
   b. demonstrating work habits.
   c. handling the majority of their physical care.
   d. all of the above.

8. Developmental psychologists believe that as men become more actively involved in caring for their children,
   a. children—but not necessarily their fathers—benefit.
   b. fathers—but not necessarily their children—benefit.
   c. both children and fathers benefit.
   d. children, their fathers, and other family members benefit.

9. Regarding culture and caregiving, which of the following is true?
   a. Some cultures provide fathers greater opportunity to co-parent their children than other cultures.
   b. As a general rule, fathers in developing countries have greater opportunity to co-parent than fathers in developed countries.
   c. Fathers in developed countries generally have greater opportunity to co-parent than fathers in developing countries.
   d. Throughout most of history, women and men have shared caregiving duties equally.

10. To a large extent, parenting and fathering
    a. are biologically constructed processes.
    b. are culturally constructed processes.
    c. are roles entirely shaped by the individuals that occupy them.
    d. haven't changed significantly since the dawn of human existence.

11. Compared to mothers, the amount of time that the average father spends caring for his infant is
    a. about the same.
    b. far less but of better quality.
    c. so greatly varied that it is nearly impossible to come up with an "average" amount of time.
    d. none of the above.

12. Throughout the world, children form attachments to their caregivers between _____________ of age.
    a. one and two weeks
    b. one and two months
    c. four and seven weeks
    d. four and seven months

13. Compared to the attachments mothers form with their children, fathers form attachment bonds that tend to be

    a. comparable in security.
    b. slightly less secure.
    c. less predictable.
    d. less emotional.

14. The emotional tie that develops between a child and his or her caregiver is called

    a. self-awareness.
    b. synchrony.
    c. affiliation.
    d. attachment.

15. Developmental psychologists believe that children who form multiple attachments are

    a. probably insecurely attached to each caregiver.
    b. at increased risk for a wide range of developmental problems.
    c. rare exceptions to the rule, "one child, one attachment."
    d. quite normal, and likely to benefit from having multiple attachments.

16. The most significant benefit of children and parents reading together is the

    a. cognitive development of the child.
    b. social development of the child.
    c. emotional development of the child.
    d. strengthening of the parent-child bond.

17. The typical father–child pattern of play probably helps children

    a. learn to control their states of arousal and emotional excitement.
    b. become self-aware.
    c. develop a healthy fear of strangers.
    d. develop stronger bodies.

18. Josh, who is about to become a father and primary caregiver, is worried that he will never have the natural caregiving skills that the child's mother has. Studies on father–infant relationships show that

    a. infants nurtured by single fathers are more likely to be insecurely attached.
    b. fathers can provide the emotional and cognitive nurturing necessary for healthy infant development.
    c. women are biologically predisposed to be better parents than men are.
    d. social development is usually slightly delayed in children whose fathers are the primary caregiver.

19. We are more likely to imitate the behavior of others if we particularly admire and identify with them. This belief finds expression in

    a. stage theory.
    b. sociocultural theory.
    c. social learning theory.
    d. Pavlov's experiments.

True or False Items

Write T (for true) or F (for false) on the line in front of each statement.

20. _____ Children can only become attached to one caregiver.
21. _____ Children tend to attach to whomever is providing their care.
22. _____ Children attach more readily to their mothers than they do to their fathers.
23. _____ Cross-culturally, there is relatively little variation in the roles fathers play in caring for their children.
24. _____ Despite popular belief, young children rarely mimic their parents' behavior.
25. _____ Women are biologically predisposed to be better parents than men are.

Key Terms

1. **social learning theory:** An extension of behaviorism that emphasizes the influence that other people have over a person's behavior. Even without specific reinforcement, every individual learns many things through observation and imitation of other people. (p. 44; objective 1)
2. **modeling:** The central process of social learning, by which a person observes the actions of others and then copies them. (p. 44; objective 1)
3. **attachment:** According to Ainsworth, an affectional tie that an infant forms with a caregiver—a tie that binds them together in space and endures over time. (p. 207; video lesson, segment 2; objective 3)

Summary

As noted throughout this series, the social context of development teaches infants and children when and how to express their emotions and has a powerful influence on cognitive development as well. Along with mothers and other primary caregivers in a child's social context, fathers play a key role in this social referencing. An important aspect of the social context is modeling, in which infants observe behavior and then pattern their own after it. The age-old hypothesis that mothers, and only mothers, can provide the optimal care and modeling in the first two years of life has been discounted by research on infant care. Children form multiple attachments and learn from many people, including their fathers.

Fathers can and do master caregiving and today, throughout the world, fathers are increasingly taking on a significant share of the caregiving and nurturing responsibilities for their children. When fathers are more involved with their kids, the children—and the entire family—benefit. Even so, women worldwide still spend far more time at child care than men do, especially during the earliest years. A key challenge for couples today is working together to support each other's role in caregiving.

Survey research indicates that children living with both biological parents tend to have fewer physical, emotional, or learning difficulties than do children in other family structures. As adolescents and adults, they continue to fare better. This family structure confers at least two important advantages for children: (a) two adults generally provide more complete caregiving than one, (b) two-parent homes usually have a financial advantage over other forms (especially the single-parent home) enabling better health care, housing, nutrition, and education for their children.

The apparent advantage of original two-parent homes may be overstated, however, since survey data are often confounded by the fact that a disproportionate number of one-parent families are also low-income families. Two other caveats apply: (a) not every biological father or mother is a fit parent, and (b) not every marriage creates a nurturant household. Children who live in intact families with persistently high levels of conflict are especially likely to suffer.

Answer Key

Practice Questions

Multiple-Choice Questions

1. d. is the correct answer. (objective 1)

   a. & c. are incorrect. These can be true in all types of learning.

   b. is incorrect. This was not discussed as an aspect of developmental theory.

2. a. is the correct answer. (video lesson, segment 1; objectives 1 & 2)

   d. is incorrect. Throughout history, fathers' involvement in the care of their children has been predictable.

3. d. is the correct answer. (video lesson, segment 2; objective 3)

4. c. is the correct answer. (video lesson, segment 1; objective 2)

   a. & b. are incorrect. To the extent that the "Ozzie and Harriet family" existed, it is associated with families in the 1950s.

   d. is incorrect. The lesson does not differentiate parental roles and family "styles" by ethnic group.

5. b. is the correct answer. (video lesson, segment 1; objective 2)

6. c. is the correct answer. (video lesson, segment 1; objective 2)

7. a. is the correct answer. (video lesson, segment 1; objectives 2 & 3)

8. d. is the correct answer. (video lesson, segment 2; objective 3)

9. a. is the correct answer. (video lesson, segment 1; objective 2)

   b. & c. are incorrect. The lesson does not differentiate the caregiving opportunities for fathers in developing and developed countries.

d. is incorrect. In fact, throughout history women have tended to perform more caregiving than men.

10. b. is the correct answer. (video lesson, segment 1; objective 2)

    c. is incorrect. Although individuals do help to shape the roles they occupy, cultural values and expectations also have a substantial impact.

11. c. is the correct answer. (video lesson, segment 1; objectives 2 & 3)
12. d. is the correct answer. (video lesson, segment 2; objective 3)
13. a. is the correct answer. (video lesson, segment 2; objective 3)

    b., c., & d. are incorrect. Fathers' attachment bonds are no less predictable or emotional than those mothers form with their children.

14. d. is the correct answer. (video lesson, segment 2; objective 3)

    a. is incorrect. Self-awareness refers to the child's developing sense of identity apart from that of others.

    b. is incorrect. Synchrony refers to the coordinated interaction between caregiver and infant that helps infants learn to express and read emotions.

    c. is incorrect. Affiliation refers to a general need to associate with other people; not just primary caregivers.

15. d. is the correct answer. Children can and often do form multiple attachments to the many different people who love and care for them. (video lesson, segment 2; objective 3)
16. a. is the correct answer. (video lesson, segment 3; objective 1)

    b., c., & d. are incorrect. Although children's social and emotional development certainly are likely to benefit from the close interactions involved in reading with caregivers, the question specifies the "most significant" benefit of reading.

17. a. is the correct answer. (video lesson, segment 4; objective 4)

    b., c., & d. are incorrect. The lesson does not address these issues.

18. b. is the correct answer. (video lesson, segments 1 & 2; objectives 3 & 4)
19. c. is the correct answer. (objective 1)

True or False Items

20. F Children can and often do form multiple attachments. (video lesson, segment 2; objective 3)
21. T (video lesson, segment 2; objective 3)
22. F Throughout the world, fathers readily form secure attachments with their children that are comparable to the bonds that are shared between children and their mothers. (video lesson, segment 2; objectives 1 & 3)
23. F Cultures differ significantly in the roles that fathers are encouraged to play in caring for their children. (video lesson, segment 1; objective 2)
24. F Young children model their parents' behaviors extensively. (objective 1)
25. F (video lesson, segment 2; objective 3)

Lesson Review

Lesson 10

The First Two Years
Special Topic

Please Note: Use this matrix to guide your study and achieve the learning objectives of this lesson. It will also help you to view the video, which defines and demonstrates important concepts and skills as they relate to everyday life.

Learning Objective	Textbook	Course Student Guide	Video Lesson
1. Discuss social learning theory as an extension of learning theory, focusing specifically on fathers as role models for their children.	pp. 43–44	Key Terms: 1, 2; Practice Questions: 1, 2, 16, 19, 22, 24.	Segment 2: *Attachment and Dad* Segment 3: *Bonding with Dad*
2. Summarize how culture influences a father's role in the family, and how this in turn can affect a child's development.	*	Practice Questions: 2, 4, 5, 6, 7, 9, 10, 11, 23.	Segment 1: *Fatherhood Across Culture*
3. Discuss contemporary views on the role of the father in infant psychosocial development, focusing on the development of attachment.	pp. 212–213	Key Terms: 3; Practice Questions: 3, 7, 8, 11, 12, 13, 14, 15, 18, 20, 21, 22, 25.	Segment 2: *Attachment and Dad*
4. Discuss how some mothers may interfere with the developing relationship between father and child, and list some things couples can do to effectively share parenting roles.	p. 213	Practice Questions: 17, 18.	Segment 4: *And Baby Makes Three*

* The video for this lesson offers excellent coverage of this topic.

Playing and Growing

Lesson 11

The Play Years: Biosocial Development

Preview

Lesson 11 is the first of 5 lessons covering the early childhood period, ages 2 to 6. Among other things, these lessons address the central importance of play to the biosocial, cognitive, and psychosocial development of preschoolers.

This lesson on biosocial development outlines the changes in size and shape that occur during this period. This is followed by a look at brain growth and development and its role in the development of physical and cognitive abilities and emotions. A description of the acquisition of gross and fine motor skills follows, noting that mastery of such skills develops steadily with intellectual growth during early childhood. The lesson also addresses the important issues of **injury control** and accidents, the major cause of childhood death in all but the most disease-ridden or war-torn countries. The lesson concludes with an exploration of **child maltreatment**, including its prevalence, contributing factors, consequences for future development, treatment, and prevention.

As you move through this lesson, think of children you know in this age range. Consider their size and shape, their eating habits, and their motor-skill capabilities—what they can do with their bodies and hands. Also consider any child maltreatment cases you know of or have read about. What were the circumstances? What type of maltreatment occurred? What was the response?

Prior Knowledge That Will Be Used in This Lesson

- In this lesson, physical growth and the development of gross and fine motor skills during early childhood will be compared to earlier development during infancy and toddlerhood (Lesson 6).
- This lesson will return to the topic of brain growth and development, which was introduced in Lesson 6. In children from ages 2 to 6, the growth of dendrites and axons continues, along with myelination, the insulating process that speeds up the transmission of neural impulses. This brain maturation leads to many other advances, including development of the visual pathways and eye-hand coordination that will make reading and writing possible.

Learning Objectives

Use this information to guide your reading, viewing, thinking, and studying. After successfully completing this lesson, you should be able to:

1. Describe normal physical growth during early childhood, and account for variations in height and weight.
2. Describe changes in eating habits and nutritional needs during the preschool years, noting some of the nutritional challenges and risks for children in this stage.
3. Discuss the brain processes of myelination and lateralization and their development during early childhood.
4. Describe the prevalence of accidental injuries during early childhood, describe some measures that have significantly reduced accidental death rates for children, and identify several factors that contribute to this problem.
5. Describe the maturation of the prefrontal cortex and the regulation of attention in early childhood.
6. Distinguish between gross and fine motor skills, and discuss the development of each during early childhood.
7. Discuss the significance of artistic expression during early childhood.
8. Identify the various categories and consequences of child maltreatment.
9. Discuss several factors that contribute to maltreatment, and describe current treatment and prevention efforts.
10. Describe how the expression and regulation of emotions are fostered by brain development and influenced by brain damage.

Textbook Reading & Video Viewing

For the most effective study of this lesson, complete the assignments in the sequence listed below.

Before viewing the video program:

Read Chapter 8, "Early Childhood: Biosocial Development," pages 225–255.

View the video for Lesson 11, "Playing and Growing."

Segment 1: *Body and Brain Growth*

Segment 2: *Motor Skills*

Segment 3: *Maltreatment*

After viewing the video program:

Review all reading assignments for this lesson.

Complete the "Practice Questions" and "Applying Your Knowledge" sections to reinforce your understanding of important terms and concepts and measure your achievement of the Learning Objectives. Check your answers with the feedback given and review when necessary.

Practice Questions I

Multiple-Choice Questions

1. During the preschool years, ages 2 to 6, the weight gained by the average child is
   a. less than in previous years but greater than in following years.
   b. more than during other age periods.
   c. less than during other age periods.
   d. more than in previous years but less than in following years.

2. The brain center for speech is usually located in the
   a. right brain.
   b. left brain.
   c. corpus callosum.
   d. space just below the right ear.

3. Ethnic differences in childhood size and shape
   a. are consistent throughout the world.
   b. vary from one culture to another.
   c. are more pronounced in Western cultures.
   d. are more pronounced today than in the past.

4. Which of the following is **NOT** true regarding injury control?
   a. Tertiary prevention measures are rarely useful in controlling injury.
   b. Many experts now would agree with the adage, "Accidents happen."
   c. Automatic safety regulations tend to be more effective than educational measures.
   d. Accidental deaths of one- to five-year-olds have held steady in the United States over the past two decades.

5. Children in the United States tend to have too much ___________ in their diet.
   a. iron
   b. calcium
   c. sugar
   d. zinc

6. Skills that involve large body movements, such as running and jumping, are called
   a. activity-level skills.
   b. fine motor skills.
   c. gross motor skills.
   d. left-brain skills.

7. The brain's ongoing myelination during childhood helps children
   a. control their actions more precisely.
   b. react more quickly to stimuli.
   c. coordinate and control muscles.
   d. do all of the above.
8. Worldwide, a major cause of death in childhood is
   a. accidental injury.
   b. cancer.
   c. malnutrition.
   d. iron deficiency anemia.
9. Regarding lateralization, which of the following is **NOT** true?
   a. Many cognitive skills require only one side of the brain.
   b. Brain centers for generalized emotional impulses can be found in the right hemisphere.
   c. The left hemisphere contains brain areas dedicated to logic.
   d. The right side of the brain controls the left side of the body.
10. Which of the following factors is most responsible for differences in height and weight between children in developed and developing countries?
    a. the child's genetic background
    b. health care
    c. nutrition
    d. age of weaning
11. The so-called "executive" area of the brain that directs and controls the other areas is the
    a. corpus callosum.
    b. myelin sheath.
    c. prefrontal cortex.
    d. temporal lobe.
12. Children's art provides opportunities to practice
    a. gross motor skills.
    b. fine motor skills.
    c. learning the colors.
    d. large muscle skills.

13. Which of the following is true of the corpus callosum?
    a. It enables short-term memory.
    b. It connects the two halves of the brain.
    c. It must be fully myelinated before gross motor skills can be acquired.
    d. All of the above are correct.
14. The improvements in eye-hand coordination that allow preschoolers to catch and then throw a ball occur, in part, because
    a. the brain areas associated with this ability become more fully myelinated.
    b. the corpus callosum begins to function.
    c. fine motor skills have matured by age 2.
    d. gross motor skills have matured by age 2.
15. The increased activity in early childhood of which of the following is a reason for nightmares and the development of irrational fears?
    a. amygdala
    b. prefrontal cortex
    c. hippocampus
    d. hypothalamus

True or False Items

Write T (for true) or F (for false) on the line in front of each statement.

16. _____ If given the choice between a nutritious snack (like carrots and milk) or one with empty calories and lots of salt, fat, and sugar (like potato chips and fruit punch), most children will naturally choose the healthier option.
17. _____ Brain weight increases more slowly than body weight during early childhood.
18. _____ Urbanization poses a threat to young children's biosocial development because of its resulting environmental and safety concerns.
19. _____ The health care, genetic background, and nutrition of the preschool child are major influences on growth.
20. _____ Memories of location are fragile in early childhood because the hippocampus is still developing.
21. _____ Fine motor skills are usually easier for preschoolers to master than are gross motor skills.
22. _____ Most serious childhood injuries truly are "accidents."
23. _____ Children often fare as well in kinship care as they do in conventional foster care.

24. _____ Developmentalists believe that every culture probably has values that are destructive to children.

25. _____ Child maltreatment includes both child abuse and child neglect.

Practice Questions II

Multiple-Choice Questions

1. Each year from ages 2 to 6, the average child gains and grows, respectively
   a. 2 pounds and 1 inch.
   b. 3 pounds and 2 inches.
   c. 4.5 pounds and 3 inches.
   d. 6 pounds and 6 inches.

2. The ability to grasp "the big picture" is usually located in the brain's
   a. right hemisphere.
   b. left hemisphere.
   c. right or left hemisphere.
   d. corpus callosum.

3. Which of the following is **NOT** associated with an increased risk of child maltreatment?
   a. depressed mothers
   b. financial stress
   c. mothers who feel sufficiently in control
   d. infant fragility

4. A lack of which of the following is particularly helpful to young children's artistic expression?
   a. well-developed fine motor skills
   b. inclination to be self-critical
   c. developing gross motor skills
   d. realistic perception

5. Which of the following is an example of secondary prevention of child maltreatment?
   a. removing a child from an abusive home
   b. jailing a maltreating parent
   c. home visitation of families with infants by health professionals
   d. public-policy measures aimed at creating stable neighborhoods

6. When parents or caregivers do not provide adequate food, shelter, attention, or supervision, it is specifically referred to as
   a. abuse.
   b. neglect.
   c. endangering.
   d. maltreatment.
7. Which of the following is true of a developed nation in which many ethnic groups live together?
   a. Ethnic variations in height and weight disappear.
   b. Ethnic variations in stature persist, but are substantially smaller.
   c. Children of African descent tend to be tallest, followed by Europeans, Asians, and Latinos.
   d. Cultural patterns exert a stronger-than-normal impact on growth patterns.
8. Which of the following is an example of a fine motor skill?
   a. kicking a ball
   b. running
   c. drawing with a pencil
   d. jumping
9. Most gross motor skills can be learned by healthy children by about age
   a. 2.
   b. 3.
   c. 5.
   d. 7.
10. The perseveration and impulsiveness that is common in early childhood are both symptoms of _________________, resulting from an undeveloped _________________.
    a. poor source memory; amygdala
    b. poor source memory; prefrontal cortex
    c. a lack of self-control; amygdala
    d. a lack of self-control; prefrontal cortex
11. Over the past two decades in the United States, the accidental death rate for children between the ages of 1 and 5 has
    a. decreased, largely as a result of new city, state, and federal safety laws.
    b. decreased, largely because parents are more knowledgeable about safety practices.
    c. increased.
    d. remained unchanged.

12. During early childhood, because growth is slow, children's appetites seem ________________ they were in the first two years of life.

    a. larger than
    b. smaller than
    c. about the same as
    d. erratic, sometimes smaller and sometimes larger than

Matching Items

Match each definition or description with its corresponding term.

Terms

13. __________ corpus callosum
14. __________ gross motor skills
15. __________ fine motor skills
16. __________ myelination
17. __________ lateralization
18. __________ injury control
19. __________ perseveration
20. __________ prefrontal cortex
21. __________ child abuse
22. __________ child neglect
23. __________ primary prevention
24. __________ secondary prevention
25. __________ tertiary prevention

Definitions or Descriptions

a. an insulating process that speeds up neural transmission
b. the differentiation of the two sides of the brain
c. the tendency to repeat thoughts or actions
d. called the "executive" of the brain
e. procedures to prevent child maltreatment from ever occurring
f. running and jumping
g. actions that are deliberately harmful to a child's well-being
h. procedures for spotting and treating the early warning signs of child maltreatment
i. painting a picture or tying shoelaces
j. failure to appropriately meet a child's basic needs
k. an approach emphasizing "accident" prevention
l. procedures to halt maltreatment that has already occurred
m. band of nerve fibers connecting the right and left hemispheres of the brain

Applying Your Knowledge

1. When Jonathan was three, his parents noticed his apparent left-hand preference for most activities and set about teaching him to use his right hand instead, believing this would be better for him in the long run. Which of the following outcomes should be expected?

   a. Jonathan will eventually learn to do most things with his right hand, but his brain will never be fully reprogrammed.

   b. Because his parents began teaching him to use his right hand when he was young, Jonathan will develop no differently than a natural right-hander.

   c. Jonathan will not be able to learn to use his right hand—handedness is unchangeable.

   d. Jonathan will become fully ambidextrous, able to complete any task with either hand.

2. Four-year-old Carrie is hyperactive, often confused between fantasy and reality, and jumps at any sudden noise. Her pediatrician suspects that she is suffering from

   a. shaken baby syndrome.

   b. failure to thrive.

   c. post-traumatic stress disorder.

   d. child neglect.

3. Following an automobile accident, Amira developed severe problems with her speech. Her doctor believes that the accident injured the _______________ of her brain.

   a. left side

   b. right side

   c. communication pathways

   d. corpus callosum

4. Two-year-old Ali is quite clumsy, falls down frequently, and often bumps into stationary objects. Ali most likely

   a. has a neuromuscular disorder.

   b. has an underdeveloped right hemisphere of the brain.

   c. is suffering from iron deficiency anemia.

   d. is a normal two-year-old whose gross motor skills will improve dramatically during the preschool years.

5. Climbing a fence is an example of a

   a. fine motor skill.

   b. gross motor skill.

   c. circular reaction.

   d. launching event.

6. To prevent accidental death in childhood, some experts urge forethought and planning for safety and measures to limit the damage of such accidents as do occur. This approach is called

   a. protective analysis.

   b. safety education.

   c. injury control.

   d. childproofing.

7. Which of the following activities would probably be the **MOST** difficult for a five-year-old child?

   a. climbing a ladder

   b. running and then jumping

   c. throwing a ball

   d. tracing a drawing of an animal

8. Most child maltreatment

   a. includes both child abuse and child neglect.

   b. involves a rare outburst from the perpetrator.

   c. involves a mentally ill perpetrator.

   d. can be predicted entirely from the victim's personality characteristics.

9. A mayoral candidate is calling for sweeping policy changes to help ensure the well-being of children by promoting home ownership, high-quality community centers, and more stable neighborhoods. If these measures are effective in reducing child maltreatment, they would be classified as

   a. primary prevention.

   b. secondary prevention.

   c. tertiary prevention.

   d. permanency planning.

10. Which of the following factors would likely figure **LEAST** into the development of fine motor skills?

    a. strength

    b. muscular control

    c. patience

    d. dexterity of fingers

11. Parents who were abused as children

    a. almost always abuse their children.

    b. almost always neglect their children.

    c. are no more likely than anyone else to mistreat their children.

    d. are somewhat more likely than others to abuse their children.

12. Three-year-old Kyle's parents are concerned because Kyle, who generally seems healthy, doesn't seem to have the hefty appetite or rate of growth he had as an infant. Should they be worried?

    a. Yes, because both appetite and growth rate normally increase throughout the preschool years.

    b. Yes, because appetite (but not necessarily growth rate) normally increases during the preschool years.

    c. No, because growth rate (and hence caloric need) is slower during the preschool years than during infancy.

    d. There is not enough information to determine whether Kyle is developing normally.

Key Terms

1. **myelination:** The process by which axons become coated with myelin, a fatty substance that speeds the transmission of nerve impulses from neuron to neuron. (p. 230; objective 3)
2. **corpus callosum:** A long, thick band of nerve fibers that connects the left and right hemispheres of the brain and allows communication between them. (p. 231; objective 3)
3. **lateralization:** Literally, sidedness, referring to the specialization in certain functions by each side of the brain, with one side dominant for each activity. The left side of the brain controls the right side of the body, and vice versa. (p. 231; objective 3)
4. **perseveration:** The tendency to persevere in, or stick to, one thought or action for a long time. (p. 234; objective 5)

   Memory aid: To persevere is to continue, or persist, at something.
5. **amygdala:** A tiny brain structure that registers emotions, particularly fear and anxiety. (p. 235; objective 10)
6. **hippocampus:** A brain structure that is a central processor of memory, especially the memory of locations. (p. 235; objective 10)
7. **hypothalamus:** A brain area that responds to the amygdala and the hippocampus to produce hormones that activate other parts of the brain and body. (p. 235; objective 10)
8. **injury control/harm reduction:** Practices that are aimed at anticipating, controlling, and preventing dangerous activities; these practices reflect the beliefs that accidents are not random and that injuries can be made less harmful if proper controls are in place. (p. 243; objective 4)
9. **primary prevention:** Actions that change overall background conditions to prevent some unwanted event or circumstance, such as injury, disease, or abuse. (p. 244; objective 4)
10. **secondary prevention:** Actions that avert harm in a high-risk situation, such as stopping a car before it hits a pedestrian. (p. 244; objective 4)

11. **tertiary prevention:** Actions, such as immediate and effective medical treatment, that are taken after an adverse event (such as illness or injury) occurs and that are aimed at reducing the harm or preventing disability. (p. 244; objective 4)
12. **child maltreatment:** Intentional harm to, or avoidable endangerment of, anyone under age 18. (p. 247; objective 8)
13. **child abuse:** Deliberate action that is harmful to a child's physical, emotional, or sexual well-being. (p. 247; objective 8)
14. **child neglect:** Failure to meet a child's basic physical, educational, or emotional needs. (p. 248; objective 8)
15. **reported maltreatment:** Harm or endangerment about which someone has notified the authorities. (p. 248; objective 8)
16. **substantiated maltreatment:** Harm or endangerment that has been reported, investigated, and verified. (p. 248; objective 8)
17. **post-traumatic stress disorder (PTSD):** An anxiety disorder that develops as a delayed reaction to having experienced or witnessed a profoundly shocking or frightening event, such as rape, severe beating, war, or natural disaster. Its symptoms may include flashbacks to the event, hyperactivity and hypervigilance, displaced anger, sleeplessness, nightmares, sudden terror or anxiety, and confusion between fantasy and reality. (p. 250; objective 8)
18. **permanency planning:** An effort by child-welfare authorities to find a long-term living situation that will provide stability and support for a maltreated child. A goal is to avoid repeated changes of caregiver or school, which can be particularly harmful to the child. (p. 252; objective 9)
19. **foster care:** A legal, publicly supported system in which a maltreated child is removed from the parents' custody and entrusted to another adult or family, which is reimbursed for expenses incurred in meeting the child's needs. (p. 252; objective 9)
20. **kinship care:** A form of foster care in which a relative of a maltreated child, usually a grandparent, becomes the child's legal caregiver. (p. 252; objective 9)
21. **adoption:** A legal proceeding in which an adult or couple unrelated to a child is granted the joys and obligations of being that child's parent(s). (p. 253; objective 9)

Summary

Children grow steadily taller and slimmer during the preschool years, with their genetic background and nutrition being responsible for most of the variation seen in children from various parts of the world. Paradoxically, young children the world over face significant threats from both malnutrition and overnutrition due to their propensity for filling up with unhealthy foods and their caregivers' overfeeding them in countries where food is abundant. Overweight children tend to become overweight adults, and this trend has lead to an epidemic of heart disease and diabetes. Teaching and providing good nutrition to young children is the most important preventative factor in this worldwide problem.

The most significant aspect of growth is the continued maturation of the nervous system and the refinement of the visual, muscular, and cognitive skills that will be necessary for the child to function in school. The brain becomes more specialized as it matures, with the left half usually becoming the center for speech, and the right the center for visual, spatial, and artistic skills. Such **lateralization** is noticed most readily in the approximately ten percent of children who possess a genetically encoded preference to use the left hand. Cultural norms may result in a smaller percentage of adults who claim to be left-handed.

Gross motor skills, such as running, climbing, jumping, and throwing, improve dramatically between ages 2 and 6, making it essential that children have access to safe play space and guided practice to assist in this developmental process. Fine motor skills, such as pouring, holding a pencil, and using a knife and fork, are much harder for preschoolers to master. This difficulty is due to several factors, including incomplete myelination of the nervous system and incomplete muscular control. In spite of these challenges, many preschool-aged-children love engaging in creative expression. Doing so is a powerful stimulus to the development of the fine motor skills, as children are drawn to practice these skills in order to produce the artistic results they desire.

Throughout childhood, accidental injuries are the leading cause of death. The accident risk for a particular child depends on several factors. Boys, as a group, and low-socioeconomic status (SES) children suffer more serious injuries and accidental deaths than girls, and high-SES children. Three levels of preventative measure are used for **injury control**: **primary prevention**, **secondary prevention**, and **tertiary prevention**.

Child maltreatment takes many forms, including physical, emotional, or sexual **abuse**, and emotional or physical **neglect**. Although certain conditions are almost universally harmful, some practices that are considered neglectful or abusive in one culture are acceptable in others. Maltreatment is especially likely if the family context is either too rigid in its schedules and role demands that no one can measure up to them or so chaotic and disorganized that no one knows what is expected. Maltreatment is also especially likely to develop in isolated families in which the parents are unusually suspicious or distrustful of outsiders.

The consequences of maltreatment to children include impaired learning, self-esteem, social relationships, and emotional control. Many people erroneously believe that maltreated children automatically become adults who abuse or neglect their own children. The most effective prevention strategies for maltreatment are those that enhance community support and address the specific material and emotional needs of troubled families. Adoption is the final option when families are inadequate and children are young.

The phenomenon of maltreated children invariably growing up to become abusive or neglectful parents themselves is a widely held, and very destructive, misconception. Experts believe that between 30 and 40 percent of children who were abused actually become child abusers themselves. Still, this rate is much higher than that in the general population, so it is safest to conclude that it is a real, although often-exaggerated, problem.

Special Note: We will discuss the topic of child maltreatment (pp. 247–253) in more detail in Lesson 15, "Hazards Along the Way."

Answer Key

Practice Questions I

Multiple-Choice Questions

1. c. is the correct answer. Serious malnutrition is much more likely to occur in infancy or in adolescence than in early childhood. (objective 1)

   a. is incorrect..

2. b. is the correct answer. (objective 5)

   a. & d. are incorrect. The right brain is the location of areas associated with recognition of visual configurations.

   c. is incorrect. The corpus callosum helps integrate the functioning of the two halves of the brain; it does not contain areas specialized for particular skills.

3. b. is the correct answer. (video lesson, segment 1; objective 1)
4. c. is the correct answer. (objective 4)

   a. is incorrect. All three levels of prevention measures are effective.

   b. is incorrect. Experts believe that injuries are not accidental, but rather predictable and avoidable.

   d. is incorrect. In fact, accident rates have decreased during this time period.

5. c. is the correct answer. (objective 2)
6. c. is the correct answer. (video lesson, segment 2; objective 6)
7. d. is the correct answer. (video lesson, segment 1; objectives 3 & 6)
8. a. is the correct answer. (objective 4)
9. a. is the correct answer. (objective 3)
10. c. is the correct answer. (video lesson, segment 1; objective 1)
11. c. is the correct answer. (objective 5)

    a. is incorrect. The corpus callosum is the band of fibers that link the two halves of the brain.

    b. is incorrect. The myelin sheath is the fatty insulation that surrounds some axons in the brain.

    d. is incorrect. The temporal lobes of the brain contain the primary centers for hearing.

12. b. is the correct answer. Children with lower socioeconomic status have higher accident rates. (objective 7)
13. b. is the correct answer. (video lesson, segment 1; objective 3)

    a. is incorrect. The corpus callosum is not directly involved in memory.

    c. is incorrect. Myelination of the central nervous system is important to the mastery of fine motor skills.

14. a. is the correct answer. (objective 3)

    b. is incorrect. The corpus callosum begins to function long before early childhood.

    c. & d. are incorrect. Neither fine nor gross motor skills have fully matured by age 2.

15. a. is the correct answer. (objective 10)

True or False Items

16. F Young children need to be taught healthy choices and given the means to make them. (video lesson, segment 1; objective 2)
17. F During childhood, the brain develops faster than any other part of the body. (video lesson, segment 1; objective 3)
18. T (objective 6)
19. T (video lesson, segment 1; objective 1)
20. T (objective 10)
21. F Fine motor skills are more difficult for preschoolers to master than are gross motor skills. (video lesson, segment 2; objective 6)
22. F Most serious accidents involve someone's lack of forethought. (objective 4)
23. T (objective 9)
24. T (objective 9)
25. T (video lesson, segment 3; objective 8)

Practice Questions II

Multiple-Choice Questions

1. c. is the correct answer. (video lesson, segment 1; objective 1)
2. a. is the correct answer. (objective 3)

   b. & c. are incorrect. The left hemisphere of the brain contains areas associated with language development.

   d. is incorrect. The corpus callosum does not contain areas for specific behaviors.

3. c. is the correct answer. Mothers who feel like their lives or their infants are out of their control are more likely to be abusive. (objective 9)
4. b. is the correct answer. (objective 7)
5. c. is the correct answer. (objective 9)

   a. & b. are incorrect. These are examples of tertiary prevention.

   d. is incorrect. This is an example of primary prevention.

6. b. is the correct answer. (video lesson, segment 3; objective 8)

   a. is incorrect. Abuse is deliberate, harsh injury to the body.

   c. & d. are incorrect. Maltreatment and endangerment are too broad.

7. c. is the correct answer. (objective 1)

8. c. is the correct answer. (video lesson, segment 2; objective 6)

   a., b., & d. are incorrect. These are gross motor skills.

9. c. is the correct answer. (video lesson, segment 2; objective 6)

10. d. is the correct answer. (objective 5)

11. a. is the correct answer. (objective 4)

    b. is incorrect. Although safety education is important, the decrease in accident rate is largely the result of new safety laws.

12. b. is the correct answer. (objective 2)

Matching Items

13. m (video lesson, segment 1; objective 3)
14. f (video lesson, segment 2; objective 6)
15. i (video lesson, segment 2; objective 6)
16. a (video lesson, segment 1; objective 3)
17. b (objective 3)
18. k (objective 4)
19. c (objective 5)
20. d (objective 5)
21. g (video lesson, segment 3; objective 8)
22. j (video lesson, segment 3; objective 8)
23. e (objectives 4 & 9)
24. h (objectives 4 & 9)
25. l (objectives 4 & 9)

Applying Your Knowledge

1. a. is the correct answer. (objective 3)

2. c. is the correct answer. Carrie's specific symptoms may be caused by neglect or maltreatment, but they are most directly signs of PTSD. (objectives 8 & 9)

3. a. is the correct answer. In most people, the left hemisphere of the brain contains centers for language, including speech. (objective 3)

4. d. is the correct answer. (objective 6)

5. b. is the correct answer. (video lesson, segment 2; objective 6)

   a. is incorrect. Fine motor skills involve small body movements, such as the hand movements used in painting.

   c. & d. are incorrect. These events were not discussed in this chapter.

6. c. is the correct answer. (objective 4)

7. d. is the correct answer. (video lesson, segment 2; objective 6)

   a., b., & c. are incorrect. Preschoolers find these gross motor skills easier to perform than fine motor skills such as that described in d.

8. a. is the correct answer. (video lesson, segment 3; objective 8)

9. a. is the correct answer. (objective 9)

   b. is incorrect. Had the candidate called for measures to spot the early warning signs of maltreatment, this answer would be true.

   c. is incorrect. Had the candidate called for jailing those who maltreat children or providing greater counseling and health care for victims, this answer would be true.

   d. is incorrect. Permanency planning is the term for a long-term plan for a child who has experienced substantiated maltreatment.

10. a. is the correct answer. Strength is a more important factor in the development of gross motor skills. (video lesson, segment 2; objective 6)

11. d. is the correct answer. Approximately 30 percent of adults who were abused as children themselves become abusive parents. (video lesson, segment 3; objective 8)

12. c. is the correct answer. (objective 2)

Lesson Review

Lesson 11

The Play Years
Biosocial Development

Please Note: Use this matrix to guide your study and achieve the learning objectives of this lesson. It will also help you to view the video, which defines and demonstrates important concepts and skills as they relate to everyday life.

Learning Objective	Textbook	Course Student Guide	Video Lesson
1. Describe normal physical growth during early childhood, and account for variations in height and weight.	pp. 225–226	Practice Questions I: 1, 3, 10, 19; Practice Questions II: 1, 7.	Segment 1: *Body and Brain Growth*
2. Describe changes in eating habits and nutritional needs during the preschool years, noting some of the nutritional challenges and risks for children in this stage.	pp. 226–229	Practice Questions I: 5, 16; Practice Questions II: 12; Applying Your Knowledge: 12.	Segment 1: *Body and Brain Growth*
3. Discuss the brain processes of myelination and lateralization and their development during early childhood.	pp. 229–233	Key Terms: 1, 2, 3; Practice Questions I: 7, 9, 13, 14, 17; Practice Questions II: 2, 13, 16, 17; Applying Your Knowledge: 1, 3.	Segment 1: *Body and Brain Growth*
4. Describe the prevalence of accidental injuries during early childhood, describe some measures that have significantly reduced accidental death rates for children, and identify several factors that contribute to this problem.	pp. 242–247	Key Terms: 8, 9, 10, 11; Practice Questions I: 4, 8, 22; Practice Questions II: 11, 18, 23, 24, 25; Applying Your Knowledge: 6.	
5. Describe the maturation of the prefrontal cortex and the regulation of attention in early childhood.	pp. 233–235	Key Terms: 4; Practice Questions I: 2, 11, 18; Practice Questions II: 10, 19.	

Learning Objective	**Textbook**	**Course Student Guide**	**Video Lesson**
6. Distinguish between gross and fine motor skills, and discuss the development of each during early childhood.	pp. 238–241	Practice Questions I: 6, 7, 21; Practice Questions II: 8, 9, 14, 15; Applying Your Knowledge: 4, 5, 7, 10.	Segment 1: *Body and Brain Growth* Segment 2: *Motor Skills*
7. Discuss the significance of artistic expression during early childhood.	p. 241	Practice Questions I: 12; Practice Questions II: 4.	
8. Identify the various categories and consequences of child maltreatment.	pp. 247–251	Key Terms: 12, 13, 14, 15, 16, 17; Practice Questions I: 25; Practice Questions II: 6, 21, 22; Applying Your Knowledge: 2, 8, 11.	Segment 3: *Maltreatment*
9. Discuss several factors that contribute to maltreatment, and describe current treatment and prevention efforts.	pp. 251–253	Key Terms: 18, 19, 20, 21; Practice Questions I: 23, 24; Practice Questions II: 3, 5, 23, 24, 25; Applying Your Knowledge: 2, 9.	Segment 3: *Maltreatment*
10. Describe how the expression and regulation of emotions are fostered by brain development and influenced by brain damage.	pp. 235–237	Key Terms: 5, 6, 7; Practice Questions I: 15, 20.	

Playing and Learning

Lesson 12

The Play Years: Cognitive Development

Preview

Young children reveal themselves to be remarkably thoughtful, insightful, and perceptive thinkers in countless everyday instances, as well as in findings of numerous research studies. Their memory of the past and mastery of language are sometimes astonishing. Lesson 12 begins by comparing Jean Piaget's and Lev Vygotsky's views of cognitive development at this age. According to Piaget, young children's thought is prelogical: between the ages of 2 and 6, they are unable to use logical principles and are limited by irreversible and static thinking. Lev Vygotsky, a contemporary of Piaget, saw learning more as a product of social interaction than of individual discovery.

The lesson next focuses on what preschoolers can do, including their competence in understanding number concepts, storing and retrieving memories, and theorizing about the world. This leads into a description of language development during early childhood. Although young children demonstrate rapid improvement in vocabulary and grammar, they have difficulty with abstractions, metaphorical speech, and certain rules of grammar. The lesson concludes with a discussion of preschool education, including a description of "quality" preschool programs and an evaluation of their lifelong impact on children.

As you complete this lesson, consider the cognitive development of any children you know in this age group (2 to 6). Consider what these children understand already and what they have yet to learn. Observe how they think—how they look at the world, interpret events, draw conclusions, and make decisions. Note how these children discover knowledge on their own and how they learn new skills through the guidance of parents, caregivers, and other children. Also, consider the memory skills of these children. For instance, how well can they remember events of their day and how well can they describe them? Consider their language skills—the extent of their vocabulary and their use of grammar. Finally, do any of these children go to day care or preschool? If so, what type of care are they receiving? What sort of learning experiences are they exposed to and how might that exposure affect their development later in life?

Prior Knowledge That Will Be Used in This Lesson

- This lesson will return to Piaget's theory of cognitive development (from Lesson 1) with a discussion of *preoperational thought*. Recall that Piaget's theory specifies four major periods of cognitive development:
  1. Sensorimotor (birth to 2 years)
  2. **Preoperational (2 to 6 years) ←The Play Years**
  3. Concrete Operational (7 to 11 years)
  4. Formal Operational (12 years through adulthood)
- This lesson will return to the sociocultural theories of Lev Vygotsky (from Lesson 1). Recall that Vygotsky emphasized the importance of **guided participation**, a process in which an individual learns through social interaction with a mentor who offers assistance, models strategies, and provides explicit instruction as needed.

Learning Objectives

Use this information to guide your reading, viewing, thinking, and studying. After successfully completing this lesson, you should be able to:

1. Describe the major characteristics of preoperational thought, according to Piaget.
2. Contrast Vygotsky's views on cognitive development with those of Piaget, focusing on the concept of guided participation.
3. Explain the significance of the zone of proximal development and scaffolding in promoting cognitive growth.
4. Describe Vygotsky's view of the role of language in cognitive growth.
5. Discuss more recent research on conservation, and explain why these and other findings have led to qualification or revision of Piaget's description of cognition during early childhood.
6. Discuss young children's memory abilities and limitations, noting the role of prior knowledge in their ability to recall events.
7. Describe the concept of a theory-theory, and explain the typical young child's theory of mind, noting how it is affected by culture and context.
8. Outline the sequence by which vocabulary and grammar develop during early childhood, and discuss limitations in the young child's language abilities.
9. Explain the role of fast-mapping in children's acquisition of language.
10. Describe the costs and benefits of bilingualism and the concept of balanced bilingualism.
11. Identify the characteristics of high-quality early-childhood education programs, and describe the different types of programs and the benefits of each type.

Textbook Reading & Video Viewing

For the most effective study of this lesson, complete the assignments in the sequence listed below.

Before viewing the video program:

Read Chapter 9, "Early Childhood: Cognitive Development," pages 257–287.

View the video for Lesson 12, "Playing and Learning."

Segment 1: *How Preschoolers Think*

Segment 2: *Words and Memories*

Segment 3: *Early Childhood Education*

After viewing the video program:

Review all reading assignments for this lesson.

Complete the "Practice Questions" and "Applying Your Knowledge" sections to reinforce your understanding of important terms and concepts and measure your achievement of the Learning Objectives. Check your answers with the feedback given and review when necessary.

Practice Questions I

Multiple-Choice Questions

1. Piaget believed that children are in the preoperational stage from ages
   a. 6 months to 1 year.
   b. 1 to 3 years.
   c. 2 to 6 years.
   d. 5 to 11 years.

2. Which of the following is **NOT** a characteristic of preoperational thinking?
   a. focus on appearance
   b. static reasoning
   c. lack of imagination
   d. centration

3. Which of the following provides evidence that early childhood is a sensitive period, rather than a critical period, for language learning?
   a. People can and do master language after early childhood.
   b. Vocabulary, grammar, and pronunciation are acquired especially easily during early childhood.
   c. Neurological characteristics of the young child's developing brain facilitate language acquisition.
   d. a and b
   e. a, b, and c

4. Which of the following is **NOT** associated with a more advanced theory of mind?
   a. having a younger sibling
   b. neurological maturation
   c. mother–child conversations that include thoughts and wishes
   d. certain cultural contexts
5. The vocabulary of preschool children consists primarily of
   a. metaphors.
   b. self-created words.
   c. abstract nouns.
   d. verbs and concrete nouns.
6. Preschoolers sometimes apply the rules of grammar even when they shouldn't. This tendency is called
   a. overregularization.
   b. centration.
   c. fast-mapping.
   d. conservation.
7. The Russian psychologist Lev Vygotsky emphasized that
   a. language advances children's thoughts.
   b. children form concepts first, then find words to express them.
   c. language and other cognitive developments are unrelated at this stage.
   d. preschoolers learn language only for egocentric purposes.
8. Private speech can be described as
   a. a way of formulating ideas to oneself.
   b. fantasy.
   c. an early learning difficulty.
   d. the beginnings of deception.
9. The child who has not yet grasped the principle of conservation is likely to
   a. insist that a tall, narrow glass contains more liquid than a short, wide glass, even though both glasses actually contain the same amount.
   b. be incapable of egocentric thought.
   c. be able to reverse an event.
   d. do all of the above.

10. Research on the benefits of Head Start have demonstrated
    a. that Head Start produces better report cards, but more behavioral problems.
    b. that children's IQ scores significantly improve.
    c. varied results, with benefits most readily apparent for children who would not otherwise have access to early education programs.
    d. children's alienation from their original neighborhoods and families.

11. The best preschool programs are generally those that provide the greatest amount of
    a. behavioral control.
    b. adult-child conversation.
    c. instruction in conservation and other logical principles.
    d. demonstration of toys by professionals.

12. Relatively recent experiments have demonstrated that preschoolers can succeed at tests of conservation when
    a. they are allowed to work cooperatively with other children.
    b. the test is presented as a competition.
    c. the children are informed that their parents are observing them.
    d. the test is presented in a simple, gamelike way.

13. Through the process called fast-mapping, children
    a. immediately assimilate new words by connecting them through their assumed meaning to categories of words they have already mastered.
    b. acquire the concept of conservation at an earlier age than Piaget believed.
    c. are able to move beyond egocentric thinking.
    d. become skilled in the practical use of language.

True or False Items

Write T (for true) or F (for false) on the line in front of each statement.

14. _____ Piaget's description of cognitive development in early childhood has been universally rejected by contemporary developmentalists.

15. _____ Fast-mapping is nearly always precise.

16. _____ In conservation problems, many preschoolers are unable to understand the transformation because they focus exclusively on appearances.

17. _____ Preschoolers who use private speech have slower cognitive growth than those who do not.

18. _____ According to theory-theory, young children are continually seeking reasons, causes, and underlying principles.

19. _____ According to expert Kay Bussey in the video for this lesson, one of the most important limitations preschoolers have in terms of memory ability is their inability to report what they remember because of their limited language skills.

20. _____ Piaget believed that preschoolers' acquisition of language makes possible their cognitive development.

21. _____ With the beginning of preoperational thought, most preschoolers can understand abstract words.

22. _____ A preschooler who says "You comed up and hurted me" is demonstrating a lack of understanding of English grammar.

23. _____ Successful preschool programs generally have a low teacher-to-child ratio.

24. _____ Vygotsky believed that cognitive growth is largely a social activity.

Practice Questions II

Multiple-Choice Questions

1. When three-year-old Megan's parents tell her about the day they got married, she is confused about why she wasn't there, not understanding that her parents existed before she was born. Megan is demonstrating
   a. a lack of understanding of conservation.
   b. a focus on appearance.
   c. centration.
   d. static reasoning.

2. According to the textbook, scaffolding has such a powerful influence on children's behavior that it can even lead to the error of
   a. overimitation.
   b. fast-mapping.
   c. overregularization.
   d. all of the above.

3. A preschooler who focuses his or her attention on only one feature of a situation is demonstrating a characteristic of preoperational thought called
   a. centration.
   b. overregularization.
   c. reversibility.
   d. egocentrism.

4. One characteristic of preoperational intelligence is
   a. the ability to categorize objects.
   b. the ability to count in multiples of 5.
   c. the inability to perform logical operations.
   d. difficulty adjusting to changes in routine.

5. The zone of proximal development represents the
   a. skills or knowledge that are within the potential of the learner but are not yet mastered.
   b. influence of a child's peers on cognitive development.
   c. explosive period of language development during early childhood.
   d. normal variations in children's language proficiency.

6. According to Vygotsky, language advances thinking through private speech and by
   a. helping children to review privately what they know.
   b. helping children explain events to themselves.
   c. serving as a mediator of the social interaction that is a vital part of learning.
   d. facilitating the process of fast-mapping.

7. Irreversibility refers to the
   a. inability to understand that other people view the world from a different perspective than one's own.
   b. inability to think about more than one idea at a time.
   c. failure to understand that changing the arrangement of a group of objects doesn't change their number.
   d. failure to understand that undoing a process will restore the original conditions.

8. According to Piaget
   a. it is impossible for preoperational children to grasp the concept of conservation, no matter how carefully it is explained.
   b. preschoolers fail to solve conservation problems because they center their attention on the transformation that has occurred and ignore the changed appearances of the objects.
   c. with special training, even preoperational children are able to grasp some aspects of conservation.
   d. preschoolers fail to solve conservation problems because they have no theory of mind.

9. In order to scaffold a child's cognitive skills, parents
   a. simplify tasks.
   b. interpret the activity.
   c. help children find answers, while anticipating mistakes.
   d. do all of the above.

10. Which theorist would be likely to agree with the statement, "Learning is a social activity more than it is a matter of individual discovery"?

    a. Piaget
    b. Vygotsky
    c. both a and b
    d. neither a nor b

11. Children first demonstrate some understanding of grammar

    a. as soon as the first words are produced.
    b. once they begin to use language for practical purposes.
    c. through the process called fast-mapping.
    d. in their earliest two-word sentences.

12. Preschoolers sometimes seem forgetful because they

    a. are unable to benefit from private speech.
    b. have difficulty reporting what they have committed to memory.
    c. are egocentric in their thinking.
    d. have all of the above limitations.

13. During the preschool years, vocabulary increases exponentially, from about 500 words at age ________ to __________ at age 6.

    a. 2; about 7,000
    b. 2; more than 10,000
    c. 3; more than 20,000
    d. 3; about 25,000

14. Overregularization indicates that a child

    a. is clearly applying rules of grammar.
    b. persists in egocentric thinking.
    c. has not yet mastered the principle of conservation.
    d. does not yet have a theory of mind.

15. Regarding the value of preschool education, most developmentalists believe that

    a. most disadvantaged children will not benefit from an early preschool education.
    b. most disadvantaged children will benefit from an early preschool education.
    c. because of sleeper effects, the early benefits of preschool education are likely to disappear by grade 3.
    d. the relatively small benefits of antipoverty measures such as Head Start do not justify their huge costs.

Matching Items

Match each definition or description with its corresponding term.

Terms

16. __________ Reggio Emilia approach
17. __________ scaffolding
18. __________ theory of mind
19. __________ zone of proximal development
20. __________ overimitation
21. __________ fast-mapping
22. __________ irreversibility
23. __________ teacher-directed
24. __________ symbolic thought
25. __________ private speech
26. __________ guided participation
27. __________ child-directed

Definitions or Descriptions

a. understanding that words and items can stand for something else
b. a program of early childhood education that encourages creativity in a carefully designed setting
c. the cognitive distance between a child's actual and potential levels of development
d. an approach to preschool that stresses school readiness
e. the process whereby the child learns through social interaction with a "tutor"
f. our understanding of mental processes in ourselves and others
g. the process by which words are learned after only one hearing
h. when children copy irrelevant and/or inefficient actions modeled by adults
i. the internal use of language to form ideas
j. the inability to understand that original conditions are restored by the undoing of some process
k. structuring a child's participation in learning encounters
l. an approach to preschool that stresses children's development and growth

Applying Your Knowledge

1. An experimenter first shows a child two rows of checkers that each have the same number of checkers. Then, with the child watching, the experimenter elongates one row and asks the child if each of the two rows still has an equal number of checkers. This experiment tests the child's understanding of

   a. reversibility.
   b. conservation of matter.
   c. conservation of number.
   d. centration.

2. A preschooler believes that a "party" is the one and only attribute of a birthday. She says that Daddy doesn't have a birthday because he never has a party. This thinking demonstrates the tendency Piaget called

   a. egocentrism.
   b. centration.
   c. conservation of events.
   d. mental representation.

3. A child who understands that $3 + 4 = 7$ means that $7 - 4 = 3$ has had to master the concept of

   a. reversibility.
   b. number.
   c. conservation.
   d. egocentrism.

4. A four-year-old tells the teacher that a clown should not be allowed to visit the class because "Pat is 'fraid of clowns." The four-year-old thus shows that he can anticipate how another will feel. This is evidence of the beginnings of

   a. egocentrism.
   b. deception.
   c. a theory of mind.
   d. overimitation.

5. Which of the following examples **BEST** demonstrates scaffolding?

   a. Elizabeth helps her son prepare meatloaf for dinner. She gives him specific instructions and simplifies whenever possible.
   b. Roberto buys his daughter ice cream when she rides her two-wheel bike successfully.
   c. Carla decides not to ask her daughter for help, because she knows her daughter does not have much patience.
   d. Jason makes his son, Peter, go to bed early, because Peter swore at school.

6. An early childhood educator is given the job of selecting holiday entertainment for a group of preschool children. If the teacher agrees with the ideas of Vygotsky, of the following, she is **MOST** likely to select

   a. a simple television show that every child can understand.
   b. a hands-on experience that requires little adult supervision.
   c. brief, action-oriented play activities that the children and teachers will perform together.
   d. holiday puzzles for children to work on individually.

7. Which of the following children who live in the United States is **MOST** likely to achieve balanced bilingualism?

   a. Adam, whose parents speak English and who learns Spanish in school starting at age 5
   b. Martin, whose parents speak Spanish and whose teachers and peers speak English
   c. Carlos, whose mother speaks English to him and whose father speaks Spanish to him
   d. All of these children will be equally likely to achieve balanced bilingualism.

8. That a child produces sentences that follow such rules of word order as "the initiator of an action precedes the verb, the receiver of an action follows it" demonstrates a knowledge of

   a. grammar.
   b. semantics.
   c. pragmatics.
   d. phrase structure.

9. The two-year-old child who says, "We goed to the store," is making a grammatical

   a. overextension.
   b. overregularization.
   c. underextension.
   d. irreversibility.

10. An experimenter who makes two balls of clay of equal amount, then rolls one into a long, skinny rope and asks the child if the amounts are still the same, is testing the child's understanding of

    a. conservation.
    b. egocentrism.
    c. perspective.
    d. centration.

11. Dr. Jones, who believes that children's language growth greatly contributes to their cognitive growth, evidently is a proponent of the ideas of

    a. Piaget.
    b. Chomsky.
    c. Flavell.
    d. Vygotsky.

12. Jack constantly "talks down" to his three-year-old son's speech level. Jack's speech is

    a. appropriate because three-year-olds have barely begun to comprehend grammatical rules.
    b. commendable, given the importance of scaffolding in promoting cognitive growth.
    c. unnecessary because preschoolers are able to comprehend more complex grammar and vocabulary than they can produce.
    d. clearly within his son's zone of proximal development.

13. Four-year-old Annalee attends an early-childhood education program that follows the Reggio Emilia approach. Which of the following is **MOST** likely to be part of her experience?

    a. whole-class instruction in writing letters
    b. individualized projects
    c. emphasis on listening to the teacher
    d. drama and pretending

14. A preschooler fails to put together a difficult puzzle on her own, so her mother encourages her to try again, this time guiding her by asking questions such as, "For this space do we need a big piece or a little piece?" With Mom's help, the child successfully completes the puzzle. Lev Vygotsky would attribute the child's success to

    a. additional practice with the puzzle pieces.
    b. imitation of her mother's behavior.
    c. the social interaction with her mother that restructured the task to make its solution more attainable.
    d. modeling and reinforcement.

15. Mark is answering an essay question that asks him to "discuss the positions of major developmental theorists regarding the relationship between language and cognitive development." To help organize his answer, Mark jots down a reminder that _______________ contended that language is essential to the advancement of thinking, as private speech, and as a _______________ of social interactions.

    a. Piaget; mediator
    b. Vygotsky; mediator
    c. Piaget; theory
    d. Vygotsky; theory

Key Terms

1. **preoperational thought:** Piaget's term for cognitive development between the ages of about 2 and 6; it includes language and imagination (which involve symbolic thought), but logical, operational thinking is not yet possible at this stage. (p. 257; video lesson, segment 1; objective 1)

Memory aid: Operations are mental transformations involving the manipulation of ideas and symbols. Preoperational children, who lack the ability to perform transformations, are "before" this developmental milestone.

2. **symbolic thought:** A major accomplishment of preoperational intelligence that allows a child to think symbolically, including understanding that words can refer to things not seen and that an item, such as a flag, can symbolize something else (in this case, for instance, a country). (p. 258; objective 1)
3. **centration:** A characteristic of preoperational thought in which a young child focuses (centers) on one idea, excluding all others. (p. 258; video lesson, segment 1; objective 1)
4. **egocentrism:** Piaget's term for children's tendency to think about the world entirely from their own personal perspective. (p. 258; video lesson, segment 1; objective 1)
5. **focus on appearance:** A characteristic of preoperational thought in which a young child ignores all attributes that are not apparent. (p. 258; objective 1)
6. **static reasoning:** A characteristic of preoperational thought in which a young child thinks that nothing changes. Whatever is now has always been and always will be. (p. 258; objective 1)
7. **irreversibility:** A characteristic of preoperational thought in which a young child thinks that nothing can be undone. A thing cannot be restored to the way it was before a change occurred. (p. 258; video lesson, segment 1; objective 1)
8. **conservation:** The principle that the amount of a substance remains the same (i.e., is conserved) even when its appearance changes. (p. 259; video lesson, segment 1; objectives 1 & 5)
9. **animism:** The belief that natural objects and phenomena are alive. (p. 259; objective 1)
10. **guided participation:** The process by which people learn from others who guide their experiences and explorations. (p. 262; video lesson, segment 1; objective 2)
11. **zone of proximal development (ZPD):** Vygotsky's term for the skills—cognitive as well as physical—that a person can exercise only with assistance, not yet independently. (p. 262; video lesson, segment 1; objective 3)
12. **scaffolding:** Temporary support that is tailored to a learner's needs and abilities and aimed at helping the learner master the next task in a given learning process. (p. 262; video lesson, segment 1; objective 3)
13. **overimitation:** Occurs when a person imitates an action that is not a relevant part of the behavior to be learned. Overimitation is common among 2- to 6-year-olds when they imitate adult actions that are irrelevant and inefficient. (p. 263; objective 3)
14. **private speech:** The internal dialogue in which a person talks to himself or herself (either silently or out loud). Preschoolers' private speech, which often is uttered aloud, helps them think, review what they know, and decide what to do. (p. 263; objective 4)

15. **social mediation:** Human interaction that expands and advances understanding, often through words that one person uses to explain something to another. (p. 264; objective 4)
16. **theory-theory:** The idea that children attempt to explain everything they see and hear by constructing theories. (p. 266; objective 7)
17. **theory of mind:** A person's theory of what other people might be thinking. In order to have a theory of mind, children must realize that other people are not necessarily thinking the same thoughts that they themselves are. That realization seldom occurs before age 4. (p. 267; video lesson, segment 2; objective 7)
18. **fast-mapping:** The speedy and sometimes imprecise way in which children learn new words by tentatively placing them in mental categories according to their perceived meaning. (p. 270; video lesson, segment 2; objective 9)
19. **overregularization:** The application of rules of grammar even when exceptions occur, making the language seem more "regular" than it actually is. (p. 272; video lesson, segment 2; objective 8)
20. **balanced bilingual:** A person who is equally fluent in two languages and does not favor one or the other. (p. 274; objective 10)
21. **Montessori schools:** Institutions that offer early childhood education based on the philosophy of Maria Montessori, which emphasizes careful work and tasks that each young child can do (p. 277; objective 11)
22. **Reggio Emilia approach:** A famous program of early childhood education that originated in the town of Reggio Emilia, Italy. This approach encourages each child's creativity in a carefully designed setting. (p. 278; objective 11)
23. **Head Start:** A federally funded early-childhood intervention program for low-income children of preschool age. (p. 281; objective 11)
24. **apprentice in thinking:** Vygotsky's term describing young children, whose intellectual growth is stimulated by more skilled members of society. (video lesson, segment 1; objective 2)

Summary

Symbolic thought, which enables children to form mental representations of things and events they are not immediately experiencing, develops rapidly throughout the preschool years. Both language and imagination become tools of thought, making the typical four-year-old much more verbal and creative than the typical one-year-old.

Although preschool children can think symbolically, they cannot perform what Jean Piaget called "logical operations." One characteristic of this **preoperational intelligence** is **irreversibility**: Preschoolers do not generally understand that reversing a process will restore the original conditions. **Egocentrism** also limits the preschooler's ideas about the world to his or her own point of view. Preoperational children also fail to answer correctly problems involving **conservation**, indicating that they do not yet understand the idea that the amount of a substance is unaffected by changes in its shape or placement.

Centration refers to the tendency of preschoolers to focus or center their analysis on one aspect of a problem, for instance, the appearance of liquid in a glass. In tests of conservation, Piaget believed, the problem is that preschoolers center on only the height of the liquid and fail to consider the shape and diameter of the glass it is in. Another example of centration is the preschooler's tendency toward egocentrism—to see the world only from his or her perspective.

Piaget focused on the individual child's innate curiosity. In general, he believed that children will find a way to learn when they are ready to do so. In contrast, Lev Vygotsky emphasized the impact of cultural and social factors in learning, including the effects of mentors and teachers. For instance, Vygotsky believed that—for each individual and each skill—there is a **zone of proximal development**, which represents the cognitive distance between the child's actual and potential levels of development. To encourage development, mentors can **scaffold** learning—in other words, provide structured assistance to help the child master new skills. Vygotsky also believed that language advances thinking in two ways: through **private speech** that an individual child uses to assist his or her thinking, and as **social mediation**, a tool of verbal interaction between mentor and apprentice. While these approaches are sometimes described as contradictory, a closer examination reveals that they may simply emphasize two different aspects of cognitive development.

Recent experiments have shown that preschoolers are not as illogical as Piaget believed. For example, under certain circumstances, young children can demonstrate the concept of conservation. They also develop an elementary theory of mind about their own and others' mental processes.

During early childhood, children are gaining a better understanding of their own thoughts and feelings. In addition, they are beginning to develop informal theories about why other people act the way they do. In time this develops into what psychologists call a **theory of mind**, an understanding of human mental processes. This understanding helps children explain basic everyday questions, such as how a person's knowledge and emotions affect his or her actions and how people can have such different perceptions, intentions, and desires. The development of a theory of mind appears to be influenced by a number of factors, including brain maturation, language proficiency, having older siblings, and culture.

Language development during early childhood includes learning 10,000 words or more, in a predictable sequence according to parts of speech. Words are often learned after only one hearing, through the process called **fast-mapping**. By age 3, children demonstrate extensive grammatical knowledge, although they often apply grammatical rules even when they should not (**overregularization**).

There is much controversy about whether language-minority children should be encouraged to develop fluency in both the minority language and the majority language and how this is associated with cognitive development. Being a **balanced bilingual**, that is, equally fluent in two languages, appears to be the best solution.

Changes in family composition and work patterns have resulted in great increases in early-childhood education programs. A high-quality preschool program is characterized by a low child-teacher ratio, a staff with training and credentials in early-childhood education, a curriculum geared toward cognitive development rather than behavioral control, and an organization of space that facilitates creative and constructive play.

There are notable differences among early-childhood education programs. Child-directed programs stress children's development and growth and focus on children's play and exploration. Teacher-directed programs, in contrast, stress preparation for school. Longitudinal evaluations have demonstrated that early education programs such as **Head Start** can have substantial long-term benefits.

Answer Key

Practice Questions I

Multiple-Choice Questions

1. c. is the correct answer. (video lesson, segment 1; objective 1)
2. c. is the correct answer. In fact, preoperational children have excellent imaginations, as revealed by their symbolic play. (objective 1)
3. e. is correct the answer. (objective 8)
4. a. is the correct answer. (objective 7)

   b., c., & d. are incorrect. Brain maturation, mother–child conversations that include thoughts and wishes, and cultural variations such as the amount of time a child spends being read to versus watching television are all associated with a more advanced theory of mind.
5. d. is the correct answer. (objective 9)

   a. & c. are incorrect. Preschoolers generally have great difficulty understanding, and therefore using, metaphors and abstract nouns.

   b. is incorrect. Other than the grammatical errors of overregularization, the textbook does not indicate that preschoolers use a significant number of self-created words.
6. a. is the correct answer. (video lesson, segment 2; objective 8)

   b. & d. are incorrect. These terms refer to the thinking of preoperational children.

   c. is incorrect. This term refers to how young children often learn new words.
7. a. is the correct answer. (objective 4)

   b. is incorrect. This expresses the views of Piaget.

   c. is incorrect. Because he believed that language facilitates thinking, Vygotsky clearly believed that language and other cognitive developments are intimately related.

   d. is incorrect. Vygotsky did not hold this view.
8. a. is the correct answer. (objective 4)
9. a. is the correct answer. (video lesson, segment 1; objective 1)

   b., c., & d. are incorrect. Failure to conserve is the result of thinking that is centered on appearances. Egocentrism and irreversibility are also examples of centered thinking.
10. c. is the correct answer. (objective 11)
11. b. is the correct answer. (video lesson, segment 3; objective 11)

12. d. is the correct answer. (video lesson, segment 1; objective 5)
13. a. is the correct answer. (video lesson, segment 2; objective 9)

True or False Items

14. F More recent research has found that children may understand conservation earlier than Piaget thought, given a more gamelike presentation. His theory has not been rejected overall, however. (video lesson, segment 1; objective 5)
15. F (objective 9)
16. T (video lesson, segment 1; objective 1)
17. F In fact, just the opposite is true. Children who have learning difficulties tend to be slower to develop private speech. (objective 4)
18. T (objective 7)
19. T (video lesson, segment 2; objective 6)
20. F This was Vygotsky's hypothesis. (objectives 1 & 4)
21. F Preschoolers have difficulty understanding abstract words because they have no concrete referent. (video lesson, segment 2; objective 8)
22. F In adding "ed" to form a past tense, the child has indicated an understanding of the grammatical rule for making past tenses in English, even though the construction in these two cases is incorrect. (video lesson, segment 2; objective 8)
23. T (video lesson, segment 3; objective 11)
24. T (video lesson, segment 1; objective 2)

Practice Questions II

Multiple-Choice Questions

1. d. is the correct answer. (objective 1)

   a., b., & c. are incorrect. Although these *are* characteristics of preoperational thinking, they are not the source of Megan's confusion.

2. a. is the correct answer. (objective 1)

   b. & c. are incorrect. Fast-mapping and overregularization are characteristics of language development during early childhood and are not necessarily dependant on scaffolding.

3. a. is the correct answer. (video lesson, segment 1; objective 1)

   b. is incorrect. Overregularization is the child's tendency to apply grammatical rules even when he or she shouldn't.

   c. is incorrect. Reversibility is the concept that reversing an operation, such as addition, will restore the original conditions.

   d. is incorrect. This term is used to refer to the young child's belief that people think as he or she does.

4. c. is the correct answer. This is why the stage is called preoperational. (video lesson, segment 1; objective 1)
5. a. is the correct answer. (video lesson, segment 1; objective 3)

6. c. is the correct answer. (objective 4)

   a. & b. are incorrect. These are both advantages of private speech.

   d. is incorrect. Fast-mapping is the process by which new words are acquired, often after only one hearing.

7. d. is the correct answer. (video lesson, segment 1; objective 1)

   a. is incorrect. This describes egocentrism.

   b. is incorrect. This is the opposite of centration.

   c. is incorrect. This defines conservation of number.

8. a. is the correct answer. (objective 5)

   b. is incorrect. According to Piaget, preschoolers fail to solve conservation problems because they focus on the appearance of objects and ignore the transformation that has occurred.

   c. is incorrect. Piaget believed that preoperational children are entirely unable to conserve.

   d. is incorrect. Piaget did not relate conservation to a theory of mind.

9. d. is the correct answer. (video lesson, segment 1; objective 3)

10. b. is the correct answer. (video lesson, segment 1; objective 2)

    a. is incorrect. Piaget believed that learning is a matter of individual discovery.

11. d. is the correct answer. Preschoolers almost always put subject before verb in their two-word sentences. (video lesson, segment 2; objective 8)

12. b. is the correct answer. (video lesson, segment 2; objective 6)

    a. is incorrect. Preschoolers do tend to use private speech.

    c. is incorrect. Although this type of thinking is somewhat characteristic of preschoolers, it has no impact on memory per se.

13. b. is the correct answer. (objective 8)

14. a. is the correct answer. (video lesson, segment 2; objective 8)

    b., c., & d. are incorrect. Overregularization is a linguistic phenomenon rather than a characteristic type of thinking (b & d), or a logical principle (c).

15. b. is the correct answer. (objective 11)

Matching Items

16. b (objective 11)
17. k (video lesson, segment 1; objective 3)
18. f (video lesson, segment 2; objective 7)
19. c (video lesson, segment 1; objective 3)
20. h (objective 4)
21. g (video lesson, segment 2; objective 9)
22. j (video lesson, segment 1; objective 1)
23. d (objective 11)
24. a (objective 1)

25. i (objective 4)
26. e (video lesson, segment 1; objective 2)
27. l (objective 11)

Applying Your Knowledge

1. c. is the correct answer. (video lesson, segment 1; objective 1)

   a. is incorrect. A test of reversibility would ask a child to perform an operation, such as adding 4 to 3, and then reverse the process (subtract 3 from 7) to determine whether the child understood that the original condition
   (the number 4) was restored.

   b. is incorrect. A test of conservation of matter would transform the appearance of an object, such as a ball of clay, to determine whether the child understood that the object remained the same.

   d. is incorrect. A test of centration would involve the child's ability to see various aspects of a situation.

2. b. is the correct answer. (video lesson, segment 1; objective 1)

   a. is incorrect. Egocentrism is thinking that is self-centered.

   c. is incorrect. This is not a concept in Piaget's theory.

   d. is incorrect. Mental representation is an example of symbolic thought.

3. a. is the correct answer. (objective 1)
4. c. is the correct answer. (video lesson, segment 2; objective 7)

   a. is incorrect. Egocentrism is self-centered thinking.

   b. is incorrect. Although deception provides evidence of a theory of mind, the child in this example is not deceiving anyone.

   d. is incorrect. Overimitation is the tendency for children to mimic even the unhelpful elements of modeled behavior.

5. a. is the correct answer. (objective 3)
6. c. is the correct answer. In Vygotsky's view, learning is a social activity more than a matter of individual discovery. Thus, social interaction that provides motivation and focuses attention facilitates learning. (video lesson, segment 1; objective 2)

   a., b., & d. are incorrect. These situations either provide no opportunity for social interaction (b & d) or do not challenge the children (a).

7. c. is the correct answer. (objective 10)
8. a. is the correct answer. (video lesson, segment 2; objective 8)

   b. & d. are incorrect. The textbook does not discuss these aspects of language.

   c. is incorrect. Pragmatics, which is not mentioned in the text, refers to the practical use of language in varying social contexts.

9. b. is the correct answer. (video lesson, segment 2; objective 8)
10. a. is the correct answer. (video lesson, segment 1; objective 1)

11. d. is the correct answer. (objective 4)

    a. is incorrect. Piaget believed that cognitive growth precedes language development.

    b. & c. are incorrect. Chomsky focused on the acquisition of language, and Flavell emphasizes cognition.

12. c. is the correct answer. (objective 8)
13. d. is the correct answer. (objective 11)
14. c. is the correct answer. (video lesson, segment 1; objective 3)
15. b. is the correct answer. (objective 4)

Lesson Review

Lesson 12

The Play Years
Cognitive Development

Please Note: Use this matrix to guide your study and achieve the learning objectives of this lesson. It will also help you to view the video, which defines and demonstrates important concepts and skills as they relate to everyday life.

Learning Objective	Textbook	Course Student Guide	Video Lesson
1. Describe the major characteristics of preoperational thought, according to Piaget.	pp. 257–260	Key Terms: 1, 2, 3, 4, 5, 6, 7, 8, 9; Practice Questions I: 1, 2, 9, 16, 20; Practice Questions II: 1, 2, 3, 4, 7, 22, 24; Applying Your Knowledge: 1, 2, 3, 10.	Segment 1: *How Preschoolers Think*
2. Contrast Vygotsky's views on cognitive development with those of Piaget, focusing on the concept of guided participation.	pp. 261–262	Key Terms: 10, 24; Practice Questions I: 24; Practice Questions II: 10, 26; Applying Your Knowledge: 6.	Segment 1: *How Preschoolers Think*
3. Explain the significance of the zone of proximal development and scaffolding in promoting cognitive growth.	pp. 262–263	Key Terms: 11, 12, 13; Practice Questions II: 5, 9, 17, 19; Applying Your Knowledge: 14.	Segment 1: *How Preschoolers Think*
4. Describe Vygotsky's view of the role of language in cognitive growth.	pp. 263–265	Key Terms: 14, 15; Practice Questions I: 7, 8, 17, 20; Practice Questions II: 6, 25; Applying Your Knowledge: 11, 15.	
5. Discuss more recent research on conservation, and explain why these and other findings have led to qualification or revision of Piaget's description of cognition during early childhood.	pp. 260–261	Key Terms: 8; Practice Questions I: 12, 14; Practice Questions II: 8; Applying Your Knowledge: 3.	Segment 1: *How Preschoolers Think*

Learning Objective	Textbook	Course Student Guide	Video Lesson
6. Discuss young children's memory abilities and limitations, noting the role of prior knowledge in their ability to recall events.	*	Practice Questions I: 19; Practice Questions II: 12.	Segment 2: *Words and Memories*
7. Describe the concept of a theory-theory, and explain the typical young child's theory of mind, noting how it is affected by culture and context.	pp. 266–269	Key Terms: 16, 17; Practice Questions I: 4, 18; Practice Questions II: 18; Applying Your Knowledge: 4.	Segment 2: *Words and Memories*
8. Outline the sequence by which vocabulary and grammar develop during early childhood, and discuss limitations in the young child's language abilities.	pp. 269–272	Key Terms: 19; Practice Questions I: 3, 6, 12, 21, 22; Practice Questions II: 11, 13, 14, 20; Applying Your Knowledge: 8, 9, 12.	Segment 2: *Words and Memories*
9. Explain the role of fast-mapping in children's acquisition of language.	pp. 270–271	Key Terms: 18; Practice Questions I: 5, 13, 15; Practice Questions II: 21.	Segment 2: *Words and Memories*
10. Describe the costs and benefits of bilingualism and the concept of balanced bilingualism.	pp. 272–274	Key Terms: 20; Applying Your Knowledge: 7.	
11. Identify the characteristics of high-quality early-childhood education programs, and describe the different types of programs and the benefits of each type.	pp. 275–285	Key Terms: 21, 22, 23; Practice Questions I: 10, 11, 23; Practice Questions II: 15, 16, 23, 27; Applying Your Knowledge: 13.	Segment 3: *Early Childhood Education*

* The video for this lesson offers excellent coverage of this topic.

Playing and Socializing

Lesson 13

The Play Years: Psychosocial Development

Preview

Lesson 13 explores the ways in which young children begin to relate to others in an ever-widening social environment. The lesson begins with emotional development and the continuing emergence of the sense of self. With their increasing social awareness, children become more concerned with how others evaluate them and better able to regulate their emotions.

Next, the lesson explores the origins of helpful, cooperative behaviors in young children, as well as aggression and other hurtful behaviors. These social skills reflect many influences, including the quality of early attachments and learning from playmates through various types of play, as well as from television.

The lesson also describes the increasing complexity of children's interactions with others, paying special attention to the different styles of parenting and how factors such as the cultural, ethnic, and community contexts influence parenting.

The lesson concludes with a description of children's emerging awareness of male-female differences and gender identity. Several major theories of gender-role development are considered.

As you complete this lesson, consider the psychosocial development of one or more preschoolers you know. Consider their self-understanding—what do they think and feel about themselves? How do they interact with adults and other children? What sort of play activities do they engage in, and how might this affect their development? How good are they at controlling their own emotions and behavior? Finally, consider the relationship these children have with their parents. How do the parents support and guide their kids, and how to they handle discipline and punishment?

Prior Knowledge That Will Be Used in This Lesson

- This lesson will return to Erik Erikson's theory (introduced in Lesson 1) that specifies eight stages of psychosocial development, each of which is characterized by a particular challenge, or developmental crisis, which is central to that stage of life and must be resolved:

1. Trust vs. Mistrust (birth to 1 year)
2. Autonomy vs. Shame and Doubt (1 to 3 years)
3. **Initiative vs. Guilt (3 to 6 years) ←The Play Years**
4. Industry vs. Inferiority (7 to 11 years)
5. Identity vs. Role Confusion (adolescence)
6. Intimacy vs. Isolation (adulthood)
7. Generativity vs. Stagnation (adulthood)
8. Integrity vs. Despair (adulthood)

- Several major developmental theories (from Lesson 1) will be used to help explain gender-role development during early childhood. Recall that:
  1. Freud's theory specifies stages of psychosexual development, during which the child battles unconscious, biological impulses.
  2. Behaviorism emphasizes the effect of conditioning, as the child responds to stimuli, reinforcement and modeling in his or her immediate environment.
  3. Cognitive theory emphasizes how the child's intellectual processes and thinking affect his or her beliefs and actions.
  4. Sociocultural theory reminds us that development is embedded in a rich cultural context, and is often influenced by the guidance of parents and mentors.
  5. Evolutionary theory emphasizes the driving power of the basic urges to survive and reproduce that all living things possess.

Learning Objectives

Use this information to guide your reading, viewing, thinking, and studying. After successfully completing this lesson, you should be able to:

1. Discuss emotional development during early childhood, focusing on emotional regulation.
2. Discuss the importance of positive self-evaluation during this period, noting the child's developing self-concept, self-esteem, intrinsic motivation, and extrinsic motivation.
3. Describe the development of empathy and antipathy, and define and give examples of prosocial and antisocial behaviors.
4. Describe the different forms of aggression demonstrated by young children, and discuss the role of television and video games in encouraging these and other antisocial behaviors.
5. Discuss the role of play in the development of social skills, focusing on the benefits of rough-and-tumble and sociodramatic play.
6. Compare the three classic styles of parenting, and discuss the factors that might account for variations in parenting style.

7. Discuss the pros and cons of the most common methods of discipline, and describe the most effective methods for disciplining a child regarding both short-term and long-term behavioral modification as well as overall moral development.
8. Distinguish between sex differences and gender differences, and describe the developmental progression of gender awareness in young children.
9. Summarize the three grand theories' and the newer theories' take on gender-role development during early childhood, noting important contributions of each.

Textbook Reading & Video Viewing

For the most effective study of this lesson, complete the assignments in the sequence listed below.

Before viewing the video program:

Read Chapter 10, "Early Childhood: Psychosocial Development," pages 289–318.

View the video for Lesson 13, "Playing and Socializing."

Segment 1: *Social Awareness*

Segment 2: *Emotional Regulation*

Segment 3: *Parenting Styles*

After viewing the video program:

Review all reading assignments for this lesson.

Complete the "Practice Questions" and "Applying Your Knowledge" sections to reinforce your understanding of important terms and concepts and measure your achievement of the Learning Objectives. Check your answers with the feedback given and review when necessary.

Practice Questions I

Multiple-Choice Questions

1. Preschool children have a clear (but not necessarily accurate) concept of self. Typically, the preschooler believes that she or he

   a. owns all objects in sight.

   b. is great at almost everything.

   c. is much less competent than peers and older children.

   d. is more powerful than her or his parents.

2. According to Freud, the third stage of psychosexual development, during which the penis is the focus of psychological concern and pleasure, is the

   a. oral stage.

   b. anal stage.

   c. phallic stage.

   d. latency period.

3. Because it helps children rehearse social roles, work out fears and fantasies, and learn cooperation, an important form of social play is

   a. sociodramatic play.

   b. mastery play.

   c. rough-and-tumble play.

   d. sensorimotor play.

4. The three basic patterns of parenting described by Diana Baumrind are

   a. hostile, loving, and harsh.

   b. authoritarian, permissive, and authoritative.

   c. positive, negative, and punishing.

   d. abusive, democratic, and traditional.

5. Authoritative parents are receptive and loving, and they also

   a. set limits and enforce rules.

   b. have difficulty communicating.

   c. withhold praise and affection.

   d. encourage aggressive behavior.

6. Children who watch a lot of violent television

   a. are more likely to be aggressive.

   b. are particularly susceptible to its effects if they are already aggressive.

   c. tend to spend less time in social and educational activities.

   d. have all of the above characteristics.

7. During early childhood, a child's self-concept includes all of the following **EXCEPT** his or her

   a. expanding range of skills and competencies.

   b. physical appearance.

   c. gender.

   d. realistic assessment of abilities.

8. Behaviorists emphasize the importance of ________________ in the development of the preschool child.

   a. identification

   b. praise and blame

   c. initiative

   d. a theory of mind

9. Children apply gender labels consistently as early as age
   a. 2.
   b. 3.
   c. 4.
   d. 5.

10. When a child demonstrates understanding of another person's feelings and concerns, he or she possesses _______________ toward that person.
    a. antipathy
    b. prosocial
    c. empathy
    d. sympathy

11. Six-year-old Elijah has superior verbal ability rivaling that of most girls his age. Dr. Laurent believes that although his sex is predisposed to slower language development, Elijah's upbringing in a linguistically rich home enhanced his biological capabilities. Dr. Laurent is evidently a proponent of
    a. cognitive theory.
    b. gender-schema theory.
    c. sociocultural theory.
    d. evolutionary theory.

12. Three-year-old Jake, who lashes out at the family pet in anger, is displaying signs of _______________ problems and that he is emotionally _______________.
    a. internalizing; overcontrolled
    b. internalizing; undercontrolled
    c. externalizing; overcontrolled
    d. externalizing; undercontrolled

13. When her friend hurts her by stepping on her foot, Lauren impulsively shouts that she is a "mean old stinker!" Lauren's behavior is an example of
    a. instrumental aggression.
    b. reactive aggression.
    c. bullying aggression.
    d. relational aggression.

True or False Items

Write T (for true) or F (for false) on the line in front of each statement.

14. _____ According to Diana Baumrind, only authoritarian parents make maturity demands on their children.

15. _____ Children of authoritative parents tend to be successful, happy with themselves, and generous with others.

16. _____ Differences between males and females that are truly sex differences are more apparent in childhood than in adulthood.

17. _____ Spanking is associated with higher rates of aggression toward peers.

18. _____ Preschool children are generally extrinsically motivated.

19. _____ When young children behave in ways that demonstrate they understand another person's sadness or frustration, they are indicating that they feel empathy for that other person.

20. _____ Developmentalists do not agree about how children acquire gender roles.

21. _____ Identification was defined by Freud as a defense mechanism in which people ally themselves with others by taking on their behaviors and attitudes.

Practice Questions II

Multiple-Choice Questions

1. Of the following, what is particularly likely to be lacking in children of permissive parents is
   a. social skills.
   b. self-control.
   c. initiative and guilt.
   d. care and concern.

2. Children learn negotiation and cooperation most readily from their interaction with
   a. their mothers.
   b. their fathers.
   c. peers.
   d. dolls and action figures.

3. The initial advantages of an authoritative parenting style
   a. do not persist past middle childhood.
   b. remain apparent through adolescence.
   c. are likely to be even stronger over time.
   d. have an unpredictable impact later in children's lives.

4. True prosocial behavior is possible as early as _________________; true antisocial behavior is possible as early as _________________.
   a. toddlerhood; toddlerhood
   b. toddlerhood; age 4 or 5
   c. age 4 or 5; toddlerhood
   d. age 4 or 5; age 4 or 5

5. According to Freud, a young boy's jealousy of his father's relationship with his mother, and the guilt feelings that result, are part of the
   a. Electra complex.
   b. Oedipus complex.
   c. phallic complex.
   d. penis envy complex.
6. The style of parenting in which the parents make few demands on children, the discipline is lax, and the parents are nurturant and accepting is
   a. authoritarian.
   b. authoritative.
   c. permissive.
   d. rejecting-neglecting.
7. Cooperating with a playmate is to ________________ as insulting a playmate is to ________________.
   a. antisocial behavior; prosocial behavior
   b. prosocial behavior; antisocial behavior
   c. emotional regulation; antisocial behavior
   d. prosocial behavior; emotional regulation
8. Of the following types of play identified by Mildred Parten (1932), which is the most social?
   a. cooperative play
   b. parallel play
   c. onlooker play
   d. associative play
9. Which of the following theories advocates the development of gender identification as a means of avoiding guilt over feelings for the opposite-sex parent?
   a. learning
   b. sociocultural
   c. psychoanalytic
   d. social learning
10. A parent who wishes to use a time-out to discipline her son for behaving aggressively on the playground would be advised to
   a. have the child sit quietly indoors for a few minutes.
   b. tell her son that he will be punished later at home.
   c. tell the child that he will not be allowed to play outdoors for the rest of the week.
   d. choose a different disciplinary technique since time-outs are ineffective.

11. Which of the following explanations of gender identity and gender differences is consistent with cognitive theory?
    a. Compliance with gender roles is reinforced, punished, and modeled.
    b. Children identify with their same-sex parent, adopting that parent's attitudes and behavior.
    c. Children's self-concept and self-esteem lead them to categorize themselves as either male or female, and that categorization then leads them to behave in a way that is consistent with the category.
    d. Every culture teaches to their children the values and attitudes regarding appropriate behavior for males and females.
12. Emotional regulation is in part related to maturation of a specific portion of the brain in the
    a. prefrontal cortex.
    b. parietal cortex.
    c. temporal lobe.
    d. occipital lobe.
13. In which style of parenting is the parents' word law and misbehavior strictly punished?
    a. permissive
    b. authoritative
    c. authoritarian
    d. uninvolved
14. Erikson noted that preschoolers eagerly begin many new activities but are vulnerable to criticism and feelings of failure; in other words, they experience the crisis of
    a. identity versus role confusion.
    b. initiative versus guilt.
    c. basic trust versus mistrust.
    d. efficacy versus helplessness.

Matching Items

Match each theorist, term, or concept with its corresponding description or definition.

Theorists, Terms, and Concepts

15. __________ rough-and-tumble play
16. __________ imaginary friends
17. __________ sociodramatic play
18. __________ prosocial behavior
19. __________ antisocial behavior
20. __________ Electra complex
21. __________ Oedipus complex
22. __________ authoritative
23. __________ authoritarian
24. __________ identification
25. __________ instrumental aggression

Descriptions or Definitions

a. aggressive behavior whose purpose is to obtain an object desired by another
b. Freudian theory that every daughter secretly wishes to replace her mother
c. parenting style associated with high maturity demands and low parent-child communication
d. an action performed for the benefit of another person without the expectation of reward
e. Freudian theory that every son secretly wishes to replace his father
f. parenting style associated with high maturity demands and high parent-child communication
g. two children wrestle without serious hostility
h. an action that is intended to harm someone else
i. two children act out roles in a story of their own creation
j. a defense mechanism through which children cope with their feelings of guilt during the phallic stage
k. help children develop emotional regulation and combat loneliness

Applying Your Knowledge

1. According to Freud, Jana eventually copes with the fear and anger she feels over her hatred of her mother and love of her father by
   a. identifying with her mother.
   b. copying her brother's behavior.
   c. adopting her father's moral code.
   d. competing with her brother for her father's attention.

2. A little girl who says she wants her mother to go on vacation so that she can marry her father is voicing a fantasy consistent with the ________________ described by Freud.
   a. Oedipus complex
   b. Electra complex
   c. theory of mind
   d. crisis of initiative versus guilt

3. According to Erikson, *before* the preschool years children are incapable of feeling guilt because
   a. guilt depends on a sense of self, which is not sufficiently established in toddlerhood.
   b. they do not yet understand that they are male or female for life.
   c. this emotion is unlikely to have been reinforced at such an early age.
   d. guilt is associated with the resolution of the Oedipus complex, which occurs later in life.

4. Parents who are strict and aloof are most likely to make their children
   a. cooperative and trusting.
   b. obedient but unhappy.
   c. violent.
   d. withdrawn and anxious.
5. When four-year-old Bonita wants Aldo's beanie baby, she slaps Aldo's hand away, displaying an example of
   a. bullying aggression.
   b. reactive aggression.
   c. instrumental aggression.
   d. relational aggression.
6. The belief that almost all sexual patterns are learned rather than inborn would find its strongest adherents among
   a. cognitive theorists.
   b. behaviorists.
   c. psychoanalytic theorists.
   d. evolutionary theorists.
7. In explaining the origins of gender distinctions, Dr. Christie notes that every society teaches its children its values and attitudes regarding preferred behavior for men and women. Dr. Christie is evidently a proponent of
   a. gender-schema theory.
   b. sociocultural theory.
   c. evolutionary theory.
   d. psychoanalytic theory.
8. Which of the following is **LEAST** likely to be true of four-year-old Keshawn?
   a. His developing attention span allows him to complete projects, for which he can then be proud of accomplishing.
   b. He is more willing to try new experiences than when he was younger.
   c. He is self-critical and believes that he cannot do complicated tasks, such as difficult puzzles.
   d. He believes that whatever he is (dark skinned, male) is good.
9. An angry four-year-old might stop herself from hitting another child because she has developed
   a. social referencing.
   b. self-esteem.
   c. identification.
   d. emotional regulation.

10. Concerning children's concept of gender, which of the following statements is true?
    a. Before the age of 3 or so, children think that boys and girls can change gender as they get older.
    b. Children as young as age 1 have a clear understanding of the physical differences between girls and boys and can consistently apply gender labels.
    c. Not until age 5 or 6 do children show a clear preference for gender-typed toys.
    d. All of the above are true.
11. Which of the following is **NOT** one of the features of parenting used by Diana Baumrind to differentiate authoritarian, permissive, and authoritative parents?
    a. maturity demands for the child's conduct
    b. efforts to control the child's actions
    c. nurturance
    d. adherence to stereotypic gender roles
12. Which of the following is true regarding the effects of spanking?
    a. Spanking seems to reduce reactive aggression.
    b. When administered appropriately, spanking promotes psychosocial development.
    c. Spanking is associated with increased aggression.
    d. None of the above is true.
13. Rodney and Jack are wrestling and hitting each other without intent to hurt. Although this rough-and-tumble play mimics negative, aggressive behavior, it serves a useful purpose, which is to
    a. rehearse social roles.
    b. develop interactive skills.
    c. improve fine motor skills.
    d. do both b and c.

Key Terms

1. **emotional regulation:** The ability to control when and how emotions are expressed. (p. 289; video lesson, segment 2; objective 1)
2. **initiative versus guilt:** Erikson's third psychosocial crisis, in which children undertake new skills and activities and feel guilty when they do not succeed at them. (p. 289; objective 1)
3. **self-concept:** A person's understanding of who he or she is, in relation to self-esteem, appearance, personality, and various traits. (p. 290; video lesson, segment 2; objective 2)

4. **intrinsic motivation:** A drive, or reason to pursue a goal, that comes from inside a person, such as the need to feel smart or competent. (p. 291; objective 2)
5. **extrinsic motivation:** A drive, or reason to pursue a goal, that arises from the need to have one's achievements rewarded from outside, perhaps by receiving material possessions or another person's esteem. (p. 291; objective 2)
6. **imaginary friends:** Make-believe friends who exist only in a child's imagination; increasingly common from ages 3 through 7, they combat loneliness and aid emotional regulation. (p. 291; objective 2)
7. **psychopathology:** Defined in the Berger textbook as an illness or disorder of the mind. (p. 293; objective 1)
8. **externalizing problems:** Difficulty with emotional regulation that involves expressing powerful feelings through uncontrolled physical or verbal outbursts, as by lashing out at other people or breaking things. (p. 293; objective 1)
9. **internalizing problems:** Difficulty with emotional regulation that involves turning one's emotional distress inward, as by feeling excessively guilty, ashamed, or worthless. (p. 293; objective 1)
10. **rough-and-tumble play:** Play that mimics aggression through wrestling, chasing, or hitting, but in which there is no intent to harm. (p. 296; video lesson, segment 1; objective 5)
11. **sociodramatic play:** Pretend play in which children act out various roles and themes in stories of their own creation, allowing them to examine personal concerns in a nonthreatening manner. (p. 297; video lesson, segment 1; objective 5)
12. **authoritarian parenting:** An approach to child rearing that is characterized by high behavioral standards, strict punishment of misconduct, and little communication. (p. 299; video lesson, segment 3; objective 6)

    Memory aid: Someone who is an authoritarian demands unquestioning obedience and acts in a dictatorial way.
13. **permissive parenting:** An approach to child rearing that is characterized by high nurturance and communication but little discipline, guidance, or control. Also called *indulgent parenting*. (p. 299; video lesson, segment 3; objective 6)
14. **authoritative parenting:** An approach to child rearing in which the parents set limits but listen to the child and are flexible. (p. 299; video lesson, segment 3; objective 6)

    Memory aid: Authoritative parents act as authorities do on a subject—by discussing and explaining why certain family rules are in place.
15. **neglectful-uninvolved parenting:** An approach to childrearing in which the parents are indifferent toward their children and unaware of what is going on in their children's lives. (p. 300; objective 6)
16. **empathy:** The ability to understand the emotions and concerns of another person, especially when they differ from one's own. (p. 305; objective 3)

17. **antipathy:** Feelings of anger, dislike, or hatred toward another person. (p. 305; objective 3)
18. **prosocial behavior:** Actions that are helpful and kind but are of no obvious benefit to oneself. (p. 306; video lesson, segment 2; objective 3)
19. **antisocial behavior:** Actions that are deliberately hurtful or destructive to another person. (p. 306; video lesson, segment 2; objective 3)
20. **instrumental aggression:** Behavior that hurts someone else because the aggressor wants to get or keep a possession or a privilege. (p. 306; objective 4)
21. **reactive aggression:** An impulsive retaliation for another person's intentional or accidental action, verbal or physical. (p. 306; objective 4)

    Memory aid: Instrumental aggression is behavior that is instrumental in allowing a child to retain a favorite toy. Reactive aggression is a reaction to another child's behavior.
22. **relational aggression:** Nonphysical acts, such as insults or social rejection, aimed at harming the social connection between the victim and other people. (p. 306; objective 4)
23. **bullying aggression:** Unprovoked, repeated physical or verbal attack, especially on victims who are unlikely to defend themselves. (p. 307; objective 4)
24. **psychological control:** A form of discipline that involves threatening to withdraw love and support and that relies on a child's feelings of guilt and gratitude to the parents. (p. 308; objective 7)
25. **time-out:** A form of discipline in which a child is required to stop all activity and sit quietly for a few minutes. (p. 308; objective 7)
26. **sex differences:** Biological differences between females and males, in organs, hormones, and body type. (p. 311; objective 8)
27. **gender differences:** Cultural differences in the roles and behavior of males and females. (p. 311; objective 8)
28. **phallic stage:** In psychoanalytic theory, the third stage of psychosexual development, in which the penis becomes the focus of psychological concerns and physiological pleasure. (p. 313; objective 9)
29. **Oedipus complex:** According to Freud, the unconscious desire of young boys to replace their father and win their mother's romantic love. (p. 313; objective 9)
30. **superego:** In psychoanalytic theory, the self-critical and judgmental part of personality that internalizes the moral standards set by parents and society. (p. 313; objective 9)
31. **Electra complex:** According to Freud, the unconscious desire of girls to replace their mother and win their father's romantic love. (p. 313; objective 9)
32. **identification:** An attempt to defend one's self-concept by taking on the behaviors and attitudes of someone else. (p. 313; objective 9)

33. **gender schema:** A cognitive concept or general belief that is based on one's experiences—in this case, a child's understanding of sex differences. (p. 315; objective 9)
34. **self-esteem:** Refers to how a child *feels* about himself or herself; it has to do with how lovable the child feels. (video lesson, segment 2; objective 2)

Summary

During the preschool years, a child's self-confidence, social skills, and social roles become more fully developed. This growth coincides with the child's increased capacity for communication, imagination, and understanding of his or her social context. Much of this development occurs through play activities.

Play provides crucial experiences not only for motor and cognitive development but also for self-understanding and social interaction. Apparent in important types of play include **rough-and-tumble play**, in which children mimic aggression but actually have no intent to harm, and **sociodramatic play**, in which children act out various roles and themes in stories of their own creation. This exploration through play enables children to test their ability to convince others of their ideas and examine personal concerns in a nonthreatening manner.

In Erik Erikson's theory, the crisis of early childhood is **initiative versus guilt**. The child is turning away from an exclusive attachment to parents and moving toward membership in the larger culture. A crucial factor in this developmental progression is learning **emotional regulation**—a key aspect of the child's developing **emotional intelligence**. Because of brain maturation, children gain a much greater ability to direct or modify their feelings, particularly feelings of fear, frustration, and anger.

The development of **empathy** and **antipathy** during the preschool years leads to **prosocial behaviors,** such as sharing and cooperating, which are performed to benefit other people, and **antisocial behaviors,** such as hitting or insulting. Antisocial behaviors are those that are intended to hurt someone else. Developmental psychologists differentiate among at least four types of aggression: **instrumental aggression**, **reactive aggression**, **relational aggression**, and **bullying aggression**.

The three classic styles of parenting include **authoritarian** parents, whose word is law and who often show little affection or nurturance; **permissive** parents, who make few demands on their children, but display high levels of communication and connection; and **authoritative** parents, who set limits and enforce rules but do so more democratically by listening to their children's ideas and being willing to make compromises. Among the reasons for parenting variations are culture, religion, ethnicity, and the family's economic well-being.

Even at age 2, children know whether they are boys or girls and apply gender labels consistently. Each of the major developmental theories has a somewhat different explanation for gender differences. Psychoanalytic theorists focus on fears and fantasies that motivate children to initially adore their opposite-sex parent and then later identify with their same-sex parent. Behaviorists maintain that gender roles are instilled because parents and society provide models and reinforcement for appropriate gender-role behavior and punishment for inappropriate behavior. In explaining gender identity and gender-role development, cognitive theorists focus on children's growing understanding of male-female differences. Sociocultural theorists emphasize the influence of cultural differences. Evolutionary theorists point out that gender-role behavior is instrumental in sexual attraction, the cornerstone of the reproductive drive.

Special Note: We will cover the effects of television, video games, and other electronic media (pp. 303–304) in more detail in Lesson 15, "Hazards Along the Way."

Answer Key

Practice Questions I

Multiple-Choice Questions

1. b. is the correct answer. (video lesson, segment 2; objective 2)
2. c. is the correct answer. (objective 9)

   a. & b. are incorrect. In Freud's theory, the oral and anal stages are associated with infant and early childhood development, respectively.

   d. is incorrect. In Freud's theory, the latency period is associated with development during the school years.
3. a. is the correct answer. (video lesson, segment 1; objective 5)

   b. is incorrect. Mastery play is play that helps children develop new physical and intellectual skills.

   c. is incorrect. Rough-and-tumble play is physical play that mimics aggression.

   d. is incorrect. Sensorimotor play captures the pleasures of using the senses and motor skills.
4. b. is the correct answer. (video lesson, segment 3; objective 6)

   d. is incorrect. These styles were uncovered by later research.
5. a. is the correct answer. (video lesson, segment 3; objective 6)

   b. & c. are incorrect. Authoritative parents communicate very well and are quite affectionate.

   d. is incorrect. This is not typical of authoritative parents.
6. d. is the correct answer. (video lesson, segment 2; objective 4)
7. d. is the correct answer. (objective 2)
8. b. is the correct answer. (objective 9)

   a. is incorrect. This is the focus of Freud's phallic stage.

   c. is incorrect. This is the focus of Erikson's psychosocial theory.

   d. is incorrect. This is the focus of cognitive theorists.
9. a. is the correct answer. (objective 8)
10. c. is the correct answer. (objective 3)

11. d. is the correct answer. In accounting for Elijah's verbal ability, Dr. Laurent alludes to both genetic and environmental factors, a dead-giveaway for evolutionary theory. (objective 9)

    a., b., & c. are incorrect. These theories do not address biological or genetic influences on development.

12. d. is the correct answer. (objective 1)

13. b. is the correct answer. (objective 4)

    a. is incorrect. Instrumental aggression is intended to get something someone else has.

    c. is incorrect. Bullying aggression is unprovoked.

    d. is incorrect. Relational aggression is aimed at hurting the victim's social relationships.

True or False Items

14. F All parents make some maturity demands on their children; maturity demands are high in both the authoritarian and authoritative parenting styles. (video lesson, segment 3; objective 6)
15. T (video lesson, segment 3; objective 6)
16. F Just the opposite is true. (objective 8)
17. T (objective 7)
18. F (objective 2)
19. T (objective 3)
20. T (objective 9)
21. T (objective 9)

Practice Questions II

Multiple-Choice Questions

1. b. is the correct answer. (objective 6)

2. c. is the correct answer. (video lesson, segment 1; objective 5)

   a. & b. are incorrect. Adults tend to be either too accommodating or too domineering with children, and learning emotional regulation is best done in context.

3. c. is the correct answer. (objective 6)

4. d. is the correct answer. Prior to this age, deliberate prosocial and antisocial behaviors are not possible because the self-concept is not sufficiently developed. (objective 3)

5. b. is the correct answer. (objective 9)

   a. & d. are incorrect. These are Freud's versions of phallic-stage development in little girls.

   c. is incorrect. There is no such thing as the "phallic complex."

6. c. is the correct answer. (video lesson, segment 3; objective 6)

   a. & b. are incorrect. Both authoritarian and authoritative parents make high demands on their children.

   d. is incorrect. Rejecting-neglecting parents are quite cold and unengaged.

7. b. is the correct answer. (video lesson, segment 2; objective 3)

8. a. is the correct answer. This type of play involves a joint activity or taking turns. (objective 5)

   b. is incorrect. In this type of play, children play near each other but not together.

   c. is incorrect. In this type of play, children watch each other play.

   d. is incorrect. In this type of play, children interact but play is not mutual or reciprocal.

9. c. is the correct answer. (objective 9)

   a. & d. are incorrect. Learning and social learning theories emphasize that children learn about gender by rewards and punishments and by observing others.

   b. is incorrect. Sociocultural theory focuses on the impact of the environment on gender identification.

10. a. is the correct answer. (objective 7)

    b. & c. are incorrect. Time-outs involve removing a child from a situation in which misbehavior has occurred. Moreover, these threats of future punishment would likely be less effective because of the delay between the behavior and the consequence.

    d. is incorrect. Although developments stress the need to prevent misdeeds instead of punishing them, and warn that time-outs may have unintended consequences, they nevertheless can be an effective form of discipline.

11. c. is the correct answer. (objective 9)

    a. is incorrect. This is the belief of behaviorists.

    b. is incorrect. This is consistent with psychoanalytic theory.

    d. is incorrect. This is consistent with sociocultural theory.

12. a. is the correct answer. (objective 1)

13. c. is the correct answer. (video lesson, segment 3; objective 6)

14. b. is the correct answer. (objective 1)

    a. & c. are incorrect. According to Erikson, these are the crises of adolescence and infancy, respectively.

    d. is incorrect. This is not a crisis described by Erikson.

Matching Items

15. g (video lesson, segment 1; objective 5)
16. k (objective 2)
17. i (video lesson, segment 1; objective 5)
18. d (video lesson, segment 2; objective 3)

19. h (video lesson, segment 2; objective 3)
20. b (objective 9)
21. e (objective 9)
22. f (video lesson, segment 3; objective 6)
23. c (video lesson, segment 3; objective 6)
24. j (objective 9)
25. a (objective 4)

Applying Your Knowledge

1. a. is the correct answer. (objective 9)
2. b. is the correct answer. (objective 9)

   a. is incorrect. According to Freud, the Oedipus complex refers to the male's sexual feelings toward his mother and resentment toward his father.

   c. & d. are incorrect. These are concepts introduced by cognitive theorists and Erik Erikson, respectively.
3. a. is the correct answer. (objectives 1 & 2)

   b. is incorrect. Erikson did not equate gender constancy with the emergence of guilt.

   c. & d. are incorrect. These reflect the viewpoints of behaviorism and Freud, respectively.
4. b. is the correct answer. (objective 6)
5. c. is the correct answer. The purpose of Bonita's action is clearly to get the beanie baby, rather than to retaliate (b, which is incorrect), or bully Aldo (a, which is incorrect). (objective 4)

   d. is incorrect. Relational aggression generally takes the form of a verbal insult.
6. b. is the correct answer. (objective 9)
7. b. is the correct answer. (objective 9)
8. c. is the correct answer. Self-criticism is not common at this age, and children naively believe they can accomplish more than they can. (objective 2)
9. d. is the correct answer. (objective 1)
10. a. is the correct answer. (objective 8)

    b. is incorrect. Not until about age 2 can children consistently apply gender labels.

    c. is incorrect. By age 2, children prefer gender-typed toys.
11. d. is the correct answer. (video lesson, segment 3; objective 6)
12. c. is the correct answer. (objective 7)
13. b. is the correct answer. (objective 5)

Lesson Review

Lesson 13

The Play Years
Psychosocial Development

Please Note: Use this matrix to guide your study and achieve the learning objectives of this lesson. It will also help you to view the video, which defines and demonstrates important concepts and skills as they relate to everyday life.

Learning Objective	Textbook	Course Student Guide	Video Lesson
1. Discuss emotional development during early childhood, focusing on emotional regulation.	pp. 289–295	Key Terms: 1, 2, 7, 8, 9; Practice Questions I: 12; Practice Questions II: 12, 14; Applying Your Knowledge: 3, 9.	Segment 2: *Emotional Regulation*
2. Discuss the importance of positive self-evaluation during this period, noting the child's developing self-concept, self-esteem, intrinsic motivation, and extrinsic motivation.	pp. 289–292	Key Terms: 3, 4, 5, 6, 34; Practice Questions I: 1, 7, 18; Practice Questions II: 16; Applying Your Knowledge: 3, 8.	Segment 2: *Emotional Regulation*
3. Describe the development of empathy and antipathy, and define and give examples of prosocial and antisocial behaviors.	pp. 305–307	Key Terms: 16, 17, 18, 19; Practice Questions I: 10, 19; Practice Questions II: 4, 7, 18, 19.	Segment 2: *Emotional Regulation*
4. Describe the different forms of aggression demonstrated by young children, and discuss the role of television and video games in encouraging these and other antisocial behaviors.	pp. 303–304, 306–307	Key Terms: 20, 21, 22, 23; Practice Questions I: 6, 13; Practice Questions II: 25; Applying Your Knowledge: 5.	Segment 2: *Emotional Regulation*
5. Discuss the role of play in the development of social skills, focusing on the benefits of rough-and-tumble and sociodramatic play.	pp. 295–298	Key Terms: 10, 11; Practice Questions I: 3; Practice Questions II: 2, 8, 15, 17; Applying Your Knowledge: 13.	Segment 1: *Social Awareness*

Learning Objective	Textbook	Course Student Guide	Video Lesson
6. Compare the three classic styles of parenting, and discuss the factors that might account for variations in parenting style.	pp. 299–302	Key Terms: 12, 13, 14, 15; Practice Questions I: 4, 5, 13, 14, 15; Practice Questions II: 1, 3, 6, 13, 22, 23; Applying Your Knowledge: 4, 11.	Segment 3: *Parenting Styles*
7. Discuss the pros and cons of the most common methods of discipline and describe the most effective methods for disciplining a child regarding both short-term and long-term behavioral modification as well as overall moral development.	pp. 307–311	Key Terms: 24, 25; Practice Questions I: 17; Practice Questions II: 10; Applying Your Knowledge: 12.	
8. Distinguish between sex differences and gender differences, and describe the developmental progression of gender awareness in young children.	pp. 311–312	Key Terms: 26, 27; Practice Questions I: 9, 16; Applying Your Knowledge: 10.	
9. Summarize the three grand theories' and the newer theories' take on gender-role development during early childhood, noting important contributions of each.	pp. 312–316	Key Terms: 28, 29, 30, 31, 32, 33; Practice Questions I: 2, 8, 11, 20, 21; Practice Questions II: 5, 9, 11, 20, 21, 24; Applying Your Knowledge: 1, 2, 6, 7.	

Developing Through Play

Lesson 14
The Play Years:
Summary

Preview

Lesson 14, which is the second of the unit summary lessons, reviews biosocial, cognitive, and psychosocial development during early childhood between ages 2 and 6.

The overall theme of this lesson is that as preschoolers grow, their physical, cognitive, and psychosocial development makes possible new types of play activities. These new types of play activities create more opportunities for growth in each domain of development. During early childhood, play is a catalyst for development.

In the program, this interwoven nature of play and development is revealed in the stories of four children: three-year-old Jordan, who is flourishing in the care offered by an extended family; four-year-olds Maddy and Alex, fraternal twins who are following their own unique developmental paths; and four-and-a-half-year-old C.C., who was badly burned as an infant and then spent a year in **foster care** before being adopted by a loving family.

Prior Knowledge That Will Be Used in This Lesson

- This lesson will return to the dual influences of heredity and environment (from Lesson 3). Recall that all human development is a product of the interaction between nature (our genes) and nurture (our environment).
- Biosocial development during early childhood (from Lesson 11) will be referred to as we review brain and motor skill development and the subject of child maltreatment.
- This lesson will also review cognitive development during early childhood (from Lesson 12) as we discuss language development, theory of mind, and the theories of Lev Vygotsky (guided participation, scaffolding).
- Psychosocial development during early childhood (from Lesson 13) will be referred to as we return to the concepts of self-concept, self-esteem, emotional regulation, and the different types of types of play that children engage in.

Learning Objectives

Use this information to guide your reading, viewing, thinking, and studying. After successfully completing this lesson, you should be able to:

1. Summarize biosocial development in early childhood, giving examples of brain and motor-skill development and childhood maltreatment.
2. Discuss the general pattern of cognitive development during early childhood, focusing on language development, theory of mind, and the role of caregivers.
3. Summarize psychosocial development during early childhood, focusing on self-concept, emotional regulation, and the various types of play and their influence.
4. Offer examples of how a child's development in any one domain (biosocial, cognitive, or psychosocial) can affect development in a different domain.
5. Discuss some things that parents can do to encourage the healthy development of their preschooler.

Textbook Reading & Video Viewing

For the most effective study of this lesson, complete the assignments in the sequence listed below.

Before viewing the video program:

Read Chapter 8, "Summary: Early Childhood: Biosocial Development," page 254; Chapter 9, "Summary: Early Childhood: Cognitive Development," page 286; Chapter 10, "Summary: Early Childhood: Psychosocial Development," pages 316–317, and "The Developing Person So Far: Early Childhood," page 319.

View the video for Lesson 14, "Developing Through Play."

Segment 1: *Jordan*

Segment 2: *Maddy and Alex*

Segment 3: *C.C.*

Video Viewing Tips

The video for Lesson 14 will feature four preschool children who offer living examples of some concepts you've learned in the previous three lessons. As you view the video, watch for the following issues and situations.

This video will clearly demonstrate the importance of *play* in early childhood. Note differences in the types of play these children engage in, and consider the range of effects on their biosocial, cognitive, and psychosocial development. Also, consider the level of gross and fine motor skills in these children and how that might affect their preference for certain play activities.

Pay close attention to the role of parents and other caregivers in this video, and try to guess their parenting style (authoritarian, permissive, authoritative). Also, look for examples of how these caregivers structure or scaffold individual learning situations for their children through a process of guided participation.

As you watch, consider how the heredity of these children and environmental factors interact to influence their development. For example, Maddy and Alex in segment two of the video are fraternal twins. Remember that fraternal (dizygotic) twins come from two different ova fertilized by two separate sperm. So, they have different genes just like any other siblings. While Maddy and Alex live in very similar environments, you'll see how their genetic differences have produced two very different young girls.

As always in these "Summary" videos, keep an eye out for any interaction between domains—how development in one domain can effect changes in a different domain. Before you watch this lesson, it may help you to review the vocabulary in the Key Terms section.

After viewing the video program:

Review all reading assignments for this lesson.

Complete the "Practice Questions" section to reinforce your understanding of important terms and concepts and measure your achievement of the Learning Objectives. Check your answers with the feedback given and review when necessary.

Practice Questions

Multiple-Choice Questions

1. ___________________ refers to the tendency of young children to view the world exclusively from their own perspective.

   a. Egocentrism
   b. Centration
   c. Symbolic thought
   d. Theory of mind

2. When a child demonstrates understanding of another person's feelings and concerns, he or she possesses ______________ toward that person.

   a. antipathy
   b. prosocial
   c. empathy
   d. sympathy

3. Skills that involve large body movements, such as running and jumping, are called

   a. activity-level skills.
   b. fine motor skills.
   c. gross motor skills.
   d. left-brain skills.

4. The brain's ongoing myelination during childhood helps children
   a. control their actions more precisely.
   b. react more quickly to stimuli.
   c. coordinate and control muscles.
   d. do all of the above.
5. Worldwide, a major cause of death in childhood is
   a. accidental injury.
   b. cancer.
   c. malnutrition.
   d. iron deficiency anemia.
6. When parents or caregivers do not provide adequate food, shelter, attention, or supervision, it is specifically referred to as
   a. abuse.
   b. neglect.
   c. endangering.
   d. maltreatment.
7. Which of the following activities would probably be the **MOST** difficult for a five-year-old child?
   a. climbing a ladder
   b. running and then jumping
   c. throwing a ball
   d. tracing a drawing of an animal
8. The Russian psychologist Lev Vygotsky emphasized that
   a. language advances children's thoughts.
   b. children form concepts first, then find words to express them.
   c. language and other cognitive developments are unrelated at this stage.
   d. preschoolers learn language only for egocentric purposes.
9. A four-year-old tells the teacher that a clown should not be allowed to visit the class because "Pat is 'fraid of clowns." The four-year-old thus shows that he can anticipate how another will feel. This is evidence of the beginnings of
   a. egocentrism.
   b. deception.
   c. a theory of mind.
   d. conservation.

10. Relatively recent experiments have demonstrated that preschoolers can succeed at tests of conservation when
    a. they are allowed to work cooperatively with other children.
    b. the test is presented as a competition.
    c. the children are informed that their parents are observing them.
    d. the test is presented in a simple, gamelike way.

11. A preschooler who focuses his or her attention on only one feature of a situation is demonstrating a characteristic of preoperational thought called
    a. centration.
    b. overregularization.
    c. reversibility.
    d. egocentrism.

12. One characteristic of preoperational thought is
    a. the ability to categorize objects.
    b. the ability to count in multiples of 5.
    c. the inability to perform logical operations.
    d. difficulty adjusting to changes in routine.

13. In order to scaffold a child's cognitive skills, parents
    a. simplify tasks.
    b. interpret the activity.
    c. help children find answers, while anticipating mistakes.
    d. do all of the above.

14. Regarding the value of preschool education, most developmentalists believe that
    a. most disadvantaged children will not benefit from an early preschool education.
    b. most disadvantaged children will benefit from an early preschool education.
    c. because of sleeper effects, the early benefits of preschool education are likely to disappear by grade 3.
    d. the relatively small benefits of antipoverty measures such as Head Start do not justify their huge costs.

15. A preschooler fails to put together a difficult puzzle on her own, so her mother encourages her to try again, this time guiding her by asking questions such as, "For this space do we need a big piece or a little piece?" With Mom's help, the child successfully completes the puzzle. Lev Vygotsky would attribute the child's success to

    a. additional practice with the puzzle pieces.
    b. imitation of her mother's behavior.
    c. the social interaction with her mother that restructured the task to make its solution more attainable.
    d. modeling and reinforcement.

16. Preschool children have a clear (but not necessarily accurate) concept of self. Typically, the preschooler believes that she or he

    a. owns all objects in sight.
    b. is great at almost everything.
    c. is much less competent than peers and older children.
    d. is more powerful than her or his parents.

17. Because it helps children rehearse social roles, work out fears and fantasies, and learn cooperation, an important form of social play is

    a. sociodramatic play.
    b. mastery play.
    c. rough-and-tumble play.
    d. sensorimotor play.

18. The three basic patterns of parenting described by Diana Baumrind are

    a. hostile, loving, and harsh.
    b. authoritarian, permissive, and authoritative.
    c. positive, negative, and punishing.
    d. abusive, democratic, and traditional.

19. Authoritative parents are receptive and loving, but they also normally

    a. set limits and enforce rules.
    b. have difficulty communicating.
    c. withhold praise and affection.
    d. encourage aggressive behavior.

20. An angry four-year-old might stop herself from hitting another child because she has developed
    a. social referencing.
    b. self-esteem.
    c. identification.
    d. emotional regulation.
21. The initial advantages of an authoritative parenting style
    a. do not persist past middle childhood.
    b. remain apparent through adolescence.
    c. are likely to be even stronger over time.
    d. have an unpredictable impact later in children's lives.
22. Which of the following is **LEAST** likely to be true of four-year-old Keshawn?
    a. His developing attention span allows him to complete projects, for which he can then be proud of accomplishing.
    b. He is more willing to try new experiences than when he was younger.
    c. He is self-critical and believes that he cannot do complicated tasks, such as difficult puzzles.
    d. He believes that whatever he is (dark skinned, male) is good.
23. Erikson noted that preschoolers eagerly begin many new activities but are vulnerable to criticism and feelings of failure; in other words, they experience the crisis of
    a. identity versus role confusion.
    b. initiative versus guilt.
    c. basic trust versus mistrust.
    d. efficacy versus helplessness.
24. Rodney and Jack are wrestling and hitting each other without intent to hurt. Although this rough-and-tumble play mimics negative, aggressive behavior, it serves a useful purpose, which is to
    a. rehearse social roles.
    b. develop interactive skills.
    c. improve fine motor skills.
    d. do both b and c.

True or False Items

Write T (for true) or F (for false) on the line in front of each statement.

25. ____ Children tend to gain proportionately more fat than muscle during the period between the ages of 2 and 6.

26. ____ The health care, genetic background, and nutrition of the preschool child are major influences on growth.

27. ____ Fine motor skills are usually easier for preschoolers to master than are gross motor skills.

28. ____ Most child maltreatment involves both child abuse and child neglect.

29. ____ With the beginning of preoperational thought, most preschoolers can understand abstract words.

30. ____ A preschooler who says "You comed up and hurted me" is demonstrating a lack of understanding of English grammar.

31. ____ Vygotsky believed that cognitive growth is largely a social activity.

32. ____ Children of authoritative parents tend to be successful, happy with themselves, and generous with others.

Questions for Reflection

1. Considering the physical, cognitive, linguistic, and social development of children during early childhood, describe the type of toy that would be suitable for a three- or four-year-old child. In your description of the toy, be sure to include its design and construction, the play value of the toy, and the domain(s) of development the toy is intended to stimulate.

2. According to the lesson, the United States is one of the most violent nations in the world. In what ways does this context of violence promote child maltreatment? If it were in your power to completely shape the social context in which a child grew up, what steps would you take to help ensure that he or she would be protected from maltreatment?

3. Visit the children's section of your local library or bookstore. Ask the librarian or salesperson to guide you to a book that is a "classic" or well-loved storybook for children from 3 to 6 years of age. Examine the book carefully. If possible, read it aloud to a child or someone else. Then complete the following items.

   a. Give the title, name of the author and illustrator, and date of publication of the book.

   b. Summarize what the librarian or salesperson told you about why this book is a "classic" for this age group.

   c. Give examples of any of the following story elements that appear in the book: rhyme and repetition; egocentrism (for example, animals that dress and talk like a child); centration (for example stories about characters who have only one prominent feature); story elements that reassure the child about the strong ties of family and friendship.

4. Give examples of how a child's development in any one domain (biosocial, cognitive, or psychosocial) can affect development in a different domain.

Key Terms

1. **injury control/harm reduction:** Practices that are aimed at anticipating, controlling, and preventing dangerous activities; these practices reflect the beliefs that accidents are not random and that injuries can be made less harmful if proper controls are in place. (p. 243; objective 1)
2. **child maltreatment:** Intentional harm to, or avoidable endangerment of, anyone under age 18. (p. 247; video lesson, segment 3; objective 1)
3. **child abuse:** Deliberate action that is harmful to a child's physical, emotional, or sexual well-being. (p. 247; objective 1)
4. **foster care:** A legal, publicly supported system in which a maltreated child is removed from the parents' custody and entrusted to another adult or family, which is reimbursed for expenses incurred in meeting the child's needs. (p. 252; video lesson, segment 3; objective 1)
5. **child neglect:** Failure to meet a child's basic physical, educational, or emotional needs. (p. 248; objective 1)
6. **preoperational thought:** Piaget's term for cognitive development between the ages of about 2 and 6; it includes language and imagination (which involve symbolic thought), but logical, operational thinking is not yet possible at this stage. (p. 257; objective 2)
7. **egocentrism:** Piaget's term for children's tendency to think about the world entirely from their own personal perspective. (p. 258; objective 2)
8. **irreversibility:** A characteristic of preoperational thought in which a young child thinks that nothing can be undone. A thing cannot be restored to the way it was before a change occurred. (p. 258; objective 2)
9. **conservation:** The principle that the amount of a substance remains the same (i.e., is conserved) even when its appearance changes. (p. 259; objective 2)
10. **guided participation:** The process by which people learn from others who guide their experiences and explorations. (p. 262; video lesson, segment 1; objective 2)
11. **scaffolding:** Temporary support that is tailored to a learner's needs and abilities and aimed at helping the learner master the next task in a given learning process. (p. 262; video lesson, segment 1; objective 2)
12. **theory of mind:** A person's theory of what other people might be thinking. In order to have a theory of mind, children must realize that other people are not necessarily thinking the same thoughts that they themselves are. That realization seldom occurs before age 4. (p. 267; video lesson, segments 1 & 2; objective 2)
13. **fast-mapping:** The speedy and sometimes imprecise way in which children learn new words by tentatively placing them in mental categories according to their perceived meaning. (p. 270; video lesson, segment 1; objective 2)
14. **overregularization:** The application of rules of grammar even when exceptions occur, making the language seem more "regular" than it actually is. (p. 272; objective 2)

15. **self-concept:** A person's understanding of who he or she is, in relation to self-esteem, appearance, personality, and various traits. (p. 290; video lesson, segment 1; objective 3)
16. **initiative versus guilt:** Erikson's third psychosocial crisis, in which children undertake new skills and activities and feel guilty when they do not succeed at them. (p. 289; objective 3)
17. **emotional regulation:** The ability to control when and how emotions are expressed. (p. 289; objective 3)
18. **prosocial behavior:** Actions that are helpful and kind but are of no obvious benefit to oneself. (p. 306; video lesson, segment 3; objective 3)
19. **antisocial behavior:** Actions that are deliberately hurtful or destructive to another person. (p. 306; objective 3)
20. **rough-and-tumble play:** Play that mimics aggression through wrestling, chasing, or hitting, but in which there is no intent to harm. (p. 296; objective 3)
21. **sociodramatic play:** Pretend play in which children act out various roles and themes in stories of their own creation, allowing them to examine personal concerns in a nonthreatening manner. (p. 297; objective 3)
22. **authoritarian parenting:** An approach to child rearing that is characterized by high behavioral standards, strict punishment of misconduct, and little communication. (p. 299; objective 3)
23. **permissive parenting:** An approach to child rearing that is characterized by high nurturance and communication but little discipline, guidance, or control. (Also called indulgent parenting.) (p. 299; objective 3)
24. **authoritative parenting:** An approach to child rearing in which the parents set limits but listen to the child and are flexible. (p. 299; objective 3)
25. **self-esteem:** Refers to how a child *feels* about himself or herself; it has to do with how lovable the child feels. (Lesson 13 video lesson; objective 3)

Summary

Children grow steadily taller and slimmer during the preschool years, and genetic background and nutrition are responsible for most of the variation seen in children throughout the world. The most significant aspect of growth is the continued maturation of the nervous system and the refinement of the visual, muscular, and cognitive skills that will be necessary for the child to function in school. Gross motor skills—such as running, jumping, and other key elements of play—improve dramatically during these years while fine motor skills, such as writing and drawing, develop more slowly.

Child maltreatment, including the abuse and neglect revealed in the poignant story of C.C., may cast a long shadow on the developing child. These problems are likely to occur in homes with immature parents, many children, and few personal and community resources.

Cognitive skills flourish during early childhood, especially in homes such as Jordan's, where the guided participation offered by loving family members stimulates memory, problem solving, and reasoning about number and theory of mind. In countless everyday instances, preschoolers reveal themselves to be remarkably thoughtful, insightful, and perceptive thinkers whose grasp of the causes of everyday events, memory of the past, and mastery of language is sometimes astounding. Still, you may recall Jordan's reaction when his father tried to get him to spell "house," which may be beyond his zone of proximal development. It's important for caregivers to provide age-appropriate activities that encourage development without demanding too much.

During the preschool years a child's self-confidence, social skills, and social roles become more fully developed. This growth coincides with the child's increased capacity for communication, imagination, and understanding of his or her social context. Self-concept emerges, as does the child's ability to regulate his or her emotions. As their social and cognitive skills develop, preschoolers engage in ever more imaginative types of play, which further stimulates development in each domain.

Answer Key

Practice Questions

Multiple-Choice Questions

1. a. is the correct answer. (objective 2)
2. c. is the correct answer. (objective 3)
3. c. is the correct answer. (video lesson, segments 1, 2, & 3; objective 1)
4. d. is the correct answer. (objective 1)
5. a. is the correct answer. (objective 1)
6. b. is the correct answer. (video lesson, segment 3; objectives 1 & 5)

   a. is incorrect. Abuse is deliberate, harsh injury to the body.

   c. & d. are incorrect. Endangerment and maltreatment are too broad a term.
7. d. is the correct answer. (objective 1)

   a., b., & c. are incorrect. Preschoolers find these gross motor skills easier to perform than fine motor skills such as that described in d.
8. a. is the correct answer. (objective 2)

   b. is incorrect. This expresses the views of Piaget.

   c. is incorrect. Because he believed that language facilitates thinking, Vygotsky obviously felt that language and other cognitive developments are intimately related.

   d. is incorrect. Vygotsky did not hold this view.
9. c. is the correct answer. (objective 2)

   a. is incorrect. Egocentrism is self-centered thinking.

   b. is incorrect. Although deception provides evidence of a theory of mind, the child in this example is not deceiving anyone.

   d. is incorrect. Conservation is the understanding that the amount of a substance is unchanged by changes in its shape or placement.

10. d. is the correct answer. (objective 2)
11. a. is the correct answer. (objective 2)

    b. is incorrect. Overregularization is the child's tendency to apply grammatical rules even when he or she shouldn't.

    c. is incorrect. Reversibility is the concept that reversing an operation, such as addition, will restore the original conditions.

    d. is incorrect. This term is used to refer to the young child's belief that people think as he or she does.
12. c. is the correct answer. This is why the stage is called preoperational. (objective 2)
13. d. is the correct answer. (video lesson, segment 1; objective 2)
14. b. is the correct answer. (objectives 2 & 5)
15. c. is the correct answer. (objectives 2 & 5)
16. b. is the correct answer. (objective 3)
17. a. is the correct answer. (objective 3)

    b. is incorrect. Mastery play is play that helps children develop new physical and intellectual skills.

    c. is incorrect. Rough-and-tumble play is physical play that mimics aggression.

    d. is incorrect. Sensorimotor play captures the pleasures of using the senses and motor skills.
18. b. is the correct answer. (objective 3)

    d. is incorrect. These styles were uncovered by later research.
19. a. is the correct answer. (objective 3)

    b. & c. are incorrect. Authoritative parents communicate very well and are quite affectionate.

    d. is incorrect. This is not typical of authoritative parents.
20. d. is the correct answer. (objective 3)
21. c. is the correct answer. (objectives 3 & 5)
22. c. is the correct answer. Self-criticism is not common at this age, and children naively believe they can accomplish more than they can. (objective 3)
23. b. is the correct answer. (objective 3)

    a. & c. are incorrect. According to Erikson, these are the crises of adolescence and infancy, respectively.

    d. is incorrect. This is not a crisis described by Erikson.
24. b. is the correct answer. (objective 3)

True or False Items

25. F In fact, the BMI (body mass index) is the lowest of the entire life span during this period. (video lesson, segment 1; objective 1)
26. T (objectives 1 & 5)

27. F Fine motor skills are more difficult for preschoolers to master than are gross motor skills. (video lesson, segments 1, 2, & 3; objective 1)
28. T (objective 1)
29. F Preschoolers have difficulty understanding abstract words; their vocabulary consists mainly of concrete nouns and verbs. (objective 2)
30. F In adding "ed" to form a past tense, the child has indicated an understanding of the grammatical rule for making past tenses in English, even though the construction in these two cases is incorrect. (objective 2)
31. T (video lesson, segment 1; objective 2)
32. T (objectives 3 & 5)

Lesson Review

Lesson 14

The Play Years
Summary

Please Note: Use this matrix to guide your study and achieve the learning objectives of this lesson. It will also help you to view the video, which defines and demonstrates important concepts and skills as they relate to everyday life.

Learning Objective	Textbook	Course Student Guide	Video Lesson
1. Summarize biosocial development in early childhood, giving examples of brain and motor-skill development and childhood maltreatment.	pp. 223–253	Key Terms: 1, 2, 3, 4, 5; Practice Questions: 3, 4, 5, 6, 7, 25, 26, 27, 28.	all segments
2. Discuss the general pattern of cognitive development during early childhood, focusing on language development, theory of mind, and the role of caregivers.	pp. 257–285	Key Terms: 6, 7, 8, 9, 10, 11, 12, 13, 14; Practice Questions: 1, 8, 9, 10, 11, 12, 13, 14, 15, 29, 30, 31.	all segments
3. Summarize psychosocial development during early childhood, focusing on self-concept, emotional regulation, and the various types of play and their influence.	pp. 289–316	Key Terms: 15, 16, 17, 18, 19, 20, 21, 22, 23, 24, 25; Practice Questions: 2, 16, 17, 18, 19, 20, 21, 22, 23, 24, 32.	all segments
4. Offer examples of how a child's development in any one domain (biosocial, cognitive, or psychosocial) can affect development in a different domain.	*		all segments
5. Discuss some things that parents can do to encourage the healthy development of their preschooler.	*	Practice Questions: 6, 14, 15, 21, 26, 32.	all segments

* The video for this lesson offers excellent coverage of these topics.

Hazards Along the Way

Lesson 15

The Play Years: Special Topic

Preview

This lesson explores two hazards along a child's development path: media and maltreatment. Although television and video games provide ready "babysitters," they also put children at risk. Research has linked media overexposure to a variety of negative effects. Although all children may not be adversely affected, electronic media can be hazardous to a child's biological, cognitive, and psychosocial well-being.

This lesson will also focus on the disturbing subject of child maltreatment, including an in-depth exploration of its prevalence, contributing factors, consequences for future development, treatment, and prevention. In this context, appropriate discipline for children is also discussed.

As you complete this lesson, consider the relevant experiences of any child you know. About how many hours of television does this child watch per week? About how many hours does he or she spend playing video games? What is the nature of these programs and games? How much violence is presented and in what context? Has anyone you know experienced maltreatment as a child? What were the circumstances? What type of treatment (if any) did the child receive? What could have been done to prevent this maltreatment? How was this child disciplined in the home? Was physical punishment ever used?

Prior Knowledge That Will Be Used in This Lesson

- This lesson returns to the topic of child maltreatment, which was introduced in Lesson 11. Recall that maltreatment includes both *abuse* (deliberate action that causes harm) and *neglect* (inaction, inattention, or general failure to meet a child's basic needs).
- This lesson will also discuss different strategies for disciplining a child (from Lesson 13), which can include explanation, criticism, persuasion, and/or physical punishment.

Learning Objectives

Use this information to guide your reading, viewing, thinking, and studying. After successfully completing this lesson, you should be able to

1. Discuss the effects of television and the media on a child's development.
2. Identify the various categories of child maltreatment, and discuss several factors that contribute to its occurrence.
3. Discuss the consequences, prevention, and approaches to treating child maltreatment, which includes both abuse and neglect.
4. Discuss permanency planning including foster care, kinship care, and adoption as long-term intervention options in cases of child maltreatment.
5. Discuss the impact of punishment on a child's development and describe alternative methods for disciplining a child.

Textbook Reading & Video Viewing

For the most effective study of this lesson, complete the assignments in the sequence listed below.

Before viewing the video program:

Review Chapter 8, "Early Childhood: Biosocial Development," pages 225–255; and Chapter 10, "Early Childhood: Psychosocial Development," pages 289–318.

View the video for Lesson 15, "Hazards Along the Way."

Segment 1: *Media Influences*

Segment 2: *Child Maltreatment: Causes and Consequences*

Segment 3: *Child Maltreatment: Treatment and Prevention*

After viewing the video program:

Review all reading assignments for this lesson.

Complete the "Practice Questions" section to reinforce your understanding of important terms and concepts and measure your achievement of the Learning Objectives. Check your answers with the feedback given and review when necessary.

Practice Questions

Multiple-Choice Questions

1. Children who watch a lot of violent television
   a. are likely to be less creative.
   b. are more likely to become violent in certain social situations.
   c. are more likely to become lower achieving teens.
   d. have all of the above characteristics.

2. Which of the following is true regarding the effects of spanking?
   a. Spanking immediately stops a child's misbehavior.
   b. Some studies have found that children who are physically punished (spanked) are more likely to become bullies later in life.
   c. Many children who are spanked as children do not become violent adults.
   d. All of the above are true.
3. Which of the following is an example of tertiary prevention of child maltreatment?
   a. removing a child from an abusive home
   b. home visitation of families with infants by health professionals
   c. new laws establishing stiff penalties for child maltreatment
   d. public-policy measures aimed at creating stable neighborhoods
4. Which of the following is an example of secondary prevention of child maltreatment?
   a. removing a child from an abusive home
   b. jailing a maltreating parent
   c. home visitation of families with infants by health professionals
   d. public-policy measures aimed at creating stable neighborhoods
5. When parents or caregivers do not provide adequate food, shelter, attention, or supervision, it is specifically referred to as
   a. abuse.
   b. neglect.
   c. endangering.
   d. maltreatment.
6. Which of the following is **NOT** true regarding foster care?
   a. Foster children often have behavioral problems.
   b. The number of foster children in the United States is increasing.
   c. Most foster children become maltreating caregivers.
   d. The average stay in foster care has decreased.
7. Children who have been maltreated often
   a. regard other children and adults as hostile and exploitative.
   b. are less friendly and more aggressive.
   c. are more isolated than other children.
   d. are all of the above.

8. Most child maltreatment
   a. includes both child abuse and child neglect.
   b. involves a rare outburst from the perpetrator.
   c. involves a mentally ill perpetrator.
   d. can be predicted entirely from the victim's personality characteristics.

9. A mayoral candidate is calling for sweeping policy changes to help ensure the well-being of children by promoting home ownership, high-quality community centers, and more stable neighborhoods. If these measures are effective in reducing child maltreatment, they would be classified as
   a. primary prevention.
   b. secondary prevention.
   c. tertiary prevention.
   d. permanency planning.

10. Parents who were abused as children
   a. almost always abuse their children.
   b. neglect, but not necessarily abuse, their children.
   c. are no more likely than anyone else to mistreat their children.
   d. are somewhat more likely than others to abuse their children.

11. One sign of child _______________, in which a young child seems fearful, is startled by noise, defensive and quick to attack, and confused between fantasy and reality is referred to as _______________.
   a. maltreatment; post-traumatic stress disorder (PTSD)
   b. neglect; failure to thrive
   c. abuse; hypervigilance
   d. neglect; hypervigilance

12. Most young children of all ethnic and economic backgrounds in the United States spend more than _______ hours each day using one electronic medium or another.
   a. 3
   b. 4.5
   c. 5
   d. 6

Matching Items

Match each definition or description with its corresponding term.

Terms

13. __________ kinship care
14. __________ foster care
15. __________ child abuse
16. __________ child neglect
17. __________ primary prevention
18. __________ secondary prevention
19. __________ tertiary prevention
20. __________ time-out

Definitions or Descriptions

a. legal placement of a child in the care of someone other than his or her biological parents
b. a form of care in which a relative of a maltreated child takes over from the biological parents
c. procedures to prevent child maltreatment from ever occurring
d. actions that are deliberately harmful to a child's well-being
e. procedures for spotting and treating the early warning signs of child maltreatment
f. failure to appropriately meet a child's basic needs
g. procedures to halt maltreatment that has already occurred
h. a disciplinary technique that does not require physical punishment

Key Terms

1. **child maltreatment:** Intentional harm to, or avoidable endangerment of, anyone under age 18. (p. 247; video lesson, segment 2; objective 2)
2. **child abuse:** Deliberate action that is harmful to a child's physical, emotional, or sexual well-being. (p. 247; video lesson, segment 2; objective 2)
3. **child neglect:** Failure to meet a child's basic physical, educational, or emotional needs. (p. 248; video lesson, segment 2; objective 2)
4. **reported maltreatment:** Harm or endangerment about which someone has notified the authorities. (p. 248; objective 2)
5. **substantiated maltreatment:** Harm or endangerment that has been reported, investigated, and verified. (p. 248; objective 2)
6. **post-traumatic stress disorder (PTSD):** An anxiety disorder that develops as a delayed reaction to having experienced or witnessed a profoundly shocking or frightening event, such as rape, severe beating, war, or natural disaster. Its symptoms may include flashbacks to the event, hyperactivity and hypervigilance, displaced anger, sleeplessness, nightmares, sudden terror or anxiety, and confusion between fantasy and reality. (p. 250; objective 3)
7. **permanency planning:** An effort by child-welfare authorities to find a long-term living situation that will provide stability and support for a maltreated

child. A goal is to avoid repeated changes of caregiver or school, which can be particularly harmful to the child. (p. 252; objective 4)

8. **foster care:** A legal, publicly supported system in which a maltreated child is removed from the parents' custody and entrusted to another adult or family, which is reimbursed for expenses incurred in meeting the child's needs. (p. 252; objective 4)
9. **kinship care:** A form of foster care in which a relative of a maltreated child, usually a grandparent, becomes the child's legal caregiver. (p. 252; objective 4)
10. **adoption:** A legal proceeding in which an adult or couple unrelated to a child is granted the joys and obligations of being that child's parent(s). (p. 253; objective 4)
11. **primary prevention:** Actions that change overall background conditions to prevent some unwanted event or circumstance, such as injury, disease, or abuse. (p. 244; video lesson, segment 3; objective 3)
12. **secondary prevention:** Actions that avert harm in a high-risk situation, such as stopping a car before it hits a pedestrian. (p. 244; video lesson, segment 3; objective 3)
13. **tertiary prevention:** Actions, such as immediate and effective medical treatment, that are taken after an adverse event (such as illness or injury) occurs and that are aimed at reducing the harm or preventing disability. (p. 244; video lesson, segment 3; objective 3)
14. **time-out:** A disciplinary technique in which the child is required to stop all activity and sit in a corner or stay indoors for a few minutes. (p. 308; objective 5)

Summary

A typical child in the United States watches more than three hours of television per day, more than any other age group. Among the criticisms of video watching are that it takes time from active and imaginative play; sends faulty messages about nutrition; provides sexist, racist, and ageist stereotypes; undermines sympathy for emotional pain; and undercuts attributes, skills, and values that lead to prosocial activity.

One longitudinal study found that teenagers who had watched educational television as young children earned higher grades and did more reading than others, especially if they were boys. On the other hand, teenagers who watched violent television programs as young children had lower grades than others, especially if they were girls. For these reasons, allowing a child unlimited and unsupervised media exposure could be seen as a form of **child maltreatment**.

Child maltreatment includes all intentional harm to, or avoidable endangerment of someone under age 18. Maltreatment falls into one of two broad categories: **abuse** and **neglect**. **Child abuse** includes all deliberate actions that are harmful to a child's well-being, including all physical, sexual, and emotional abuse. **Child neglect** refers to failures to act appropriately to meet a child's basic needs.

Although it is difficult to estimate the prevalence of maltreatment (reporting sources often are biased), the number of substantiated cases of child maltreatment in the United States is estimated to be about 1 million. Before a particular practice can be considered abusive, customs and community standards must be taken into account.

Communities vary in customs and goals regarding child-rearing, which means that what may be considered maltreatment in one place may not be in another. Two aspects of the overall context that seem conducive to maltreatment are poverty and social isolation.

Maltreated children often have difficulties in several areas. They may have trouble learning because maltreatment can cause the development of abnormal brain patterns that make learning difficult.

Children who are chronically maltreated tend to be slower to talk, underweight, less able to concentrate, and delayed in academic growth. They also tend to regard others as hostile and exploitive, and hence they are less friendly, more aggressive, and more isolated than other children. As adolescents and adults, they are more likely to engage in self-destructive and/or other destructive behaviors.

New laws requiring teachers, social workers, and other professionals to report possible maltreatment have resulted in increased reporting. Out of their concern that reporting does not create enough protection for a maltreated child, some experts advocate a policy of differential response that separates high-risk cases that may require complete investigation and removal of the child from low-risk cases that may only require some sort of supportive measure.

Permanency planning refers to the process of finding a long-term solution to the care of a child who has been abused. One option is **foster care**, a legal plan which transfers care of the child from the family to someone else. In one type of foster care, called **kinship care**, a relative of the maltreated child becomes the approved caregiver. A final option is **adoption**, which may be best when families are inadequate and children are young.

Public policy measures and other efforts designed to prevent maltreatment from ever occurring are called **primary prevention**. **Secondary prevention** focuses on spotting and treating the first symptoms of maltreatment. Last-ditch measures such as removing a child from an abusive home, jailing the perpetrator, and so forth constitute **tertiary prevention**.

For some, the difference between physical punishment and child abuse may be hard to distinguish. How a parent disciplines a child is an integral aspect of parenting style. To be effective, discipline should be more proactive than punitive. And, although most parents continue to believe that physical discipline is necessary at times, research suggests that children who are physically punished may learn to be more aggressive.

Answer Key

Practice Questions

Multiple-Choice Questions

1. d. is the correct answer. (video lesson, segment 1; objective 1)
2. d. is the correct answer. (video lesson, segment 3; objective 5)
3. a. is the correct answer. (video lesson, segment 3; objective 3)

   b. is incorrect. This is an example of secondary prevention.

   c. & d. are incorrect. These are examples of primary prevention.
4. c. is the correct answer. (video lesson, segment 3; objective 3)

   a. & b. are incorrect. These are examples of tertiary prevention.

   d. is incorrect. This is an example of primary prevention.
5. b. is the correct answer. (video lesson, segment 2; objective 2)

   a. is incorrect. Abuse is deliberate, harsh injury to the body.

   c. & d. are incorrect. Maltreatment and endangerment are too broad.
6. c. is the correct answer. Foster children often become good, nonmaltreating caregivers. (objective 4)
7. d. is the correct answer. (video lesson, segment 2; objective 3)
8. a. is the correct answer. (video lesson, segment 2; objective 2)
9. a. is the correct answer. (video lesson, segment 3; objective 3)

   b. is incorrect. Had the candidate called for measures to spot the early warning signs of maltreatment, this answer would be true.

   c. is incorrect. Had the candidate called for jailing those who maltreat children or providing greater counseling and health care for victims, this answer would be true.

   d. is incorrect. Permanency planning is the term for a long-term plan for a child who has experienced substantiated maltreatment.
10. d. is the correct answer. Approximately 30 percent of adults who were abused as children themselves become abusive parents. (video lesson, segment 3; objective 2)
11. b. is the correct answer. (objective 3)
12. a. is the correct answer. (Figure 10.1, p. 304; video lesson, segment 1; objective 1)

Matching

13. b. is the correct answer (objective 4)
14. a. is the correct answer (objective 4)
15. d. is the correct answer (video lesson, segment 2; objective 2)
16. f. is the correct answer (video lesson, segment 2; objective 2)
17. c. is the correct answer (video lesson, segment 3; objective 3)
18. e. is the correct answer (video lesson, segment 3; objective 3)
19. g is the correct answer (video lesson, segment 3; objective 3)
20. h is the correct answer (objective 5)

Lesson Review

Lesson 15

The Play Years
Special Topic

Please Note: Use this matrix to guide your study and achieve the learning objectives of this lesson. It will also help you to view the video, which defines and demonstrates important concepts and skills as they relate to everyday life.

Learning Objective	Textbook	Course Student Guide	Video Lesson
1. Discuss the effects of television and the media on a child's development.	pp. 303–304	Practice Questions: 1, 12.	Segment 1: *Media Influences*
2. Identify the various categories of child maltreatment, and discuss several factors that contribute to its occurrence.	pp. 247–253	Key Terms: 1, 2, 3, 4, 5; Practice Questions: 5, 8, 10, 15, 16.	Segment 2: *Child Maltreatment: Causes & Consequences*
3. Discuss the consequences, prevention, and approaches to treating child maltreatment, which includes both abuse and neglect.	pp. 250–253	Key Terms: 6, 11, 12, 13; Practice Questions: 3, 4, 7, 9, 11, 17, 18, 19.	Segment 2: *Child Maltreatment: Causes & Consequences* Segment 3: *Child Maltreatment: Treatment & Prevention*
4. Discuss permanency planning including foster care, kinship care, and adoption as long-term intervention options in cases of child maltreatment.	pp. 252–253	Key Terms: 7, 8, 9, 10; Practice Questions: 6, 13, 14.	
5. Discuss the impact of punishment on a child's development and describe alternative methods for disciplining a child.	pp. 307–311	Key Terms: 14; Practice Questions: 2, 20.	Segment 3: *Child Maltreatment: Treatment & Prevention*

The Golden Years of Childhood

Lesson 16

The School Years: Biosocial Development

Preview

This lesson introduces **middle childhood**, the years from about 6 to 11. Changes in physical size and shape are described, and the problem of **obesity** is addressed. The discussion then turns to the continuing development of the brain and motor skills. A final section examines the experiences of **children with special needs**, such as those diagnosed with **learning disabilities** or **attention-deficit/hyperactivity disorder (ADHD)**. The causes of and treatments for these problems are discussed, with emphasis placed on insights arising from the **developmental psychopathology** perspective. This perspective makes it clear that the manifestations of any special childhood problem will change, as the child grows older and that treatment must often focus on all three domains of development.

As you complete this lesson, think about any children you know in this age range. Consider their height and weight relative to other children of the same age (and younger). Are any of these children overweight? If so, speculate on the possible causes. Also, observe the motor skills of these children—how does their coordination compare with younger and older children? Do any of these children have a special problem or disorder, such as a learning disability or ADHD? If so, how are they being treated? What kind of special services or treatment do they receive at school?

Prior Knowledge That Will Be Used in This Lesson

- Biosocial development during infancy and toddlerhood (Lesson 6), as well as that during early childhood (Lesson 11) will be referred to as we discuss variations in physique and the development of motor skills during the school years.
- This lesson will return to the concept of *self-esteem* (Lesson 13), how a child feels about him- or herself. A child's perception of his or her biological development (especially relative to peers) can affect self-evaluation in both positive and negative ways.

Learning Objectives

Use this information to guide your reading, viewing, thinking, and studying. After successfully completing this lesson, you should be able to:

1. Describe normal physical growth and development during the school years, and account for the factors that help ensure health in the school years.
2. Define BMI and discuss the problem of childhood obesity and its potential effects on a child's physical and psychological health.
3. Identify the major causes of obesity, and outline the best approaches for treatment.
4. Discuss the common health problem called asthma, focusing on its causes, prevention, treatment, and impact on development.
5. Describe brain maturation during the school years, including the concepts of automatization, selective attention, and reaction time.
6. Describe the methods used to measure developmental changes in brain function and mental processes, which include achievement tests, aptitude, and IQ testing.
7. Outline the developmental psychopathology perspective, and discuss its value in treating children with special needs.
8. Discuss the characteristics and possible causes of learning disabilities, emphasizing autism spectrum disorder.
9. Describe the symptoms and possible causes of attention-deficit/hyperactivity disorder (ADHD) and bipolar disorder, noting the challenges of distinguishing between the two, and discuss the types of treatment available for children with these disorders.
10. Describe techniques that have been tried in efforts to educate children with special needs.

Textbook Reading & Video Viewing

For the most effective study of this lesson, complete the assignments in the sequence listed below.

Before viewing the video program:

Read Chapter 11, "The School Years: Biosocial Development," pages 321–349.

View the video for Lesson 16, "The Golden Years of Childhood."

Segment 1: *Physical Growth*

Segment 2: *Motor-Skill Development*

Segment 3: *Special Needs*

After viewing the video program:

Review all reading assignments for this lesson.

Complete the "Practice Questions" and "Applying Your Knowledge" sections to reinforce your understanding of important terms and concepts and measure your achievement of the Learning Objectives. Check your answers with the feedback given and review when necessary.

Practice Questions I

Multiple-Choice Questions

1. As children move into middle childhood,
   a. the rate of accidental death increases.
   b. sexual urges intensify.
   c. the rate of weight gain increases.
   d. biological growth slows and steadies.

2. During middle childhood,
   a. girls tend to be stronger than boys.
   b. girls and boys have significantly different patterns of motor development.
   c. boys and girls are very similar in physical development.
   d. the development of girls' and boys' motor skills slows drastically.

3. To help obese children, nutritionists usually recommend
   a. strenuous dieting to counteract early overfeeding.
   b. the use of amphetamines and other drugs.
   c. more exercise and time to "grow out" of the fat.
   d. no specific actions.

4. Dyslexia is a learning disability that affects the ability to
   a. do math.
   b. read.
   c. write.
   d. speak.

5. In relation to weight in later life, childhood obesity is
   a. not an accurate predictor of adolescent or adult weight.
   b. predictive of adolescent but not adult weight.
   c. predictive of adult but not adolescent weight.
   d. predictive of both adolescent and adult weight.

6. The developmental psychopathology perspective is characterized by its
   a. study of normal development.
   b. emphasis on individual therapy.
   c. emphasis on the cognitive domain of development.
   d. concern with all of the above.

7. The time—usually measured in fractions of a second—it takes for a person to respond to a particular stimulus is called

   a. the interstimulus interval.

   b. reaction time.

   c. the stimulus-response interval.

   d. response latency.

8. Which of the following are considered causes of childhood obesity?

   a. parenting practices

   b. genes

   c. social influences

   d. all the above

9. The underlying problem in attention-deficit/hyperactivity disorder is

   a. low overall intelligence.

   b. a brain abnormality resulting in difficulty paying attention.

   c. a learning disability in a specific academic skill.

   d. the existence of a conduct disorder.

10. The process by which thoughts and actions are repeated so often that they require little or no conscious thought is referred to as

   a. the Flynn effect.

   b. selective attention.

   c. automatization.

   d. myelination.

11. Which of the following is an example of primary prevention of asthma?

   a. a suggestion to a family with a history of allergies to breastfeed their newborn

   b. proper ventilation of homes and schools

   c. prompt use of medications when an asthma attack begins

   d. all of the above

12. Children's increasing ability to read without painstakingly sounding out letters and words is an example of

   a. selective attention.

   b. reaction time.

   c. dyslexia.

   d. automatization.

13. Which of the following testing methods are used to measure brain function and mental processes according to the Berger textbook?

    a. IQ tests
    b. brain scans
    c. aptitude and achievement tests
    d. all of the above

True or False Items

Write T (for true) or F (for false) on the line in front of each statement.

14. _____ The increasing myelination that occurs in middle childhood allows for the development of selective attention.
15. _____ Bipolar disorder can only be diagnosed in adulthood.
16. _____ During middle childhood, children experience slower growth and stronger muscles.
17. _____ The quick reaction time that is crucial in some sports can be readily achieved with practice.
18. _____ Despite the efforts of teachers and parents, most children with learning disabilities can expect their disabilities to persist and even worsen as they enter adulthood.
19. _____ The best way for children to lose weight is through strenuous dieting.
20. _____ Children with dyslexia will have the most favorable outcome if they are given individualized instruction before age 6 so that they can form new neurological patterns.
21. _____ The best educational approach for gifted children is learning alongside peers with the same mental age, regardless of chronological age.
22. _____ The drugs sometimes given to children to reduce hyperactive behaviors are most effective in combination with counseling and adequate teacher training.
23. _____ Response to intervention (RTI) is an educational strategy that targets low achievers in early grades with special intervention.

Practice Questions II

Multiple-Choice Questions

1. During the years from age 6 to 11, the average child

    a. becomes slimmer.
    b. gains about 12 pounds a year.
    c. has decreased lung capacity.
    d. is more likely to become obese than at any other period in the life span.

2. Among the factors that are known to contribute to obesity are activity level, quantity of food eaten, and

   a. quality of food.
   b. television-watching.
   c. social policies.
   d. all of the above.

3. A specific learning disability that becomes apparent when a child experiences unusual difficulty in learning to read is

   a. dyslexia.
   b. dyscalculia.
   c. ADHD.
   d. autism.

4. Specific problems in learning to write, to read, or to do math are collectively referred to as

   a. learning disabilities.
   b. attention-deficit/hyperactivity disorder.
   c. hyperactivity.
   d. dyscalculia.

5. A measure of obesity in which weight in kilograms is divided by the square of height in meters is the

   a. basal metabolic rate (BMR).
   b. body mass index (BMI).
   c. body fat index (BFI).
   d. basal fat ratio (BFR).

6. The most effective form of help for children with ADHD is

   a. medication.
   b. psychological therapy.
   c. environmental change.
   d. a combination of some or all of the above.

7. A key factor in reaction time is

   a. whether the child is male or female.
   b. brain maturation.
   c. whether the stimulus to be reacted to is an auditory or visual one.
   d. all of the above.

8. Which of the following is true of children with a diagnosed learning disability?
   a. A child might have an average or above average IQ.
   b. Children find ways to compensate for their disability.
   c. The child may receive "scattered" scores when tested—high on some, low on others.
   d. All of the above are true.
9. During the school years,
   a. boys are, on average, at least a year ahead of girls in the development of physical abilities.
   b. girls are, on average, at least a year ahead of boys in the development of physical abilities.
   c. boys and girls are about equal in physical abilities.
   d. motor-skill development proceeds at a slower pace, since children grow more rapidly at this age than at any other time.
10. Which of the following is **NOT** a lesson provided by developmental psychopathology?
   a. Adolescence and adulthood make disabilities worse.
   b. Abnormality is normal.
   c. Diagnosis depends on the social context.
   d. Disability changes over time.
11. Which approach to education may seem more effective in meeting the needs of children with learning disabilities in terms of social skills and academic achievement?
   a. mainstreaming
   b. special education
   c. inclusion
   d. resource rooms
12. Which of the following factors are considered true in most cases of ADHD?
   a. More boys than girls are diagnosed.
   b. Other disorders are often comorbid with ADHD.
   c. Some comorbid conditions can be consequences of undiagnosed ADHD.
   d. All of the above are true.

Matching Items

Match each term or concept with its corresponding description or definition.

Terms or Concepts

13. ______ individual education plan (IEP)
14. ______ dyslexia
15. ______ dyscalculia
16. ______ learning disability
17. ______ attention-deficit/hyperactivity disorder (ADHD)
18. ______ asthma
19. ______ developmental psychopathology
20. ______ equifinality
21. ______ multifinality

Descriptions or Definitions

a. an unexpected difficulty with one or more specific academic skills
b. the principle that holds that one symptom can have many causes
c. a document specifying the educational goals of a child with special needs
d. the principle that holds that one cause can have many final manifestations
e. difficulty in reading
f. chronic inflammation of the airways
g. behavior problem involving difficulty in concentrating, as well as excitability and impulsivity
h. difficulty in math
i. applies insights from studies of normal development to the study of childhood disorders

Applying Your Knowledge

1. According to developmentalists, the best game for a typical group of eight-year-olds would be
   a. football or baseball.
   b. basketball.
   c. one in which reaction time is not crucial.
   d. a game involving one-on-one competition.
2. Dr. Rutter, who believes that "we can learn more about an organism's normal functioning by studying its pathology and, likewise, more about its pathology by studying its normal condition," evidently is working from which of the following perspectives?
   a. clinical psychology
   b. developmental psychopathology
   c. behaviorism
   d. psychoanalysis

3. Nine-year-old Paul, who lives in the United States, has difficulty concentrating on his class work for more than a few moments, repeatedly asks his teacher irrelevant questions, and is constantly disrupting the class with loud noises. If his difficulties persist, Paul is likely to be diagnosed as suffering from

   a. dyslexia.

   b. dyscalculia.

   c. conduct disorder.

   d. attention-deficit/hyperactivity disorder.

4. Britta is an average, healthy eight-year-old girl. She should be able to carry out which of the following tasks alone?

   a. brush her teeth

   b. button her jacket

   c. make her own lunch

   d. all of the above

5. Ten-year-old Clarence frequently experiences extreme mood swings that are not caused by circumstantial factors. Clarence may be suffering from

   a. dyslexia.

   b. dyscalculia.

   c. autism.

   d. bipolar disorder.

6. Of the following individuals, who is likely to have the fastest reaction time?

   a. a seven-year-old

   b. a nine-year-old

   c. an eleven-year-old

   d. a young adult

7. Les is a child with special needs who attends public school in the United States. Which of the following is **MOST** likely to be true of his education?

   a. He spends a great deal of time in the resource room with special education teachers.

   b. He is included in a general education classroom and has a specially trained aide.

   c. His learning context complies with the mandate of the most encouraging environment.

   d. He is in a class made up of other children with special needs.

8. In determining whether an eight-year-old has a learning disability, a teacher looks primarily for
   a. discrepant performance in a particular subject area.
   b. the exclusion of other explanations.
   c. both a and b.
   d. none of the above.
9. A friend's child has just been diagnosed with ADHD. On the basis of what you have learned from the Berger textbook, you might emphasize to your friend the importance of
   a. accepting that the child will always be a slow learner.
   b. finding the proper classroom environment.
   c. teaching compliance to the child to reduce behavioral disturbances at home and in school.
   d. avoiding prescription drugs.
10. Danny has been diagnosed as having attention-deficit/hyperactivity disorder. Every day his parents make sure that he takes the proper dose of Ritalin. His parents should
    a. continue this behavior until Danny is an adult.
    b. try different medications when Danny seems to be reverting to his normal overactive behavior.
    c. make sure that Danny also has psychotherapy.
    d. not worry about Danny's condition; he will outgrow it.
11. In concluding her presentation entitled "Facts and falsehoods regarding childhood obesity," Cheryl states that, contrary to popular belief, ___________ is not a common cause of childhood obesity.
    a. television-watching
    b. lack of exercise
    c. overeating of high-fat foods
    d. a prenatal teratogen
12. Curtis is 8 years old, 48 inches (1.22 meters) tall, and weighs 58 pounds (26.4 kilograms). His BMI equals __________, making him statistically ___________.
    a. 20; obese
    b. 20; overweight
    c. 17.7; normal body weight
    d. 17.7; obese

13. For a ten-year-old, some mental activities have become so familiar or routine as to require little mental work. This development is called

    a. selective attention.

    b. identity.

    c. metacognition.

    d. automatization.

14. Claire and Tiana, both seven years old, experienced high levels of stress hormones as infants because of domestic violence. As a result, Claire is hypervigilant, while Tiana is unusually calm. This difference is an illustration of the basic principle of developmental psychopathology known as

    a. multifinality.

    b. variability.

    c. equifinality.

    d. multiple intelligences.

Key Terms

1. **middle childhood:** The period between early childhood and early adolescence, approximately from ages 6 to 11. (p. 323; objective 1)
2. **body mass index (BMI):** A measure of obesity in which a person's weight in kilograms is divided by his or her height squared in meters. (p. 328; video lesson, segment 1; objective 2)
3. **overweight:** In a child, having a BMI above the 85th percentile, according to the U.S. Centers for Disease Control's 1980 standards for children of a given age. (p. 328; video lesson, segment 1; objective 1).
4. **obesity:** In a child, having a BMI above the 95th percentile, according to the U.S. Centers for Disease Control's 1980 standards for children of a given age. (p. 328; video lesson, segment 1; objective 1)
5. **asthma:** A chronic disease of the respiratory system in which inflammation narrows the airways from the nose and mouth to the lungs, causing difficulty in breathing. Signs and symptoms include wheezing, shortness of breath, chest tightness, and coughing. (p. 330; objective 4)
6. **reaction time:** The time it takes to respond to a stimulus, either physically (with a reflexive movement such as an eyeblink) or cognitively (with a thought). (p. 333; objective 5)
7. **selective attention:** The ability to concentrate on some stimuli while ignoring others. (p. 333; objective 5)
8. **automatization:** A process in which repetition of a sequence of thoughts and actions makes the sequence routine, so that it no longer requires conscious thought. (p. 334; objective 5)
9. **aptitude:** The potential to master a specific skill or to learn a certain body of knowledge. (p. 334; objective 6)

10. **IQ tests:** Tests designed to measure intellectual aptitude, or ability to learn in school. Originally, intelligence was defined as mental age divided by chronological age, times 100—hence the term *intelligence quotient*, or IQ. (p. 334; objective 6)
11. **achievement tests:** A measurement of mastery or proficiency in reading, math, writing, science, or some other subject. (p. 334; objective 6)
12. **Flynn effect:** The rise in average IQ scores that has occurred over the decades in many nations. (p. 335; objective 6)
13. **multiple intelligences:** The idea that human intelligence is comprised of a varied set of abilities rather than a single, all-encompassing one. (p. 335; objective 6)
14. **developmental psychopathology:** The field that uses insights into typical development to understand and remediate developmental disorders. (p. 337; video lesson, segment 3; objective 7)
15. **comorbid:** The presence of two or more unrelated disease conditions at the same time in the same person. (p. 338; objective 7)
16. **multifinality:** A basic principle of developmental psychopathology that holds that one cause can have many (multiple) final manifestations. (p. 338; objective 7)
17. **equifinality:** A basic principle of developmental psychopathology that holds that one symptom can have many causes. (p. 338; objective 7)
18. **attention-deficit/hyperactivity disorder (ADHD):** A condition in which a person not only has great difficulty concentrating for more than a few moments but also is inattentive, impulsive, and overactive. (p. 338; video lesson, segment 3; objective 9)
19. **bipolar disorder:** A condition characterized by extreme mood swings, from euphoria to deep depression, not caused by outside experiences. (p. 339; objective 9)
20. **learning disability:** A marked delay in a particular area of learning that is not caused by an apparent physical disability, by mental retardation, or by an unusually stressful home environment. (p. 341; video lesson, segment 3; objective 8)
21. **dyslexia:** An unusual difficulty with reading; thought to be the result of some neurological underdevelopment. (p. 341; video lesson, segment 3; objective 8)
22. **autism:** A developmental disorder marked by an inability to relate to other people normally, extreme self-absorption, and an inability to acquire normal speech. (p. 342; objective 8)
23. **autism spectrum disorder:** Any of several disorders characterized by inadequate social skills, impaired communication, and unusual play. (p. 342; objective 8)
24. **least restrictive environment (LRE):** A legally required school setting that allows children with special needs to benefit from the instruction available to most children (often in traditional classrooms). (p. 344; objective 10)

25. **response to intervention (RTI):** An educational strategy intended to help children in early grades who demonstrate below average achievement by means of special intervention. (p. 345; objective 10)
26. **individual education plan (IEP):** A legal document that specifies the educational goals and plans for a child with special needs. (p. 345; objective 10)
27. **acceleration:** The strategy of educating gifted children alongside other children of the same mental, not chronological, age. (p. 346; objective 10)
28. **children with special needs:** Children who require particular physical, intellectual, or social accommodations in order to learn. (pp. 337–338; objectives 7 & 10)
29. **dyscalculia:** A learning disability in math. Also called *dyscalcula*. (video lesson, segment 3; objective 8)
30. **mainstreaming:** An educational approach in which children with special needs are included in regular classrooms. (video lesson, segment 3; objective 10)

Summary

For most boys and girls, the years of the school years are a time when biosocial development is smooth and uneventful. Children become slimmer than in earlier years, their limbs lengthen, their body proportions change, their muscles become stronger, and their lung capacity increases. Brain and body maturation coupled with sufficient practice enables school-age children to master many motor skills.

Diet interacts with heredity, activity level, and other factors to create obesity in some cases. Obesity is a growing problem in North American children during the school years. Obese children are at increased risk of serious orthopedic and respiratory problems. The best way to get children to lose weight is to increase their physical activity and change their eating patterns. In some cases, a family-based treatment program of exercise and nutrition education is necessary. It is better to treat obesity early in life before habits that contribute to weight gain become well established.

Another serious problem for many children is **asthma**—a disorder characterized by chronic inflammation of the airways. Asthma is becoming increasingly prevalent in developed nations, indicating that environmental factors are to blame. Several aspects of modern life contribute to asthma, including crowded living conditions, airtight windows, carpeted floors, more bedding, dogs and cats living inside the house, and so forth.

Motor habits that rely on coordinating both sides of the body improve because the corpus callosum between the brain's hemispheres continues to mature. In addition, rough-and-tumble play may help boys overcome their tendencies toward hyperactivity and learning disabilities because it helps with regulation in the frontal lobes of the brain. Motor-skill development is also influenced by culture, national policies, and genetic endowment.

For children with special needs, development can be limited by the difficulties posed by physical or mental disabilities. The field of **developmental psychopathology** applies insights from studies of normal development to the origins and treatment of childhood disorders to help these children learn and reach their full potential.

Children are said to have a **learning disability** when their difficulty with a particular skill is in surprising contrast with their overall intelligence level. One of the most puzzling problems in childhood is **attention-deficit/hyperactivity disorder (ADHD)**, a behavior problem characterized by excessive activity, an inability to concentrate, and impulsive, sometimes aggressive behavior. Further complicating the puzzle is the frequently **comorbid** mood disorder known as **bipolar disorder**, which shares many symptoms with ADHD. Bipolar disorder is characterized by extreme mood swings, from the highest highs to the lowest lows, with no external cause. Both ADHD and bipolar disorder may arise from several factors, including genetic differences, teratogens, and family and environmental influences.

Special Note: We will discuss the topics of developmental psychopathology and autism (pp. 337–344) in more detail in Lesson 26, "Different Paths."
We will cover multiple intelligences and the use of tests (pp. 334–337) in Lesson 20, "School Days."

Answer Key

Practice Questions I

Multiple-Choice Questions

1. d. is the correct answer. (video lesson, segment 1; objective 1)
2. c. is the correct answer. (video lesson, segments 1 & 2; objective 1)

   a. & b. are incorrect. At this age, physical and motor development is quite similar.

   d. is incorrect. Motor-skill development improves greatly during middle childhood.
3. c. is the correct answer. (video lesson, segment 1; objective 3)

   a. is incorrect. Dieting is not recommended, as it can be physically harmful and may increase the desire for the forbidden foods.

   b. is incorrect. The use of amphetamines to control weight is not recommended at any age.
4. b. is the correct answer. (video lesson, segment 3; objective 8)

   a. is incorrect. This is dyscalcula (or dyscalculia).

   c. & d. are incorrect. The textbook does not give labels for learning disabilities in writing or speaking.
5. d. is the correct answer. (video lesson, segment 1; objective 2)
6. a. is the correct answer. (video lesson, segment 3; objective 7)

   b. & c. are incorrect. Because of its contextual approach, developmental psychopathology emphasizes group therapy and all domains of development.

7. b. is the correct answer. (objective 5)
8. d. is the correct answer. (video lesson, segment 1; objective 3)
9. b. is the correct answer. (video lesson, segment 3; objective 9)
10. c. is the correct answer. (objective 5)

    a. is incorrect. Overweight children tend to begin puberty earlier than children of average weight.

    b. is incorrect. In fact, just the opposite is true.

    d. is incorrect. Children tend to do best when they mature at the same rate as their peers.
11. b. is the correct answer. (objective 4)

    a. is incorrect. This is an example of secondary prevention.

    c. is incorrect. This is an example of tertiary prevention.
12. d. is the correct answer. (objective 5)

    a. is incorrect. Selective attention refers to the ability to only concentrate on particular stimuli when many stimuli are present.

    b. is incorrect. Reaction time refers to the length of time it takes a person to respond to a particular stimulus.

    c. is incorrect. Dyslexia is a learning disability in reading.
13. d. is the correct answer. (objective 6)

True or False Items

14. T (objective 5)
15. F Although difficult to accurately diagnose, bipolar disorder is seen in some children and adolescents. (objective 9)
16. T (objective 1)
17. F In childhood, reaction time depends primarily on brain maturation, which is related to age. (objective 5)
18. F With the proper assistance, many children with learning disabilities develop into adults who are virtually indistinguishable from other adults in their educational and occupational achievements. (video lesson, segment 3; objective 8)
19. F Strenuous dieting during childhood can be dangerous. The best way to get children to lose weight is by increasing their activity level. (video lesson, segment 1; objective 3)
20. T (video lesson, segment 3; objective 8)
21. F This approach, known as acceleration, has fallen out of favor due to its negative impact on self-esteem and the development of social skills. (objective 10)
22. T (objective 9)
23. T (objective 10)

Practice Questions II

Multiple-Choice Questions

1. a. is the correct answer. (video lesson, segment 1; objective 1)

   b. & c. are incorrect. During this period children gain about 5 pounds per year and experience increased lung capacity.

   d. is incorrect. Although childhood obesity is a common problem, the textbook does not indicate that a person is more likely to become obese at this age than at any other.

2. d. is the correct answer. (video lesson, segment 1; objective 3)
3. a. is the correct answer. (video lesson, segment 3; objective 8)

   b. is incorrect. This learning disability involves math rather than reading.

   c. & d. are incorrect. These disorders do not manifest themselves in a particular academic skill.

4. a. is the correct answer. (video lesson, segment 3; objective 8)

   b. is incorrect. ADHD is a general learning disability that usually does not manifest itself in specific subject areas. Hyperactivity is a facet of this disorder.

   d. is incorrect. Dyscalcula (or dyscalculia) is a learning disability in math only.

5. b. is the correct answer. (video lesson, segment 1; objective 2)
6. d. is the correct answer. (video lesson, segment 3; objective 9)
7. b. is the correct answer. (objective 5)
8. d. is the correct answer. (video lesson, segment 3; objective 8)
9. c. is the correct answer. (video lesson, segment 1; objective 1)
10. a. is the correct answer. Adolescence and adulthood can make disabilities better or worse. (objective 7)
11. c. is the correct answer. (objective 10)

    a. is incorrect. Many general education teachers are unable to cope with the special needs of some children.

    b. & d. are incorrect. These approaches undermined the social integration of children with special needs.

12. d. is the correct answer. (objective 9)

Matching Items

13. c (objective 10)
14. e (video lesson, segment 3; objective 8)
15. h (video lesson, segment 3; objective 8)
16. a (video lesson, segment 3; objective 8)
17. g (video lesson, segment 3; objective 9)
18. f (objective 4)
19. i (video lesson, segment 3; objective 7)

20. b (objective 7)
21. d (objective 7)

Applying Your Knowledge

1. c. is the correct answer. (objective 5)

   a. & b. are incorrect. Each of these games involves skills that are hardest for schoolchildren to master.

   d. is incorrect. Because one-on-one sports are likely to accentuate individual differences in ability, they may be especially discouraging to some children.
2. b. is the correct answer. (video lesson, segment 3; objective 7)
3. d. is the correct answer. (video lesson, segment 3; objective 9)

   a. & b. are incorrect. Paul's difficulty is in concentrating, not in reading (dyslexia) or math (dyscalcula or dyscalculia).

   c. is incorrect. These symptoms are characteristic of ADHD.
4. d. is the correct answer. (objective 1)
5. d. is the correct answer. (video lesson, segment 3; objective 9)
6. d. is the correct answer. (objective 5)
7. b. is the correct answer. (objective 10)

   a. & d. are incorrect. These arrangements are no longer common.

   c. is incorrect. The mandate is referred to as the least restrictive environment.
8. c. is the correct answer. (video lesson, segment 3; objective 8)
9. b. is the correct answer. (video lesson, segment 3; objective 9)
10. c. is the correct answer. Medication alone cannot ameliorate all the problems of ADHD. (video lesson, segment 3; objective 9)
11. d. is the correct answer. There is no evidence that teratogens have anything to do with obesity. (objective 3)
12. c. is the correct answer. BMI = weight/height squared. Therefore, BMI for Curtis = 26.4/1.49, or 17.7. For children at age 8, obesity begins at about 18 BMI. (video lesson, segment 1; objective 2)
13. d. is the correct answer. (objective 5)

    a. is incorrect. Selective attention is the ability to focus on important information and screen out distractions.

    b. is incorrect. Identity is the logical principle that certain characteristics of an object remain the same even when other characteristics change.

    c. is incorrect. Metacognition is the ability to evaluate a task and to monitor one's performance of it.
14. a. is the correct answer. (objective 7)

Lesson Review

Lesson 16

The School Years
Biosocial Development

Please Note: Use this matrix to guide your study and achieve the learning objectives of this lesson. It will also help you to view the video, which defines and demonstrates important concepts and skills as they relate to everyday life.

Learning Objective	Textbook	Course Student Guide	Video Lesson
1. Describe normal physical growth and development during middle childhood, and account for the factors that ensure health in middle childhood.	pp. 323-328	Key Terms: 1, 3, 4; Practice Questions I: 1, 2, 16; Practice Questions II: 1, 9; Applying Your Knowledge: 4.	Segment 1: *Physical Growth* Segment 2: *Motor-Skill Development*
2. Define BMI and discuss the problem of childhood obesity and its potential effects on a child's physical and psychological health.	pp. 328-329	Key Terms: 2; Practice Questions I: 5; Practice Questions II: 5; Applying Your Knowledge: 12.	Segment 1: *Physical Growth*
3. Identify the major causes of obesity, and outline the best approaches for treatment.	pp. 329-330	Practice Questions I: 3, 8, 19; Practice Questions II: 2; Applying Your Knowledge: 11.	Segment 1: *Physical Growth*
4. Discuss the common health problem called asthma, focusing on its causes, prevention, treatment, and impact on development.	pp. 330-332	Key Terms: 5; Practice Questions I: 11; Practice Questions II: 18.	
5. Describe brain maturation during middle childhood, including the concepts of automatization, selective attention, and reaction time.	pp. 332-334	Key Terms: 6, 7, 8; Practice Questions I: 7, 10, 12, 14, 17; Practice Questions II: 7; Applying Your Knowledge: 1, 6, 13.	
6. Describe the methods used to measure developmental changes in brain function and mental processes, which include achievement tests, aptitude, and IQ testing.	pp. 334-337	Key Terms: 9, 10, 11, 12, 13; Practice Questions I: 13.	Segment 2: *Motor-Skill Development*

Learning Objective	Textbook	Course Student Guide	Video Lesson
7. Outline the developmental psychopathology perspective, and discuss its value in treating children with special needs.	pp. 337–338	Key Terms: 14, 15, 16, 17, 28; Practice Questions I: 6; Practice Questions II: 10, 19, 20, 21; Applying Your Knowledge: 2, 14.	Segment 3: *Special Needs*
8. Discuss the characteristics and possible causes of learning disabilities, emphasizing autism spectrum disorders.	pp. 341–344	Key Terms: 20, 21, 22, 23, 29; Practice Questions I: 4, 18, 20; Practice Questions II: 3, 4, 8, 14, 15, 16; Applying Your Knowledge: 8.	Segment 3: *Special Needs*
9. Describe the symptoms and possible causes of attention-deficit/hyperactivity disorder (ADHD) and bipolar disorder, noting the challenges of distinguishing between the two, and discuss the types of treatment available for children with these disorders.	pp. 338–341	Key Terms: 18, 19; Practice Questions I: 9, 15, 22; Practice Questions II: 6, 12, 17; Applying Your Knowledge: 3, 5, 9, 10.	Segment 3: *Special Needs*
10. Describe techniques that have been tried in efforts to educate children with special needs.	pp. 344–347	Key Terms: 24, 25, 26, 27, 28, 30; Practice Questions I: 21, 23; Practice Questions II: 11, 13, 23; Applying Your Knowledge: 7.	Segment 3: *Special Needs*

The Age of Reason

Lesson 17

The School Years: Cognitive Development

Preview

Lesson 17 looks at the development of cognitive abilities in children from age 6 to 11. The first part of the lesson focuses on Jean Piaget's view of the child's cognitive development in this period, which involves a growing ability to use logic and reasoning. Next, we discuss Lev Vygotsky's perspective, with its emphasis on the role of instruction and sociocultural contexts. Concluding the section on theories, the information-processing perspective details changes in the child's **control processes**, processing speed and capacity, memory strategies, **knowledge base**, and problem-solving strategies.

The lesson also looks at moral reasoning and language learning in middle childhood. During this time, children develop a more analytic understanding of words and show a marked improvement in **pragmatics**, such as changing from one form of speech to another when the situation so demands. The linguistic and cognitive advantages of bilingualism are discussed, as are educational and environmental conditions that are conducive to fluency in a second language.

The final part of the lesson describes a variety of teaching methods, some of which are derived from the developmental theories of Piaget, Vygotsky, and others. Comparing education in the United States and other countries illuminates several possible reasons for the disparities. The lesson concludes by examining measures of cognitive growth, such as tests, and variations in cultural standards.

As you complete this lesson, consider the cognitive development of a child you know and/or interview the parent of a child in this age range (about age 6 to 11). Describe the cognitive skills of this child. In other words, how well can he or she focus attention, solve problems, and apply logical principles to the world? How well can this child recall facts, events and other memories? Describe the language skills of this child relative to younger and older children, including vocabulary and grammar. Does he or she speak a second language? Now, consider this child's moral development. Describe his or her moral code and how it applies to everyday decisions? Finally, how well does this child perform in school? Speculate on why. What techniques are used in the classroom to teach subjects such as reading and math.

Prior Knowledge That Will Be Used in This Lesson

- This lesson will introduce "**concrete operational thought**," the third stage in Jean Piaget's theory of cognitive development (from Lesson 1). Recall that Piaget's theory specifies four major periods of cognitive development:
    1. Sensorimotor (birth to 2 years)
    2. Preoperational (2 to 6 years)
    3. **Concrete Operational (7 to 11 years) ←The School Years**
    4. Formal Operational (12 years through adulthood)
- During its exploration of school learning, this lesson will return to Lev Vygotsky's theory of development (from Chapter 2/Lesson 1). Recall that Vygotsky emphasized the importance of *guided participation,* a learning process in which an individual learns through social interaction with a mentor.
- Recall the information processing model of cognition from Lesson 7. As children's brains continue to develop through middle childhood, they are capable of increasingly complex mental processes.
- Recall from Lesson 16 that middle childhood is the time of significant advances in selective attention and automatization.

Learning Objectives

Use this information to guide your reading, viewing, thinking, and studying. After successfully completing this lesson, you should be able to:

1. Identify and describe the elements of Piaget's and Vygotsky's theories about middle childhood, comparing and contrasting the two with particular attention to issues such as concrete operational thought, the role of instruction, and cultural variations.
2. Describe the components of the information-processing system, noting how they interact.
3. Discuss advances in the knowledge base, processing speed and capacity, and memory skills during middle childhood.
4. Discuss advances in cognitive control processes and metacognition during middle childhood.
5. Describe language development during middle childhood, noting changing abilities in vocabulary and pragmatics and causes of differences in language learning.
6. Outline Kohlberg's stage theory of moral development and describe several criticisms of the theory.
7. Compare the academic performance of children in countries around the world, and identify differences in culture, school, and home life that may account for differences in academic performance.
8. Identify several conditions that foster the learning of a second language, and describe different strategies for teaching another language to school-age children.

9. Differentiate several approaches to teaching reading and math, and discuss evidence regarding the effectiveness of these methods.

10. Discuss the determining factors in educational practice and describe three alternatives to public school, detailing the pros and cons of each.

Textbook Reading & Video Viewing

For the most effective study of this lesson, complete the assignments in the sequence listed below.

Before viewing the video program:

Read Chapter 12, "Middle Childhood: Cognitive Development," pages 351–375.

View the video for Lesson 17, "The Age of Reason."

Segment 1: *How School-Age Children Think*

Segment 2: *Language Development*

After viewing the video program:

Review all reading assignments for this lesson.

Complete the "Practice Questions" and "Applying Your Knowledge" sections to reinforce your understanding of important terms and concepts and measure your achievement of the Learning Objectives. Check your answers with the feedback given and review when necessary.

Practice Questions I

Multiple-Choice Questions

1. According to Piaget, the stage of cognitive development in which a person understands specific logical ideas and can apply them to concrete problems is called
   a. preoperational thought.
   b. operational thought.
   c. concrete operational thought.
   d. formal operational thought.

2. Which of the following is a reason why thinking speed increases during middle childhood?
   a. the increasing myelination of neural axons
   b. repeated sequences of neuron firing
   c. learning from experience
   d. all of the above

3. The idea that an object that has been transformed in some way can be restored to its original form by undoing the process is
   a. identity.
   b. reversibility.
   c. total immersion.
   d. automatization.
4. Information-processing theorists contend that major advances in cognitive development occur during the school years because
   a. the child's mind becomes more like a computer as he or she matures.
   b. children become better able to process and analyze information.
   c. most mental activities become automatic by the time a child is about 13 years old.
   d. the major improvements in reasoning that occur during the school years involve increased long-term memory capacity.
5. The ability to evaluate a cognitive task in order to best determine how to accomplish it is called
   a. metacognition.
   b. information processing.
   c. selective attention.
   d. decentering.
6. Concrete operational thought is Piaget's term for the school-age child's ability to
   a. reason logically about things and events he or she perceives.
   b. think about thinking.
   c. understand that certain characteristics of an object remain the same when other characteristics are changed.
   d. understand that moral principles may supersede the standards of society.
7. The term for the ability to monitor one's cognitive performance—to think about thinking—is
   a. pragmatics.
   b. information processing.
   c. selective attention.
   d. metacognition.
8. Long-term memory is ___________ permanent and ___________ limited than working memory.
   a. more; less
   b. less; more
   c. more; more
   d. less; less

9. In making moral choices, according to Gilligan, females are more likely than males to
   a. score at a higher level in Kohlberg's system.
   b. emphasize the needs of others.
   c. judge right and wrong in absolute terms.
   d. formulate abstract principles.

10. Compared to language development among more advantaged children, children from low-income families show deficits in
   a. vocabulary.
   b. syntax.
   c. sentence length.
   d. all of the above.

11. The formal code that children use in the classroom is characterized by
   a. limited use of vocabulary and syntax.
   b. context-bound grammar.
   c. extensive use of gestures and intonation to convey meaning.
   d. correct grammar, full sentences, and good pronunciation.

12. Which of the following is **NOT** an approach used in the United States to avoid the shock of complete immersion in the teaching of English?
   a. reverse immersion
   b. English as a second language
   c. bilingual schooling
   d. heritage language classes

13. Code-switching occurs among
   a. low-income children.
   b. affluent children.
   c. ethnic minority children.
   d. all of the above; children of all backgrounds and ethnicities code-switch.

14. Between 9 and 11 years of age, children are **MOST** likely to demonstrate moral reasoning at which of Kohlberg's stages?
   a. preconventional
   b. conventional
   c. postconventional
   d. It is impossible to predict based on a child's age.

15. Of the following, which was **NOT** identified as an important factor in the difference between success and failure in second-language learning?

    a. the age of the child
    b. the attitudes of the parents
    c. community values regarding second-language learning
    d. the difficulty of the language

True or False Items

Write T (for true) or F (for false) on the line in front of each statement.

16. _____ One major objection to Piaget's theory is that it describes the schoolchild as an active learner, a term appropriate only for preschoolers.

17. _____ Learning a second language fosters children's overall linguistic and cognitive development.

18. _____ During middle childhood, children are particularly concerned with issues of right and wrong.

19. _____ In an international math test, the average ten-year-old in Singapore was ahead of the top 5 percent of U.S. students.

20. _____ The process of telling a joke involves pragmatic language skills usually not mastered before age 7.

21. _____ Code-switching, especially the occasional use of slang, is a behavior characteristic primarily of children in the lower social strata.

22. _____ Middle childhood is a good time to learn a new language because 7- to 11-year-olds are eager to communicate.

23. _____ Most information that comes into sensory memory is lost or discarded.

24. _____ Information-processing theorists believe that advances in the thinking of school-age children occur primarily because of changes in long-term memory.

25. _____ New standards of math education in the United States emphasize problem-solving skills rather than simple memorization of formulas.

26. ____ Vygotsky believed that instruction is critical in children's development of necessary skills and knowledge.

27. ____ Unlike regular public schools, both private schools and charter schools charge tuition for attendance.

Practice Questions II

Multiple-Choice Questions

1. According to Piaget, eight- and nine-year-olds can reason only about concrete things in their lives. "Concrete" means
   a. logical.
   b. abstract.
   c. tangible or visible.
   d. mathematical or classifiable.

2. Recent research regarding Piaget's theory has found that
   a. as Vygotsky believed, cognitive development seems to be considerably more affected by sociocultural factors than Piaget's descriptions imply.
   b. the movement to a new level of thinking is much less erratic than Piaget predicted.
   c. there is a dramatic logical shift that occurs between ages 5 and 7, as Piaget predicted.
   d. all of the above are true.

3. The increase in processing speed that occurs during middle childhood is partly the result of
   a. ongoing myelination of axons.
   b. neurological development in the limbic system.
   c. the streamlining of the knowledge base.
   d. all of the above.

4. When psychologists look at the ability of children to receive, store, and organize information, they are examining cognitive development from a view based on
   a. the observations of Piaget.
   b. information processing.
   c. learning theory.
   d. Vygotsky's model.

5. Kohlberg's stage theory of moral development is based on his research on a group of boys and on
   a. psychoanalytic ideas.
   b. Piaget's theory of cognitive development.
   c. Carol Gilligan's research on moral dilemmas.
   d. questionnaires distributed to a nationwide sample of high school seniors.

6. The logical operations of concrete operational thought are particularly important to an understanding of the elementary-school subject of

   a. spelling.
   b. reading.
   c. math.
   d. social studies.

7. Although older school-age children are generally at the conventional level of moral reasoning, when they reach a particular level depends on

   a. the specific context and the child's opportunity to discuss moral issues.
   b. the level of moral reasoning reached by their parents.
   c. how strongly their peers influence their thinking.
   d. whether they are male or female.

8. Piaget studied the ability to figure out (infer) the unspoken link between one fact and another. He called this ability

   a. reversibility.
   b. reciprocity.
   c. transitive inference.
   d. operational thought.

9. Working memory capacity refers to

   a. the ability to selectively attend to more than one thought.
   b. the amount of information that a person is able to use for current conscious mental activity.
   c. the size of the child's knowledge base.
   d. all of the above.

10. The retention of new information is called

    a. retrieval.
    b. storage.
    c. automatization.
    d. metacognition.

11. According to Kohlberg, a person whose morality involves being a dutiful citizen and obeying the laws set down by society is at which level of moral reasoning?

    a. preconventional stage one
    b. preconventional stage two
    c. conventional
    d. postconventional

12. Which aspect of the information-processing system assumes an executive role in regulating the analysis and transfer of information?
    a. sensory memory
    b. working memory
    c. long-term memory
    d. control processes
13. An example of schoolchildren's growth in metacognition is their understanding that
    a. transformed objects can be returned to their original state.
    b. rehearsal is a good strategy for memorizing, but outlining is better for understanding.
    c. objects may belong to more than one class.
    d. they can use different language styles in different situations.
14. Which of the following most accurately states the relative merits of the phonics approach and the whole-language approach to teaching reading?
    a. The phonics approach is more effective.
    b. The whole-language approach is more effective.
    c. Both approaches have merit.
    d. Both approaches have been discarded in favor of newer, more interactive methods of instruction.
15. Regarding bilingual schooling, many contemporary developmentalists believe that
    a. the attempted learning of two languages seriously delays proficiency in both languages.
    b. bilingual schooling can be cognitively advantageous to children.
    c. second-language education is most effective when the child has not yet mastered the native language.
    d. bilingual schooling programs are too expensive to justify the few developmental advantages they confer.

Matching Items

Match each term or concept with its corresponding description or definition.

Terms or Concepts

16. __________ phonics approach
17. __________ reversibility
18. __________ conventional
19. __________ identity
20. __________ information processing
21. __________ whole-language approach
22. __________ voucher
23. __________ retrieval
24. __________ storage
25. __________ metacognition
26. __________ immersion
27. __________ postconventional
28. __________ preconventional
29. __________ home schooling

Descriptions or Definitions

a. a method that encourages drawing, writing with inventive spelling, talking, and listening
b. the idea that a transformation process can be undone to restore the original conditions
c. the idea that certain characteristics of an object remain the same even when other characteristics change
d. developmental perspective that conceives of cognitive development as the result of changes in the processing and analysis of information
e. moral reasoning in which the individual focuses on his or her own welfare
f. moral reasoning in which the individual follows principles that supersede the standards of society
g. an educational technique in which instruction occurs entirely in the second language
h. accessing previously learned information
i. holding information in memory
j. moral reasoning in which the individual considers social standards and laws to be primary
k. method that requires children to sound out words
l. the ability to evaluate a cognitive task and to monitor one's performance on it
m. while authorities set the learning standards, parents select the curriculum and schedules in this approach to schooling
n. can be used by parents to pay for tuition at a private school in some jurisdictions

Applying Your Knowledge

1. Of the following statements made by children, which best exemplifies the logical principle of identity?
   a. "You can't leave first base until the ball is hit!"
   b. "See how the jello springs back into shape after I poke my finger into it?"
   c. "I know it's still a banana, even though it's mashed down in my sandwich."
   d. "You're my friend, so I don't have talk politely like I do with adults."
2. Which of the following statements is the clearest indication that the child has grasped the principle of reversibility?
   a. "See, the lemonade is still the same in both our glasses; if I pour mine back into that glass, it will look the same again."
   b. "Even though your dog looks funny, I know it's still a dog."
   c. "I have one sister and no brothers. My parents have two children."
   d. "I don't cheat because I don't want to be punished."

3. Compared to her four-year-old sister, nine-year-old Andrea is more likely to seek explanations that are

   a. intuitive.

   b. generalizable.

   c. subjective.

   d. all of the above.

4. Dr. Larsen believes that the cognitive advances of middle childhood occur because of basic changes in children's thinking speed, knowledge base, and memory retrieval skills. Dr. Larsen evidently is working from the ___________ perspective.

   a. Piagetian

   b. Vygotskian

   c. information-processing

   d. psychoanalytic

5. Some researchers believe that cognitive processing speed and capacity increase during middle childhood because of

   a. the myelination of nerve pathways.

   b. the maturation of the prefrontal cortex.

   c. better use of cognitive resources.

   d. all of the above.

6. A child's ability to tell a joke that will amuse his or her audience always depends on

   a. the child's mastery of reciprocity and reversibility.

   b. code switching.

   c. the child's intellectual flexibility.

   d. an expansion of the child's processing capacity.

7. Immersion is an approach to learning a second language in which

   a. the child is taught entirely in the second language.

   b. the second language is taught as a foreign language in middle school.

   c. all children receive bilingual and bicultural education.

   d. the child is taught entirely in his or her original language.

8. Lana is age 4, and her brother Roger is 7. The fact that Roger remembers what their mother just told them about playing in the street while Lana is more interested in the children playing across the street at the time is partially the result of improvements in Roger's

   a. code-switching.

   b. automatization.

   c. selective attention.

   d. long-term memory.

9. Which of the following statements is the best example of stage 1 of Kohlberg's preconventional level of moral reasoning?
   a. "Might makes right."
   b. "Law and order."
   c. "Nice boys do what is expected of them."
   d. "Look out for number one."
10. According to Carol Gilligan, a girl responding to the hypothetical question of whether an impoverished child should steal food to feed her starving dog is most likely to
   a. respond according to a depersonalized standard of right and wrong.
   b. hesitate to take a definitive position based on the abstract moral premise of "right and wrong."
   c. immediately respond that the child was justified in stealing the food.
   d. respond unpredictably, based on her own personal experiences.
11. Four-year-old Tasha, who is learning to read by sounding out the letters of words, evidently is being taught using which approach?
   a. phonics
   b. whole-language
   c. immersion
   d. heritage language learning
12. As compared with her five-year-old brother, seven-year-old Althea has learned to adjust her vocabulary to her audience. This is known as
   a. selective attention.
   b. a retrieval strategy.
   c. code-switching.
   d. classification.
13. Critics of Kohlberg's theory of moral development argue that it
   a. places too much emphasis on sociocultural factors.
   b. places too much emphasis on traditional, religious beliefs.
   c. is biased toward liberal, Western cultural beliefs.
   d. can't be tested.
14. Which of the following is an example of a component of a hidden curriculum?
   a. using a whole-language approach
   b. having a security guard at the front door
   c. emphasizing basic math skills
   d. teaching a second language beginning in first grade

15. The style of reading instruction that involves children developing all their language skills at the same time is called

    a. a whole-language approach.
    b. phonics.
    c. linguistics.
    d. rote language.

16. When given the word problem, "Brandon's dog weighs more than Gabrielle's dog and Bryan's dog weighs less than Gabrielle's dog. Which dog is the heaviest?" 9-year-old Trevor can answer confidently thanks to his mastery of the logical process known as

    a. reversibility.
    b. transitive inference.
    c. identity.
    d. pragmatics.

17. Seven-year-old Minh is a first-generation American whose parents immigrated to the United States before he was born. Both parents work long hours in minimum wage jobs in order to put food on the table and keep a roof over their family's heads, but they are sometimes unable to meet even those basic needs. Minh is delayed in his language development compared to same-age peers. Potential causes of this delay include

    a. limited early exposure to words.
    b. teachers' and parents' expectations.
    c. family poverty.
    d. all of the above.

18. Six-year-old Sibylla began reading sooner than her sister Isobel (who is two years older). In fact, she has achieved a number of developmental milestones earlier than her big sister. Vygotsky might attribute this accelerated achievement to

    a. superior educational practices in Sibylla's kindergarten classroom.
    b. Sibylla's parents reading to her more than they read to Isobel.
    c. Isobel engaging Sibylla in her zone of proximal development.
    d. Sibylla's genetic makeup.

19. In the United States, who determines educational practice?

    a. the federal government
    b. local jurisdictions
    c. parents
    d. all of the above

Key Terms

1. **concrete operational thought:** During Piaget's stage, lasting from ages 7 to 11, children can think logically about concrete events and objects but are not able to reason abstractly. (p. 351; video lesson, segment 1; objective 1)
2. **classification:** The logical principle that things can be organized into groups (or categories or classes) according to some characteristic they have in common. (p. 352; objective 1)
3. **transitive inference:** The ability to figure out the unspoken link between one fact and another. (p. 352)
4. **sensory memory:** The component of the information-processing system in which incoming stimulus information is stored for a split second to allow it to be processed. Also called *sensory register* and *short-term memory*. (p. 356; video lesson, segment 1; objective 2)
5. **working memory:** The component of the information-processing system in which current conscious mental activity occurs. Formerly called *short-term memory*. (p. 356; video lesson, segment 1; objective 2)
6. **long-term memory:** The component of the information-processing system in which virtually limitless amounts of information can be stored indefinitely. (p. 358; video lesson, segment 1; objective 2)
7. **knowledge base:** A body of knowledge in a particular area that makes it easier to master new information in that area. (p. 358; objective 3)
8. **control processes:** Mechanisms (including selective attention, metacognition, and emotional regulation) that combine memory, processing speed, and knowledge to regulate the analysis and flow of information within the information-processing system. Also called *executive processes*. (p. 358; objective 4)
9. **metacognition:** "Thinking about thinking," or the ability to evaluate a cognitive task in order to determine how best to accomplish it, and then to monitor and adjust one's performance on that task. (p. 358; objective 4)
10. **pragmatics:** The practical use of language that includes the ability to adjust language communication according to audience and context. (p. 361; objective 5)
11. **ELLs (English Language Learners):** Children in the United States whose proficiency in English is low—usually below a cutoff score on an oral or written test. This term replaces *ESL* (English as a Second Language) because many children who primarily speak a non-English language at home are also capable in English; they are *not* ELLs. (p. 362; objective 8)
12. **hidden curriculum:** The unofficial, unstated, or implicit rules and priorities that influence the academic curriculum and every other aspect of learning in a school. (p. 366; objective 7)
13. **immersion:** A strategy in which instruction in all school subjects occurs in the second (majority) language that a child is learning. (p. 366; video lesson, segment 2; objective 8)

14. **bilingual schooling:** A strategy in which school subjects are taught in both the learner's original language and the second (majority) language. (p. 366; video lesson, segment 2; objective 8)
15. **Trends in Math and Science Study (TIMSS):** An international assessment of the math and science skills of fourth- and eighth-graders. Although the TIMSS is very useful, different countries' scores are not always comparable because sample selection, test administration, and content validity are hard to keep uniform. (p. 367; objective 7)
16. **Progress in International Reading Literacy Study (PIRLS):** A planned five-year cycle of international trend studies in the reading ability of fourth-graders. (p. 367; objectives 7 & 9)
17. **No Child Left Behind Act:** A U.S. law enacted in 2001 that was intended to increase accountability in education by requiring states to qualify for federal educational funding by administering standardized tests to measure school achievement. (p. 368; objective 7)
18. **National Assessment of Educational Progress (NAEP):** An ongoing and nationally representative measure of U.S. children's achievement in reading, mathematics, and other subjects over time; nicknamed "the Nation's Report Card." (p. 369; objective 7)
19. **phonics approach:** A method of teaching reading by first teaching the sounds of each letter and of various letter combinations. (p. 369; objective 9)
20. **whole-language approach:** A method of teaching reading by encouraging early use of all language skills—talking and listening, reading and writing. (p. 369; objective 9)
21. **charter school:** A public school with its own set of standards that is funded and licensed by the state or local district in which it is located. (p. 372; objective 7)
22. **private school:** A school funded by tuition charges, endowments, and often religious or other nonprofit sponsors. (p. 372; objective 7)
23. **voucher:** A public subsidy for tuition payment at a non-public school. Vouchers vary a great deal from place to place, not only in amount and availability but also in restrictions as to who gets them and what schools accept them. (p. 372; objective 7)
24. **home schooling:** Education in which children are taught at home, usually by their parents. (p. 372; objective 7)
25. **code-switching:** A pragmatic communication skill involving changing from one form of speech to another. (video lesson, segment 2; objective 5)
26. **conservation:** The principle that the amount of a substance is unaffected by changes in its appearance. (video lesson, segment 1; objective 1)
27. **reciprocity:** The logical principle that two objects, quantities, or actions can be mutually related, such that a change in one can be compensated for by a corresponding or opposite change in another. (video lesson, segment 1; objective 1)

28. **preconventional moral reasoning:** Kohlberg's first level of moral reasoning, which emphasizes obedience to authority in order to avoid punishment (stage 1) and being nice to other people so they will be nice to you (stage 2). (video lesson, segment 1; objective 6)

29. **conventional moral reasoning:** Kohlberg's second level of moral reasoning, which emphasizes winning the approval of others (stage 3) and obeying the laws set down by those in power (stage 4). (video lesson, segment 1; objective 6)

30. **postconventional moral reasoning:** Kohlberg's third level, which emphasizes the social and contractual nature of moral principles (stage 5) and the existence of universal ethical principles (stage 6). (video lesson, segment 1; objective 6)

31. **identity:** In Piaget's theory, the logical principle that certain characteristics of an object remain the same even when other characteristics change. (video lesson, segment 1; objective 1)

32. **reversibility:** The logical principle that a transformation process can be reversed to restore the original conditions. (video lesson, segment 1; objective 1)

33. **information-processing theory:** A perspective that compares human thinking processes, by analogy, to computer analysis of data—from sensory input through brain reactions, connections, and stored memories, to output. (video lesson, segment 1; objective 2)

34. **English as a second language (ESL):** An approach to teaching English in which English is the only language of instruction for students who speak many other native languages. (video lesson, segment 2; objective 8)

Summary

Cognitive development between the ages of 6 and 11 is impressive. Developmental highlights include children's improved reasoning strategies, mastery of school-related skills, and increasingly sophisticated use of language. For children around the world, the transition into middle childhood marks a passage into a new phase of cognitive development some call the "age of reason." For Piaget, the age of reason begins with the shift from preoperational to **concrete operational thought**. When this transition is complete, children are much better able to understand logical principles, as long as they are applied to tangible, concrete examples.

Among the logical operations schoolchildren acquire are the ability to categorize objects into groups according some property they have in common (**classification**), that certain characteristics of an object remain the same when other characteristics are changed (**identity**), that something that has been changed can be returned to its original state by reversing the process (**reversibility**), and that a change in one object can be compensated for by a corresponding change in another (**reciprocity**). By the process of **transitive inference**, children in this stage can deduce implied connections between facts, an impossible feat for preoperational children. Research has shown that such logical processes are made possible by the continued maturation of brain structures, notably the hippocampus.

Like Piaget, Vygotsky theorized about the development of children's thought processes during middle childhood. However, unlike Piaget, he believed instruction (*guided participation*) from parents, peers, and educators to be crucial for children to reach their developmental potential. Additionally, Vygotsky emphasized the importance of the sociocultural context of learning, maintaining that culture affects both *what* and *how* children learn, in contrast to Piaget's universal theory of development.

International research supports the merits of both approaches—universal changes do take place at various points in child development and culture-bound instruction plays a significant part in the process. The information-processing view of cognitive development bridges these two models. The ability to selectively attend to, rehearse, store, organize, and retrieve information improves steadily during middle childhood. Schoolchildren also have an improved **working memory** and a larger **long-term memory**. The ability to evaluate a cognitive task and to monitor one's performance, called **metacognition**, also improves during middle childhood. The information-processing approach emphasizes that the most effective way to teach is to adapt teaching materials and sequence of instruction to fit the needs of the individual child.

As discussed in the video for this lesson, logical thought processes also foster moral development, as school-age children become better able to grasp moral laws and ethical principles. Lawrence Kohlberg identified three levels of moral reasoning (each level including two stages):

- Preconventional: Emphasis on avoiding punishment and obtaining rewards. *Stage 1*: Might makes right. *Stage 2*: Look out for number one.
- Conventional: Emphasis on social rules. *Stage 3:* "good girl" and "nice boy." *Stage 4*: "law and order."
- Postconventional: Emphasis on moral principles. *Stage 5:* social contract. *Stage 6:* universal ethical principles.

Language development during these years is also extensive, with children showing improvement in vocabulary, grammar, and pragmatic use of language. This is clearly indicated by their newly found delight in words and their growing sophistication in telling jokes. School-age children can also easily engage in **code-switching** (**pragmatics**), from the formal code used with teachers to the informal code used with friends. However, poverty and low parental expectations can stifle the language development that takes place in this stage.

Given the right environment, children are particularly open to learning a second language during middle childhood. The specifics of how that **bilingual schooling** should occur, however, remain controversial.

There is controversy also as to the best methods for educating children. Variability exists both across cultures, as has been examined with international assessments, and within the United States, as is demonstrated by the "reading wars" and "math wars." Alternatives to public schooling include **charter schools**, **private schools**, and **home schooling**. Each approach has advantages and drawbacks and it is often up to parents to decide the best learning environment for their children.

Special Note: We will cover the topic of school learning in more detail in Lesson 20, "School Days."

Answer Key

Practice Questions I

Multiple-Choice Questions

1. c. is the correct answer. (video lesson, segment 1; objective 1)

   a. is incorrect. Preoperational thought is "pre-logical" thinking.

   b. is incorrect. There is no such stage in Piaget's theory.

   d. is incorrect. Formal operational thought extends logical reasoning to abstract problems.

2. d. is the correct answer. (objective 3)

3. b. is the correct answer. (video lesson, segment 1; objective 1)

   a. is incorrect. This is the concept that certain characteristics of an object remain the same even when other characteristics change.

   c. is incorrect. This is the concept that refers to a bilingual schooling method.

   d. is incorrect. This is the process by which familiar mental activities become routine and automatic.

4. b. is the correct answer. (video lesson, segment 1; objectives 2, 3, & 4)

   a. is incorrect. Information-processing theorists use the mind-computer metaphor at every age.

   c. is incorrect. Although increasing automatization is an important aspect of development, the information-processing perspective does not suggest that most mental activities become automatic by age 13.

   d. is incorrect. Most of the important changes in reasoning that occur during middle childhood are the result of the improved processing capacity of the person's working memory.

5. a. is the correct answer. (objective 4)

   b. is incorrect. Information processing is a perspective on cognitive development that focuses on how the mind analyzes, stores, retrieves, and reasons about information.

   c. is incorrect. Selective attention is the ability to choose which stimuli or topic to concentrate on.

   d. is incorrect. Decentering, which refers to the school-age child's ability to consider more than one aspect of a problem simultaneously, is not discussed in this chapter.

6. a. is the correct answer. (video lesson, segment 1; objective 1)

   b. is incorrect. This refers to metacognition.

   c. is incorrect. This refers to Piaget's concept of identity.

   d. is incorrect. This is characteristic of Kohlberg's postconventional moral reasoning.

7. d. is the correct answer. (objective 4)

   a. is incorrect. Pragmatics refers to the practical use of language to communicate with others.

b. is incorrect. The information-processing perspective views the mind as being like a computer.

c. is incorrect. This is the ability to screen out distractions in order to focus on important information.

8. a. is the correct answer. (video lesson, segment 1; objective 2)
9. b. is the correct answer. (video lesson, segment 1; objective 6)
10. d. is the correct answer. (objective 5)
11. d. is the correct answer. (video lesson, segment 2; objective 5)
12. a. is the correct answer. (objective 8)
13. d. is the correct answer. (video lesson, segment 2; objective 1)
14. b. is the correct answer. (video lesson, segment 1; objective 6)
15. d. is the correct answer. (video lesson, segment 2; objective 8)

True or False Items

16. F Most educators agree that the school-age child, like the preschooler, is an active learner. (objective 2)
17. T (video lesson, segment 2; objective 8)
18. T (video lesson, segment 1; objective 6)
19. T (objective 7)
20. T (video lesson, segment 2; objective 5)
21. F Code-switching (including occasional use of slang) is a behavior demonstrated by all children. (video lesson, segment 2; objective 5)
22. F (objective 8)
23. T (video lesson, segment 1; objective 2)
24. F They believe that the changes are the result of basic changes in control processes. (video lesson, segment 1; objective 4)
25. T (objectives 7 & 9)
26. T (objective 1)
27. F While private schools are funded by tuition charges, charter schools are free to students because they are funded by states and/or local school districts. (objective 10)

Practice Questions II

Multiple-Choice Questions

1. c. is the correct answer. (video lesson, segment 1; objective 1)
2. a. is the correct answer. (objective 1)
3. a. is the correct answer. (video lesson, segment 1; objective 3)

   b. is incorrect. Neurological development in the prefrontal cortex facilitates processing speed during middle childhood. The limbic system, which was not discussed in this chapter, is concerned with emotions.

   c. is incorrect. Processing speed is facilitated by growth, rather than streamlining, of the knowledge base.

4. b. is the correct answer. (video lesson, segment 1; objective 2)
5. b. is the correct answer. (video lesson, segment 1; objective 6)
6. c. is the correct answer. (video lesson, segment 1; objective 1)
7. a. is the correct answer. (video lesson, segment 1; objective 6)

   b., c., & d. are incorrect. Although these may be factors, they don't necessarily determine the child's level of moral reasoning.
8. c. is the correct answer. (video lesson, segment 1; objective 1)
9. b. is the correct answer. (video lesson, segment 1; objective 2)
10. b. is the correct answer. (video lesson, segment 1; objective 3)

    a. is incorrect. This is the accessing of already learned information.

    c. is incorrect. Automatization is the process by which well-learned activities become routine and automatic.

    d. is incorrect. This is the ability to evaluate a task and to monitor one's performance of it.
11. c. is the correct answer. (video lesson, segment 1; objective 6)
12. d. is the correct answer. (video lesson, segment 1; objective 2)

    a. is incorrect. Sensory memory stores incoming information for a split second.

    b. is incorrect. Working memory is the part of memory that handles current, conscious mental activity.

    c. is incorrect. Long-term memory stores information for days, months, or years.
13. b. is the correct answer. (objective 4)
14. c. is the correct answer. (objective 9)
15. b. is the correct answer. (video lesson, segment 2; objective 8)

Matching Items

16. k (objective 9)
17. b (video lesson, segment 1; objective 1)
18. j (video lesson, segment 1; objective 6)
19. c (video lesson, segment 1; objective 1)
20. d (video lesson, segment 1; objective 2)
21. a (objective 9)
22. n (objective 10)
23. h (video lesson, segment 1; objective 3)
24. i (video lesson, segment 1; objective 3)
25. l (objective 4)
26. g (video lesson, segment 2; objective 8)
27. f (video lesson, segment 1; objective 6)
28. e (video lesson, segment 1; objective 6)
29. m (objective 10)

Applying Your Knowledge

1. c. is the correct answer. (video lesson, segment 1; objective 1)

   a., b., & d. are incorrect. Identity is the logical principle that certain characteristics of an object (such as the shape of a banana) remain the same even when other characteristics change.

2. a. is the correct answer. (video lesson, segment 1; objective 1)

   b., c., & d. are incorrect. Reversibility is the logical principle that something that has been changed (such as the height of lemonade poured from one glass into another) can be returned to its original shape by reversing the process of change (pouring the liquid back into the other glass)

3. b. is the correct answer. (video lesson, segment 1; objective 1)

4. c. is the correct answer. (video lesson, segment 1; objective 2)

   a. is incorrect. This perspective emphasizes the logical, active nature of thinking during middle childhood.

   b. is incorrect. This perspective emphasizes the importance of social interaction in learning.

   d. is incorrect. This perspective does not address the development of cognitive skills.

5. d. is the correct answer. (objective 3)

6. c. is the correct answer. Joke-telling is one of the clearest demonstrations of schoolchildren's improved pragmatic skills, including the ability to know what someone else will think is funny. (video lesson, segment 2; objective 5)

7. a. is the correct answer. (video lesson, segment 2; objective 8)

8. c. is the correct answer. (objective 4)

   a. is incorrect. Control processes regulate the analysis and flow of information.

   b. is incorrect. Automatization refers to the tendency of well-rehearsed mental activities to become routine and automatic.

   d. is incorrect. Long-term memory is the part of memory that stores information for days, months, or years.

9. a. is the correct answer. (video lesson, segment 1; objective 6)

   b. & c. are incorrect. These exemplify conventional moral reasoning.

   d. is incorrect. This exemplifies stage 2 preconventional moral reasoning.

10. b. is the correct answer. Gilligan contends that females' morality of care makes them reluctant to judge right and wrong in absolute terms because they are socialized to be nurturing and caring. (video lesson, segment 1; objective 6)

11. a. is the correct answer. (objective 5)

    b. is incorrect. This approach encourages children to develop all their language skills at the same time.

    c. & d. are incorrect. These are approaches to bilingual instruction, not reading instruction.

12. c. is the correct answer. (video lesson, segment 2; objective 5)

13. c. is the correct answer. (video lesson, segment 1; objective 6)
14. b. is the correct answer. The hidden curriculum is the unspoken and often unrecognized lessons that children learn in school. (objective 7)

    a., c., & d. are incorrect. These are aspects of the official curriculum.
15. a. is the correct answer. (objective 9)
16. b. is the correct answer. (objective 1)
17. d. is the correct answer. (objective 5)
18. c. is the correct answer. (objective 1)

    a. & b. are incorrect. There is no reason to assume Sibylla's schooling or the parenting she received would be dramatically different than those of her sister.

    d. is incorrect. Vygotsky did not theorize about genetics.
19. d. is the correct answer. (objective 10)

Lesson Review

Lesson 17

The School Years
Cognitive Development

Please Note: Use this matrix to guide your study and achieve the learning objectives of this lesson. It will also help you to view the video, which defines and demonstrates important concepts and skills as they relate to everyday life.

Learning Objective	Textbook	Course Student Guide	Video Lesson
1. Identify and describe the elements of Piaget's and Vygotsky's theories about middle childhood, comparing and contrasting the two with particular attention to issues such as concrete operational thought, the role of instruction, and cultural variations.	pp. 351–355	Key Terms: 1, 2, 3, 26, 27, 31, 32; Practice Questions I: 1, 3, 6, 13, 26; Practice Questions II: 1, 2, 6, 8, 17, 19; Applying Your Knowledge: 1, 2, 3, 16, 18.	Segment 1: *How School-Age Children Think* Segment 2: *Language Development*
2. Describe the components of the information-processing system, noting how they interact.	pp. 356–360	Key Terms: 4, 5, 6, 33; Practice Questions I: 4, 8, 16, 23; Practice Questions II: 4, 9, 12, 20; Applying Your Knowledge: 4.	Segment 1: *How School-Age Children Think*
3. Discuss advances in the knowledge base, processing speed and capacity, and memory skills during middle childhood.	pp. 356–358	Key Terms: 7; Practice Questions I: 2, 4; Practice Questions II: 3, 10, 23; Applying Your Knowledge: 5.	Segment 1: *How School-Age Children Think*
4. Discuss advances in cognitive control processes and metacognition during middle childhood.	pp. 358–360	Key Terms: 8, 9; Practice Questions I: 4, 5, 7, 24; Practice Questions II: 13, 24; Applying Your Knowledge: 8.	Segment 1: *How School-Age Children Think*
5. Describe language development during middle childhood, noting changing abilities in vocabulary and pragmatics and causes of differences in language learning.	pp. 360–364	Key Terms: 10, 24, 25; Practice Questions I: 10, 11, 20, 21; Applying Your Knowledge: 6, 11, 12, 17.	Segment 2: *Language Development*

Learning Objective	Textbook	Course Student Guide	Video Lesson
6. Outline Kohlberg's stage theory of moral development, and describe several criticisms of the theory.	*	Key Terms: 28, 29, 30; Practice Questions I: 9, 14, 18; Practice Questions II: 5, 7, 11, 18, 26, 27; Applying Your Knowledge: 9, 10, 13.	Segment 1: *How School-Age Children Think*
7. Compare the academic performance of children in countries around the world, and identify differences in culture, school, and home life that may account for differences in academic performance.	pp. 364–369	Key Terms: 12, 15, 16, 17, 18, 21, 22, 23, 24; Practice Questions I: 19, 25; Applying Your Knowledge: 14.	
8. Identify several conditions that foster the learning of a second language, and describe different strategies for teaching another language to school-age children.	pp. 366–367	Key Terms: 11, 13, 14, 34; Practice Questions I: 12, 15, 17, 22; Practice Questions II: 15, 25; Applying Your Knowledge: 7.	Segment 2: *Language Development*
9. Differentiate several approaches to teaching reading and math, and discuss evidence regarding the effectiveness of these methods.	pp. 369–371	Key Terms: 16, 19, 20; Practice Questions I: 25; Practice Questions II: 14, 16, 21; Applying Your Knowledge: 15.	
10. Discuss the determining factors in educational practice and describe three alternatives to public school, detailing the pros and cons of each.	pp. 371–373	Key Terms: 21, 22, 23; Practice Questions I: 27; Practice Questions II: 22, 29; Applying Your Knowledge: 19.	

* The video for this lesson offers excellent coverage of these topics.

A Society of Children

Lesson 18

The School Years: Psychosocial Development

Preview

We have seen that from about ages 6 to 11, the child becomes stronger and more competent, mastering the biosocial and cognitive abilities that are important in his or her culture. The psychosocial accomplishments of middle childhood are equally impressive.

This lesson begins by exploring the growing social competence of school-age children. Starting with the theories of Freud and Erikson, the lesson continues with a discussion of the school-age child's growing social awareness and self-understanding.

Children's interaction with peers and others in their ever-widening social world is the next subject of this lesson. In addition to the changing nature of friendships, the problem of bullies and their victims is discussed.

The lesson also explores the structure and function of families in middle childhood, including the experience of parental divorce and remarriage. The lesson closes with a discussion of the ways in which children cope with stressful situations.

As you complete this lesson, recall some of your own social experiences during this age range (6 to 11). How did you spend a typical day? Were you a "social animal" or more of a loner? Who were the friends you spent time with? How do you think your peers at school would have described you during this period? Did you have a school or neighborhood bully? Did you grow up in a family with both of your biological parents or in some other **family structure**? What challenges did you face during this period of life and how did you handle them?

Prior Knowledge That Will Be Used in This Lesson

- The developmental theories of Erik Erikson (from Lesson 1) will be used to help explain psychosocial development during the school years. Recall that Erikson's theory specifies eight stages of psychosocial development, each of which is characterized by a particular challenge, or developmental crisis, which is central to that stage of life and must be resolved. This lesson will highlight Erikson's fourth stage, "Industry vs. Inferiority":

1. Trust vs. Mistrust (birth to 1 year)
2. Autonomy vs. Shame and Doubt (1 to 3 years)
3. Initiative vs. Guilt (3 to 6 years)
4. **Industry vs. Inferiority (7 to 11 years) ← The School Years**
5. Identity vs. Role Confusion (adolescence)
6. Intimacy vs. Isolation (adulthood)
7. Generativity vs. Stagnation (adulthood)
8. Integrity vs. Despair (adulthood)

- This lesson will revisit the concept of theory of mind (from Lesson 12), an understanding of human mental processes. During the school years, children gain an increasingly better understanding of the thoughts, emotions, needs, and motivations of others—which allows them to interact more effectively in their social world.

Learning Objectives

Use this information to guide your reading, viewing, thinking, and studying. After successfully completing this lesson, you should be able to:

1. Describe the rising competence and independence of middle childhood from different theoretical perspectives, including Erikson's crisis of "industry vs. inferiority."
2. Define social cognition, and explain how children's theory of mind and emotional understanding evolve during middle childhood.
3. Describe the development of self-understanding during middle childhood and its implications for children's self-esteem.
4. Discuss the importance of peer groups, providing examples of how school-age children develop their own subculture and explaining the importance of this development.
5. Discuss how peer acceptance and friendships change during the school years.
6. Describe the special problems of unpopular children, bullies and their victims, and discuss possible ways of helping such children.
7. Define shared and nonshared environments, and identify five essential ways in which families nurture school-age children.
8. Differentiate among various basic family structures, describe how family structures have changed in recent decades, describe the connection between family structure and function, and discuss the impact of these factors on the development of school-age children.
9. Summarize how low income and high conflict can interfere with good family function, and discuss the potential impact of divorce on children.
10. Identify the variables that influence the impact of stresses on schoolchildren, and discuss those factors that seem especially important in helping children to cope with problems.
11. Outline Kohlberg's stage theory of moral development and describe one criticism of the theory as stated in the textbook.

Textbook Reading & Video Viewing

For the most effective study of this lesson, complete the assignments in the sequence listed below.

Before viewing the video program:

Read Chapter 13, "Middle Childhood: Psychosocial Development," pages 377–406.

View the video for Lesson 18, "A Society of Children."

Segment 1: *Peers*

Segment 2: *Family*

Segment 3: *Coping*

After viewing the video program:

Review all reading assignments for this lesson.

Complete the "Practice Questions" and "Applying Your Knowledge" sections to reinforce your understanding of important terms and concepts and measure your achievement of the Learning Objectives. Check your answers with the feedback given and review when necessary.

Practice Questions I

Multiple-Choice Questions

1. Social cognition is defined as
   a. a person's awareness and understanding of human personality, motives, emotions, and interactions.
   b. the ability to form friendships easily.
   c. a person's skill in persuading others to go along with his or her wishes.
   d. the ability to learn by watching another person.

2. Throughout the world, the child culture encourages
   a. a period of latency.
   b. the emergence of a theory of mind.
   c. independence from adults.
   d. increasingly positive self-esteem.

3. The best strategy for helping children who are at risk of developing serious psychological problems because of multiple stresses would be to
   a. obtain assistance from a psychiatrist.
   b. change the household situation.
   c. increase the child's competencies or social supports.
   d. reduce the peer group's influence.

4. Compared with the self-concepts of preschoolers, the self-concepts of older children are
   a. more positive.
   b. less tied to their parents' perspective.
   c. severely negative.
   d. less realistic.
5. Research has suggested that school-age children are _____________ by violations in a contract between a mother and a child and are _____________ by violations in a contract between friends.
   a. not particularly upset; not particularly upset
   b. not particularly upset; upset
   c. upset; particularly upset
   d. upset; upset
6. Compared with average or popular children, rejected children tend to
   a. be brighter and more competitive.
   b. be affluent and "stuck-up."
   c. be economically disadvantaged.
   d. misinterpret others' social behavior.
7. A family that consists of two parents, at least one of whom has children from another union, is called a(n) __________ family.
   a. nuclear
   b. extended
   c. blended
   d. single-parent
8. Single parenthood can be less difficult for children when
   a. fathers pay child support.
   b. the child has numerous siblings.
   c. the parent has a live-in boyfriend or girlfriend.
   d. stepchildren are included as siblings.
9. Older schoolchildren tend to be __________ vulnerable to the stresses of life than children who are just beginning middle childhood because they __________.
   a. more; tend to overpersonalize their problems
   b. less; have better developed skills for coping with problems
   c. more; are more likely to compare their well-being with that of their peers
   d. less; are less egocentric

10. Compared to preschool children, the frequency of emotional problems in school-age children
    a. increases in both boys and girls.
    b. decreases in both boys and girls.
    c. increases in boys and decreases in girls.
    d. decreases in boys and increases in girls.
11. Children who are considered popular are likely to be
    a. arrogant.
    b. dominant.
    c. kind.
    d. all of the above.
12. During the school years, children become ____________ selective about their friends, and close friendships increasingly involve children who are ____________ them.
    a. less; similar to
    b. more; similar to
    c. less; different from
    d. more; different from
13. Erikson sees the crisis of the school years as that of
    a. industry versus inferiority.
    b. acceptance versus rejection.
    c. initiative versus guilt.
    d. male versus female.
14. Lawrence Kohlberg measured morality by
    a. analyzing the words people chose when explaining their answers.
    b. watching how people behave in morally ambiguous situations.
    c. analyzing how people reason about what is right and wrong.
    d. determining what people felt was right or wrong.

True or False Items

Write T (for true) or F (for false) on the line in front of each statement.

15. _____ As they evaluate themselves according to increasingly complex self-theories, school-age children typically experience a rise in self-esteem.
16. _____ During middle childhood, acceptance by the peer group is valued more than having a close friend.
17. _____ The child culture tends to mirror the values of adults.
18. _____ The degree of harmony and stability in the family appears to be a more powerful predictor of children's development than the actual structure of the family.

19. _____ Children who are considered to be popular are always well-liked by their peers.

20. _____ School-age children are less able than younger children to cope with the chronic stresses that are troublesome at any age.

21. _____ Being neglected by the peer group tends to be more damaging than being rejected by the peer group.

22. _____ Friendships become more selective and exclusive as children grow older.

Practice Questions II

Multiple-Choice Questions

1. Children who are categorized as ___________ are particularly vulnerable to being bullied.
   a. aggressive-rejected
   b. passive-aggressive
   c. withdrawn-rejected
   d. passive-rejected

2. The main reason for the special vocabulary, dress codes, and behaviors that flourish within the child culture is that they
   a. lead to clubs and gang behavior.
   b. are unknown to or unapproved by adults.
   c. imitate adult-organized society.
   d. provide an alternative to useful work in society.

3. In the area of social cognition, developmentalists are impressed by the school-age child's increasing ability to
   a. identify and take into account other people's viewpoints.
   b. develop an increasingly wide network of friends.
   c. relate to the opposite sex.
   d. resist social models.

4. Which of the following helps school-age children protect their self-esteem?
   a. devaluing what they are not good at
   b. overvaluing what they are good at
   c. comparing themselves to their friends
   d. comparing themselves to children with whom they are not friends

5. Typically, children in middle childhood experience a decrease in self-esteem as a result of
   a. a wavering self-theory.
   b. increased awareness of personal shortcomings and failures.
   c. rejection by peers.
   d. difficulties with members of the opposite sex.

6. Neglected children are
   a. also withdrawn-rejected.
   b. not avoided by their peers.
   c. at major risk of adjustment problems.
   d. picked as friends by a few kids.
7. Which of the following most accurately describes how friendships change during the school years?
   a. Friendships become more casual and less intense.
   b. Older children demand less of their friends.
   c. Older children change friends more often.
   d. Close friendships increasingly involve members of the same sex, ethnicity, and socioeconomic status.
8. Which of the following is an accurate statement about school-age bullies?
   a. They are socially perceptive.
   b. They usually have friends who abet, fear, and admire them.
   c. They are adept at not getting into immediate trouble.
   d. All of the above are accurate statements.
9. From early childhood to middle childhood, children become
   a. less impulsive.
   b. more able to control their emotions.
   c. more susceptible to emotional problems.
   d. all of the above.
10. Two factors that most often help the child cope well with multiple stresses are social support and
    a. social comparison.
    b. competence in a specific area.
    c. remedial education.
    d. referral to mental health professionals.
11. How are social acceptance and social understanding associated?
    a. Social acceptance leads to advances in social understanding.
    b. Advances in social understanding lead to social acceptance.
    c. Social acceptance and social understanding develop independently.
    d. Social acceptance and social understanding develop simultaneously.
12. Family ____________________ is more crucial to children's well-being than is family ____________________.
    a. structure; socioeconomic status
    b. socioeconomic status; stability
    c. stability; socioeconomic status
    d. functioning; structure

13. According to Freud, the period between ages 7 and 11 when a child's sexual drives are relatively quiet is the
    a. phallic stage.
    b. genital stage.
    c. period of latency.
    d. period of industry versus inferiority.

14. Which of the following is the **LEAST** likely to reduce the incidence of bullying in school-age children?
    a. social skills training for victims
    b. ensuring that victims have at least one protective peer
    c. intervening with the whole school
    d. providing adult supervision in lunchroom, playground, and restrooms

15. Kohlberg's theory was criticized because
    a. it emphasizes differences between men and women.
    b. it is seen as too narrow and too restrictive.
    c. it does not emphasize the stages strongly enough.
    d. his "universal" stages do not reflect Western values.

Matching Items

Match each term or concept with its corresponding description or definition.

Terms or Concepts

16. __________ family structure
17. __________ social cognition
18. __________ social comparison
19. __________ effortful control
20. __________ child culture
21. __________ aggressive-rejected
22. __________ withdrawn-rejected
23. __________ resilience
24. __________ family function
25. __________ blended family
26. __________ extended family
27. __________ preconventional moral reasoning

Descriptions or Definitions

a. the legal and genetic connections among related people living in the same household
b. adults living with their children from previous marriages as well as their own biological children
c. an awareness and understanding of others' motives and emotions
d. one parent, usually the father, sets strict guidelines and rules
e. a positive adaptation to stress
f. children who are disliked because of their confrontational nature
g. evaluating one's abilities by measuring them against those of other children
h. three or more generations of biologically related individuals living together
i. contributions from every family member are valued

j. children who are disliked because of timid, anxious behavior
k. the way a family works to meet the needs of its members
l. the games, vocabulary, dress codes, and culture of children
m. the power to modify impulses and emotions
n. a stage in Kohlberg's theory that emphasizes rewards and punishments

Applying Your Knowledge

1. Eight-year-old Harry is in the cafeteria holding his lunch tray when he gets pushed from behind, spilling his milk. Harry assumes the push was purposeful, and he turns around and pushes the other child. Harry's response suggests that he is
   a. well-liked.
   b. aggressive-rejected.
   c. withdrawn-rejected.
   d. neglected.
2. Dr. Ferris believes that children develop views of themselves as either competent or incompetent in skills valued by their culture. Dr. Ferris is evidently working from the perspective of
   a. behaviorism.
   b. social learning theory.
   c. Erik Erikson's theory of development.
   d. Freud's theory of development.
3. Cheryl, who is low achieving, shy, and withdrawn, is rejected by most of her peers. Her teacher, who wants to help Cheryl increase her self-esteem and social acceptance, encourages her parents to
   a. transfer Cheryl to a different school.
   b. help their daughter improve her motor skills.
   c. help their daughter learn to accept more responsibility for her academic failures.
   d. help their daughter find even a single friend.
4. Miguel, who has no children of his own, is worried about his twelve-year-old niece because she wears unusual clothes and uses vocabulary unknown to him. What should Miguel do?
   a. Tell his niece's parents that they need to discipline their daughter more strictly.
   b. Convince his niece to find a new group of friends.
   c. Recommend that his niece's parents seek professional counseling for their daughter, because such behaviors often are the first signs of a lifelong pattern of antisocial behavior.
   d. Miguel need not necessarily be worried because children typically develop their own subculture of speech, dress, and behavior.

5. Which of the following statements would be **LEAST** likely to be part of the self-description of a school-age child?
   a. "I don't do very well in soccer compared to the other kids."
   b. "I try not to get so mad at my brother."
   c. "I help my friends when they are upset."
   d. "My parents know me better than I know myself."
6. Seven-year-old Camille fumes after a friend compliments her new dress, thinking that the comment was intended to be sarcastic. Camille's reaction is an example of
   a. egocentrism.
   b. feelings of inferiority.
   c. the distorted thought processes of an emotionally disturbed child.
   d. immature social cognition.
7. In contrast to younger children, 10-year-old children will often
   a. deny that friendships are important.
   b. state that they prefer same-sex playmates.
   c. have one "best" friend to whom they are quite loyal.
   d. be less choosy about whom they call a friend.
8. Dan is a 10-year-old bully. He is likely to
   a. use relational aggression.
   b. be small for his age.
   c. inflict harm on a particular victim repeatedly.
   d. have no friends.
9. Which of the following school-age children is most likely to be emotionally healthy in adulthood?
   a. Trevor, who has a few close friends but who is not popular
   b. Arnie, who is aggressive-rejected
   c. Nate, who is popular but who has many acquaintances and has no close friends
   d. Mica, who is not popular and who has many acquaintances and no close friends
10. Which factor is crucial in determining the effect of family income on child development?
   a. nonshared environment
   b. parents' reaction to the income
   c. exact income level
   d. all of the above

11. Ten-year-old Troy is less optimistic and self-confident than his five-year-old sister. This may be explained in part by the tendency of older children to
    a. evaluate their abilities by comparing them with their own competencies a year or two earlier.
    b. evaluate their competencies by comparing them with those of others.
    c. be less realistic about their own abilities.
    d. do both b and c.
12. Which of the following family functions is **NOT** one that school-age children require of their families?
    a. Help them develop self-respect.
    b. Encourage reliance on the family.
    c. Ensure harmony and stability.
    d. Nurture peer relationships.
13. Of the following children, who is most likely to become a bully?
    a. Callie, a girl who is taller than average
    b. Ricky, a boy who is above average in verbal assertiveness
    c. Matthew, who is withdrawn-rejected
    d. Amy, who has a history of insecure attachment
14. Monozygotic twins April and May differ in
    a. shared environment.
    b. genetics.
    c. nonshared environment.
    d. none of the above.

Key Terms

1. **industry versus inferiority:** The fourth of Erikson's eight psychosocial crises, during which children try to master many skills , developing a sense of themselves as either industrious or inferior, competent or incompetent. (p. 378; video lesson, introduction; objective 1)
2. **latency:** Freud's term for middle childhood, during which children's emotional drives and psychosexual needs are quiet (latent). Freud thought that sexual conflicts from earlier stages are only temporarily submerged, bursting forth again at puberty. (p. 379; objective 1)
3. **effortful control:** The ability to regulate impulses and emotions through effort, not simply through natural inclination. (p. 380; objective 2)
4. **resilience:** The capacity to adapt well to significant adversity and to overcome serious stress. (p. 380; objective 10)
5. **family structure:** The legal and genetic relationships among relatives living in the same home; includes nuclear family, extended family, stepfamily, and so on. (p. 385; video lesson, segment 2; objective 8)

6. **family function:** The ways in which a family works to meet the needs of its members. Children need families to provide basic material necessities, to encourage learning, to help them develop self-respect, to nurture friendships, and to foster harmony and stability. (p. 385; objective 7)
7. **nuclear family:** A family that consists of a father, a mother, and their biological children under age 18. (p. 387; video lesson, segment 2; objective 8)
8. **single-parent family:** A family that consists of only one parent and his or her biological children under age 18. (p. 387; objective 8)
9. **extended family:** A family of three or more generations living in one household. (p. 387; objective 8)
10. **polygamous family:** A family consisting of one man, several wives, and the biological children of the man and his wives. (p. 387; objective 8)
11. **blended family:** A stepparent family that includes children born to several furnishes, including biological children from spouses' previous marriages and the offspring from the new relationship. (p. 388; objective 8)
12. **child culture:** Refers to the particular habits, styles, and values that reflect the set of rules and rituals that characterize children as distinct from adult society Also called the *society of children*. (p. 395; video lesson, segment 1; objective 4)
13. **aggressive-rejected children:** Children who are rejected by peers because of antagonistic, confrontational behavior. (p. 397; video lesson, segment 1; objective 6)
14. **withdrawn-rejected children:** Children who are rejected by peers because of timid, withdrawn, and anxious behavior. (p. 397; video lesson, segment 1; objective 6)
15. **bullying:** The repeated, systematic effort to inflict harm on a child through physical, verbal, or social attack on a weaker person. (p. 397; video lesson, segment 1; objective 6)
16. **bully-victim:** Someone who attacks others and who is attacked as well. Also called *provocative victims* because they do things that elicit bullying. (p. 398; objective 6)
17. **preconditional moral reasoning:** Kohlberg's first level of moral reasoning, which emphasizes rewards and punishments. (p. 401; objective 11)
18. **conventional moral reasoning:** Kohlberg's second level of moral reasoning, which emphasizes social rules. (p. 401; objective 11)
19. **postconventional moral reasoning:** Kohlberg's third level of moral reasoning, which emphasizes moral principles. (p. 401; objective 11)
20. **peer group:** A group of individuals of roughly the same age and social status who play, work, or learn together. (video lesson, segment 1; objective 4)
21. **social comparison:** The tendency to assess one's abilities, achievements, and social status by measuring them against those of others, especially those of one's peers. (video lesson, segment 1; objective 3)

22. **social cognition:** A person's awareness and understanding of the personalities, motives, emotions, intentions, and interactions of other people and groups. (video lesson, segment 1; objective 2)

Summary

The psychoanalytic theory portrays the school-age child as an individual who is much more independent, capable, and open to the challenges of the world. Erikson, for example, refers to these years as the time of industry, while Freud says that sexual concerns are latent. Erikson's "industry" refers to children being busy learning all the skills that will make them productive adults. This means that children in the school years should be learning how to read, write, calculate, socialize with others, and trying things like sports or dance or skill-building hobbies. Learning new skills is the "work" of the school-age child.

As school-age children develop their theory of mind and powers of **social cognition**, they are increasingly aware of the motives, emotions, and personality traits that are the foundation of others' behavior. As their social skills improve, school age children also become better able to adjust their own behavior to interact appropriately with others.

The expanded social world of children in the school years is full of opportunities for growth, as children create their own subculture or "society"—complete with its own language, values, and codes of behavior—and friendships become more selective and exclusive. This expanded world also presents challenges and special problems. This lesson discusses the impact of peer rejection, **bullying**, divorce, low income, and high conflict on children's psychosocial development. Most children, however, are sufficiently resilient and resourceful to cope with the stresses they may face during middle childhood. The emotional stability of parents and the amount of attention each child receives are significant factors in their healthy adjustment to environmental stress. Likewise, social support from relatives, friends, teachers, community programs, religious institutions, and a variety of other sources fosters resilience and positive coping. How well a family nurtures and supports a child depends on how well it meets the child's basic needs, encourages learning, nurtures peer relationships, provides harmony and stability, and develops the child's self-esteem.

Special Note: We will discuss how children and adolescents react to stress and cope with problems (pp. 380–383) in more detail in Lesson 25, "Crashing Hard into Adulthood."

Answer Key

Practice Questions I

Multiple-Choice Questions

1. a. is the correct answer. (objective 2)
2. c. is the correct answer. (objective 4)
3. c. is the correct answer. (video lesson, segment 3; objective 10)

4. b. is the correct answer. (objective 3)

   a., c., & d. are incorrect. Compared with preschool children, schoolchildren are more self-critical and more realistic, but their self-esteem usually only drops slightly.
5. b. is the correct answer. (objective 4)
6. d. is the correct answer. (video lesson, segment 1; objective 6)
7. c. is the correct answer. (objective 8)
8. a. is the correct answer. (video lesson, segment 2; objective 8)

   b., c., & d. are incorrect. These factors are likely to increase, rather than decrease, stress, and therefore to have an adverse effect on children.
9. b. is the correct answer. (objective 10)
10. b. is the correct answer. (objectives 2 & 3)
11. d. is the correct answer. (objective 5)
12. b. is the correct answer. (objective 5)
13. a. is the correct answer. (video lesson, introduction; objective 1)
14. c. is the correct answer. (objective 11)

True or False Items

15. F In fact, just the opposite is true. (objective 3)
16. F In fact, just the opposite is true. (video lesson, segment 1; objectives 4 & 5)
17. F (video lesson, segment 1; objective 4)
18. T (video lesson, segment 2; objective 9)
19. F (objective 5)
20. F Because of the coping strategies that school-age children develop, they are better able than younger children to cope with stress. (objective 10)
21. F (objective 6)
22. T (video lesson, segment 1; objective 5)

Practice Questions II

Multiple-Choice Questions

1. c. is the correct answer. (video lesson, segment 1; objective 6)

   a. is incorrect. These are usually bullies.

   b. & d. are incorrect. These are not subcategories of rejected children.
2. b. is the correct answer. (objective 4)
3. a. is the correct answer. (objective 2)

   b. is incorrect. Friendship circles typically become smaller during middle childhood, as children become choosier about their friends.

   c. & d. are incorrect. These issues are not discussed in the textbook.
4. a. is the correct answer. (objective 3)

   b. is incorrect. Although children tend to appreciate their strengths, they do not typically overvalue them.

   c. & d. are incorrect. Social comparison tends to decrease, rather than increase, self-esteem.

5. b. is the correct answer. (objective 3)
   a. is incorrect. This tends to promote, rather than reduce, self-esteem.
   c. is incorrect. Only 10 percent of schoolchildren experience this.
   d. is incorrect. This issue becomes more important during adolescence.
6. b. is the correct answer. (objective 5)
   a. is incorrect. Neglected children are a separate group from withdrawn-rejected children.
   c. is incorrect. Being neglected is not necessarily harmful, especially if children have other positive aspects of their lives.
   d. is incorrect. Neglected children are not chosen as friends.
7. d. is the correct answer. (objective 5)
   a., b., & c. are incorrect. In fact, just the opposite is true of friendship during middle childhood.
8. d. is the correct answer. (objective 6)
9. b. is the correct answer. (objectives 2 & 3)
   a. is incorrect. Children do not necessarily become less impulsive with age.
   c. is incorrect. Just the opposite is true.
10. b. is the correct answer. (video lesson, segment 3; objective 10)
11. a. is the correct answer. (objective 2)
12. d. is the correct answer. (video lesson, segment 2; objectives 7 & 8)
13. c. is the correct answer. (objective 1)
14. a. is the correct answer. (objective 6)
15. b. is the correct answer. (objective 11)

Matching Items

16. a (video lesson, segment 2; objective 8)
17. c (objective 2)
18. g (video lesson, segment 1; objective 3)
19. m (objective 2)
20. l (video lesson, segment 1; objective 4)
21. f (video lesson, segment 1; objective 6)
22. j (video lesson, segment 1; objective 6)
23. e (objective 10)
24. k (objective 7)
25. b (objective 8)
26. h (objective 8)
27. n (objective 11)

Applying Your Knowledge

1. b. is the correct answer. (objective 6)
2. c. is the correct answer. The question describes what is, for Erikson, the crisis of middle childhood: industry versus inferiority. (objective 1)

3. d. is the correct answer. Having friends appears to help children develop social competence. (video lesson, introduction; objective 6)

   a. is incorrect. Because it would seem to involve "running away" from her problems, this approach would likely be more harmful than helpful.

   b. is incorrect. Improving motor skills is not a factor considered in the textbook and probably has little value in raising self-esteem in such situations.

   c. is incorrect. If Cheryl is like most school-age children, she is quite self-critical and already accepts responsibility for her failures.

4. d. is the correct answer. (video lesson, segment 1; objective 4)
5. d. is the correct answer. (objective 4)
6. d. is the correct answer. (objective 2)

   a. is incorrect. Egocentrism is self-centered thinking. In this example, Camille is misinterpreting her friend's comment.

   b. & c. are incorrect. There is no reason to believe that Camille is suffering from an emotional disturbance or that she is feeling inferior.

7. c. is the correct answer. (video lesson, segment 1; objective 5)
8. c. is the correct answer. (objective 6)

   a. is incorrect. This is typical of female bullies, but male bullies typically use physical attraction.

   b. is incorrect. The opposite is true.

   d. is incorrect. Bullies usually have a few admiring friends.

9. a. is the correct answer. (objective 5)
10. b. is the correct answer. (objective 9)
11. b. is the correct answer. (objective 3)

    a. & c. are incorrect. These are more typical of preschoolers than school-age children.

12. b. is the correct answer. (video lesson, segment 2; objective 7)
13. d. is the correct answer. (video lesson, segment 1; objective 6)

    a. & b. are incorrect. It is taller-than-average boys and verbally assertive girls who are more likely to bully others.

    c. is incorrect. Bullies are certainly not withdrawn.

14. c. is the correct answer. (objective 7)

Lesson Review

Lesson 18

The School Years
Psychosocial Development

Please Note: Use this matrix to guide your study and achieve the learning objectives of this lesson. It will also help you to view the video, which defines and demonstrates important concepts and skills as they relate to everyday life.

Learning Objective	Textbook	Course Student Guide	Video Lesson
1. Describe the rising competence and independence of middle childhood from different theoretical perspectives, including Erikson's crisis of "industry vs. inferiority."	pp. 378–379	Key Terms: 1, 2; Practice Questions I: 13; Practice Questions II: 13; Applying Your Knowledge: 2.	Introduction
2. Define social cognition, and explain how children's theory of mind and emotional understanding evolve during middle childhood.	p. 396	Key Terms: 3, 22; Practice Questions I: 1, 10; Practice Questions II: 3, 9, 11, 17, 19; Applying Your Knowledge: 6.	Segment 1: *Peers*
3. Describe the development of self-understanding during middle childhood and its implications for children's self-esteem.	pp. 379–380	Key Terms: 21; Practice Questions I: 4, 10, 15; Practice Questions II: 4, 5, 9; Applying Your Knowledge: 11.	Segment 1: *Peers*
4. Discuss the importance of peer groups, providing examples of how school-age children develop their own subculture and explaining the importance of this development.	pp. 395–396	Key Terms: 12, 20; Practice Questions I: 2, 5, 16, 17; Practice Questions II: 2, 20; Applying Your Knowledge: 4, 5.	Segment 1: *Peers*
5. Discuss how peer acceptance and friendships change during the school years.	p. 396	Practice Questions I: 11, 12, 16, 19, 22; Practice Questions II: 6, 7; Applying Your Knowledge: 7, 9.	Segment 1: *Peers*

Learning Objective	Textbook	Course Student Guide	Video Lesson
6. Describe the special problems of unpopular children, bullies and their victims, and discuss possible ways of helping such children.	pp. 397–400	Key Terms: 13, 14, 15, 16; Practice Questions I: 6, 21; Practice Questions II: 1, 8, 14, 21, 22; Applying Your Knowledge: 1, 3, 8, 13.	Introduction Segment 1: *Peers*
7. Define shared and nonshared environments, and identify five essential ways in which families nurture school-age children.	pp. 384–385	Key Terms: 6; Practice Questions II: 12, 24; Applying Your Knowledge:12, 14.	Segment 2: *Family*
8. Differentiate among various basic family structures, describe how family structures have changed in recent decades, describe the connection between family structure and function, and discuss the impact of these factors on the development of school-age children.	pp. 385–392	Key Terms: 5, 7, 8, 9, 10, 11; Practice Questions I: 7, 8; Practice Questions II: 12, 16, 25, 26.	Segment 2: *Family*
9. Summarize how low income and high conflict can interfere with good family function, and discuss the potential impact of divorce on children.	pp. 392–394	Practice Questions I: 18; Applying Your Knowledge: 10.	Segment 2: *Family*
10. Identify the variables that influence the impact of stresses on schoolchildren, and discuss those factors that seem especially important in helping children to cope with problems.	pp. 380–383	Key Terms: 4; Practice Questions I: 3, 9, 20; Practice Questions II: 10, 23; Applying Your Knowledge: 3.	Segment 3: *Coping*
11. Outline Kohlberg's stage theory of moral development and describe one criticism of the theory as stated in the textbook.	pp. 400–404	Key Terms: 17, 18, 19; Practice Questions I: 14; Practice Questions II: 15, 27.	

On the Road of Accomplishment

Lesson 19

The School Years:
Summary

Preview

This lesson summarizes biosocial, cognitive, and psychosocial development during the school years (ages 6 to 11).

Middle childhood is a time of achievement, when children rapidly rise from one new accomplishment to another. Erik Erikson captured this idea in his psychosocial crisis for this age period: *industry vs. inferiority*. School-age children are busy trying to master whatever their culture values. Depending on how successful they are, they judge themselves as either competent or incompetent. In the video for this lesson, the developmental issues and accomplishments of middle childhood are revealed in the stories of four individual children.

Although children grow more slowly during this period, they learn to use their bodies in new, more complex ways. Cognitive development between the ages of 6 and 11 is equally impressive, as revealed in children's reasoning strategies, mastery of school-related skills, and use of language. Psychosocial development during middle childhood is characterized by an expanding social world of peer relationships and friendships, along with children's growing awareness of their own personalities, motives, and emotions, as well as those of others.

Prior Knowledge That Will Be Used in This Lesson

- Biosocial development during middle childhood (from Lesson 16) will be referred to as we discuss the development of motor skills and children with special needs.
- Cognitive development during middle childhood (from Lesson 17) will be referred to as language development is discussed, including the development of a second language.
- Psychosocial development during middle childhood (from Lesson 18) will be referred to as we discuss the child's expanding social world and different family structures (nuclear, single-parent, and blended).

- In the last video segment, you'll see the process of "conditioning" used to treat Sean, a boy with ADHD (attention-deficit/hyperactivity disorder). Recall from the discussion of behaviorism (in Lesson 1) that *operant conditioning* occurs when a response is gradually learned via *reinforcement*, such as offering a child rewards for positive behavior.

Learning Objectives

Use this information to guide your reading, viewing, thinking, and studying. After successfully completing this lesson, you should be able to:

1. Give examples of the basic pattern of motor-skill development, and discuss variations in biosocial development during middle childhood.
2. Describe cognitive development during middle childhood, focusing on language development and the advantages and challenges of learning English as a second language during this time.
3. Discuss psychosocial development during middle childhood, and give examples of the main developments in the child's social life and self-understanding.
4. Describe the symptoms of ADHD (attention-deficit/hyperactivity disorder), and discuss the types of treatment available for children with this disorder.

Textbook Reading & Video Viewing

For the most effective study of this lesson, complete the assignments in the sequence listed below.

Before viewing the video program:

Read Chapter 11, "Summary: Middle Childhood: Biosocial Development," page 348; Chapter 12, "Summary: Middle Childhood: Cognitive Development," page 374; and Chapter 13, "Summary: Middle Childhood: Psychosocial Development," page 405, and "The Developing Person So Far: Middle Childhood, Ages 6 Through 11," page 407.

View the video for Lesson 19, "On the Road of Accomplishment."

Segment 1: *Jazzmyn*

Segment 2: *Nikki*

Segment 3: *Truong*

Segment 4: *Sean*

Video Viewing Tips

The video for this lesson will feature four school-age children—Jazzmyn (9), Nikki (9), Truong (7), and Sean (11). Each has individual talents, interests, and backgrounds that make his or her journey unique. As you watch each segment, look for these key issues and themes:

Consider how the biosocial development of these four children may have affected their social interactions and self-concept. For example, a child's physical accomplishments can often influence his or her social status and self-esteem (something you're likely to remember if you've ever stood in line to "choose up sides" for a ballgame). Note any significant challenges these children face in their biological development and how these challenges may affect other domains.

Listen to how these children use language, and consider how this might affect their development in other domains. Improved language skills combined with a developing "theory of mind" and social cognition can allow the school-age child to see another person's point of view. This can lead to more sophisticated social interactions and negotiations—crucial skills in the development of relations within the peer group.

Also, note the influence of the school experience on these children. Teachers, the classroom, and the playground provide contexts for development outside the secure and accepting home environment. Watch for evidence of social comparison within the "society of children." How the child handles these often-unforgiving environments can influence his or her self-concept for years to come.

Finally, consider each child's family structure and function. A family that delivers all the basic needs provides a child with the security and confidence to explore the greater physical and social world. Also, note the parenting style in each family and speculate on how this may have affected each child's development. Relationships with parents often provide the prototype for relations with authority figures outside the home.

After viewing the video program:

Review all reading assignments for this lesson.

Complete the "Practice Questions" section to reinforce your understanding of important terms and concepts and measure your achievement of the Learning Objectives. Check your answers with the feedback given and review when necessary.

Practice Questions

Multiple-Choice Questions

1. As children move into middle childhood,
   a. the rate of accidental death increases.
   b. sexual urges intensify.
   c. the rate of weight gain increases.
   d. biological growth slows and steadies.

2. The increase in processing speed that occurs during middle childhood is partly the result of
   a. ongoing myelination of axons.
   b. neurological development in the limbic system.
   c. the streamlining of the knowledge base.
   d. all of the above.

3. To help obese children, nutritionists usually recommend
    a. strenuous dieting to counteract early overfeeding.
    b. the use of amphetamines and other drugs.
    c. more exercise and time to "grow out" of the fat.
    d. no specific actions.
4. The most effective form of help for children with ADHD is
    a. medication.
    b. psychological therapy.
    c. environmental change.
    d. a combination of some or all of the above.
5. Which of the following is true of children with a diagnosed learning disability?
    a. A child might have an average or above average IQ.
    b. Children find ways to compensate for their disability.
    c. The child may receive "scattered" scores when tested—high on some, low on others.
    d. All of the above are true.
6. A key factor in reaction time is
    a. whether the child is male or female.
    b. brain maturation.
    c. whether the stimulus to be reacted to is an auditory or visual one.
    d. all of the above.
7. Which approach to education may seem more effective in meeting the needs of children with learning disabilities in terms of social skills and academic achievement?
    a. mainstreaming
    b. special education
    c. inclusion
    d. resource rooms
8. In determining whether an eight-year-old has a learning disability, a teacher looks primarily for
    a. discrepant performance in a particular subject area.
    b. the exclusion of other explanations.
    c. both a and b.
    d. none of the above.

9. According to Carol Gilligan, a girl responding to the hypothetical question of whether an impoverished child should steal food to feed her starving dog is most likely to
   a. respond according to a depersonalized standard of right and wrong.
   b. hesitate to take a definitive position based on the abstract moral premise of "right and wrong."
   c. immediately respond that the child was justified in stealing the food.
   d. respond unpredictably, based on her own personal experiences.

10. According to developmentalists, the best game for a typical group of eight-year-olds would be
    a. football or baseball.
    b. basketball.
    c. one in which reaction time is not crucial.
    d. a game involving one-on-one competition.

11. According to Piaget, eight- and nine-year-olds can reason only about concrete things in their lives. "Concrete" means
    a. logical.
    b. abstract.
    c. tangible or visible.
    d. mathematical or classifiable.

12. The logical operations of concrete operational thought are particularly important to an understanding of the elementary-school subject of
    a. spelling.
    b. reading.
    c. math.
    d. social studies.

13. Piaget studied the ability to figure out (infer) the unspoken link between one fact and another. He called this ability
    a. reversibility.
    b. reciprocity.
    c. transitive inference.
    d. operational thought.

14. An example of schoolchildren's growth in metacognition is their understanding that
    a. transformed objects can be returned to their original state.
    b. rehearsal is a good strategy for memorizing, but outlining is better for understanding.
    c. objects may belong to more than one class.
    d. they can use different language styles in different situations.

15. Social cognition is defined as

    a. a person's awareness and understanding of human personality, motives, emotions, and interactions.
    b. the ability to form friendships easily.
    c. a person's skill in persuading others to go along with his or her wishes.
    d. the ability to learn by watching another person.

16. Throughout the world, the child culture encourages

    a. a period of latency.
    b. the emergence of a theory of mind.
    c. independence from adults.
    d. increasingly positive self-esteem.

17. The best strategy for helping children who are at risk of developing serious psychological problems because of multiple stresses would be to

    a. obtain assistance from a psychiatrist.
    b. change the household situation.
    c. increase the child's competencies or social supports.
    d. reduce the peer group's influence.

18. Compared with average or popular children, rejected children tend to

    a. be brighter and more competitive.
    b. be affluent and "stuck-up."
    c. be economically disadvantaged.
    d. misinterpret others' social behavior.

19. Compared to preschool children, the frequency of emotional problems in school-age children

    a. increases in both boys and girls.
    b. decreases in both boys and girls.
    c. increases in boys and decreases in girls.
    d. decreases in boys and increases in girls.

20. Erikson sees the crisis of the school years as that of

    a. industry versus inferiority.
    b. acceptance versus rejection.
    c. initiative versus guilt.
    d. male versus female.

21. In the area of social cognition, developmentalists are impressed by the school-age child's increasing ability to

    a. identify and take into account other people's viewpoints.
    b. develop an increasingly wide network of friends.
    c. relate to the opposite sex.
    d. resist social models.

22. Which of the following helps school-age children protect their self-esteem?

    a. devaluing what they are not good at
    b. overvaluing what they are good at
    c. comparing themselves to their friends
    d. comparing themselves to children with whom they are not friends

23. Which of the following school-age children is most likely to be emotionally healthy in adulthood?

    a. Trevor, who has a few close friends but who is not popular
    b. Arnie, who is aggressive-rejected
    c. Nate, who is popular but who has many acquaintances and has no close friends
    d. Mica, who is not popular and who has many acquaintances and no close friends

24. Which of the following statements would be **LEAST** likely to be part of the self-description of a school-age child?

    a. "I don't do very well in soccer compared to the other kids."
    b. "I try not to get so mad at my brother."
    c. "I help my friends when they are upset."
    d. "My parents know me better than I know myself."

True or False Items

Write T (for true) or F (for false) on the line in front of each statement.

25. ____ As they evaluate themselves according to increasingly complex self-theories, school-age children typically experience a rise in self-esteem.

26. ____ During middle childhood, acceptance by the peer group is valued more than having a close friend.

27. ____ Vygotsky believed that all children can achieve their developmental potential on their own and without the aid of instruction.

28. ____ School-age children are adept at tasks important in second-language acquisition.

29. ____ Code-switching, especially the occasional use of slang, is a behavior characteristic primarily of children in the lower social strata.

30. ____ The increasing myelination that occurs in middle childhood allows for the development of selective attention.

31. ____ Children can master almost any motor skill partly because of slower growth and stronger muscles.

32. ____ Despite the efforts of teachers and parents, most children with learning disabilities can expect their disabilities to persist and even worsen as they enter adulthood.

Questions for Reflection

1. Did any of the children's stories in the video lesson provide insight into your own childhood or (for those who are parents) that of your children? What did you learn about yourself or your children?
2. Which qualities and experiences of the children in the program would you hope to see in any children you might have? Why? Which qualities and experiences would you prefer not to see?
3. What experiences of middle childhood were *not* portrayed in the program? Which of these should have been included?
4. What are some of the losses that occur during middle childhood? What new potentials emerge during this stage of life? In what ways do these losses and gains relate to developmental events specific to childhood?

Key Terms

1. **learning disability:** A marked delay in a particular area of learning that is not caused by an apparent physical disability, by mental retardation, or by an unusually stressful home environment. (p. 341; objective 1)
2. **attention-deficit/hyperactivity disorder (ADHD):** A condition in which a person not only has great difficulty concentrating for more than a few moments but also is inattentive, impulsive, and overactive. (p. 338; video lesson, segment 4; objective 4)
3. **middle childhood:** The period between early childhood and early adolescence, approximately from ages 6 or 7 to 11. (p. 323; objectives 1, 2, & 3)
4. **developmental psychopathology:** The field of study that uses insights into typical development to understand and remediate developmental disorders. (p. 337; objective 1)
5. **least restrictive environment (LRE):** A legally required school setting in which children with special needs are offered as much freedom as possible to benefit from the instruction available to other children. (p. 344; objective 2)
6. **concrete operational thought:** Piaget's term for the ability to reason logically about direct experiences and perceptions. (p. 351; objective 2)
7. **immersion:** A strategy in which instruction in all school subjects occurs in the second (majority) language that a child is learning. (p. 366; objective 2)

8. **industry versus inferiority:** The fourth of Erikson's eight psychosocial crises, during which children attempt to master many skills, developing a sense of themselves as either industrious or inferior, competent or incompetent. (p. 378; objective 3)
9. **child culture:** The particular habits, styles, and values that reflect the set of rules and rituals that characterize children as distinct from adult society. Also called the *society of children*. (p. 395; video lesson, segment 3; objective 3)
10. **nuclear family:** A family that consists of a father, a mother, and their biological children under age 18. (p. 387; video lesson, segments 3 & 4; objective 3)
11. **single-parent family:**. A family that consists of only one parent and his or her biological children under age 18. (p. 387; video lesson, segment 1; objective 3)
12. **extended family:** A family of three or more generations living in one household is called an extended family. (p. 387; objective 3)
13. **code-switching:** A pragmatic communication skill involving changing from one form of speech to another. (video lesson, segment 2; objective 2)
14. **mainstreaming:** An educational approach in which children with special needs are included in regular classrooms. (video lesson, segment 3; objective 1)
15. **social cognition:** A person's awareness and understanding of the personalities, motives, emotions, intentions, and interactions of other people and groups. (Lesson 18 video lesson, segment 1; objective 3)
16. **social comparison:** The tendency to assess one's abilities, achievements, and social status by measuring them against those of others, especially those of one's peers. (Lesson 18 video; objective 3)
17. **blended family:** A family consisting of two parents, at least one with biological children from another union. (p. 388; objective 3)

Summary

Many children, including Nikki in the video lesson, benefit from their parents' authoritative style that encourages communication and independent thinking. For this and other reasons, Nikki is growing up to be a very independent young lady. For children such as Truong, growing up in a family of recent immigrants to the United States poses special challenges in learning to speak a new language and adjust to a new culture. Yet, Truong is meeting these challenges well. A new language is generally learned more easily prior to adolescence, which is why Truong can pick up English more easily than his parents can. Children who have ADHD (attention-deficit/hyperactivity disorder), such as Sean, find that development in each of the three domains is much more difficult for them than for children without the disorder. With the help of a special form of behavioral conditioning, however, Sean is regaining his developmental stride. It should be noted that not all children with attention deficit exhibit hyperactive behavior like Sean.

Although most children follow a similar path of growth in each of the three domains of development, their individual achievements depend on their own unique combination of interests, genetics, and talents, as well as the environmental influences exerted by their family, friends, school, and culture. For most boys and girls, the years of middle childhood are a time when biosocial development is smooth and uneventful. Body maturation coupled with sufficient practice enables school-age children to master many motor skills.

Cognitive development between the ages of 6 and 11 is impressive, as reflected by children's reasoning strategies, mastery of school-related skills, and use of language. For children around the world, the transition into middle childhood marks a passage into a new phase of cognitive development some call the "age of reason." For Piaget, the age of reason begins with the shift from preoperational to concrete operational thought. When this transition is complete, children are much better able to understand logical principles, as long as they are applied to concrete examples.

As school-age children develop a more complex view of social interactions, their social awareness and theory of mind begin to mature, and they become increasingly aware of the motives, emotions, and personality traits that are the foundation of others' behavior. As their social skills improve, school-age children also become better able to adjust their own behavior to interact appropriately with others. As they do so, children further develop their self-concept and self-esteem through social comparison—especially with peers.

Answer Key

Practice Questions

Multiple-Choice Questions

1. d. is the correct answer. (objective 1)
2. a. is the correct answer. (objective 2)

   b. is incorrect. Neurological development in the frontal cortex facilitates processing speed during middle childhood. The limbic system, which was not discussed in this lesson, is concerned with emotions.

   c. is incorrect. Processing speed is facilitated by growth, rather than streamlining, of the knowledge base.
3. c. is the correct answer. (video lesson, segment 4; objective 4)

   a. is incorrect. Dieting is not recommended, as it can be physically harmful and may increase the desire for the forbidden foods.

   b. is incorrect. The use of amphetamines to control weight is not recommended at any age.
4. d. is the correct answer. (video lesson, segment 4; objective 4)
5. d. is the correct answer. (objective 1)
6. b. is the correct answer. (objective 1)
7. c. is the correct answer. (objective 1)

   a. is incorrect. Many general education teachers are unable to cope with the special needs of some children.

   b. & d. are incorrect. These approaches undermined the social integration of children with special needs.
8. c. is the correct answer. (objective 1)

9. b. is the correct answer. Gilligan contends that females' morality of care makes them reluctant to judge right and wrong in absolute terms because they are socialized to be nurturing and caring. (objective 3)

10. c. is the correct answer. (objective 1)

    a. & b. are incorrect. Each of these games involves skills that are hardest for schoolchildren to master.

    d. is incorrect. Because one-on-one sports are likely to accentuate individual differences in ability, they may be especially discouraging to some children.

11. c. is the correct answer. (video lesson, segment 2; objective 2)

12. c. is the correct answer. (objective 2)

13. c. is the correct answer. (objective 2)

14. b. is the correct answer. (objective 2)

15. a. is the correct answer. (objective 3)

16. c. is the correct answer. (objective 3)

17. c. is the correct answer. (objective 3)

18. d. is the correct answer. (objective 3)

19. b. is the correct answer. (objective 3)

20. a. is the correct answer. (objective 3)

21. a. is the correct answer. (video lesson, segment 2; objective 3)

    b. is incorrect. Friendship circles typically become smaller during middle childhood, as children become choosier about their friends.

    c. & d. are incorrect. These issues are not discussed in the lesson.

22. c. is the correct answer. (objective 3)

23. b. is the correct answer. (objective 3)

24. c. is the correct answer. Although emotional maturity is an important factor in family functioning, the textbook does not suggest that biological parents are more mature than other parents. (objective 3)

True or False Items

25. F In fact, just the opposite is true. (objective 3)

26. F In fact, just the opposite is true. (objective 3)

27. F Vygotsky believed that instruction is crucial in children's development. (objective 2)

28. T (video lesson, segment 3; objective 2)

29. F Code-switching (including occasional use of slang) is a behavior demonstrated by all children. (objective 2)

30. F Physical variations in children from developed countries are caused primarily by heredity. (objective 1)

31. T (objective 1)

32. F With the proper assistance, many children with learning disabilities develop into adults who are virtually indistinguishable from other adults in their educational and occupational achievements. (objective 1)

Lesson Review

Lesson 19

The School Years
Summary

Please Note: Use this matrix to guide your study and achieve the learning objectives of this lesson. It will also help you to view the video, which defines and demonstrates important concepts and skills as they relate to everyday life.

Learning Objective	Textbook	Course Student Guide	Video Lesson
1. Give examples of the basic pattern of motor-skill development, and discuss variations in biosocial development during middle childhood.	pp. 323–328, 337–347	Key Terms: 1, 3, 4, 5, 6; Practice Questions: 1, 5, 6, 7, 8, 10, 30, 31, 32.	all segments
2. Describe cognitive development during middle childhood, focusing on language development and the advantages and challenges of learning English as a second language during this time.	pp. 311, 317–322, 330–333, 338, 342–346, 348–351, 372–373	Key Terms: 4, 7, 8, 9, 18; Practice Questions: 2, 11, 12, 13, 14, 27, 28, 29.	all segments
3. Discuss psychosocial development during middle childhood, and give examples of the main developments in the child's social life and self-understanding.	pp. 311, 371–380, 391–395, 399–401	Key Terms: 4, 10, 11, 12, 13, 14, 15, 16, 17; Practice Questions: 9, 15, 16, 17, 18, 19, 20, 21, 22, 23, 24, 25, 26.	all segments
4. Describe the symptoms of ADHD (attention-deficit/hyperactivity disorder), and discuss the types of treatment available for children with this disorder.	pp. 338–341	Key Terms: 2; Practice Questions: 3, 4.	Segment 4: *Sean*

School Days

Lesson 20

The School Years:
Special Topic

Preview

This lesson follows the story of Mario, a fifth grade student, who struggled socially and academically until he met a devoted teacher, Erik Rossman, who found a way to motivate and encourage the boy. Mario's transformation poignantly illustrates the powerful influence that teachers and schools can have on children. It also raises a number of questions that are addressed in this lesson: What should we teach our children and who should decide? What is "good teaching"? Is there too much emphasis on testing today? How do the major developmental theories inform and guide teachers?

While you're studying this lesson, talk to a schoolteacher and/or a child you know who attends a public or private elementary school. How is the school day organized, what's the typical schedule each day? How many children are in each class? What subjects are taught? How does the instructor teach each subject, what techniques are used? How does the teacher assess and evaluate student learning? What type of tests are given and how often? How does the teacher motivate students to study? In what other ways can the school experience shape a child's development, both inside and outside the classroom?

Prior Knowledge That Will Be Used in This Lesson

- The theories of Jean Piaget, Lev Vygotsky, and B. F. Skinner (from Lesson 1) will be discussed as we explore the various methods used by skilled teachers.

Learning Objectives

Use this information to guide your reading, viewing, thinking, and studying. After successfully completing this lesson, you should be able to:

1. Summarize how curriculum and academic standards are typically selected in formal school systems, and how these choices can ultimately affect a child's development.
2. Outline the constructivist philosophy, describe emergent curriculum, and discuss the potential advantages and disadvantages of this approach to education.
3. Discuss the socializing influence of school and identify the social skills that children learn at school both inside and outside the classroom.
4. Explain how the theories of Jean Piaget, Lev Vygotsky, and B. F. Skinner have shaped how children are taught in the classroom.
5. Define the concept of multiple intelligences, identify different types of intelligence, and discuss the possible benefits and challenges of applying this theory in classroom situations.
6. Summarize what parents can do to support the learning experience of their school-age children.
7. Differentiate between achievement and aptitude tests and discuss the pros and cons of using tests to evaluate student knowledge and performance.

Textbook Reading & Video Viewing

For the most effective study of this lesson, complete the assignments in the sequence listed below.

Before viewing the video program:

Review Chapter 11, "Middle Childhood: Biosocial Development," pages 334–337 ("Measuring the Mind"), and Chapter 12, "Middle Childhood: Cognitive Development," pages 365–366 and 369–373 ("Differences by Nation," "Reading Wars, Math Wars, and Cognitive Theory," and "Who Determines Educational Practice?").

View the video for Lesson 20, "School Days."

Segment 1: *What Do We Teach?*

Segment 2: *How Do We Teach?*

Segment 3: *How Do We Measure Success?*

After viewing the video program:

Review all reading assignments for this lesson.

Complete the "Practice Questions" section to reinforce your understanding of important terms and concepts and measure your achievement of the Learning Objectives. Check your answers with the feedback given and review when necessary.

Practice Questions

Multiple-Choice Questions

1. Tests that measure a child's potential to learn a new subject are called _______________ tests.
   a. aptitude
   b. achievement
   c. norm-referenced
   d. criterion-referenced
2. In the earliest IQ tests, a child's score was calculated by dividing the child's __________________ age by his or her ________________age to find the __________________ quotient.
   a. mental; chronological; intelligence
   b. chronological; mental; intelligence
   c. intelligence; chronological; mental
   d. intelligence; mental; chronological
3. Aptitude and achievement testing are controversial because
   a. they don't provide valid and reliable results.
   b. test performance can be affected by many factors other than the child's intellectual potential or academic achievement.
   c. they often fail to identify serious learning problems.
   d. of all of the above reasons.
4. Tests that measure what a child has already learned are called __________________ tests.
   a. aptitude
   b. vocational
   c. achievement
   d. intelligence
5. Which of the following is **NOT** a type of intelligence identified in Robert Sternberg's theory?
   a. academic
   b. practical
   c. achievement
   d. creative

6. Angela was born in 1984. In 1992, she scored 125 on an intelligence test. Using the original formula, what was Angela's mental age when she took the test?

   a. 6
   b. 8
   c. 10
   d. 12

7. Raymond's score on a test indicated that his ability equals that of a typical fifth-grade student. The test Raymond took evidently was

   a. criterion-referenced.
   b. norm-referenced.
   c. an aptitude test.
   d. all of the above.

8. Howard Gardner and Robert Sternberg would probably be most critical of traditional aptitude and achievement tests because they

   a. inadvertently reflect certain nonacademic competencies.
   b. do not reflect knowledge of cultural ideas.
   c. measure only a limited set of intellectual abilities.
   d. underestimate the intellectual potential of disadvantaged children.

9. During the school board meeting, a knowledgeable parent proclaimed that the board's position on achievement testing and class size was an example of the district's "hidden curriculum." The parent was referring to

   a. unofficial and unstated educational priorities of the school district.
   b. political agendas of individual members of the school board.
   c. legal mandates for testing and class size established by the state board of education.
   d. none of the above.

10. Judy's mother has some questions about the curriculum in her daughter's school. The principal informs her that the curriculum is set by

    a. each teacher.
    b. each school
    c. the State Board of Education.
    d. the National Education Association.

11. Today, most public schools primarily teach

    a. standards-based curriculum.
    b. an emergent curriculum.
    c. constructivist curriculum.
    d. none of the above.

12. The idea that reinforcing a desired classroom behavior makes that behavior more likely to happen again stems most directly from the ideas of
    a. Lev Vygotsky.
    b. Jean Piaget.
    c. Howard Gardner.
    d. B. F. Skinner.
13. The idea that children learn best through active participation and exploration based on their natural curiosity stems most directly from the ideas of
    a. Lev Vygotsky.
    b. Jean Piaget.
    c. Howard Gardner.
    d. B. F. Skinner.
14. A middle school science teacher who mentors students and structures her lessons to emphasize social interaction and cooperative learning is apparently an advocate of the ideas of
    a. Lev Vygotsky.
    b. Jean Piaget.
    c. Howard Gardner.
    d. B. F. Skinner.

True or False Items

Write T (for true) or F (for false) on the line in front of each statement.

15. _____ In the United States, children are required by law to attend school.
16. _____ Emergent curriculum has its roots in behaviorism.
17. _____ Today, most educators have discarded emergent curriculum because it is ineffective.
18. _____ Sadly, there is little connection between educational curriculum in the United States and the ideas of developmental theorists.
19. _____ Jean Piaget emphasized the role of social interaction in the learning process.
20. _____ Most teachers believe that "good teaching is good teaching," and that all children should be taught the same way.
21. _____ Most school districts use aptitude tests to measure how much and how well a child has learned in a specific subject area.
22. _____ A test that is graded "on a curve" is an example of a norm-referenced test.
23. _____ Research shows that standardized testing tends to expand the curriculum to subjects such as art and music that might otherwise be excluded.

24. _____ Research shows clearly that children learn better when there are fewer children in each class.

Key Terms

1. **curriculum:** The subjects and topics that children are taught in a particular grade. (video lesson, segment 1; objective 1)
2. **hidden curriculum:** The unofficial, unstated, or implicit rules and priorities that influence the academic curriculum and every other aspect of learning in a school. (p. 366; objective 1)
3. **standards-based curriculum:** A curriculum that is based on a level of competency for each subject, typically set by the state and local school boards. (video lesson, segment 1; objective 1)
4. **emergent curriculum:** A curriculum that derives more from the needs, abilities, and interests of each individual student than from a standard set of competencies deemed important for all students. (video lesson, segment 1; objective 2)
5. **constructivist philosophy:** The idea that knowledge is "constructed" in the mind of each individual. It suggests that children learn best from direct interactions and first-hand experiences, which take into account their previous knowledge and personal interests. (video lesson, segment 1; objective 2)
6. **operant conditioning:** As described by B. F. Skinner, the learning process by which a particular action is followed by something desired (which makes the person or animal more likely to repeat the action) or by something unwanted (which makes the action less likely to be repeated). (p. 43; video lesson, segment 2; objective 4)
7. **multiple intelligences:** As proposed by Howard Gardner and Robert Sternberg, the idea that humans have different types of intellectual aptitudes and abilities, rather than a single, underlying ability (as emphasized in standard IQ tests). (p. 335; video lesson, segment 2; objective 5)
8. **IQ tests:** Tests designed to measure intellectual aptitude, or ability to learn in school. Originally, intelligence was defined as mental age divided by chronological age, times 100—hence the term *intelligence quotient*, or IQ. (p. 334; objective 7)
9. **aptitude:** The potential to master a specific skill or to learn a certain body of knowledge. (p. 335; objective 7)
10. **achievement tests:** Tests that measure what a child has already learned about a particular subject. (p. 334; video lesson, segment 3; objective 7)
11. **norm-referenced:** An achievement test that is based on a certain level of achievement that is usual, such as grade level. A student's performance is compared to the performance of other students. (video lesson, segment 3; objective 7)

12. **standards-based or criterion-referenced:** An achievement test that is based on a specific standard of performance, such as how well a child reads. A child's performance is compared to the standard rather than the performance of other students. (video lesson, segment 3; objective 7)

Summary

While schooling of some sort is required by law in most communities worldwide, who receives instruction, in what subjects, and how they receive this instruction varies enormously. In addition to teaching academic subjects, school is a major socializing force that helps children find their places in society.

Although the specific styles of education will vary, depending on teacher personality and cultural assumptions, any developmental approach to education attempts to engage every student in the learning process. In the United States, the content of K–12 (kindergarten through 12th grade) instruction—what we call **curriculum**—is mandated separately by each state's Board of Education, which also establishes levels of competency—or standards—in reading, math, social studies, and all other academic subjects. These competency levels form a **standards-based curriculum** that guides instruction in the classroom.

An alternative approach is **emergent curriculum**, which attempts to address the needs and abilities of each individual student more directly. This approach has its roots in **constructivist philosophy**, which proposes that knowledge is constructed and not transmitted. Those who follow this philosophy believe that children learn best through active interactions with their environment. A new emergent approach in math—for example—replaces rote learning with hands-on materials and active discussion that relates directly to the students interests and prior experience. Such an approach promotes problem solving and a deeper level of understanding. Although standards-based and emergent curricula each have their strengths and weaknesses, both depend on the child's motivation for learning.

Each of the major theories of development has had an impact on contemporary education. For instance, the use of goals and rewards or **reinforcement** in the classroom stems from B. F. Skinner's principles of **operant conditioning**, and the emphasis on learning through active participation and exploration of the environment derives from the ideas of Jean Piaget. As a third example, teachers who pay particular attention to the role of social interaction in learning are following the ideas of Lev Vygotsky. Finally, most teachers recognize that each child has a unique style of learning and demonstrates what Howard Gardner and Robert Sternberg have called "multiple intelligences." Sternberg believes that there are three distinct types of intelligence: academic, creative, and practical. Similarly, Howard Gardner describes seven distinct intelligences: linguistic, logical-mathematical, musical, spatial, body-kinesthetic, interpersonal, and intrapersonal.

The issue of testing in education remains controversial because a child's test performance can be affected by nonacademic factors, such as the capacity to pay attention and concentrate, emotional stress, health, language difficulties, and test-taking anxiety. **Achievement tests** are designed to measure what a child has learned, while **aptitude tests** are designed to measure learning potential. Achievement tests take one of two forms. A **norm-referenced** test compares student performance to an average set by other students who have taken the same test. Instead of comparing to others, a **standards-based** or **criterion-referenced** test compares each student's performance to predetermined standards or competencies.

The most commonly used aptitude tests are intelligence tests or **IQ tests**. In some versions of these tests, a person's score is translated into a mental age, which is divided by the person's chronological age and multiplied by 100 to determine his or her IQ. IQ scores may seriously underestimate the intellectual potential of a disadvantaged child or overestimate that of a child from an advantaged background.

Answer Key

Practice Questions

Multiple-Choice Questions

1. a. is the correct answer. (video lesson, segment 3; objective 7)

   b. is incorrect. Achievement tests measure what has already been learned.

   c. is incorrect. Vocational tests, which, as their name implies, measure what a person has learned about a particular trade, are achievement tests.

   d. is incorrect. Intelligence tests measure general aptitude, rather than aptitude for a specific subject.
2. a. is the correct answer. (objective 7)
3. b. is the correct answer. (video lesson, segment 3; objective 7)
4. c. is the correct answer. (video lesson, segment 3; objective 7)
5. c. is the correct answer. (objective 5)
6. c. is the correct answer. (objective 7)
7. b. is the correct answer. (video lesson, segment 3; objective 7)

   a. is incorrect. Criterion-referenced tests specify a certain standard of performance rather than comparing performance to that of others.

   c. is incorrect. Aptitude tests measure the potential to learn rather than how much material has already been mastered.
8. c. is the correct answer. Both Sternberg and Gardner believe that there are multiple intelligences rather than the narrowly defined abilities measured by traditional aptitude and achievement tests. (video lesson, segment 2; objective 5)

   a., b., & d. are incorrect. Although these criticisms are certainly valid, they are not specifically associated with Sternberg or Gardner.
9. a. is the correct answer. (objective 1)
10. c. is the correct answer. (video lesson, segment 1; objective 1)
11. a. is the correct answer. (video lesson, segment 1; objective 1)

12. d. is the correct answer. (video lesson, segment 2; objective 4)

    a. is incorrect. Lev Vygotsky emphasized the role of social interaction in learning.

    b. is incorrect. Jean Piaget emphasized the importance of active participation and exploration in learning.

    c. is incorrect. Howard Gardner is known for his theory that there are multiple intelligences.

13. b. is the correct answer. (video lesson, segment 2; objective 4)

    a. is incorrect. Lev Vygotsky emphasized the role of social interaction in learning.

    c. is incorrect. Howard Gardner is known for his theory that there are multiple intelligences.

    d. is incorrect. B. F. Skinner is known for his theory of operant conditioning, which emphasizes the influence of reinforcement on classroom behaviors.

14. a. is the correct answer. (video lesson, segment 2; objective 4)

True-False Items

15. T (video lesson, introduction; objective 1)
16. F Emergent curriculum has its roots in constructivist philosophy. (video lesson, segment 1; objective 2)
17. F Emergent curriculum is increasingly being used with positive results, often in conjunction with standards-based curriculum. (video lesson, segment 1; objective 2)
18. F The major theories of development are highly evident in contemporary education. (video lesson, segment 2; objective 4)
19. F Lev Vygotsky emphasized the role of social interaction in learning; Piaget emphasized active exploration and experimentation. (video lesson, segment 2; objective 4)
20. F Most teachers agree that children differ in their intelligences and learning styles. (video lesson, segment 2; objective 5)
21. F Most school districts use achievement tests for this purpose; aptitude tests measure a student's *potential* to learn. (video lesson, segment 3; objective 7)
22. T (video lesson, segment 3; objective 7)
23. F Testing generally *narrows* the curriculum to exclude subjects such as these, which tend not to be covered on standardized achievement tests. (video lesson, segment 3; objective 7)
24. F Despite this widespread belief, research support is mixed, at best. (objective 1)

Lesson Review

Lesson 20

The School Years
Special Topic

Please Note: Use this matrix to guide your study and achieve the learning objectives of this lesson. It will also help you to view the video, which defines and demonstrates important concepts and skills as they relate to everyday life.

Learning Objective	Textbook	Course Student Guide	Video Lesson
1. Summarize how curriculum and academic standards are typically selected in formal school systems, and how these choices can ultimately affect a child's development.	pp. 368–373	Key Terms: 1, 2, 3; Practice Questions: 9, 10, 11, 15, 24.	Introduction Segment 1: *What Do We Teach?*
2. Outline the constructivist philosophy, describe emergent curriculum, and discuss the potential advantages and disadvantages of this approach to education.	*	Key Terms: 4, 5; Practice Questions: 16, 17.	Segment 1: *What Do We Teach?*
3. Discuss the socializing influence of school and identify the social skills that children learn at school both inside and outside the classroom.	*		Segment 2: *How Do We Teach?*
4. Explain how the theories of Jean Piaget, Lev Vygotsky, and B. F. Skinner have shaped how children are taught in the classroom.	*	Key Terms: 6; Practice Questions: 12, 13, 14, 18, 19.	Segment 2: *How Do We Teach?*
5. Define the concept of multiple intelligences, identify different types of intelligence, and discuss the possible benefits and challenges of applying this theory in classroom situations.	pp. 335–336	Key Terms: 7; Practice Questions: 5, 8, 20.	Segment 2: *How Do We Teach?*
6. Summarize what parents can do to support the learning experience of their school-age children.	*		Segment 2: *How Do We Teach?*
7. Differentiate between achievement and aptitude tests and discuss the pros and cons of using tests to evaluate student knowledge and performance.	pp. 334–336	Key Terms: 8, 9, 10, 11, 12; Practice Questions: 1, 2, 3, 4, 6, 7, 21, 22, 23.	Segment 3: *How Do We Measure Success?*

* The video for this lesson offers excellent coverage of these topics.

Explosions

Lesson 21

Adolescence:
Biosocial Development

Preview

Between the ages of 11 and 18, young people cross the great divide between childhood and adulthood that we call **adolescence**. This crossing encompasses all three domains of development—biosocial, cognitive, and psychosocial. Lesson 21 focuses on the dramatic changes that occur in the biosocial domain, beginning with **puberty** and the **growth spurt**. The biosocial metamorphosis of the adolescent is discussed in detail, with emphasis on sexual maturation, nutrition, and the effects of the timing of puberty, including possible problems arising from early or late maturation.

Although adolescence is, in many ways, a healthy time of life, this lesson addresses three health hazards that too often affect children of this age: sexual abuse, poor nutrition, and use of alcohol, tobacco, and other drugs.

As you begin this lesson, reflect on your own experience in adolescence. Recall your physical growth and development during this period (i.e., height, weight, voice changes, hair growth, developing curves/shoulders). Did you develop any earlier or later than your peers? How did these changes make you feel? How well did you eat and take care of yourself physically? What pressures did you feel regarding sex and the use of drugs and alcohol?

Prior Knowledge That Will Be Used in This Lesson

- Biosocial development during infancy (Lesson 6), early childhood (Lesson 11), and middle childhood (Lesson 16) will be referred to as we discuss physical developments during adolescence. As you'll learn, the rate of growth in adolescence is second only to the rapid growth experienced prenatally (in the womb) and postnatally (during the first year of life).

Learning Objectives

Use this information to guide your reading, viewing, thinking, and studying. After successfully completing this lesson, you should be able to:

1. Identify and describe the biological events of puberty.
2. Identify several factors that influence the timing of puberty.
3. Discuss the consequences for boys and girls who experience early or late onset of puberty.
4. Describe the growth spurt experienced during adolescence by both boys and girls, including changes in weight, height, and the body's internal organ system.
5. Describe the sexual maturation that occurs in males and females during puberty, distinguish between primary and secondary sex characteristics, and discuss what some experts believe regarding sexual impulses at this age.
6. Discuss the emotional and psychological impact of pubertal hormones and how this impact is influenced by social context.
7. Describe factors that have an impact on the adolescent's development of a positive body image.
8. Describe the biosocial hazards associated with early sexual activity, and discuss the prevalence and consequences of childhood sexual abuse.
9. Discuss neurological development during this period, noting the factors at play in adolescent risk taking as well as the unique benefits of this phase of development.
10. Discuss the nutritional needs and problems of adolescents, define the major types of eating disorders, and discuss how different theories of development might explain them.
11. Discuss the use and abuse of alcohol, tobacco, and other drugs among adolescents today, including prevalence, significance for development, and the best methods of prevention.
12. Describe how adolescent brain activity affects body rhythms in regard to stress, appetite, and sleep patterns.

Textbook Reading & Video Viewing

For the most effective study of this lesson, complete the assignments in the sequence listed below.

Before viewing the video program:

Read Chapter 14, "Adolescence: Biosocial Development," pages 409–437, and pages 497–500, "Drug Use and Abuse," in Chapter 16.

View the video for Lesson 21, "Explosions."

Segment 1: *Puberty*

Segment 2: *Body Image*

Segment 3: *Health*

After viewing the video program:

Review all reading assignments for this lesson.

Complete the "Practice Questions" and "Applying Your Knowledge" sections to reinforce your understanding of important terms and concepts and measure your achievement of the Learning Objectives. Check your answers with the feedback given and review when necessary.

Practice Questions I

Multiple-Choice Questions

1. Which of the following most accurately describes the sequence of pubertal development in girls?
   a. breast buds; weight spurt begins; first menstrual period; ovulation
   b. weight spurt begins; breast buds; first menstrual period; ovulation
   c. first menstrual period; breast buds; weight spurt begins; ovulation
   d. breast buds; weight spurt begins; ovulation; first menstrual period

2. Although both sexes grow rapidly during adolescence, boys typically begin their accelerated growth about
   a. a year or two later than girls.
   b. a year earlier than girls.
   c. the time they reach sexual maturity.
   d. the time facial hair appears.

3. For boys, the first readily observable signs of the onset of puberty include
   a. lowered voice.
   b. initial appearance of pubic hair.
   c. growth of testes.
   d. both b and c.

4. More than any other group in the population, adolescent girls are likely to have
   a. asthma.
   b. acne.
   c. iron-deficiency anemia.
   d. testosterone deficiency.

5. The HPA axis is the
   a. route followed by many hormones to regulate stress, growth, sleep, and appetite.
   b. pair of sex glands in humans.
   c. cascade of sex hormones in females and males.
   d. area of the brain that regulates the pituitary gland.

6. For males, the secondary sex characteristic that usually occurs last is

   a. breast enlargement.

   b. the appearance of facial hair.

   c. growth of the testes.

   d. the appearance of pubic hair.

7. For girls, the specific event that is taken to indicate sexual maturity is ______________. For boys, it is _________________.

   a. the growth of breast buds; voice deepening

   b. menarche; spermarche

   c. an ovulation; the testosterone surge

   d. the growth spurt; pubic hair

8. The most significant hormonal changes of puberty include a marked increase of ___________________ in boys and a marked increase of ___________________ in girls.

   a. progesterone; estrogen

   b. estrogen; testosterone

   c. estrogen; progesterone

   d. testosterone; estrogen

9. In general, most adolescents are

   a. overweight.

   b. satisfied with their appearance.

   c. dissatisfied with their appearance.

   d. unaffected by cultural attitudes about beauty.

10. Of the following, who is most likely to suffer from bulimia?

    a. Bill, a 23-year-old professional football player

    b. Florence, a 30-year-old account executive

    c. Lynn, an 18-year-old college student

    d. Carl, a professional wrestler

11. Potential hazards of early sexual activity include higher incidence of all of the following **EXCEPT**

    a. drug abuse.

    b. obesity.

    c. sexually transmitted infections.

    d. depression.

12. Earlier-than-average physical growth and sexual maturation
    a. tend to be equally difficult for girls and boys.
    b. tend to be more difficult for boys than for girls.
    c. tend to be more difficult for girls than for boys.
    d. are easier for both girls and boys than late maturation.
13. A fully grown person with a body mass index (BMI) of 18 or lower is considered
    a. anorexic.
    b. average.
    c. overweight.
    d. obese.
14. The emotional turbulence of adolescence
    a. is entirely explained by the direct links with hormone surges.
    b. begins as young as age 8 or 9, when hormone production begins.
    c. are often the result of the interaction between visible sexual maturation and others' reactions.
    d. is entirely explained by the social pressures placed on adolescents to behave more adult-like.
15. All creatures have a day/night cycle of biological activity that occurs approximately every 24 hours that affects tiredness, hunger, alertness, elimination, body temperature, and nutrient balance. This cycle is referred to as
    a. diurnal rhythm.
    b. nocturnal rhythm.
    c. circadian rhythm.
    d. biorhythm.

True or False Items

Write T (for true) or F (for false) on the line in front of each statement.

16. ____ Anorexia is suspected if a person's BMI is 18 or lower.
17. ____ The first indicator of reproductive potential in males is menarche.
18. ____ Lung capacity, heart size, and total volume of blood increase significantly during adolescence.
20. ____ Puberty generally begins sometime between ages 8 and 15.
21. ____ Girls who mature late and are thinner than average tend to be satisfied with their weight.

22. ____ The strong emphasis on physical appearance is unique to adolescents and finds little support from teachers, parents, and the larger culture.

23. ____ Childhood habits of overeating and underexercising usually lessen during adolescence.

24. ____ The problems of the early-maturing girl tend to be temporary.

25. ____ Both the sequence and timing of pubertal events vary greatly from one young person to another.

26. ____ Children grow taller in summer and heavier in winter.

Practice Questions II

Multiple-Choice Questions

1. Which of the following is the correct sequence of pubertal events in boys?
   a. growth spurt; pubic hair; first ejaculation; lowering of voice
   b. pubic hair; first ejaculation; growth spurt; lowering of voice
   c. lowering of voice; pubic hair; growth spurt; first ejaculation
   d. growth spurt; lowering of voice; pubic hair; first ejaculation

2. Which of the following statements about adolescent physical development is **NOT** true?
   a. Hands and feet generally lengthen before the torso.
   b. Facial features usually grow before the head itself reaches adult size and shape.
   c. Oil, sweat, and odor glands become more active.
   d. The lymphoid system increases slightly in size, and the heart increases by nearly half.

3. In puberty, a hormone that increases markedly in girls (and only somewhat in boys) is
   a. estradiol.
   b. testosterone.
   c. androgen.
   d. menarche.

4. Nutritional deficiencies in adolescence are frequently the result of
   a. eating red meat.
   b. poor food choices.
   c. an ovulatory menstruation.
   d. excessive exercise.

5. In females, puberty is typically marked by a(n)
   a. significant widening of the shoulders.
   b. significant widening of the hips.
   c. enlargement of the torso and upper chest.
   d. decrease in the size of the eyes and nose.
6. Nonreproductive sexual characteristics, such as the deepening of the voice and the development of breasts, are called
   a. gender-typed traits.
   b. primary sex characteristics.
   c. secondary sex characteristics.
   d. pubertal prototypes.
7. Puberty is initiated when hormones are released from the ______________, then from the __________________, and then from the adrenal glands and the ___________________.
   a. hypothalamus; pituitary; gonads
   b. pituitary; gonads; hypothalamus
   c. gonads; pituitary; hypothalamus
   d. pituitary; hypothalamus; gonads
8. The typical bulimic patient is a
   a. college-age woman.
   b. teenage girl who starves herself to the point of emaciation.
   c. woman in her late forties.
   d. teenager who suffers from life-threatening obesity.
9. With regard to appearance, adolescent girls are most commonly dissatisfied with
   a. timing of maturation.
   b. eyes and other facial features.
   c. weight.
   d. legs.
10. To predict the age at which a girl first has sexual intercourse, it would be useful to know
   a. her race or ethnic group.
   b. her religious beliefs.
   c. her age at menarche.
   d. all of the above.

11. Individuals who experiment with drugs early are
    a. typically affluent teenagers who are experiencing an identity crisis.
    b. more likely to become addicted.
    c. less likely to have alcohol-abuse problems later on.
    d. usually able to resist later peer pressure leading to long-term addiction.
12. Data on substantiated child sexual abuse in the United States confirms that the rate is higher among
    a. toddlers.
    b. 10- to 12-year-olds.
    c. 4- to 8-year-olds.
    d. 12- to 15-year-olds.
13. Puberty is most accurately defined as the period
    a. of rapid physical growth that occurs during adolescence.
    b. during which sexual maturation is attained.
    c. of rapid physical growth and sexual maturation that ends childhood.
    d. during which adolescents establish identities separate from their parents.
14. Which of the following does **NOT** typically occur during puberty?
    a. The lungs increase in size and capacity.
    b. Heart rate increases.
    c. Blood volume increases.
    d. The lymphoid system decreases in size.
15. Teenagers' susceptibility to respiratory ailments typically ________________ during adolescence, due to a(n) ________________ in the size of the lymphoid system.
    a. increases; increase
    b. increases; decrease
    c. decreases; increase
    d. decreases; decrease

Matching Items

Match each definition or description with its corresponding term.

Terms

16. _______ leptin
17. _______ hormone
18. _______ testosterone
19. _______ estradiol
20. _______ growth spurt
21. _______ primary sex characteristics
22. _______ menarche
23. _______ spermarche
24. _______ secondary sex characteristics
25. _______ body image
26. _______ anorexia nervosa
27. _______ bulimia nervosa

Definitions or Descriptions

a. onset of menstruation
b. a hormone that stimulates appetite and has been implicated in the timing of puberty
c. hormone that increases dramatically in boys during puberty
d. puberty begins with the cascading of these through the bloodstream
e. an affliction characterized by binge-purge eating
f. hormone that increases dramatically in girls during puberty
g. first sign is increased bone length and density
h. attitude toward one's physical appearance
i. an affliction characterized by self-starvation
j. physical characteristics not involved in reproduction
k. the sex organs involved in reproduction
l. first ejaculation containing sperm

Applying Your Knowledge

1. Girls who live with a stepfather or their mother's boyfriend experience ______________ menarche because of increased ______________.

   a. earlier; stress
   b. earlier; body fat
   c. later; stress
   d. later; body fat

2. Thirteen-year-old Rosa, an avid runner and dancer, is worried because most of her friends have begun to menstruate regularly. Her doctor tells her
   a. that she should have a complete physical exam, because female athletes usually menstruate earlier than average.
   b. not to worry, since female athletes usually menstruate later than average.
   c. that she must stop running immediately, because the absence of menstruation is a sign of a serious health problem.
   d. that the likely cause of her delayed menarche is an inadequate diet.
3. Twelve-year-old Kwan is worried because his twin sister has suddenly grown taller and more physically mature than he. His parents should
   a. reassure him that the average boy is one or two years behind the average girl in the onset of the growth spurt.
   b. tell him that within a year or less he will grow taller than his sister.
   c. tell him that one member of each fraternal twin pair is always shorter.
   d. encourage him to exercise more to accelerate the onset of his growth spurt.
4. Calvin boasts that because his beard has begun to grow, he is more virile than his male classmates. Jacob informs him that
   a. the tendency to grow facial and body hair has nothing to do with virility.
   b. beard growth is determined by heredity.
   c. girls also develop some facial hair and more noticeable hair on their arms and legs, so it is clearly not a sign of masculinity.
   d. all of the above are true.
5. The most likely source of status for a late-maturing, middle-socioeconomic status boy would be
   a. academic achievement or vocational goal.
   b. physical build.
   c. athletic prowess.
   d. success with the opposite sex.
6. Which of the following students is most likely to be well-adjusted?
   a. Vicki, an early-maturing girl
   b. Sandra, a late-maturing girl
   c. Brad, an early-maturing boy
   d. Dan, a late-maturing boy

7. Regarding the effects of early and late maturation on boys and girls, which of the following is **NOT** true?

    a. Early maturation is usually easier for boys to manage than it is for girls.

    b. Late maturation is usually easier for girls to manage than it is for boys.

    c. Late-maturing girls may be drawn into older peer groups and may exhibit problem behaviors such as early sexual activity.

    d. Late-maturing boys may not "catch up" physically, or in terms of their self-images, for many years.

8. Adolescent Maya goes to sleep much later than her parents and has a lot of trouble getting up in the morning for school. Maya's sleep pattern is most likely to be a result of

    a. depression.

    b. normal hormonal shifts.

    c. behavioral problems.

    d. laziness.

9. Which of the following adolescents is likely to begin puberty at the earliest age?

    a. Aretha, an African-American female who hates exercise

    b. Todd, a male football player of European ancestry

    c. Kyu, an Asian-American male honors student

    d. There is too little information to make a prediction.

10. If adolescents Jack and Diane, who live in the United States, are typical of their peers, which of the following is likely to be true of the age of first intercourse for each of them?

    a. Jack will be *younger* when he first has intercourse than Diane will be.

    b. Jack will be *older* when he first has intercourse than Diane will be.

    c. Jack and Diane will be at about the *same* age when each of them first has intercourse, and they will each experience their first intercourse with an *older* individual.

    d. Jack and Diane will be at about the *same* age when each of them first has intercourse, and they will each experience their first intercourse with an individual of the *same* age.

11. Brain development is implicated in which of the following characteristics of typical adolescents?

    a. impulsivity

    b. emotionality

    c. lightning-fast reflexes

    d. all of the above

12. Eleven-year-old Linda, who has just begun to experience the first signs of puberty, laments, "When will the agony of puberty be over?" You tell her that the major events of puberty typically end about _______________ after the first visible signs appear.

    a. 5 to 6 years
    b. 3 to 5 years
    c. 2 years
    d. 1 year

Key Terms

1. **puberty:** The time between the first onrush of hormones and full adult physical development. Puberty usually lasts three to five years. Many more years are required to achieve psychosocial maturity. (p. 411; video lesson, segment 1; objective 1)
2. **menarche:** Refers to a girl's first menstrual period, which signals that she has begun ovulation. Pregnancy is biologically possible, but ovulation and menstruation are often irregular for years after menarche. (p. 411; video lesson, segment 1; objectives 1 & 5)
3. **spermarche:** Refers to a boy's first ejaculation of seminal fluid containing sperm. Erections can occur as early as infancy, but ejaculation signals sperm production. Spermarche may occur during sleep (in a "wet dream") or via direct stimulation. (p. 411; video lesson, segment 1; objectives 1 & 5)
4. **hormone:** An organic chemical substance that is produced by one body tissue and conveyed via the bloodstream to another to affect some physiological function. (p. 412; objective 1)
5. **pituitary gland:** Under the influence of the hypothalamus, this gland produces hormones that regulate growth and control other glands, among them the adrenal and sex glands. (p. 412; objective 1)
6. **adrenal glands:** Two glands, located above the kidneys, that produce hormones (including the "stress hormones" epinephrine [adrenaline] and norepinephrine). (p. 412; objective 1)
7. **HPA (hypothalamus-pituitary-adrenal) axis:** A sequence of hormone production originating in the hypothalamus and moving to the pituitary and then to the adrenal glands. It is the route followed by many hormones to trigger puberty, regulate stress, growth, and other bodily changes. (p. 412; objective 1)
8. **gonads:** The paired sex glands (ovaries in females, testicles in males) that produce hormones and gametes. (p. 413; video lesson, segment 1; objectives 2 & 5)
9. **HPG (hypothalamus–pituitary–gonad) axis:** A sequence of hormone production originating in the hypothalamus and moving to the pituitary and then to the gonads. (p. 413; objectives 1 & 5)
10. **estradiol:** Considered the chief estrogen, this sex hormone is secreted in greater amounts by females than males. (p. 413; objectives 1 & 5)

11. **testosterone:** The best known of the androgens (male hormones), this sex hormone is secreted in far greater amounts by males than by females. (p. 413; objectives 1 & 5)
12. **circadian rhythm:** A day–night cycle of biological activity that occurs approximately every 24 hours (*circadian* means "about a day"). (p. 414; objective 12)
13. **leptin:** A hormone that affects appetite and is believed to affect the onset of puberty. Leptin levels increase during childhood and peak at around age 12. (p. 416; objective 2)
14. **secular trend:** The long-term upward or downward direction of a certain set of statistical measurements, as opposed to a smaller, shorter cyclical variation. For example, over the last two centuries, because of improved nutrition and medical care, children have tended to reach their adult height earlier and their adult height has increased. (p. 416; objective 2)
15. **body image:** refers to adolescents' mental conception of, and attitude toward, their physical appearance. (p. 421; video lesson, segment 2; objective 7)
16. **anorexia nervosa:** A serious eating disorder in which a person restricts eating to the point of emaciation and possible starvation. (p. 422; objective 10)
17. **bulimia nervosa:** An eating disorder in which the person engages repeatedly in episodes of binge eating followed by purging through induced vomiting or the abuse of laxatives. (p. 422; objective 10)
18. **growth spurt:** This change, which begins with an increase in bone length and density and includes rapid weight gain and organ growth, is one of the many observable signs of puberty. (p. 423; video lesson, segment 1; objective 4)
19. **primary sex characteristics:** During puberty, changes involving those sex organs that are directly involved in reproduction. (p. 425; video lesson, segment 1; objective 5)
20. **secondary sex characteristics:** During puberty, changes involving parts of the body that are not directly involved in reproduction but that signify sexual development. (p. 425; video lesson, segment 1; objective 5)
21. **child sexual abuse:** Any activity in which an adult uses a child for his or her own sexual stimulation or pleasure—even if the use does not involve physical contact and regardless of whether the victim protests. (p. 430; objective 8)
22. **sexually transmitted infection (STI):** A disease, such as syphilis, gonorrhea, herpes, and AIDS, that is spread by sexual contact. (p. 429; objective 8)
23. **generational forgetting:** The tendency of each new generation to ignore lessons (such as the hazards of drug use) learned by the previous cohort. (p. 435; objective 11)
24. **adolescence:** The period of biological, cognitive, and psychosocial transition from childhood to adulthood. (video lesson, segment 1; objective 1)
25. **drug use:** The ingestion of a drug, regardless of the amount or effect of ingestion. (video lesson, segment 3; objective 11)

26. **drug abuse:** The ingestion of a drug to the extent that it impairs the user's well-being. (video lesson, segment 3; objective 11)
27. **drug addiction:** A person's dependence on a drug or a behavior in order to feel physically or psychologically at ease. (video lesson, segment 3; objective 11)

Summary

Puberty begins when a hormonal signal from the hypothalamus stimulates hormone production in the pituitary gland, which, in turn, triggers **hormone** production by the adrenal glands and by the **gonads** (sex glands). The major physical changes of puberty generally occur in the same sequence for everyone and are usually complete three to five years after they have begun. Variation in the age of the onset of puberty is related to sex, genetic inheritance, level of body fat, and stress.

The sequence of physical growth during puberty is from the extremities inward, making many adolescents temporarily big-footed, long-legged, and short-waisted. Internal organs also grow, including the lungs (which triple in weight) and the heart (which doubles in size and slows in rate). These changes give the adolescent increased physical endurance. The lymphoid system—including the tonsils and adenoids—decreases in size at adolescence, making teenagers less susceptible than children to respiratory ailments. The growth and maturation of the sex organs, called **primary sex characteristics**, that result in the development of reproductive potential are signaled by the first menstrual period (**menarche**) in girls and by the first ejaculation (**spermarche**) in boys.

Puberty is accompanied by many emotions, some of which are a direct result of hormonal shifts and many of which are the result of an interaction between adolescents' physical changes and others' reactions to the changes.

Young people who experience puberty at the same time as their friends tend to view the experience more positively than those who do not. The effects of early and late maturation differ for boys and girls. Girls find *early* maturation more difficult because of the added pressures that accompany sexual maturation. Boys find *late* maturation particularly difficult because of the correlation between peer status and a mature build.

The psychological effects of **sexual abuse** depend on the extent and duration of the abuse, the age of the child, and the reactions of family members and authorities once the abuse is known. Unlike younger victims of abuse, adolescents are prone to becoming self-destructive through substance abuse or eating disorders, running away from home, risking AIDS through unsafe sex, or even attempting suicide.

Uneven brain maturation in adolescence leads adolescents to seek intense emotional experiences, but their rational thought often develops at a slower pace.

The two main eating disorders, **anorexia nervosa** and **bulimia nervosa**, emerge any time from about age 10 to age 30, but the most hazardous periods are at the beginning of adolescence (about age 13) and just after high school (age 18).

Drug abuse always harms physical and psychological development. **Drug use** may or may not be harmful, depending in part on how mature the drug user is and his or her reason for using the drug. Drug use is also increasing among younger adolescents. This is cause for particular concern because research has shown that adolescent drug use is particularly likely to lead to **drug addiction**.

Special Note: We will cover the topics of unwanted pregnancy and sexual abuse (pp. 428–431) in more detail in Lesson 25, "Crashing Hard into Adulthood."

Answer Key

Practice Questions I

Multiple-Choice Questions

1. a. is the correct answer. (video lesson, segment 1; objective 1)
2. a. is the correct answer. (video lesson, segment 1; objectives 1 & 2)
3. d. is the correct answer. (video lesson, segment 1; objective 1)
4. c. is the correct answer. This is because each menstrual period depletes some iron from the body and because teenage girls rarely eat enough iron-rich foods. (objective 10)
5. a. is the correct answer. (objectives 1 & 3)

   b. is incorrect. This describes the gonads.

   c. is incorrect. These include estrogen and testosterone.

   d. is incorrect. This is the hypothalamus.
6. b. is the correct answer. (video lesson, segment 1; objectives 1 & 5)
7. b. is the correct answer. (video lesson, segment 1; objectives 1 & 5)
8. d. is the correct answer. (video lesson, segment 1; objective 1)
9. c. is the correct answer. (video lesson, segment 2; objective 7)

   a. is incorrect. Although some adolescents become overweight, many diet and lose weight in an effort to attain a desired body image.

   d. is incorrect. On the contrary, cultural attitudes about beauty are an extremely influential factor in the formation of a teenager's body image.
10. c. is the correct answer. (objective 10)

    a. & d. are incorrect. Eating disorders are more common in women than in men.

    b. is incorrect. Eating disorders are more common in younger women.
11. b. is the correct answer. The textbook does not mention a direct causal link between obesity and early sexual activity. (objective 8)
12. c. is the correct answer. (objective 3)
13. a. is the correct answer. A BMI of 18 or lower in a fully grown person indicates anorexia. (objective 10)
14. c. is the correct answer. (objective 6)
15. c. is the correct answer. (objective 12)

True or False Items

16. T (objective 10)
17. T (objective 10)
18. F The first indicator of reproductive potential in males is ejaculation of seminal fluid containing sperm (spermarche). Menarche (the first menstrual period) is the first indication of reproductive potential in females. (video lesson, segment 1; objectives 1 & 5)
19. T (objective 4)
20. T (video lesson, segment 1; objectives 1 & 2)
21. F Studies show that the majority of adolescent girls, even those in the thinnest group, want to lose weight. (objectives 3 & 7)
22. F The strong emphasis on appearance is reflected in the culture as a whole; for example, teachers (and, no doubt, prospective employers) tend to judge people who are physically attractive as being more competent than those who are less attractive. (video lesson, segment 2; objective 7)
23. F These habits generally worsen during adolescence. (objectives 7)
24. F (objective 3)
25. F Although there is great variation in the timing of pubertal events, the sequence is very similar for all young people. (video lesson, segment 1; objective 2)
26. T (objective 12)

Practice Questions II

Multiple-Choice Questions

1. b. is the correct answer. (objective 1)
2. d. is the correct answer. During adolescence, the lymphoid system decreases in size and the heart doubles in size. (video lesson, segment 1; objective 4)
3. a. is the correct answer. (video lesson, segment 1; objective 1)

   b. is incorrect. Testosterone increases markedly in boys.

   c. is incorrect. Androgen is another name for testosterone.

   d. is incorrect. Menarche is the first menstrual period.
4. b. is the correct answer. (video lesson, segment 3; objective 10)
5. b. is the correct answer. (video lesson, segment 1; objective 1)

   a. is incorrect. The shoulders of males tend to widen during puberty.

   c. is incorrect. The torso typically lengthens during puberty.

   d. is incorrect. The eyes and nose increase in size during puberty.
6. c. is the correct answer. (video lesson, segment 1; objective 5)

   a. is incorrect. Although not a term used in the textbook, a gender-typed trait is one that is typical of one sex but not of the other.

   b. is incorrect. Primary sex characteristics are those involving the reproductive organs.

   d. is incorrect. This is not a term used by developmental psychologists.

7. a. is the correct answer. (video lesson, segment 1; objectives 1 & 2)
8. a. is the correct answer. (objective 10)

   b. is incorrect. This describes an individual suffering from anorexia nervosa.

   c. is incorrect. Eating disorders are much more common in younger women.

   d. is incorrect. Most individuals with bulimia nervosa are usually close to normal in weight.
9. c. is the correct answer. (video lesson, segment 2; objective 7)

   a. is incorrect. If the timing of maturation differs substantially from that of the peer group, dissatisfaction is likely; however, this is not the most common source of dissatisfaction in teenage girls.

   b. & d. are incorrect. Although teenage girls are more likely than boys to be dissatisfied with certain features, which body parts are troubling varies from girl to girl.
10. d. is the correct answer. (objectives 3 & 7)
11. b. is the correct answer. (objective 11)
12. d. is the correct answer. (objective 8)
13. c. is the correct answer. (video lesson, segment 1; objective 1)
14. b. is the correct answer. Although the size of the heart increases during puberty, heart rate decreases. (objective 4)
15. d. is the correct answer. (objective 4)

Matching Items

16. b (objective 2)
17. d (video lesson, segment 1; objective 1)
18. c (video lesson, segment 1; objective 1)
19. f (video lesson, segment 1; objective 1)
20. g (video lesson, segment 1; objective 4)
21. k (video lesson, segment 1; objective 5)
22. a (video lesson, segment 1; objectives 1 & 5)
23. l (video lesson, segment 1; objectives 1 & 5)
24. j (video lesson, segment 1; objective 5)
25. h (video lesson, segment 2; objective 7)
26. i (objective 10)
27. e (objective 10)

Applying Your Knowledge

1. a. is the correct answer. (objective 2)
2. b. is the correct answer. (objective 2)

   a. is incorrect. Because they typically have little body fat, female dancers and athletes menstruate later than average.

c. is incorrect. Delayed maturation in a young dancer or athlete is usually quite normal.

d. is incorrect. The textbook does not indicate that the age of menarche varies with diet.

3. a. is the correct answer. (objective 2)

   b. is incorrect. It usually takes longer than one year for a prepubescent male to catch up with a female who has begun puberty.

   c. is incorrect. Since adult males tend to be taller than adult females, Kwan is likely to be taller than his sister.

   d. is incorrect. The textbook does not suggest that exercise has an effect on the timing of the growth spurt.

4. d. is the correct answer. (objective 5)
5. a. is the correct answer. (video lesson, segment 2; objective 3)

   b., c., & d. are incorrect. These are more typically sources of status for early-maturing boys.

6. b. is the correct answer. (video lesson, segment 2; objective 3)
7. c. is the correct answer. It is early-maturing girls who are often drawn into older peer groups. (objective 3)
8. b. is the correct answer. (objective 4)
9. a. is the correct answer. African-Americans often begin puberty earlier than Asian-Americans or Americans of European ancestry. Furthermore, females who are inactive menstruate earlier than those who are more active. (objective 2)
10. d. is the correct answer. (objective 5)
11. d. is the correct answer. (objective 9)
12. b. is the correct answer. (video lesson, segment 1; objective 1)

Lesson Review

Lesson 21

Adolescence
Biosocial Development

Please Note: Use this matrix to guide your study and achieve the learning objectives of this lesson. It will also help you to view the video, which defines and demonstrates important concepts and skills as they relate to everyday life.

Learning Objective	Textbook	Course Student Guide	Video Lesson
1. Identify and describe the biological events of puberty.	pp. 411–415	Key Terms: 1, 2, 3, 4, 5, 6, 7, 9, 10, 11, 24; Practice Questions I: 1, 2, 3, 5, 6, 7, 8, 18, 20; Practice Questions II: 1, 3, 5, 7, 13, 17, 18, 19, 22, 23; Applying Your Knowledge: 12.	Segment 1: *Puberty*
2. Identify several factors that influence the timing of puberty.	pp. 415–418	Key Terms: 8, 13, 14; Practice Questions I: 2, 20, 25; Practice Questions II: 7, 16; Applying Your Knowledge: 1, 2, 3, 9.	Segment 1: *Puberty*
3. Discuss the consequences for boys and girls who experience early or late onset of puberty.	pp. 418–419	Practice Questions I: 5, 12, 21, 24; Practice Questions II: 10; Applying Your Knowledge: 5, 6, 7.	Segment 2: *Body Image*
4. Describe the growth spurt experienced during adolescence by both boys and girls, including changes in weight, height, and the body's internal organ system.	pp. 423–425	Key Terms: 18; Practice Questions I: 19; Practice Questions II: 2, 14, 15, 20; Applying Your Knowledge: 8.	Segment 1: *Puberty*
5. Describe the sexual maturation that occurs in males and females during puberty, distinguish between primary and secondary sex characteristics, and discuss what some experts believe regarding sexual impulses at this age.	pp. 425–427	Key Terms: 2, 3, 8, 9, 10, 11, 19, 20; Practice Questions I: 6, 7, 18; Practice Questions II: 6, 21, 22, 23, 24; Applying Your Knowledge: 4, 10.	Segment 1: *Puberty*

Learning Objective	Textbook	Course Student Guide	Video Lesson
6. Discuss the emotional and psychological impact of pubertal hormones and how this impact is influenced by social context.	pp. 413–414	Practice Questions I: 14.	Segment 1: *Puberty* Segment 2: *Body Image*
7. Describe factors that have an impact on the adolescent's development of a positive body image.	pp. 421–423	Key Terms: 15; Practice Questions I: 9, 21, 22, 23; Practice Questions II: 9, 10, 25.	Segment 2: *Body Image*
8. Describe the biosocial hazards associated with early sexual activity, and discuss the prevalence and consequences of childhood sexual abuse.	pp. 427–431	Key Terms: 21, 22; Practice Questions I: 11; Practice Questions II: 12.	
9. Discuss neurological development during this period, noting the factors at play in adolescent risk taking as well as the unique benefits of this phase of development.	pp. 431–435	Applying Your Knowledge: 11.	
10. Discuss the nutritional needs and problems of adolescents, define the major types of eating disorders, and discuss how different theories of development might explain them.	pp. 420–423	Key Terms: 16, 17; Practice Questions I: 4, 10, 13, 16, 17; Practice Questions II: 4, 8, 26, 27.	Segment 3: *Health*
11. Discuss the use and abuse of alcohol, tobacco, and other drugs among adolescents today, including prevalence, significance for development, and the best methods of prevention.	*	Key Terms: 23, 25, 26, 27; Practice Questions II: 11.	Segment 3: *Health*
12. Describe how adolescent brain activity affects body rhythms in regard to stress, appetite, and sleep patterns.	pp. 414–415	Key Terms: 12; Practice Questions I: 15, 26.	

* The video for this lesson offers excellent coverage of this topic.

What If?

Lesson 22

Adolescence: Cognitive Development

Preview

Lesson 22 begins by describing the cognitive advances of adolescence, especially the emerging ability to think in an adult way, that is, to be logical, to think in terms of possibilities, to reason scientifically and abstractly.

Not all adolescents attain this level of reasoning ability, however, and even those who do spend much of their time thinking at less advanced levels. For instance, adolescents may have difficulty thinking rationally about themselves and their immediate experiences, often seeing themselves as psychologically unique and more socially significant than they really are. **Intuitive thought** also becomes more forceful at this age and often interferes with **analytical thought**.

The lesson also addresses the question, "What kind of school best fosters adolescent intellectual growth?" Many adolescents enter secondary school feeling less motivated and more vulnerable to self-doubt than they did in elementary school. The demands and structure of most secondary schools do not, unfortunately, provide a supportive learning environment for many adolescents.

The lesson also describes the issues of **high-stakes testing**, student motivation, and school violence and how these can interfere with the benefits of high school learning.

The video lesson concludes with an example of adolescent thinking at work: decision making. The discussion relates choices made by adolescents to their cognitive abilities and typical shortcomings, and it suggests ways in which adolescents may be helped to make healthy choices.

Throughout this lesson, recall your own cognitive development during adolescence. In what ways was your thinking more like an adult's, and in what ways was it still "youthful?" Did you think about yourself, about your interests, and your future? Reflect on your experiences in middle and secondary school. Did you get what you consider to be a good education? Why or why not? Were you motivated to learn? What did you think about sex at this age? How did you make decisions regarding sex, drugs, and so forth?

Prior Knowledge That Will Be Used in This Lesson

- This lesson will return to Piaget's theory of cognitive development (from Lesson 1). Recall that Piaget's theory specifies four major periods of development, the fourth and final stage being *formal operational thought*:
    1. Sensorimotor (Birth to 2 years)
    2. Preoperational (2 to 6 years)
    3. Concrete Operational (7 to 11 years)
    4. **Formal Operational (12 years through adolescence) ← Adolescence**
- Lesson 21 included a discussion of neurological development during adolescence. Remember that the brain matures from the inside out, lending adolescents toward being emotionally liable, impulsive, and likely to engage in risk-taking behavior.

Learning Objectives

Use this information to guide your reading, viewing, thinking, and studying. After successfully completing this lesson, you should be able to:

1. Describe changes in the thinking of adolescents.
2. Describe Piaget's concept of formal operational thinking, and provide examples of adolescents' emerging ability to reason deductively and inductively.
3. Discuss adolescent egocentrism, and give three examples of egocentric fantasies or fables.
4. Describe the concept of person–environment fit, and explain how schools can be organized to more effectively meet adolescents' cognitive needs.
5. Describe some factors that can obstruct the ability of high school education to advance adolescents' thinking.
6. Identify the cognitive and emotional factors affecting adolescent thinking and/or decision making. Include in your identification the concepts of intuitive thought, analytic thought, and common fallacies.
7. Discuss the cognitive effects of neurological development during adolescence and describe why some developmentalists seek to understand the urge for thrills versus the capacity for logical thought.
8. Discuss various viewpoints regarding technology and cognition, which includes the benefits and hazards of Internet learning.

Textbook Reading & Video Viewing

For the most effective study of this lesson, complete the assignments in the sequence listed below.

Before viewing the video program:

Read Chapter 15, "Adolescence: Cognitive Development," pages 439–469.

View the video for Lesson 22, "What If?"

Segment 1: *Formal Operational Thought*

Segment 2: *Educating Adolescents*

Segment 3: *Adolescent Decision-Making*

After viewing the video program:

Review all reading assignments for this lesson.

Complete the "Practice Questions" and "Applying Your Knowledge" sections to reinforce your understanding of important terms and concepts and measure your achievement of the Learning Objectives. Check your answers with the feedback given and review when necessary.

Practice Questions I

Multiple-Choice Questions

1. Many psychologists consider the distinguishing feature of adolescent thought to be the ability to think in terms of
   a. moral issues.
   b. concrete operations.
   c. possibility, not just reality.
   d. logical principles.

2. Piaget's last stage of cognitive development is
   a. formal operational thought.
   b. concrete operational thought.
   c. universal ethical principles.
   d. symbolic thought.

3. Research has demonstrated that which of the following is beneficial to middle-school students?
   a. moving among different classrooms every 40 minutes or so
   b. having many teachers
   c. encouraging interaction among students and teachers
   d. focusing on academics rather than extracurricular activities

4. The adolescent who takes risks and feels immune to the laws of mortality is showing evidence of the
   a. invincibility fable.
   b. personal fable.
   c. imaginary audience.
   d. death instinct.

5. Imaginary audiences, invincibility fables, and personal fables are expressions of adolescent
   a. morality.
   b. thinking games.
   c. decision making.
   d. egocentrism.
6. High levels of emotions
   a. slow down rational thinking.
   b. moderately speed up rational thinking.
   c. greatly speed up rational thinking.
   d. have no effect on rational thinking.
7. Older adolescents use analytic thinking ________________ forcefully and intuitive thinking ________________ forcefully than younger adolescents.
   a. less; less
   b. less; more
   c. more; less
   d. more; more
8. Which type of thinking begins with past experience and common assumptions rather than a logical premise?
   a. cognitive economy
   b. analytic thought
   c. adolescent egocentrism
   d. intuitive thought
9. Thinking that begins with a general premise and then draws logical conclusions from it is called
   a. inductive reasoning.
   b. deductive reasoning.
   c. intuitive thought.
   d. logical thought.
10. Serious reflection on important issues is a wrenching process for many adolescents because of their newfound ability to reason
    a. inductively.
    b. deductively.
    c. hypothetically.
    d. symbolically.

11. Hypothetical-deductive thinking is to heuristic thinking as

    a. rational analysis is to intuitive thought.
    b. intuitive thought is to rational analysis.
    c. experiential thinking is to intuitive reasoning.
    d. intuitive thinking is to analytical reasoning.

12. Some adolescents believe that their effort in school will improve their intelligence. This belief is an expression of the

    a. personal fable.
    b. incremental approach to intelligence.
    c. imaginary audience.
    d. entity approach to intelligence.

13. High-stakes testing

    a. appears to increase ethnic inequality.
    b. captures the potential of males and females equally.
    c. encourages students to use deductive reasoning.
    d. does all of the above.

14. Public high school teachers in the United States are **MOST** likely to say that which of the following is their most serious problem?

    a. drugs
    b. racial tension
    c. fighting
    d. student apathy

15. Research has suggested that which of the following is the ideal high school size?

    a. 100 to 200 students
    b. 200 to 400 students
    c. 500 to 700 students
    d. 80 to 1000 students

True or False Items

Write true or false on the line in front of each statement.

16. _____ During the middle school years, academic achievement often slows down and behavioral problems become more commonplace.

17. _____ Adolescents are generally better able than eight-year-olds at recognizing the validity of arguments that clash with their own beliefs.

18. _____ The use of logic as opposed to experience to make decisions in adolescence is referred to as formal operational thought.

19. _____ Most adolescents who engage in risky behavior are unaware of the consequences, and potential costs, of their actions.

20. _____ Adolescents often create an imaginary audience as they envision how others will react to their appearance and behavior.

21. _____ Many states are banning high-stakes tests because of their negative influence on adolescents.

22. _____ Many social scientists believe that the structure of middle schools may push emotionally vulnerable children into psychopathology.

23. _____ Inductive reasoning is a hallmark of formal operational thought.

24. _____ Achievement test scores for U.S. high school students are on the rise.

25. _____ Piaget's scale balancing task demonstrated that children can systematically test hypotheses at approximately age 15.

26. _____ On a practical basis, the curriculum of high school is often disconnected from the needs and requirements of employers, colleges, and students themselves.

27. _____ The prefrontal cortex is the last part of the brain to mature.

Practice Questions II

Multiple-Choice Questions

1. All of the following are potential "cyberdangers" **EXCEPT**
   a. questioning authority.
   b. bullying.
   c. Internet addiction.
   d. cutting (self-mutilation).

2. Thinking that extrapolates from a specific experience to form a general premise is called
   a. inductive reasoning.
   b. deductive reasoning.
   c. intuitive thinking.
   d. hypothetical reasoning.

3. Teachers, researchers, and developmentalists describe adolescents in high school as generally being
   a. totally enthusiastic about their studies.
   b. eagerly engaged in social activities and clubs.
   c. bored, alienated, and disconnected from challenge.
   d. none of the above.

4. When young people overestimate their significance to others, they are displaying
   a. concrete operational thought.
   b. adolescent egocentrism.
   c. a lack of cognitive growth.
   d. immoral development.

5. The personal fable refers to adolescents imagining that
   a. they are immune to the dangers of risky behaviors.
   b. they are always being scrutinized by others.
   c. their own lives are destined to be unique, heroic, or even mythical.
   d. the world revolves around their actions.

6. In the United States, the typical high school
   a. curriculum is becoming more rigorous.
   b. emphasizes intuitive thought.
   c. focuses on the link between logic and emotion.
   d. is described by all of the above.

7. High school students demonstrate formal operational thought by understanding concepts such as
   a. $(2x)(3y)$.
   b. "gross national product."
   c. "fertility rates."
   d. all of the above.

8. All of the following is true of middle school **EXCEPT**
   a. students can stay close to teachers in ways that mimic elementary school.
   b. social relationships with friends from elementary school deteriorates.
   c. academic achievement slows down.
   d. class size is usually larger than what is considered ideal.

9. One of the hallmarks of formal operational thought is
   a. egocentrism.
   b. deductive thinking.
   c. symbolic thinking.
   d. all of the above.

10. In explaining adolescent advances in thinking, sociocultural theorists would be most likely to emphasize which of the following?
    a. the accumulated improvement in specific skills
    b. the transition from primary school to secondary school
    c. the completion of the myelination process in cortical neurons
    d. advances in metacognition

11. When studying for her first chemistry test, fifteen-year-old Louisa is quite calm and is convinced that doing well on the test will make people believe that she is the best chemistry student in the school. Louisa's thoughts are an example of
    a. the personal fable.
    b. the invincibility fable.
    c. stereotype threat.
    d. postformal thinking.

12. As with growth in the rest of the teenager's body, different parts of the brain grow at different times. Which of the following statements is true about adolescents' cognitive development?
    a. The limbic system matures before the prefrontal cortex.
    b. Myelination and maturation proceed from the back of the brain to the front.
    c. Instinctual and emotional areas develop before reflective ones.
    d. All of the above are true.

13. Which of the following is true of middle schools?
    a. Bullying decreases in comparison to elementary school levels.
    b. Grades tend to increase as students advance cognitively.
    c. Relationally aggressive children increase in popularity.
    d. All of the above are true.

14. Many researchers are convinced there are many dangers posed by adolescent use of the Internet. They include
    a. cyberbullying.
    b. self-mutilation (cutting) web sites.
    c. becoming friends with unknown people.
    d. all of the above.

Matching Items

Match each definition or description with its corresponding term.

Terms

15. __________	invincibility fable	20. __________	inductive reasoning
16. __________	imaginary audience	21. __________	formal operational thought
17. __________	person–environment fit	22. __________	volatile mismatch
18. __________	hypothetical thought	23. __________	adolescent egocentrism
19. __________	deductive reasoning	24. __________	PISA (Programme for International Student Assessment)

Definitions or Descriptions

a. the tendency of adolescents to focus on themselves to the exclusion of others

b. adolescents feel immune to the consequences of dangerous behavior

c. a creation of adolescents, who are preoccupied with how others react to their appearance and behavior

d. the correspondence between an adolescent's needs and the setting

e. reasoning about propositions that may or may not reflect reality

f. the last stage of cognitive development, according to Piaget

g. thinking that moves from premise to conclusion

h. thinking that moves from a specific experience to a general premise

i. a clash between a teenager's needs and the structure and functioning of his or her school

j. a test that measures practical thinking and knowledge

Applying Your Knowledge

1. A 13-year-old can create and solve logical problems on the computer but is not usually reasonable, mature, or consistent in his or her thinking when it comes to people and social relationships. This supports the finding that

   a. some children reach the stage of formal operational thought earlier than others.

   b. the stage of formal operational thought is not attained by age 13.

   c. formal operational thinking may be demonstrated in certain domains and not in other domains.

   d. older adolescents and adults often do poorly on standard tests of formal operational thought.

2. Blake is able to think hypothetically. He can think of an abstract concept and use logic to reach conclusions. This is characteristic of

   a. deductive reasoning.
   b. inductive reasoning.
   c. concrete operations.
   d. conventional thought.

3. Fourteen-year-old Monica is very idealistic and often develops crushes on people she doesn't even know. This reflects her newly developed cognitive ability to

   a. deal simultaneously with two sides of an issue.
   b. take another person's viewpoint.
   c. imagine possible worlds and people.
   d. see herself as others see her.

4. Which of the following is the best example of a personal fable?

   a. Adriana imagines that she is destined for a life of fame and fortune.
   b. Ben makes up stories about his experiences to impress his friends.
   c. Kalil questions his religious beliefs when they seem to offer little help for a problem he faces.
   d. Julio believes that every girl he meets is attracted to him.

5. Which of the following is the best example of the adolescent's ability to think hypothetically?

   a. Twelve-year-old Stanley feels that people are always watching him.
   b. Fourteen-year-old Mindy engages in many risky behaviors, reasoning that, "nothing bad will happen to me."
   c. Fifteen-year-old Philip feels that no one understands his problems.
   d. Thirteen-year-old Josh delights in finding logical flaws in virtually everything his teachers and parents say.

6. Frustrated because of the dating curfew her parents have set, Lucinda exclaims, "You just don't know how it feels to be in love!" Lucinda's thinking demonstrates

   a. the invincibility fable.
   b. analytical thought.
   c. the imaginary audience.
   d. adolescent egocentrism.

7. Compared to her 13-year-old brother, 17-year-old Yolanda is likely to be

   a. more critical about herself.
   b. more egocentric.
   c. less able to think analytically.
   d. more capable of reasoning hypothetically.

8. Nathan's fear that his friends will ridicule him because of a pimple that has appeared on his nose reflects a preoccupation with

   a. his personal fable.

   b. the invincibility fable.

   c. an imaginary audience.

   d. preconventional reasoning.

9. Thirteen-year-old friends Malcolm and T. J. attend seventh grade in schools in neighboring towns. Malcolm's school is a middle school with sixth through eight graders, and it is run much like a typical high school with eight 40-minute class periods, each taught by a different teacher. T. J.'s school is a kindergarten through eighth grade school, and it is run more like a typical elementary school. T. J. stays in the same classroom for the entire day, and he has three teachers who come in his classroom to teach different subjects. Research suggests that which of the following is **MOST** likely to be true?

   a. Malcolm's grades have improved since elementary school, and T. J.'s have dropped.

   b. Malcolm's and T. J.'s grades have dropped to a similar extent since elementary school.

   c. Malcolm's and T. J.'s grades have remained stable since elementary school.

   d. Malcolm's grades have dropped since elementary school, and T. J.'s have remained stable.

10. A high school principal who wished to increase the interest level and achievement of students in her school would be well advised to

    a. create more group cohesiveness.

    b. encourage greater use of standardized testing in the elementary schools that feed students to the high school.

    c. separate students into academic tracks based on achievement.

    d. do all of the above.

11. Hypothetical thought is best characterized as which of the following?

    a. "What if?"

    b. "How?"

    c. "Why not?"

    d. "When and where?"

12. From the perspective of Piaget, which of the following would be inappropriate to include in an elementary-school curriculum but appropriate in a middle-school curriculum?

    a. dividing real numbers

    b. learning a second language

    c. understanding how the body fights infection

    d. the seasonal changes of trees

13. After hearing that an unusually aggressive child has been in full-time day care since he was age 1, 16-year-old Keenan concludes that nonparental care leads to behavior problems. Keenan's conclusion is an example of

    a. inductive reasoning.
    b. deductive reasoning.
    c. hypothetical thinking.
    d. adolescent egocentrism.

14. Dr. Kayla presents 14-year-old Hina with the following problem: "If the sky is red, and all red things are made of candy, what is the sky made of?" Hina is likely to respond that

    a. the sky is blue.
    b. the sky is made of air.
    c. the sky is made of candy.
    d. she does not know how to answer the question.

15. The typical 14-year-old boy or girl

    a. cannot use deductive reasoning.
    b. can use deductive reasoning, but often fails to use it.
    c. can use deductive reasoning and always does use it.
    d. can use deductive reasoning, but often has to logically choose to think more intuitively.

Key Terms

1. **adolescent egocentrism:** A characteristic of adolescent thinking that leads young people (ages 10 to 13) to focus on themselves to the exclusion of others. (p. 440; video lesson, segment 1; objectives 1 & 3)
2. **personal fable:** An aspect of adolescent egocentrism characterized by an adolescent's belief that his or her thoughts, feelings, and experiences are unique, more wonderful or awful than anyone else's. (p. 440; video lesson, segment 1; objective 3)
3. **invincibility fable:** An adolescent's egocentric conviction that he or she cannot be overcome or even harmed by anything that might defeat a normal mortal, such as unprotected sex, drug abuse, or high-speed driving. (p. 440; video lesson, segment 1; objective 3)
4. **imaginary audience:** Consists of the other people who, in an adolescent's egocentric belief, are watching and taking note of his or her appearance, ideas, and behavior. This belief makes many teenagers very self-conscious. (p. 441; video lesson, segment 1; objective 3)
5. **formal operational thought:** In Piaget's theory, the fourth and final stage of cognitive development, which is characterized by more systematic logical thinking and by the ability to understand and systematically manipulate abstract concepts. (p. 442; video lesson, segment 1; objective 2)

6. **hypothetical thought:** The ability to reason about propositions and possibilities that may or may not reflect reality. (p. 444; video lesson, segment 1; objectives 1 & 2)
7. **deductive reasoning:** Reasoning from a general statement, premise, or principle, through logical steps, to figure out (deduce) specifics. Also called *top-down reasoning*. (p. 444; video lesson, segment 1; objective 2)
8. **inductive reasoning:** Reasoning from one or more specific experiences or facts to reach (induce) a general conclusion. Also called *bottom-up reasoning*. (p. 444; video lesson, segment 1; objective 2)
9. **sunk cost fallacy:** The mistaken belief that if money, time, or effort that cannot be recovered (a "sunk cost," in economic terms) has already been invested in some endeavor, than more should be invested in an effort to reach the goal. Because of this fallacy, people spend more money on a "lemon" of a car or send more troops to fight a losing battle. (p. 455; objective 6)
10. **base rate neglect:** A common fallacy in which the person ignores the overall frequency of some behavior or characteristic (called the base rate) in making a decision. For example, a person might bet on a "lucky" lottery number without considering the odds that that number will be selected. (p. 455; objective 6)
11. **dual-process model:** The notion that two networks exist within the human brain, one for emotional and one for analytical processing of stimuli. (p. 456; objective 6)
12. **intuitive thought:** Type of thinking that arises from an emotion or a hunch, beyond rational explanation, and is influenced by past experiences and cultural assumptions. (p. 456; objective 1)
13. **analytic thought:** Type of thinking that results from analysis, such as a systematic ranking of pros and cons, risks and consequences, possibilities and facts, and depends on logic and rationality. (p. 456; objective 1)
14. **cyberbullying:** Bullying that occurs when one person spreads insults or rumors about another by means of e-mails, text messages, anonymous phone calls, or posting embarrassing videos of the victim on the Internet. The name derives from the fact that such bullying occurs in cyberspace, the hypothetical environment in which digitized information is communicated over computer networks. (p. 453; objective 8)
15. **cutting:** An addictive form of self-mutilation that is most prevalent among adolescent girls and that correlates with depression and drug abuse. (p. 454; objective 8)
16. **secondary education:** The period after primary education—elementary or grade school—and before tertiary education (college). It usually occurs from about age 12 to 18, although there is some variation by school and nation. (p. 455; objective 6)
17. **middle school:** The years of school between elementary school and high school. Middle school usually begins with grade 6 and ends with grade 8. (p. 456; video lesson, segment 2; objective 4)
18. **entity approach to intelligence:** An approach that sees ability as innate, a fixed quantity present at birth; those who hold this view do not believe that effort enhances achievement. (p. 458; objective 5)

19. **incremental approach to intelligence:** An approach that holds that intelligence can be directly increased by effort; those who subscribe to this view believe they can master whatever they seek to learn if they pay attention, participate in class, study, complete their homework, and so on. (p. 458; objective 5)
20. **high-stakes testing:** Type of evaluation that has serious consequences for the test taker and is critical in determining success or failure. If a single test determines whether a student will graduate or be promoted, it is a high-stakes test. (p. 461; video lesson, segment 2; objective 4) A high-stakes test is an evaluation
21. **PISA (Programme for International Student Assessment):** An international test taken by 15-year-olds in 50 nations that is designed to measure problem solving and cognition in daily life. (p. 464; objective 4)
22. **person–environment fit:** Refers to the best setting for personal growth, as in the optimum educational setting. (video lesson, segment 2; objective 4)
23. **volatile mismatch:** Occurs when teenagers' individual needs do not match the size, routine, and structure of their schools. (video lesson, segment 2; objective 4)

Summary

The basic skills of thinking, learning, and remembering continue to be refined during the adolescent years. According to most developmentalists, the distinguishing feature of adolescent thought is the capacity to think in terms of possibility rather than only in terms of reality.

Piaget described the reasoning that characterizes adolescence as **formal operational thought**, which arises from maturation and experience. On the whole, adolescents are able to fantasize, speculate, and hypothesize much more readily and on a much grander scale than younger children are. With this capacity for **hypothetical thought**, the adolescent is able to consider the here and now as one among many alternative possibilities. In addition, the capacities for **deductive reasoning** (deriving conclusions from premises), and **inductive reasoning** (reasoning from one or more specific experiences or facts to a general conclusion) become refined.

Developmental psychologists have described **adolescent egocentrism** as a stage of development in which young people typically consider their own psychological experiences (love and anger, for example) to be unique. The **invincibility fable** that they are somehow immune to common dangers and the **personal fable** that their lives are unique or heroic are further examples of adolescents' egocentrism. As another part of their egocentrism, adolescents often create for themselves an **imaginary audience** that allows them to fantasize about how others will react to their appearance and behavior.

With regard to education, the optimum **person–environment fit** depends not only on the individual's developmental stage, cognitive abilities, and learning style, but also on the society's traditions, educational objectives, and future needs, which vary substantially from place to place and time to time. As students move from primary to **middle school**, their motivation and grades usually fall. One reason is that middle schools are structured in a way that is incompatible with adolescents' intellectual needs. For adolescents, smaller schools with engaging instruction that invites logical as well as personal reflections seem best. In order to avoid feelings of failure, many students simply stop trying. Those that ascribe to the **entity approach to intelligence** believe that intelligence is innate and no amount of effort will change it. As a result, their achievement tends to be low. On the other hand, individuals who believe in the **incremental approach to intelligence** tend work hard because they think their effort has a positive effect on their intelligence.

Adolescents can think about the possible and even the impossible and not just what is real. Both **analytic thought** and **intuitive thought** become more forceful at this age, and adolescents have a difficult time balancing the two types of thought.

This lesson addresses the twenty-first century phenomenon of adolescent cognition within the technological age. Computers are now widely used in schools and are considered by some to be essential tools of learning. During the 1990s, a *digital divide* or a gap between people who have access to computers and those who do not, which resulted in learning inequities between rich and poor, and boys and girls, seemed to exist. In the United States, currently, this gap has been greatly diminished because of the ubiquitous use of computers in schools. In fact, some experts believe learning via the internet is thought to improve reading and spatial skills.

Finally, the subject of high schools and their focus on the college-bound student is discussed in regards to the efficacy of **high-stakes testing**, evaluations that are critical in determining success or failure. Whether students are college-bound or not, high-stakes tests and many international tests (such as those described in Lesson 17) fail to measure practical cognition. The **PISA (Programme for International Student Assessment)** is an international test designed to do just that. Administered to 15-year-olds, it measures such practical cognition as problem-solving skills and knowledge that might be used at home or on the job.

Answer Key

Practice Questions I

Multiple-Choice Questions

1. c. is the correct answer. (video lesson, segment 1; objective 2)

   a. is incorrect. Although moral reasoning becomes much deeper during adolescence, it is not limited to this stage of development.

   b. & d. are incorrect. Concrete operational thought, which is logical, is the distinguishing feature of childhood thinking.

2. a. is the correct answer. (video lesson, segment 1; objective 2)

   b. is incorrect. In Piaget's theory, this stage precedes formal operational thought.

   c. & d. are incorrect. These are not stages in Piaget's theory.

3. c. is the correct answer. (video lesson, segment 2; objective 4)

4. a. is the correct answer. (video lesson, segment 1; objective 3)

   b. is incorrect. This refers to adolescents' tendency to imagine their own lives as unique, heroic, or even mythical.

   c. is incorrect. This refers to adolescents' tendency to fantasize about how others will react to their appearance and behavior.

   d. is incorrect. This is a concept in Freud's theory.

5. d. is the correct answer. These thought processes are manifestations of adolescents' tendency to see themselves as being much more central and important to the social scene than they really are. (video lesson, segment 1; objective 3)
6. a. is the correct answer. (objective 6)
7. d. is the correct answer. (objective 1)
8. d. is the correct answer. (objective 6)
9. b. is the correct answer. (video lesson, segment 1; objective 2)

   a. is incorrect. Inductive reasoning moves from specific facts to a general conclusion.

   c. is incorrect. Intuitive thought involves an assumption, emotions, or a hunch.

   d. is incorrect. Inductive and deductive reasoning are both logical.
10. c. is the correct answer. (video lesson, segment 1; objectives 1 & 2)
11. a. is the correct answer. (objectives 1 & 2)

    c. is incorrect. Heuristic thinking is both experiential *and* intuitive.
12. b. is the correct answer. (objective 5)

    a. is incorrect. This refers to adolescents' tendency to imagine their own lives as unique, heroic, or even mythical.

    c. is incorrect. This refers to adolescents' tendency to fantasize about how others will react to their appearance and behavior.

    d. is incorrect. This refers to the belief that effort has no bearing on intelligence.
13. a. is the correct answer. (objective 5)
14. d. is the correct answer. (objective 5)
15. b. is the correct answer. (objective 5)

True or False Items

16. T (objective 4)
17. T (video lesson, segment 1; objectives 1 & 2)
18. T (objective 6)
19. F Adolescent behavior is guided by assumptions about risks and benefits. (video lesson, segment 3; objective 3)
20. T (video lesson, segment 1; objective 3)
21. F High-stakes testing is mandated by virtually every state legislature in the United States. (objective 5)
22. T (video lesson, segment 2; objective 4)
23. F Deductive reasoning is a hallmark of formal operational thought, although adolescents continue to improve their inductive reasoning skills as well. (video lesson, segment 1; objective 2)
24. F In fact, they are stagnant. (objective 5)
25. F Children tend to succeed at this task at age 13 or 14. (objective 2)
26. T (objective 7)
27. T (objective 7)

Practice Questions II

Multiple-Choice Questions

1. a. is the correct answer. (video lesson, segment 1; objective 8)

   b., c., & d. are incorrect. The invincibility fable leads some teens to believe that they are immune to the dangers of risky behaviors; it is not necessarily linked to depression, low self-esteem, or the likelihood that an individual will drop out of school.

2. a. is the correct answer. (video lesson, segment 1; objective 2)

   b. is incorrect. Deductive reasoning begins with a general premise and then draws logical conclusions from it.

   c. is incorrect. Intuitive thought involves an assumption, emotions, or a hunch.

   d. is incorrect. Hypothetical reasoning involves the ability to think creatively about possibilities.

3. c. is the correct answer. (objective 2)

4. b. is the correct answer. (video lesson, segment 1; objective 3)

5. c. is the correct answer. (video lesson, segment 1; objective 3)

   a. is incorrect. This describes the invincibility fable.

   b. is incorrect. This describes the imaginary audience.

   d. is incorrect. This describes adolescent egocentrism in general.

6. a. is the correct answer. (objective 5)

7. d. is the correct answer. (video lesson, segment 1; objective 2)

8. a. is the correct answer. (objective 6)

9. b. is the correct answer. (video lesson, segment 1; objectives 2 & 3)

10. b. is the correct answer. (objectives 1 & 6)

    a. & d. are incorrect. These would be more likely to be emphasized by information-processing theorists.

    c. is incorrect. This reflects the biological perspective on development.

11. a. is the correct answer. (objectives 1 & 3)

    a. & b. are incorrect. These refer to the egocentric tendency of adolescents to believe their lives are heroic (personal fable) and immune to the laws of mortality (invincibility fable).

    d. is incorrect. Postformal thinking is reasoning that is well-suited to solving practical problems because it moves beyond pure logic to benefit from the wisdom of experience.

12. d. is the correct answer. (objective 7)

13. c. is the correct answer. (video lesson, segment 2; objective 4)

    a. & b. are incorrect. The opposite is true.

14. d. is the correct answer. (objective 8)

Matching Items

15. b (video lesson, segment 1; objective 3)
16. c (video lesson, segment 1; objective 3)
17. d (video lesson, segment 2; objective 4)
18. e (video lesson, segment 1; objectives 1 & 2)
19. g (video lesson, segment 1; objective 2)
20. h (video lesson, segment 1; objective 2)
21. f (video lesson, segment 1; objective 2)
22. i (video lesson, segment 2; objective 4)
23. a (video lesson, segment 1; objectives 1 & 3)
24. j (objective 4)

Applying Your Knowledge

1. c. is the correct answer. (video lesson, segment 1; objective 2)
2. a. is the correct answer. (video lesson, segment 1; objective 2)
3. c. is the correct answer. This is hypothetical thinking. (video lesson, segment 1; objectives 1 & 2)
4. a. is the correct answer. (video lesson, segment 1; objective 3)

   b. & d. are incorrect. These behaviors are more indicative of a preoccupation with the imaginary audience.

   c. is incorrect. Kalil's questioning attitude is a normal adolescent tendency that helps foster moral reasoning.
5. d. is the correct answer. (video lesson, segment 1; objectives 1 & 2)

   a. is incorrect. This is an example of the imaginary audience.

   b. is incorrect. This is an example of the invincibility fable.

   c. is incorrect. This is an example of adolescent egocentrism.
6. d. is the correct answer. Adolescent egocentrism leads adolescents to believe that they are unique. (video lesson, segment 1; objectives 1 & 3)
7. d. is the correct answer. (video lesson, segment 1; objective 2)
8. c. is the correct answer. (video lesson, segment 1; objective 3)

   a. is incorrect. In this fable adolescents see themselves destined for fame and fortune.

   b. is incorrect. In this fable young people feel that they are somehow immune to the consequences of common dangers.

   d. is incorrect. This is a stage of moral reasoning in Kohlberg's theory.
9. d. is the correct answer. (video lesson, segment 2; objective 4)
10. a. is the correct answer. (video lesson, segment 2; objective 4)
11. a. is the correct answer. (video lesson, segment 1; objective 4)

12. c. is the correct answer. This topic is somewhat abstract and cannot be observed, necessitating formal operational thought. (objective 2)
13. a. is the answer. (video lesson, segment 1; objective 2)

    b. is incorrect. Keenan is reasoning from the specific to the general, rather than vice versa.

    c. is incorrect. Keenan is thinking about an actual observation, rather than a hypothetical possibility.

    d. is incorrect. Keenan's reasoning is focused outside himself, rather than being self-centered.
14. c. is the correct answer. (objective 2)
15. b. is the correct answer. (video lesson, segment 1; objective 2)

Lesson Review

Lesson 22

Adolescence
Cognitive Development

Please Note: Use this matrix to guide your study and achieve the learning objectives of this lesson. It will also help you to view the video, which defines and demonstrates important concepts and skills as they relate to everyday life.

Learning Objective	Textbook	Course Student Guide	Video Lesson
1. Describe changes in the thinking of adolescents.	pp. 439–440	Key Terms: 1, 6, 12, 13; Practice Questions I: 7, 10, 11, 17; Practice Questions II: 10, 11, 18, 23; Applying Your Knowledge: 3, 5, 6, 13.	Segment 1: *Formal Operational Thought*
2. Describe Piaget's concept of formal operational thinking, and provide examples of adolescents' emerging ability to reason deductively and inductively.	pp. 442–446	Key Terms: 5, 6, 7, 8; Practice Questions I: 1, 2, 9, 10, 11, 17, 23, 25; Practice Questions II: 2, 3, 7, 9, 18, 19, 20, 21; Applying Your Knowledge: 1, 2, 3, 5, 7, 12, 13, 14, 15.	Segment 1: *Formal Operational Thought*
3. Discuss adolescent egocentrism, and give three examples of egocentric fantasies or fables.	pp. 440–442	Key Terms: 1, 2, 3, 4; Practice Questions I: 4, 5, 19, 20; Practice Questions II: 4, 5, 9, 11, 15, 16, 23; Applying Your Knowledge: 4, 6, 8.	Segment 1: *Formal Operational Thought* Segment 3: *Adolescent Decision-Making*
4. Describe the concept of person-environment fit, and explain how schools can be organized to more effectively meet adolescents' cognitive needs.	pp. 455–467	Key Terms: 17, 20, 21, 22, 23; Practice Questions I: 3, 16, 22; Practice Questions II: 13, 17, 22, 24; Applying Your Knowledge: 9, 10, 11.	Segment 1: *Formal Operational Thought* Segment 2: *Educating Adolescents*
5. Describe some factors that can obstruct the ability of high school education to advance adolescents' thinking.	pp. 456–463	Key Terms: 18, 19; Practice Questions I: 12, 13, 14, 15, 21, 24; Practice Questions II: 6.	

Learning Objective	Textbook	Course Student Guide	Video Lesson
6. Identify the cognitive and emotional factors affecting adolescent thinking and/or decision making. Include in your identification the concepts of intuitive thought, analytic thought, and common fallacies.	pp. 445–449	Key Terms: 9, 10, 11, 16; Practice Questions I: 6, 8, 18; Practice Questions II: 8, 10.	Segment 3: *Adolescent Decision-Making*
7. Discuss the cognitive effects of neurological development during adolescence and describe why some developmentalists seek to understand the urge for thrills versus the capacity for logical thought.	pp. 449–450	Practice Questions I: 26, 27; Practice Questions II: 12.	
8. Discuss various viewpoints regarding technology and cognition, which includes the benefits and hazards of Internet learning.	pp. 451–454	Key Terms: 14, 15; Practice Questions II: 1, 14.	Segment 1: *Formal Operational Thought*

Who Am I?

Lesson 23

Adolescence: Psychosocial Development

Preview

Adolescence brings a heightened quest for self-understanding and **identity**, a crucial process in the transition from childhood to adulthood. Lesson 23 focuses on the psychosocial development, particularly the formation of identity, required for the attainment of adult status and maturity. **Suicide**—one of the most perplexing problems of adolescence—is also explored. Finally, the special problems posed by adolescent lawbreaking are discussed.

The influences of family, peers and society on adolescent development are examined in some detail. During this period, the biological imperative of reproductive viability comes to fruition. In many cultures, the plan of life allows for an easy transition into adult life. In technologically advanced societies, another decade of preparation is needed before self-reliance becomes practical. The resulting tension can be difficult to manage.

The lesson concludes with the message that, while no other period of life except infancy is characterized by so many changes in the three domains of development, for most young people the teenage years are happy ones. Furthermore, serious problems in adolescence do not necessarily lead to lifelong problems.

As you complete this lesson, consider your own psychosocial development during adolescence. How would you define your identity at that time? What kind of person were you? What was your relationship with your parents like? Was there much friction or bickering? If so, over which kinds of issues? Describe your social circles, your peers and friends. Did these people have a positive or negative influence on your development? Did you have any romantic relationships? What were they like? Did you or someone you know ever think about suicide during this time? What were the circumstances? Did you know someone who broke the law or got arrested? What was the situation? Did you have any formal sex education in school or elsewhere?

Prior Knowledge That Will Be Used in This Lesson

- This lesson will return to Erik Erikson's theory from Lesson 1 that specifies eight stages of *psychosocial development,* each of which is characterized by a particular challenge, or *developmental crisis,* which is central to that stage of life and must be resolved. This lesson will focus on Erikson's fifth stage called "identity vs. role confusion":
    1. Trust vs. Mistrust (birth to 1 year)
    2. Autonomy vs. Shame and Doubt (1 to 3 years)
    3. Initiative vs. Guilt (3 to 6 years)
    4. Industry vs. Inferiority (7 to 11 years)
    5. **Identity vs. Role Confusion ← Adolescence**
    6. Intimacy vs. Isolation (Adulthood)
    7. Generativity vs. Stagnation (Adulthood)
    8. Integrity vs. Despair (Adulthood)
- In a discussion of family influences during adolescence, this lesson will return to the concept of "parenting styles" introduced in Lesson 13. Recall that three basic styles include *authoritarian* (parents expect unquestioning obedience and offer little affection), *permissive* (affectionate but with few demands), and *authoritative* (parents expect obedience, set appropriate limits, and offer affection).
- Recall the topic of adolescent drug use, introduced in Lesson 21. Sociocultural factors weigh heavily in adolescents' decisions regarding when, how, and what drugs to use.

Learning Objectives

Use this information to guide your reading, viewing, thinking, and studying. After successfully completing this lesson, you should be able to:

1. Define the concept of identity and describe the development of identity during adolescence, incorporating Erikson's crisis of "identity versus role confusion."
2. Describe the concepts of "possible selves" and "false self."
3. Describe the four major identity statuses or conditions, and give an example of each one.
4. Discuss the influence of society and culture on identity formation, and describe the challenges encountered by minority adolescents in achieving their identity.
5. Discuss parent–child relationships during adolescence and describe the significance of other influential adults.
6. Discuss the role of peers, friends, and romantic relationships in adolescence.
7. Discuss the emotional changes in adolescence, and describe the factors involved in adolescent depression and suicide, including prevalence, contributing factors, warning signs, and gender and cultural variations.
8. Discuss delinquency among adolescents today, noting its incidence and prevalence, and significance for later development.

9. Describe the processes of identity formation in the areas of religion, gender, and vocation.

10. Identify the role of parental advice, sex education, and peer influence in adolescent decisions about sexual activity, and summarize the historical trends in adolescent sexuality.

Textbook Reading & Video Viewing

For the most effective study of this lesson, complete the assignments in the sequence listed below.

Before viewing the video program:

Read Chapter 16, "Adolescence: Psychosocial Development," pages 471–502.

View the video for Lesson 23, "Who Am I?"

Segment 1: *Identity*

Segment 2: *Friends and Family*

After viewing the video program:

Review all reading assignments for this lesson.

Complete the "Practice Questions" and "Applying Your Knowledge" sections to reinforce your understanding of important terms and concepts and measure your achievement of the Learning Objectives. Check your answers with the feedback given and review when necessary.

Practice Questions I

Multiple-Choice Questions

1. According to Erikson, the primary task of adolescence is that of establishing
   a. basic trust.
   b. an identity.
   c. intimacy.
   d. integrity.

2. According to developmentalists who study identity formation, foreclosure involves
   a. accepting an identity prematurely, without exploration.
   b. taking time off from school, work, and other commitments.
   c. opposing parental values.
   d. failing to commit oneself to a vocational goal.

3. When adolescents adopt an identity that is the opposite of the one they are expected to adopt, they are considered to be taking on a

   a. foreclosed identity.

   b. diffused identity.

   c. negative identity.

   d. reverse identity.

4. The main sources of emotional support for most young people who are establishing independence from their parents are

   a. older adolescents of the opposite sex.

   b. older siblings.

   c. teachers.

   d. peer groups.

5. For many members of minority ethnic groups, identity achievement may be particularly complicated because

   a. their cultural ideal clashes with the Western emphasis on adolescent self-determination.

   b. democratic ideology espouses a color-blind, multiethnic society in which background is irrelevant.

   c. parents and other relatives tend to emphasize ethnicity and expect teens to honor their roots.

   d. of all of the above reasons.

6. Parents can protect their adolescents by keeping close watch over activities, friends, and so on. This practice is called

   a. generational stake.

   b. foreclosure.

   c. peer screening.

   d. parental monitoring.

7. One way adolescents work through their confusion over "who they are" is to experiment with

   a. false self.

   b. possible selves.

   c. negative identity.

   d. none of the above.

8. Fourteen-year-old Juan believes that his parents are hopelessly out of touch and old-fashioned. Juan's parents deal patiently with his acts of rebellion and believe that, at heart, Juan is a good boy. This is an example of

   a. moral judgment.
   b. emerging independence.
   c. generational stake.
   d. parental restructuring.

9. In the United States, minority identity has broadened from race to

   a. ethnicity.
   b. include political persuasion.
   c. include race relations.
   d. none of the above.

10. Gender identity refers to a person's

    a. self-definition as male or female.
    b. sexual attraction to people of the other sex, the same sex, or both sexes.
    c. sex-typed occupation.
    d. sex-typed clothing and outward appearance.

11. Seventy-year-old Mark can't understand why his daughter doesn't want her teenage son to work after school. "In my day," he says, "we learned responsibility and a useful trade by working throughout high school." You wisely point out that

    a. most after-school jobs for teens today are not very meaningful.
    b. after-school employment tends to have a more negative impact on boys than girls.
    c. attitudes are changing; today, most American parents see adolescent employment as a waste of time.
    d. teens in most European countries almost never work after school.

12. The early signs of life-course persistent offenders include all of the following **EXCEPT**

    a. signs of brain damage early in life.
    b. antisocial school behavior.
    c. delayed sexual intimacy.
    d. use of alcohol and tobacco at an early age.

13. Regarding gender differences in self-destructive acts, the rate of parasuicide is ________________ and the rate of completed suicide is ________________.

    a. higher in males; higher in females
    b. higher in females; higher in males
    c. the same in males and females; higher in males
    d. the same in males and females; higher in females

14. Conflict between parents and adolescent offspring is more likely
    a. to involve fathers than mothers.
    b. with poorly-attached pairs than with attached pairs.
    c. more likely with sons than with daughters.
    d. with tweens than with older teens.

True or False Items

Write T (for true) or F (for false) on the line in front of each statement.

15. _____ Sexual orientation refers to a person's erotic desires.
16. _____ Most adolescents have political views and educational values that are markedly different from those of their parents.
17. _____ Peer pressure is inherently destructive to the adolescent seeking an identity.
18. _____ For most adolescents, group socializing and dating precede the establishment of true intimacy with one member of the opposite sex.
19. _____ Many religions have sanctioned moratorium before individuals are expected to make a commitment.
20. _____ Parents are the only adults who have a significant impact on adolescent development.
21. _____ The majority of adolescents report that they have at some time engaged in law-breaking that might have led to arrest.
22. _____ In finding themselves, teens try to find an identity that is consistent and mature.
23. _____ Most parent–adolescent conflict centers around concerns about adolescent delinquency and sexual behavior.
24. _____ There are distinct ethnic and gender differences in adolescent suicide rates.

Practice Questions II

Multiple-Choice Questions

1. Which of the following was **NOT** identified as a factor influencing adolescent parasuicide or suicide rates?
    a. availability of lethal means (e.g., a gun)
    b. parental supervision
    c. alcohol and other drugs
    d. increased arguing with parents

2. Parent-child conflict among Asian American families often surfaces late in adolescence because these cultures
   a. emphasize family closeness.
   b. value authoritarian parenting.
   c. encourage autonomy in children.
   d. do all of the above.

3. Becoming a distinct self-determined individual is not always compatible with connections to one's heritage and peer group, causing some adolescents to experience a(n)
   a. generational stake.
   b. identity crisis.
   c. diffused identity.
   d. rejecting-neglecting identity.

4. While the rate of clinical depression more than doubles for both sexes during adolescence, it is ____________ for girls than for boys.
   a. lower
   b. much lower
   c. higher
   d. much higher

5. Which of the following is **NOT** true regarding romantic relationships among gay and lesbian adolescents?
   a. Many sexually active teenagers who have had same-sex partners self-identify as straight.
   b. Many gay teens try to conceal their homosexual orientation by becoming heterosexually involved.
   c. Many girls who will later identify themselves as lesbians have other-sex relationships before deciding their identity.
   d. Most adolescents go through an "experimental phase" in which they become romantically attached to one or more same-sex partners.

6. The adolescent experiencing role confusion is typically
   a. very apathetic.
   b. a risk-taker, anxious to experiment with alternative identities.
   c. willing to accept parental values wholesale, without exploring alternatives.
   d. one who rebels against all forms of authority.

7. Which of the following is true of most teens in the United States today?
   a. more are in school
   b. fewer use drugs
   c. almost none die of disease
   d. All of the above are true.
8. Crime statistics show that during adolescence
   a. males and females are equally likely to be arrested.
   b. males are more likely to be arrested than females.
   c. females are more likely to be arrested than males.
   d. males commit more crimes than females but are less likely to be arrested.
9. Which of the following is the most common problem among adolescents?
   a. pregnancy
   b. daily use of illegal drugs
   c. minor law-breaking
   d. attempts at suicide
10. A period during which a young person experiments with different identities, postponing important choices, is called
    a. foreclosure.
    b. a negative identity.
    c. role confusion.
    d. moratorium.
11. When adolescents' political, religious, educational, and vocational opinions are compared with their parents', the so-called "generation gap" is
    a. much smaller than when the younger and older generations are compared overall.
    b. much wider than when the younger and older generations are compared overall.
    c. wider between parents and sons than between parents and daughters.
    d. wider between parents and daughters than between parents and sons.
12. Selection and facilitation are relevant to understanding
    a. peer pressure.
    b. sex education.
    c. parent-adolescent conflict.
    d. gender identity.

13. Parent-teen conflict tends to center on issues related to
    a. politics and religion.
    b. education.
    c. vacations.
    d. daily details, such as musical tastes.

14. According to a review of studies from various nations, suicidal ideation is
    a. not as common among high school students as is popularly believed.
    b. more common among males than females.
    c. only slightly more common than parasuicide.
    d. so common among high school students that it might be considered normal.

Matching Items

Match each definition or description with its corresponding term.

Terms

15. __________ identity achievement
16. __________ foreclosure
17. __________ negative identity
18. __________ role confusion
19. __________ moratorium
20. __________ generation gap
21. __________ cluster suicide
22. __________ parental monitoring
23. __________ rumination
24. __________ parasuicide

Definitions or Descriptions

a. premature identity formation
b. dwelling on past experiences
c. the adolescent has few commitments to goals or values
d. differences between the younger and older generations
e. self-destructive act that does not result in death
f. awareness of where children are and what they are doing
g. a time-out period during which adolescents experiment with alternative identities
h. the adolescent establishes his or her own goals and values
i. several suicides committed by members of a group within a short period of time
j. an identity opposite of the one an adolescent is expected to adopt

Applying Your Knowledge

1. From childhood, Sharon thought she wanted to follow in her mother's footsteps and be a homemaker. Now, at age 40 with a home and family, she admits to herself that what she really wanted to be was a medical researcher. Erik Erikson would probably say that Sharon
   a. adopted a negative identity when she was a child.
   b. experienced identity foreclosure at an early age.
   c. never progressed beyond the obvious role confusion she experienced as a child.
   d. took a moratorium from identity formation.
2. Fifteen-year-old David is rebelling against his devoutly religious parents by taking drugs, stealing, and engaging in other antisocial behaviors. Evidently, David has
   a. foreclosed on his identity.
   b. declared an identity moratorium.
   c. adopted a negative identity.
   d. experienced role confusion.
3. Which of the following is true about parental influence on adolescents' decisions about sex?
   a. Teenagers tend to rebel against their parents' advice.
   b. Parents and teenagers tend to agree on whether they had talked to their teens about sex.
   c. Religious mothers who disapproved of sex were the most accurate in their knowledge about whether their adolescents were having sex.
   d. Adolescents take fewer risks and avoid unwanted peer pressure to have sex when they talk to their parents openly about sex.
4. In 1957, 6-year-old Raisel and her parents emigrated from Poland to the United States. Compared with her parents, who grew up in a culture in which virtually everyone held the same religious, moral, political, and sexual values, Raisel is likely to have
   a. an easier time achieving her own unique identity.
   b. a more difficult time forging her identity.
   c. a greater span of time in which to forge her own identity.
   d. a shorter span of time in which to forge her identity.
5. An adolescent exaggerates the importance of differences in her values and those of her parents. Her parents see these differences as smaller and less important. This phenomenon is called the
   a. generation gap.
   b. generational stake.
   c. family enigma.
   d. parental imperative.

6. In our society, the most obvious examples of institutionalized moratoria on identity formation are
   a. the Boy Scouts and the Girl Scouts.
   b. college and the peacetime military.
   c. marriage and divorce.
   d. bar mitzvahs and baptisms.

7. First-time parents Norma and Christopher are worried that, during adolescence, their healthy parental influence will be undone as their children are encouraged by peers to become sexually promiscuous, drug-addicted, or delinquent. Their wise neighbor, who is a developmental psychologist, tells them that
   a. during adolescence, peers are generally more likely to complement the influence of parents than they are to pull their friends in the opposite direction.
   b. research suggests that peers provide a negative influence in every major task of adolescence.
   c. only through authoritarian parenting can parents give children the skills they need to resist peer pressure.
   d. unless their children show early signs of learning difficulties or antisocial behavior, parental monitoring is unnecessary.

8. Thirteen-year-old Cassandra is constantly experimenting with different behaviors and possible identities. It is likely that she
   a. has low self-esteem.
   b. foreclosed prematurely on her identity.
   c. is normal.
   d. comes from a home environment in which there is considerable tension and conflict.

9. Maryann knows who she is. She reevaluates goals and values set by her parents, accepting some and rejecting others. This reflects
   a. individual uniqueness.
   b. peer-group membership.
   c. identity achievement.
   d. vocational identity.

10. Which of the following adults is likely to be influential in 15-year-old Shamara's identity development?
   a. her rabbi
   b. her grandmother
   c. her school counselor
   d. all of the above individuals

11. Ray was among the first of his friends to have sex, drink alcohol, and smoke cigarettes. These attributes, together with his having been hyperactive and having poor emotional control, would suggest that Ray is at high risk of

    a. becoming an adolescent-limited offender.
    b. becoming a life-course persistent offender.
    c. developing an antisocial personality.
    d. foreclosing his identity prematurely.

12. Carl is a typical 16-year-old adolescent who has no special problems. It is likely that Carl has

    a. thought about suicide.
    b. engaged in some minor illegal act.
    c. struggled with "who he is."
    d. done all of the above.

13. Statistically, which of the following adolescents is most likely to commit suicide?

    a. Micah, an African American female
    b. Yan, an Asian American male
    c. James, a Native American male
    d. Alison, a European American female

14. Coming home from work, Malcolm hears a radio announcement warning parents to be alert for possible cluster suicide signs in their teenage children. What might have precipitated such an announcement?

    a. government statistics that suicide has been on the rise since the 1990s
    b. the highly publicized suicide of a local teen
    c. the recent crash of an airliner, killing all on board
    d. any of the above

Key Terms

1. **identity versus role confusion:** Erikson's term for the fifth stage of development, in which the person tries to figure out "Who am I?" but is confused as to which of many possible roles to adopt. Also referred to as *identity versus diffusion*. (p. 472; video lesson, segment 1; objectives 1 & 3)
2. **identity achievement:** Erikson's term for the attainment of identity, or the point at which a person understands who he or she is as a unique individual, in accord with past experiences and future plans. (p. 472; video lesson, segment 1; objectives 1 & 3)
3. **role confusion:** A situation in which an adolescent does not seem to know or care what his or her identity is. Also called *identity diffusion* or *role diffusion*. (p. 472; video lesson, segment 1; objectives 1 & 3)

4. **identity foreclosure:** Erikson's term for premature identity formation, which occurs when an adolescent adopts parents' or society's roles and values wholesale, without questioning or analysis. (p. 472; video lesson, segment 1; objectives 1 & 3)
5. **moratorium:** Erikson's term for an adolescent's choice of a socially acceptable way to postpone making identity-achievement decisions. Going to college is a common example. Also called an *identity moratorium*. (p. 473; video lesson, segment 1; objectives 1 & 3)
6. **gender identity:** A person's self-identification of being female or male, including the roles and behaviors that society assigns to that sex. (p. 476; objectives 3 & 9)
7. **bickering:** The repeated, petty arguing that typically occurs in early adolescence about common, daily life activities. (p. 477; video lesson, segment 2; objective 5)
8. **parental monitoring:** Parental awareness about where one's child is and what he or she is doing, and with whom. (p. 480; objective 5)
9. **peer pressure:** The social pressure to conform to one's friends in behavior, dress, and attitude; usually considered a negative force, as when adolescent peers encourage one another to defy adult authority. (p. 483; video lesson, segment 2; objective 6)
10. **deviancy training:** Destructive peer support in which one person shows another how to rebel against authority or social norms. (p. 483; objective 6)
11. **sexual orientation:** A person's sexual attraction to members of their own sex, to the opposite sex, or to both sexes. (p. 486; objective 9)
12. **clinical depression:** An overwhelming and enduring feeling of sadness hopelessness, lethargy, and worthlessness that disrupts normal activities. (p. 490; objective 7)
13. **rumination:** Occurs when someone is repeatedly thinking and talking about past experiences; can contribute to depression. (p. 491; objective 7)
14. **suicidal ideation:** Thinking about committing suicide, usually with some serious emotional and intellectual overtones. (p. 491; objective 7)
15. **parasuicide:** Any potentially lethal action against the self that does not result in death. Also called *attempted suicide* or *failed suicide*. (p. 491; objective 7)
16. **cluster suicide:** A series of suicides or suicide attempts within a brief period of time that are precipitated by one initial suicide, usually that of a famous person or a well-known peer. (p. 493; objective 7)
17. **life-course-persistent offender:** A person whose criminal activity typically begins in early adolescence and continues throughout life; a career criminal. (p. 495; objective 8)
18. **adolescence-limited offender:** A person whose criminal activity stops by age 21. (p. 495; objective 8)

19. **identity:** As used by Erikson, refers to a person's self-definition as a separate individual in terms of roles, attitudes, beliefs, and aspirations. (video lesson, segment 1; objective 1)
20. **possible selves:** Occurs when adolescents try out variations on who they are and who they might like to become. (video lesson, segment 1; objective 2)
21. **negative identity:** According to Erikson, occurs when adolescents adopt an identity that is the opposite of the one they are expected to adopt. (video lesson, segment 1; objective 3)
22. **generation gap:** The alleged distance between generations in values, behaviors, and knowledge. (video lesson, segment 2; objective 5)
23. **generational stake:** The tendency of each family member, because of that person's different developmental stage, to see the family in a certain way. (video lesson, segment 2; objective 5)

Summary

Adolescence heightens the search for self-understanding because of the momentous changes that occur during the teenage years. Many adolescents experience the emergence of **possible selves**, or diverse perceptions of identity in different groups or settings.

According to Erik Erikson, the psychosocial challenge of adolescence is **identity versus role confusion**. The specific task of this challenge is the search for identity, both as an individual and as a member of the larger community. When the search for identify becomes overwhelming and confusing, adolescents may experience an identity crisis. The ultimate goal, **identity achievement**, occurs when adolescents establish their own goals and values by abandoning some of those set by parents and society while accepting others.

Some adolescents form an identity prematurely, a process called **foreclosure**. Other adolescents, unable to find alternative roles that are truly their own, simply rebel and become the opposite of what is expected of them, adopting a **negative identity**. Others experience **role confusion**, with few commitments to goals or values, whether those of parents, peers, or the larger society. Many adolescents declare an **identity moratorium**, often by using an institutionalized time-out such as college or voluntary military service as a means of postponing final decisions about career or marriage. While identity formation is a major task of adolescence, many people don't reach identity achievement until early adulthood (or later) and most continue to shape and refine their identities throughout the life span. Religious identity, vocational identity, gender identity, and ethnic identity can develop at different rates.

For immigrants and minority adolescents, identity formation is particularly complex because they must find the right balance between their ethnic background and the values of the society at large. This may cause them to embrace a negative identity or, as is more often the case, to foreclose on identity prematurely.

Research studies demonstrate that the **generation gap** is not as wide as it is popularly assumed to be. Indeed, studies have found substantial agreement between parents and adolescents on political, religious, educational, and vocational opinions and values. However, there is a **generational stake**, which refers to the particular needs and concerns of each generation in the parent–adolescent relationship, as well as the natural tendency to see the family in a certain way.

The adolescent's peer group is a social institution that eases the transition from childhood to adulthood by functioning in a variety of ways. Peer groups function as a source of information and social support, a group of contemporaries who are experiencing similar struggles. As adolescents associate themselves with a particular subgroup, peers help them define who they are by helping them define who they are not. Peer groups also serve as a sounding board for exploring and defining one's values and aspirations.

While the search for identity brings with it certain difficulties, most adolescents reach adulthood safe and secure. Others have special problems, including delinquent behavior and depression that may lead to suicide. Thinking about suicide (**suicidal ideation**) is quite common among high school students. Fortunately, most suicide attempts in adolescence do not result in death. Deliberate acts of self-destruction that do not cause death are referred to as **parasuicide**. Whether or not suicidal ideation leads to suicide or parasuicide depends on the availability of lethal methods, **parental monitoring**, the use of alcohol and other drugs, and the attitudes about suicide that are held by the adolescent's family, friends, and culture.

Answer Key

Practice Questions I

Multiple-Choice Questions

1. b. is the correct answer. (video lesson, segment 1; objective 1)

   a. is incorrect. According to Erikson, this is the crisis of infancy.

   c. & d. are incorrect. In Erikson's theory, these crises occur later in life.

2. a. is the correct answer. (video lesson, segment 1; objective 3)

   b. is incorrect. This describes an identity moratorium.

   c. is incorrect. This describes a negative identity.

   d. is incorrect. This describes role confusion.

3. c. is the correct answer. (video lesson, segment 1; objective 3)
4. d. is the correct answer. (video lesson, segment 2; objective 6)
5. d. is the correct answer. (video lesson, segments 1 & 2; objective 4)
6. d. is the correct answer. (objective 5)

   a. is incorrect. The generational stake refers to differences in how family members from different generations view the family.

   b. is incorrect. Foreclosure refers to the premature establishment of identity.

   c. is incorrect. Peer screening is an aspect of parental monitoring, but it was not specifically discussed in the textbook.

7. b. is the correct answer. (video lesson, segment 1; objective 2)
8. b. is the correct answer. (video lesson, segment 2; objective 5)
9. a. is the correct answer. (objective 4)
10. a. is the correct answer. (objective 9)

    b. is incorrect. This is sexual orientation.

    c. & d. are incorrect. Both of these are part of gender role.
11. a. is the correct answer. (objective 9)
12. c. is the correct answer. Most life-course persistent offenders are among the first of their cohort to have sex. (objective 8)
13. b. is the correct answer. (objective 7)
14. d. is the correct answer. (objective 5)

    a. & c. are incorrect. In fact, parent-child conflict is more likely to involve mothers and daughters.

    b. is incorrect. Conflict is indicative of the existence of a parent–child attachment, because a lack of concern would reduce conflict.

True or False Items

15. T (objective 9)
16. F Numerous studies have shown substantial agreement between parents and their adolescent children on political opinions and educational values. (video lesson, segment 2; objective 5)
17. F Just the opposite is true. (video lesson, segment 2; objective 6)
18. T (objective 6)
19. T (objective 9)
20. F (objective 5)
21. T (objective 8)
22. T (objective 1)
23. F (objective 5)
24. T (objective 7)

Practice Questions II

Multiple-Choice Questions

1. d. is the correct answer. Bickering is common in parent–teen relationships. (objective 7)
2. a. is the correct answer. (objectives 4 & 5)
3. b. is the correct answer. (video lesson, segment 1; objective 1)
4. d. is the correct answer. (video lesson, segment 2; objective 7)
5. d. is the correct answer. The textbook does not suggest that such a phase exists. Even if it did, it is not likely that "most" adolescents would experience it. (objective 10)

6. a. is the correct answer. (video lesson, segment 1; objective 3)

   b. is incorrect. This describes an adolescent undergoing an identity moratorium.

   c. is incorrect. This describes identity foreclosure.

   d. is incorrect. This describes an adolescent who is adopting a negative identity.

7. d. is the correct answer. (objective 7)
8. b. is the correct answer. (objective 8)
9. c. is the correct answer. (objective 8)
10. d. is the correct answer. (video lesson, segment 1; objective 3)

    a. is incorrect. Foreclosure occurs when the adolescent prematurely adopts an identity, without fully exploring alternatives.

    b. is incorrect. Adolescents who adopt an identity that is opposite to the one they are expected to develop have taken on a negative identity.

    c. is incorrect. Role confusion occurs when the adolescent is apathetic and has few commitments to goals or values.

11. a. is the correct answer. (video lesson, segment 2; objective 5)

    c. & d. are incorrect. The textbook does not suggest that the size of the generation gap varies with the offspring's sex.

12. a. is the correct answer. (objective 6)
13. d. is the correct answer. (objective 5)

    a., b., & c. are incorrect. In fact, on these issues parents and teenagers tend to show substantial agreement.

14. d. is the correct answer. (objective 7)

Matching Items

15. h (video lesson, segment 1; objective 1)
16. a (video lesson, segment 1; objective 1)
17. j (video lesson, segment 1; objectives 1 & 3)
18. c (video lesson, segment 1; objective 1)
19. g (video lesson, segment 1; objectives 1 & 3)
20. d (video lesson, segment 2; objective 5)
21. i (video lesson, segment 2; objective 7)
22. f (objective 5)
23. b (objective 7)
24. e (objective 7)

Applying Your Knowledge

1. b. is the correct answer. Apparently, Sharon never explored alternatives or truly forged a unique personal identity. (video lesson, segment 1; objective 1)

   a. is incorrect. Individuals who rebel by adopting an identity that is the opposite of the one they are expected to adopt have taken on a negative identity.

c. is incorrect. Individuals who experience role confusion have few commitments to goals or values. This was not Sharon's problem.

d. is incorrect. Had she taken a moratorium on identity formation, Sharon would have experimented with alternative identities and perhaps would have chosen that of a medical researcher.

2. c. is the correct answer. (video lesson, segment 1; objective 1)
3. d. is the correct answer. (objective 10)
4. b. is the correct answer. Minority adolescents struggle with finding the right balance between transcending their background and becoming immersed in it. (objectives 3 & 4)

   c. & d. are incorrect. The textbook does not suggest that the amount of time adolescents have to forge their identities varies from one ethnic group to another or has changed over historical time.
5. b. is the correct answer. (video lesson, segment 2; objective 5)
6. b. is the correct answer. (objectives 1 & 3)
7. a. is the correct answer. (video lesson, segment 2; objective 6)

   b. is incorrect. In fact, just the opposite is true.

   c. is incorrect. Developmentalists recommend authoritative, rather than authoritarian, parenting.

   d. is incorrect. Parental monitoring is important for all adolescents.
8. c. is the correct answer. (video lesson, segment 1; objective 2)

   a., b., & d. are incorrect. Experimenting with possible selves is a normal sign of adolescent identity formation.
9. c. is the correct answer. (objective 1)
10. d. is the correct answer. (objective 5)
11. b. is the correct answer. (objective 8)
12. d. is the correct answer. (objectives 1, 7, & 8)
13. c. is the correct answer. (objective 7)
14. b. is the correct answer. (objective 7)

Lesson Review

Lesson 23

Adolescence
Psychosocial Development

Please Note: Use this matrix to guide your study and achieve the learning objectives of this lesson. It will also help you to view the video, which defines and demonstrates important concepts and skills as they relate to everyday life.

Learning Objective	Textbook	Course Student Guide	Video Lesson
1. Define the concept of identity, and describe the development of identity during adolescence, incorporating Erikson's crisis of "identity versus role confusion."	pp. 472–473	Key Terms: 1, 2, 3, 4, 5, 19; Practice Questions I: 1, 22; Practice Questions II: 3, 15, 16, 17, 18, 19; Applying Your Knowledge: 1, 2, 6, 9, 12.	Segment 1: *Identity*
2. Describe the concepts of "possible selves" and "false self."	*	Key Terms: 20; Practice Questions I: 7; Applying Your Knowledge: 8.	Segment 1: *Identity*
3. Describe the four major identity statuses or conditions, and give an example of each one.	pp. 472–476	Key Terms: 1, 2, 3, 4, 5, 6, 21; Practice Questions I: 2, 3; Practice Questions II: 6, 10, 17, 19; Applying Your Knowledge: 4, 6.	Segment 1: *Identity*
4. Discuss the influence of society and culture on identity formation, and describe the challenges encountered by minority adolescents in achieving their identity.	p. 478	Practice Questions I: 5, 9; Practice Questions II: 2; Applying Your Knowledge: 4.	Segment 1: *Identity* Segment 2: *Friends and Family*
5. Discuss parent–child relationships during adolescence and describe the significance of other influential adults.	pp. 477–482	Key Terms: 7, 8, 22, 23; Practice Questions I: 6, 8, 14, 16, 20, 23; Practice Questions II: 2, 11, 13, 20, 22; Applying Your Knowledge: 5, 10.	Segment 2: *Friends and Family*

* The video for this lesson offers excellent coverage of this topic.

Learning Objective	**Textbook**	**Course Student Guide**	**Video Lesson**
6. Discuss the role of peers, friends, and romantic relationships in adolescence.	pp. 482–487	Key Terms: 9, 10; Practice Questions I: 4, 17, 18; Practice Questions II: 12; Applying Your Knowledge: 7.	Segment 2: *Friends and Family*
7. Discuss the emotional changes in adolescence, and describe the factors involved in adolescent depression and suicide, including prevalence, contributing factors, warning signs, and gender and cultural variations.	pp. 490–494	Key Terms: 12, 13, 14, 15, 16; Practice Questions I: 13, 24; Practice Questions II: 1, 4, 7, 14, 21, 23, 24; Applying Your Knowledge: 12, 13, 14.	Segment 2: *Friends and Family*
8. Discuss delinquency among adolescents today, noting its incidence and prevalence, and significance for later development.	pp. 494–496	Key Terms: 17, 18; Practice Questions I: 12, 21; Practice Questions II: 8, 9; Applying Your Knowledge: 11, 12.	
9. Describe the processes of identity formation in the areas of religion, gender, and vocation.	pp. 473–476	Key Terms: 6, 14; Practice Questions I: 10, 11, 15, 19.	
10. Identify the role of parental advice, sex education, and peer influence, and the media in adolescents' decisions about sexual activity, and summarize the historical trends in adolescent sexuality.	pp. 487–489	Practice Questions II: 5; Applying Your Knowledge: 3.	

The Home Stretch

Lesson 24

Adolescence:
Summary

Preview

Lesson 24 summarizes biosocial, cognitive, and psychosocial development during adolescence. These years are an exciting time, when the talents, abilities, and values that have been unfolding over childhood blossom and reveal the directions a teenager's life is likely to take.

In the biosocial domain of development, the changes of adolescence have a memorable and lifelong impact on our bodies and self-images. In the cognitive domain, adolescents become increasingly able to speculate, hypothesize, and use logic. Perhaps most significantly, the logical and idealistic thinking of adolescence represents a significant step in the process of creating a life story and forming an identity.

As adolescents forge an identity and try to make wise choices about their futures, their social context encourages some paths and closes others. The result of this interaction, in the ideal case, will be young people who are sure of themselves and able to pass through the vulnerable years of adolescence successfully.

Prior Knowledge That Will Be Used in This Lesson

- Biosocial development during adolescence (from Lesson 21) will be referred to as we discuss the impact of puberty, the growth spurt, and chronic illness on a teenager's development.
- Cognitive development during adolescence (from Lesson 22) will be referred to as we explore how advancing cognitive skills help teenagers make the many decisions they are faced with as they consider their futures.
- Psychosocial development during adolescence (from Lesson 23) will be referred to as we consider the formation of identity and the impact that parents, peers and mentors have on teenagers.

Learning Objectives

Use this information to guide your reading, viewing, thinking, and studying. After successfully completing this lesson, you should be able to:

1. Describe biosocial development during adolescence, focusing on the impact of puberty and sexual maturation on teenagers.
2. Explain how thinking changes during adolescence and discuss the impact of these changes on adolescent decision making.
3. Discuss psychosocial development during adolescence, focusing on the formation of identity and the influence of parents, mentors and the peer group.

Textbook Reading & Video Viewing

For the most effective study of this lesson, complete the assignments in the sequence listed below.

Before viewing the video program:

Read Chapter 14, "Summary: Adolescence: Biosocial Development," page 436; Chapter 15, "Summary: Adolescence: Cognitive Development," page 468; Chapter 6, "Summary: Adolescence: Psychosocial Development," page 501, and "The Developing Person So Far: Adolescence," page 503.

View the video for Lesson 24, "The Home Stretch."

Segment 1: *Ashley*

Segment 2: *Bayleigh*

Segment 3: *Alejandro*

Video Viewing Tips

The video for this lesson will feature three adolescent children—Ashley (16), Bayleigh (13) and Alejandro (17)—each from different backgrounds and circumstances. As you watch their stories unfold, look for these recurring issues and themes:

Note the biological development of these teens—their heredity, overall health, and the changes they are experiencing associated with puberty. Consider how this development compares with their peers, and how this might affect their body image.

Also, observe how the thinking of these adolescents compares with that of younger children, say, in middle childhood. Watch how they apply their new abilities to reason and think hypothetically to the decisions they are making about their future. Look for any evidence of egocentric thinking, including personal or invincibility fables.

Consider how these children view themselves, their identity. Listen for their goals and aspirations—their dreams of quest and conquest. Note the similarities and differences between their personalities, and any evidence of possible selves or foreclosure.

Also, observe closely how these adolescents relate to their peers—the role of friendship in their lives, their place in the friendship group, and their strength of will when challenged by peers. Consider both the positive and negative influence of their friends, and the relative value they place on friendships as opposed to personal goals.

Finally, what role do parents and other adults play in the lives of these kids? Note the different family structures (e.g., single-parent, nuclear) and how the parents are meeting the needs of these children. Also, try to discern each adult's parenting style (i.e., authoritarian, permissive, authoritative), and consider the influence of counselors, mentors and other adults.

After viewing the video program:

Review all reading assignments for this lesson.

Complete the "Practice Questions" section to reinforce your understanding of important terms and concepts and measure your achievement of the Learning Objectives. Check your answers with the feedback given and review when necessary.

Practice Questions

Multiple-Choice Questions

1. In general, most adolescents are
   a. overweight.
   b. satisfied with their appearance.
   c. dissatisfied with their appearance.
   d. unaffected by cultural attitudes about beauty.

2. Earlier-than-average physical growth and sexual maturation
   a. tend to be equally difficult for girls and boys.
   b. tend to be more difficult for boys than for girls.
   c. tend to be more difficult for girls than for boys.
   d. are easier for both girls and boys than late maturation.

3. Nutritional deficiencies in adolescence are frequently the result of
   a. eating red meat.
   b. poor food choices.
   c. anovulatory menstruation.
   d. excessive exercise.

4. Puberty is initiated when hormones are released from the _____________, then from the _______________, and then from the adrenal glands and the ___________________.
   a. hypothalamus; pituitary; gonads
   b. pituitary; gonads; hypothalamus
   c. gonads; pituitary; hypothalamus
   d. pituitary; hypothalamus; gonads

5. Individuals who experiment with drugs early are
   a. typically affluent teenagers who are experiencing an identity crisis.
   b. more likely to have multiple drug-abuse problems later on.
   c. less likely to have alcohol-abuse problems later on.
   d. usually able to resist later peer pressure leading to long-term addiction.
6. Many psychologists consider the distinguishing feature of adolescent thought to be the ability to think in terms of
   a. moral issues.
   b. concrete operations.
   c. possibility, not just reality.
   d. logical principles.
7. The adolescent who takes risks and feels immune to the laws of mortality is showing evidence of the
   a. invincibility fable.
   b. personal fable.
   c. imaginary audience.
   d. death instinct.
8. Imaginary audiences, invincibility fables, and personal fables are expressions of adolescent
   a. morality.
   b. thinking games.
   c. decision making.
   d. egocentrism.
9. High levels of emotions
   a. slow down rational thinking.
   b. moderately speed up rational thinking.
   c. greatly speed up rational thinking.
   d. have no effect on rational thinking.
10. Serious reflection on important issues is a wrenching process for many adolescents because of their newfound ability to reason
    a. inductively.
    b. deductively.
    c. hypothetically.
    d. symbolically.

11. The main sources of emotional support for most young people who are establishing independence from their parents are
    a. older adolescents of the opposite sex.
    b. older siblings.
    c. teachers.
    d. peer groups.

12. For members of minority ethnic groups, identity achievement may be particularly complicated because
    a. their cultural ideal may clash with the Western emphasis on adolescent self-determination.
    b. democratic ideology espouses a color-blind, multiethnic society in which background is irrelevant.
    c. parents and other relatives tend to emphasize ethnicity and expect teens to honor their roots.
    d. of all of the above reasons.

13. Adolescents help each other in many ways, including
    a. identity formation.
    b. independence.
    c. behavior choices.
    d. all of the above.

14. First-time parents Norma and Christopher are worried that during adolescence, their healthy parental influence will be undone as their children are encouraged by peers to become sexually promiscuous, drug-addicted, or delinquent. Their wise neighbor, who is a developmental psychologist, tells them that
    a. during adolescence, peers are generally more likely to complement the influence of parents than they are to pull their friends in the opposite direction.
    b. research suggests that peers provide a negative influence in every major task of adolescence.
    c. only through authoritarian parenting can parents give children the skills they need to resist peer pressure.
    d. unless their children show early signs of learning difficulties or antisocial behavior, parental monitoring is unnecessary.

True or False Items

Write T (for true) or F (for false) on the line in front of each statement.

15. _____ More calories are necessary during adolescence than at any other period during the life span.

16. _____ Puberty generally begins sometime between ages 8 and 15.

17. _____ Childhood habits of overeating and underexercising usually lessen during adolescence.

18. _____ The use of logic as opposed to experience to make decisions in adolescence is referred to as formal operational thought.

19. _____ Inductive reasoning is a hallmark of formal operational thought.

20. _____ In cultures where everyone's values are similar and social change is slight, identity is relatively easy to achieve.

21. _____ Peer pressure is inherently destructive to the adolescent seeking an identity.

Questions for Reflection

1. Consider your body image (your opinion about your physical appearance) when you were in the eighth or ninth grade—when you were 13 or 14 years old.
   a. What did you consider your "best feature"?
   b. What did you consider your "worst feature"—the aspect of your appearance that you felt required the most care, upgrading or camouflage?
   c. Compared to your classmates and friends, were you an average-maturing, early-maturing, or late-maturing individual? What impact do you feel the timing of your puberty had on you at the time? What impact has it had on who you are today?

2. Did any of the stories depicted in the video lesson provide insight into your own adolescence (or that of your children)? What did you learn about yourself (or your children)?

3. A central theme of this five-lesson unit is that identity formation is a primary task of adolescence. Ideally, adolescents develop a clear picture of their unique standing in the larger social world to which they belong. But the development of identity doesn't end during adolescence; rather it continues to evolve over the life span. To help you apply this truth to your own life story, write five answers to the simple question, "Who am I?" You may respond in terms of your social roles, responsibilities, or commitments; the groups to which you belong; your beliefs and values; your personality traits and abilities; and your needs, feelings, and behavior patterns. List only things that are really important to you TODAY and that would, if lost, make a real difference in your sense of who you are.

	Rank Today	Rank Five Years Ago
1. I am	________	________
2. I am	________	________
3. I am	________	________
4. I am	________	________
5. I am	________	________

After you have completed your list, RANK the importance of each item to your identity today assigning a number from 1 (most important) to 5 (least important). Then do the same for your identity five years ago. What differences do you see? What do you feel accounts for any differences you observe?

Key Terms

1. **puberty:** A period of rapid growth and sexual change that occurs in early adolescence and produces a person of adult size, shape, and sexual potential. (p. 411; video lesson, segment 2; objective 1)
2. **menarche:** A female's first menstrual period. (p. 411; video lesson, segment 2; objective 1)
3. **growth spurt:** The period of relatively sudden and rapid physical growth of every part of the body that occurs during puberty. (p. 423; video lesson, segment 2; objective 1)
4. **spermarche:** A male's first ejaculation of live sperm. (p. 411; objective 1)
5. **body image:** A person's mental concept of how his or her body appears. (p. 421; objective 1)
6. **formal operational thought:** in Piaget's theory, the fourth and final stage of cognitive development; arises from combination of maturation and experience. (p. 442; objective 2)
7. **hypothetical thought:** Thought that involves propositions and possibilities that may or may not reflect reality. (p. 444; objective 2)
8. **inductive reasoning:** Reasoning from one or more specific experiences or facts to a general conclusion. (p. 444; objective 2)
9. **deductive reasoning:** Reasoning from a general hypothesis, through logical steps, to a specific conclusion. (p. 444; objective 2)

10. **invincibility fable:** The fiction, fostered by adolescent egocentrism, that one is immune to common dangers, such as those associated with unprotected sex, drug abuse, or high-speed driving. (p. 440; video lesson, segment 2; objective 2)
11. **personal fable:** The egocentric idea, held by many adolescents, that one is destined for fame and fortune and/or great accomplishments. (p. 440; objective 2)
12. **person–environment fit:** The degree to which a particular environment is conducive to the growth of a particular individual. (video lesson, segment 1; objective 2)
13. **identity:** As used by Erikson, a consistent definition of oneself as a unique individual, in terms of roles, attitudes, beliefs, and aspirations. (video lesson, segment 2; objective 3)
14. **possible selves:** Various intellectual fantasies about what the future might bring if one or another course of action is chosen. (video lesson, segment 1; objective 3)
15. **identity versus role confusion:** Erikson's term for the fifth stage of development, in which the person tries to figure out "Who am I?" but is confused as to which of many roles to adopt. (p. 472; objective 3)
16. **identity achievement:** Erikson's term for a person's forming an identity and understanding who he or she is as a unique individual, in accord with past experiences and future plans. (p. 472; video lesson, segment 3; objective 3)
17. **foreclosure:** Erikson's term for premature identity formation, in which the young person adopts the values of parents, or other significant people, wholesale, without questioning and analysis. (p. 472; objective 3)
18. **parental monitoring:** Parental awareness of what one's children are doing, where, and with whom. (p. 480; objective 3)
19. **peer pressure:** Social pressure to conform with one's friends or contemporaries in behavior, dress, and attitude; usually considered negative, as when peers encourage each other to defy adult standards. (p. 483; video lesson, segments 1 & 3; objective 3)
20. **imaginary audience:** A teenager's false belief, stemming from adolescent egocentrism, that others are intensely interested in his or her appearance and behavior. (p. 441; objective 2)

Summary

For most people, adolescence is an eventful time of life that brings dramatic changes in each domain of development. Along with rapid physical growth, the changes associated with sexual maturation contribute a new dimension to the ways in which adolescents think about themselves and relate to others. Young people who experience puberty at the same time as their friends tend to view the experience more positively than those who experience it early or late.

Equally important changes occur in cognition as adolescents become increasingly able to think abstractly and logically. Unlike younger children, whose thinking is tied to concrete operations, adolescents (with their ability to use formal operations) are able to consider possibilities as well as reality. Adolescent thought has certain shortcomings, however, including difficulties in theoretical thinking and distortions associated with egocentrism. Because adolescent thought is egocentric, young people tend to overestimate their significance to others, a tendency that is often reflected in their belief in their own invincibility, their expectations of heroic lives, and their views about people's reactions to their appearance and behavior. As adolescents become more open to the opinions of others, their egocentrism puts them in an emotional bind—eager for lively intellectual interaction but vulnerable to self-doubt. Adolescents' cognitive immaturity makes it difficult for them to make rational decisions about many personal and emotionally charged issues, including sexuality.

In the psychosocial domain of development, adolescence brings the dawning of commitment to a personal identity and future, to other people, and to ideologies. The central psychosocial challenge of adolescence is the search for identity, both as an individual and as a member of the larger community. When the search for identity becomes overwhelming and confusing, adolescents may experience an identity crisis. Friends, family, community, and culture are powerful forces that act to help or hinder the adolescent's transition from childhood to adulthood. The peer group is a social institution that eases the transition from childhood to adulthood by functioning as a source of information and a self-help group of contemporaries who are experiencing similar struggles, and by serving as a sounding board for exploring and defining one's values and aspirations.

Answer Key

Practice Questions

Multiple-Choice Questions

1. c. is the correct answer. (objective 1)

   a. is incorrect. Although some adolescents become overweight, many diet and lose weight in an effort to attain a desired body image.

   d. is incorrect. On the contrary, cultural attitudes about beauty are an extremely influential factor in the formation of a teenager's body image.
2. c. is the correct answer. (objective 1)
3. b. is the correct answer. (objective 1)
4. a. is the correct answer. (objective 1)
5. b. is the correct answer. (objective 1)
6. c. is the correct answer. (video lesson, segments 1 & 3; objective 2)

   a. is incorrect. Although moral reasoning becomes much deeper during adolescence, it is not limited to this stage of development.

   b. & d. are incorrect. Concrete operational thought, which is logical, is the distinguishing feature of childhood thinking.

7. a. is the correct answer. (video lesson, segment 2; objective 2)

   b. is incorrect. This refers to adolescents' tendency to imagine their own lives as unique, heroic, or even mythical.

   c. is incorrect. This refers to adolescents' tendency to fantasize about how others will react to their appearance and behavior.

   d. is incorrect. This is a concept in Freud's theory.

8. d. is the correct answer. These thought processes are manifestations of adolescents' tendency to see themselves as being much more central and important to the social scene than they really are. (video lesson, segments 1, 2, & 3; objective 2)

9. a. is the correct answer. (objective 2)

10. c. is the correct answer. (objective 2)

11. d. is the correct answer. (video lesson, segment 1; objective 3)

12. d. is the correct answer. (video lesson, segments 1 & 3; objective 3)

13. d. is the correct answer. (lesson, segments 1 & 2; objective 3)

14. a. is the correct answer. (video lesson, segment 1; objective 3)

    b. is incorrect. In fact, just the opposite is true.

    c. is incorrect. Developmentalists recommend authoritative, rather than authoritarian, parenting.

    d. is incorrect. Parental monitoring is important for all adolescents.

True or False Items

15. T (objective 1)
16. T (objective 1)
17. F These habits generally worsen during adolescence. (objective 1)
18. T (objective 2)
19. F Deductive reasoning is a hallmark of formal operational thought. (video lesson, segment 1; objective 2)
20. T (objective 3)
21. F Just the opposite is true. (video lesson, segment 1; objective 3)

Lesson Review

Lesson 24

Adolescence
Summary

Please Note: Use this matrix to guide your study and achieve the learning objectives of this lesson. It will also help you to view the video, which defines and demonstrates important concepts and skills as they relate to everyday life.

Learning Objective	**Textbook**	**Course Student Guide**	**Video Lesson**
1. Describe biosocial development during adolescence, focusing on the impact of puberty and sexual maturation on teenagers.	pp. 411–435	Key Terms: 1, 2, 3, 4, 5; Practice Questions: 1, 2, 3, 4, 5, 15, 16, 17.	Segment 2 *Bayleigh*
2. Explain how thinking changes during adolescence and discuss the impact of these changes on adolescent decision making.	pp. 442–450	Key Terms: 6, 7, 8, 9, 10, 11, 12, 20; Practice Questions: 6, 7, 8, 9, 10, 18, 19.	Segment 1: *Ashley* Segment 2: *Bayleigh* Segment 3: *Alejandro*
3. Discuss psychosocial development during adolescence, focusing on the formation of identity and the influence of parents, mentors and the peer group.	pp. 472–485	Key Terms: 12, 13, 14, 15, 16, 17, 18, 19; Practice Questions: 11, 12, 13, 14, 20, 21.	Segment 1: *Ashley* Segment 2: *Bayleigh* Segment 3: *Alejandro*

Crashing Hard Into Adulthood

Lesson 25

Adolescence:
Special Topic

Preview

Although the expanding world of the teen years is filled with opportunities for growth, it can also present challenges and potential problems. This lesson discusses a few of the more significant challenges that some children and adolescents face in our society, including poverty, abuse, and parental neglect. Kids who face problems like these are often called "at-risk" because they are more vulnerable to a range of negative outcomes such as unwanted pregnancy, drug abuse, and delinquency.

But, research reveals that many "at-risk" children are able to deal with their challenges and live happy and successful lives as adults. Experts call this **resilience**, the ability to adapt and succeed in the face of adversity. Particularly important to a teen's ability to cope with problems are his or her competencies and networks of social support. With the help of positive role models and community-based intervention programs, even teenagers who have grown up under the most adverse circumstances may be sufficiently resilient and resourceful to cope with the stresses they face in life.

As you complete this lesson, think of any child or teenager you know about who has faced considerable stress or hardship in his or her life. How old is the child? What were the challenges that he or she faced? What kind of support did this child find at home? What help did he or she find outside the home? Speculate on how situations like this might be prevented.

Prior Knowledge That Will Be Used in This Lesson

- This lesson will return to the concepts of hypothetical thought, adolescent egocentrism and the invincibility fable (from Lesson 22) as it explores the relationship between adolescent thinking and high-risk behaviors. Recall that people who believe the invincibility fable think that nothing bad will happen to them.
- The concepts of false self, negative identity and peer pressure (from Lesson 23) will be discussed. A negative identity is taken on with rebellious defiance because it is the opposite of what parents or society expect.

Learning Objectives

Use this information to guide your reading, viewing, thinking, and studying. After successfully completing this lesson, you should be able to:

1. Identify the essential ways that functional families nurture children and teenagers.
2. Describe the impact of poverty, homelessness, and other adverse conditions on the development of children, and discuss ways adults can help them cope with these problems.
3. Describe the prevalence of sexual abuse in adolescence and its consequences for development.
4. Explain how adolescent thinking and decision making often promotes high-risk behaviors such as unprotected sex, drug use, and delinquency.
5. Discuss delinquency among adolescents today, noting its prevalence, and significance for later development.

Textbook Reading & Video Viewing

For the most effective study of this lesson, complete the assignments in the sequence listed below.

Before viewing the video program:

Review Chapter 13, "Middle Childhood: Psychosocial Development," pages 386–394 ("Diversity of Structures," "Family Trouble"); Chapter 14, "Adolescence: Biosocial Development," pages 427–431 (" Problems with Adolescent Sex,"); Chapter 15, "Adolescence: Cognitive Development," pages 439–448 ("Logic and Self," "Two Modes of Thinking"); Chapter 16, "Adolescence: Psychosocial Development," pages 494–496 ("Delinquency and Disobedience").

View the video for Lesson 25, "Crashing Hard Into Adulthood."

Segment 1: *Getting Off Track*

Segment 2: *Getting Back On Track*

After viewing the video program:

Review all reading assignments for this lesson.

Complete the "Practice Questions" section to reinforce your understanding of important terms and concepts and measure your achievement of the Learning Objectives. Check your answers with the feedback given and review when necessary.

Practice Questions

Multiple-Choice Questions

1. Which of the following is **NOT** identified as one of the basic elements that healthy families provide to a teenager's life?
   a. assistance in building the child's self-esteem
   b. a stable context in which to develop
   c. physical discipline
   d. monitoring peer relations
2. Teens are said to be "at risk" when
   a. one or more elements of healthy family function are missing in their lives.
   b. they experiment with "gateway" drugs.
   c. they join cliques or gangs.
   d. they establish their own "society of children."
3. The best strategy for helping children who are at risk of developing serious psychological problems because of multiple stresses would be to
   a. obtain assistance from a psychiatrist.
   b. increase the child's competencies or social supports.
   c. change the household situation.
   d. reduce the peer group's influence.
4. Older schoolchildren tend to be ______________ vulnerable to the stresses of life than children who are just beginning middle childhood because they ________________.
   a. more; tend to overpersonalize their problems
   b. less; have better developed coping skills
   c. more; are more likely to compare their well-being with that of their peers
   d. less; are less egocentric
5. Which of the following was **NOT** identified as a pivotal issue in determining whether divorce or some other problem will adversely affect a child during the school years?
   a. how many other stresses the child is already experiencing
   b. how many protective buffers are in place
   c. how much the stress affects the child's daily life
   d. the specific structure of the child's family

6. One factor that most often helps the child cope well with multiple stresses is social support and
   a. social comparison.
   b. competence in a specific area.
   c. remedial education.
   d. referral to mental health professionals.
7. Research studies have found that, as compared to children without major stress, children who are forced to cope with one serious ongoing stress (for example, poverty or large family size) are
   a. more likely to develop serious psychiatric problems.
   b. no more likely to develop problems.
   c. more likely to develop intense, destructive friendships.
   d. less likely to be accepted by their peer group.
8. The adolescent who takes risks and feels immune to the laws of mortality is showing evidence of the
   a. invincibility fable.
   b. personal fable.
   c. imaginary audience.
   d. death instinct.
9. The tendency to focus only on the pleasant outcomes of risky behaviors is an expression of adolescent
   a. morality.
   b. thinking games.
   c. decision-making.
   d. egocentrism.
10. Many adolescents seem to believe that their lovemaking will not lead to pregnancy. This belief is an expression of the
    a. personal fable.
    b. invincibility fable.
    c. imaginary audience.
    d. "volatile mismatch."
11. Adolescents who grow up in poverty or other severely adverse conditions may be more likely to
    a. engage in risky behaviors.
    b. feel worthless.
    c. have low self-esteem.
    d. experience all of the above.

12. For many teenage girls who become pregnant, pregnancy is
    a. not planned.
    b. not avoided.
    c. based on their need to find somebody to give them universal love.
    d. characterized by all of the above.

Key Terms

1. **family function:** The ways in which a family nurtures and supports its children so they can reach the full potential of their physical, cognitive and psychosocial development. (p. 385; objective 1)
2. **family structure:** The legal and genetic relationships among members of a particular family. Children can thrive in almost any family structure. (p. 385; objective 1)
3. **resilience:** A dynamic process including positive adaptation in the context of significant adversity. (p. 380; video lesson, segment 1; objective 2)
4. **nuclear family:** A family that consists of a father, a mother and their biological children under 18. (p. 387; objective 1)
5. **child sexual abuse:** Any activity in which an adult uses a child for his or her sexual pleasure. (p. 430; objective 3)
6. **single-parent family:** A family that consists of one parent and his or her biological children under 18. (p. 387; objective 1)
7. **extended family:** A family of three or more generations living in one household. (p. 387; objective 1)
8. **adolescence-limited offender:** A person whose criminal activity stops by age 21. (p. 495; objective 5)
9. **life-course-persistent offender:** A person whose criminal activity begins in adolescence and continues through life; a career criminal. (p. 495; objective 5)
10. **blended family:** A stepparent family that includes children born to several families, such as biological children from spouses' previous marriages and the biological children of the new couple. (p. 388; objective 1)
11. **sexually transmitted infection (STI):** Disease spread by sexual contact; STIs include syphilis, gonorrhea, genital herpes, chlamydia, and HIV. (p. 429; objective 3)
12. **dual-process model:** The notion that two networks exist within the human brain, one for emotional and one for analytical processing of stimuli. (p. 456; objective 4)
13. **intuitive thought:** Thought that arises from an emotion or a hunch, beyond rational explanation and is influenced by past experiences and cultural assumptions. (p. 456; objective 4)
14. **analytic thought:** Thought that results from analysis, such as a systematic ranking of pros and cons, risks and consequences, possibilities and facts. Analytic thought depends on logic and rationality. (p. 456; objective 4)

Summary

Healthy families provide for children's basic needs; they encourage and monitor peer relations, encourage and foster education, help to build the teen's self-esteem, and provide a stable context in which development can occur.

Teens who are faced with the adversity of **child sexual abuse**, violence, poverty, or negligent parents are "at risk" and face special challenges as they move into adulthood. Fortunately, social programs directed toward at-risk teens can provide the support and context that may be missing in the individual's life.

Family structure refers to the legal and genetic relationships between members of a particular family. Traditional nuclear families are not the only structures in which healthy development of children can occur. However, when the family breaks up, as in divorce or separation, children lose the harmony and stability they need.

Children who have been sexually abused at a young age, and especially those who have been abused by trusted caregivers, often experience a loss of self-esteem and do not see themselves as worthwhile individuals. Later, they may find intimate relationships difficult to establish.

Adolescent egocentrism, feelings of invincibility, and an inability to extend their newly found powers of hypothetical reasoning to all areas of their lives can explain why high-risk behaviors are particularly likely to occur during the teenage years.

The likelihood that a given stress will produce psychological fallout depends on the number of stresses the child is experiencing concurrently and on the degree to which these stresses affect the overall patterns of the child's daily life, and how many protective barriers and coping patterns are in place.

A child who is at risk because of poor parenting, difficult temperament, or poverty is likely to still be at risk as an adolescent. Particularly important to a teenager's **resilience** are his or her competencies—especially social, academic, and creative skills. Competencies boost self-esteem and often enable the child to employ various practical coping strategies. For this reason, older children are generally less vulnerable to the stresses of life than are children who are just beginning middle childhood.

Schools and teachers play a significant role in the development of competence. Another important element that helps children deal with problems is the social support they receive from friends, relatives, pets, or their religious faith and practice. Positive role models and mentors often play an important role in triggering children's native spark of resiliency. Teenagers who have grown up under adverse conditions since early childhood may need to learn new social skills to become healthy, productive adults.

Effective intervention programs often take a psychosocial approach in which the family, the school, the community, peers, and the individual him- or herself interact. Research studies show that high expectations are a hallmark of children who do well in school and in life.

Answer Key

Practice Questions

Multiple-Choice Questions

1. c. is the correct answer. (video lesson, segment 1; objective 1)
2. a. is the correct answer. (video lesson, segment 1; objective 1)
3. c. is the correct answer. (video lesson, segment 1; objective 2)
4. b. is the correct answer. (objective 2)
5. d. is the correct answer. (objective 2)
6. b. is the correct answer. (objective 2)
7. b. is the correct answer. (objective 2)

   c. & d. are incorrect. The lesson did not discuss how stress influences friendship or peer acceptance.
8. a. is the correct answer. (video lesson, segment 1; objective 4)

   b. is incorrect. This refers to adolescents' tendency to imagine their own lives as unique, heroic, or even mythical.

   c. is incorrect. This refers to adolescents' tendency to fantasize about how others will react to their appearance and behavior.

   d. is incorrect. This is a concept in Freud's theory.
9. d. is the correct answer. These thought processes are manifestations of adolescents' tendency to see themselves as being much more central and important to the social scene than they really are. (video lesson, segment 1; objective 4)
10. b. is the correct answer. (video lesson, segment 1; objective 4)

    a. is incorrect. This refers to adolescents' tendency to imagine their own lives as unique, heroic, or even mythical.

    c. is incorrect. This refers to adolescents' tendency to fantasize about how others will react to their appearance and behavior.

    d. is incorrect. This is the adolescent ability to suspend knowledge of reality in order to think playfully about possibilities.
11. d. is the correct answer. (video lesson, segment 1; objective 2)
12. d. is the correct answer. (video lesson, segment 1; objective 4)

Lesson Review

Lesson 25

Adolescence
Special Topic

Please Note: Use this matrix to guide your study and achieve the learning objectives of this lesson. It will also help you to view the video, which defines and demonstrates important concepts and skills as they relate to everyday life.

Learning Objective	Textbook	Course Student Guide	Video Lesson
1. Identify the essential ways that functional families nurture children and teenagers.	pp. 384–392	Key Terms: 1, 2, 4, 6, 7, 10; Practice Questions: 1, 2.	all segments
2. Describe the impact of poverty, homelessness, and other adverse conditions on the development of children, and discuss ways adults can help them cope with these problems.	pp. 390–395	Key Terms: 3; Practice Questions: 3, 4, 5, 6, 7, 11.	all segments
3. Describe the prevalence of sexual abuse in adolescence and its consequences for development.	pp. 429–430	Key Terms: 5, 11.	all segments
4. Explain how adolescent thinking and decision making often promotes high-risk behaviors such as unprotected sex, drug use, and delinquency.	pp. 440–442, 445–450	Key Terms: 12, 13, 14; Practice Questions: 8, 9, 10, 12.	all segments
5. Discuss delinquency among adolescents today, noting its prevalence, and significance for later development.	pp. 494–496	Key Terms: 8, 9.	all segments

Different Paths

Lesson 26

Closing:
Developmental Psychopathologies

Preview

For most boys and girls, the years of infancy, childhood, and adolescence are a time when biosocial development is smooth and uneventful. Body maturation coupled with sufficient practice enables the mastery of many motor skills. Most children follow similar paths as they grow and mature. But what about children who are born with serious disorders and disabilities? How is their development affected and what can be done to assist them?

These and related questions are the focus of this lesson, which introduces Timmy, Jonathan, and Amelia—three children born with special needs. In this final lesson, we revisit several of the major developmental themes that have guided our investigation of the biosocial, cognitive, and psychosocial changes from conception through adolescence. As we learn more about normal child development, *all* children can benefit, especially those whose developmental journey follows a different path.

Prior Knowledge That Will Be Used in This Lesson

- In its focus on children with special needs, this lesson will revisit the *developmental psychopathology* perspective (from Lesson 16). Recall that this approach uses what we know about typical development in the diagnosis and treatment of various disabilities and disorders.
- This lesson will also return to the process of *operant conditioning* (from Lesson 1). As you'll learn, this technique—sometimes called "behavior modification"—is used successfully with children who have certain disorders.
- The notions of *theory of mind* (Lesson 12) and *emotional regulation*, *self-concept*, and *self-esteem* (from Lesson 13) will be discussed as the lesson examines how different disabilities and disorders can affect a child's cognitive and psychosocial development.

Learning Objectives

Use this information to guide your reading, viewing, thinking, and studying. After successfully completing this lesson, you should be able to:

1. Explain the developmental psychopathology perspective, and discuss its value in treating children with special needs.
2. Identify the symptoms of tuberous sclerosis, autism, autistic spectrum disorder, Asperger syndrome, and epilepsy, and describe the most effective treatments for these disorders.
3. Summarize the characteristics of learning disabilities.
4. Describe the symptoms and possible causes of ADHD (attention-deficit/ hyperactivity disorder) and summarize various treatments available for children with this disorder.
5. Describe techniques that have been tried in efforts to educate children with special needs.

Textbook Reading & Video Viewing

For the most effective study of this lesson, complete the assignments in the sequence listed below.

Before viewing the video program:

Review Chapter 11, "Middle Childhood: Biosocial Development," pages 337–347.

View the video for Lesson 26, "Different Paths."

Segment 1: *Timmy*

Segment 2: *Jonathan*

Segment 3: *Amelia*

After viewing the video program:

Review all reading assignments for this lesson.

Complete the "Practice Questions" and "Applying Your Knowledge" sections to reinforce your understanding of important terms and concepts and measure your achievement of the Learning Objectives. Check your answers with the feedback given and review when necessary.

Practice Questions I

Multiple-Choice Questions

1. Dyslexia is a learning disability that primarily affects the ability to

   a. do math.

   b. read.

   c. focus attention.

   d. speak.

2. The developmental psychopathology perspective is characterized by its
   a. contextual approach.
   b. emphasis on individual therapy.
   c. emphasis on the cognitive domain of development.
   d. concern with all of the above.
3. The underlying problem in attention-deficit/hyperactivity disorder is
   a. low overall intelligence.
   b. a brain abnormality resulting in difficulty paying attention.
   c. a learning disability in a specific academic skill.
   d. the existence of a conduct disorder.
4. Comorbidity refers to
   a. the presence of more than one disorder in one person at the same time
   b. the teaching of special needs children in a special classroom.
   c. the teaching of special needs children with other children in a regular classroom.
   d. the lifelong struggle in psychological development that special needs children often face.
5. Autistic children generally have severe deficiencies in all **EXCEPT**
   a. social skills.
   b. imaginative play.
   c. gross motor skills.
   d. communication ability.
6. Psychoactive drugs are most effective in treating attention-deficit/hyperactivity disorder when they are administered
   a. before the diagnosis becomes certain.
   b. for several years after the basic problem has abated.
   c. as part of the labeling process.
   d. with psychological support or therapy.
7. Tuberous sclerosis is a chronic illness that can affect the ability to
   a. do math and write.
   b. read.
   c. pick up social cues from others.
   d. do all of the above.

8. When developmentalists say that autism is a spectrum disorder, they mean that
   a. its effects can range from mild to severe.
   b. it is treated most effectively with medication.
   c. the prognosis for recovery is slim.
   d. the disorder advances very rapidly.

9. At the time the video lesson was produced, four out of five children diagnosed with autism
   a. were boys.
   b. were girls.
   c. were undernourished.
   d. were born prematurely.

10. The neurological disorder in which a synchronized discharge of electricity occurs in one part or all of the brain is
    a. epilepsy.
    b. tuberous sclerosis.
    c. Tay-Sachs syndrome.
    d. fragile-X syndrome.

11. Autistic children are often taught scripts for how to behave in new, or difficult, situations. These scripts are called
    a. social stories.
    b. memes.
    c. discreet trials.
    d. zones of proximal development.

True or False Items

Write T (for true) or F (for false) on the line in front of each statement.

12. _____ Despite the efforts of teachers and parents, most children with learning disabilities can expect their disabilities to persist and even worsen as they enter adulthood.

13. _____ Early speech therapy might improve talking and reduce later reading problems in children with dyslexia.

14. _____ ADHD is considered a mainly neurological disorder.

15. _____ The drugs sometimes given to children are most effective in combination with counseling and adequate teacher training .

16. _____ For serious disorders such as autism, parents typically play only a small role in their children's developmental progress.

Practice Questions II

Multiple-Choice Questions

1. Autism is known as a pervasive developmental disorder because it
   a. affects all developmental domains.
   b. significantly impairs the psychosocial developmental domain.
   c. is present only during the early stages of development.
   d. accelerates development in every domain.

2. Specific problems in learning to write, to read, or to do math are collectively referred to as
   a. learning disabilities.
   b. attention-deficit/hyperactivity disorder.
   c. hyperactivity.
   d. dyscalculia.

3. The most effective form of help for children with ADHD is
   a. medication.
   b. psychological therapy.
   c. environmental change.
   d. a combination of some or all of the above.

4. The earliest noticeable symptoms of autism usually include
   a. the lack of spoken language.
   b. abnormal social responsiveness.
   c. both a. and b.
   d. unpredictable.

5. Which of the following is true of children with a diagnosed learning disability?
   a. Their aptitude is significantly higher than their achievement in that particular area.
   b. They often have a specific physical handicap, such as hearing loss.
   c. They often lack basic educational experiences.
   d. All of the above are true.

6. Which approach to education may best meet the needs of children with learning disabilities in terms of both skill remediation and social interaction with other children?
   a. mainstreaming
   b. special education
   c. inclusion
   d. resource rooms

7. Asperger syndrome is a disorder in which
    a. body weight fluctuates dramatically over short periods of time.
    b. verbal skills seem normal, but social perceptions and skills are abnormal.
    c. an autistic child is extremely aggressive.
    d. a child of normal intelligence has difficulty in mastering a specific cognitive skill.
8. Which of the following is **NOT** a lesson provided by developmental psychopathology?
    a. Adolescence and adulthood make disabilities worse.
    b. Abnormality is normal.
    c. Diagnosis depends on the social context.
    d. Disability changes over time.
9. The disorder characterized by difficulties in social interaction and verbal and nonverbal communication is
    a. epilepsy.
    b. autism.
    c. tuberous sclerosis.
    d. fragile-X syndrome.
10. One of the most effective interventions for children with autism is
    a. traditional psychotherapy.
    b. antipsychotic medication.
    c. behavior modification.
    d. none of the above.
11. The Picture Exchange Communication System (PECS) is designed to help children who
    a. are blind learn to read Braille.
    b. are autistic learn to communicate more effectively.
    c. are epileptic learn to control the severity of their seizures.
    d. have all of the above conditions succeed in life.

Matching Items

Match each definition or description with its corresponding term.

Terms

12. __________ dyslexia
13. __________ epilepsy
14. __________ mental retardation
15. __________ attention-deficit/hyperactivity disorder
16. __________ developmental psychopathology
17. __________ autism
18. __________ social story
19. __________ Braille
20. __________ learning disability
21. __________ inclusion

Definitions or Descriptions

a. speech that repeats, word for word, what has just been heard
b. a written language for the blind
c. a pervasive delay in cognitive development
d. system in which children with special needs receive individualized instruction within a regular classroom setting
e. disorder characterized by the absence of a theory of mind
f. a mental script to help children with special needs prepare for new events
g. behavior problem involving difficulty in concentrating, as well as excitability and impulsivity
h. a neurological disorder in which a synchronized discharge of electricity in one part or all of the brain makes it malfunction for the duration of the seizure
i. applies insights from studies of normal development to the study of childhood disorders
j. an unexpected difficulty with a particular area of learning
k. difficulty in reading

Applying Your Knowledge

1. Dr. Rutter, who believes that "we can learn more about an organism's normal functioning by studying its pathology and, likewise, more about its pathology by studying its normal condition," evidently is working from which of the following perspectives?
   a. clinical psychology
   b. developmental psychopathology
   c. behaviorism
   d. psychoanalysis

2. Nine-year-old Paul, who lives in the United States, has difficulty concentrating on his class work for more than a few moments, repeatedly asks his teacher irrelevant questions, and is constantly disrupting the class with loud noises. If his difficulties persist, Paul is likely to be diagnosed as suffering from
   a. dyslexia.
   b. epilepsy.
   c. conduct disorder.
   d. attention-deficit/hyperactivity disorder.

3. Ten-year-old Clarence is inattentive, easily frustrated, and highly impulsive. Clarence may be suffering from
   a. dyslexia.
   b. Rett syndrome.
   c. autism.
   d. attention-deficit/hyperactivity disorder.
4. In determining whether an eight-year-old has a learning disability, a teacher looks primarily for
   a. discrepant performance in a particular subject area.
   b. the exclusion of other explanations.
   c. both a and b.
   d. none of the above.
5. In the United States, bipolar disorder is frequently comorbid with and sometimes mistaken for which of the following diagnoses?
   a. dyslexia
   b. autism
   c. ADHD
   d. epilepsy
6. In the video lesson, doctors removed a large portion of Jonathan's left hemisphere in order to prevent
   a. epileptic seizures.
   b. blindness.
   c. autism.
   d. self-destructive behaviors.
7. Danny has been diagnosed as having attention-deficit/hyperactivity disorder. Every day his parents make sure that he takes the proper dose of Ritalin. His parents should
   a. continue this behavior until Danny is an adult.
   b. try different medications when Danny seems to be reverting to his normal overactive behavior.
   c. make sure that Danny also has psychotherapy.
   d. not worry about Danny's condition; he will outgrow it.
8. Behavior modification for children with autism focuses on teaching them
   a. how to make eye contact.
   b. how to respond to speech.
   c. how to interact with other people.
   d. all of the above.

9. Discrete trial training is a form of
   a. biomedical therapy for autistic children.
   b. teaching Braille.
   c. prenatal genetic counseling.
   d. behavior modification that breaks things down into small steps that are individually taught.

Key Terms

1. **children with special needs:** Children who require particular physical, intellectual, or social accommodations in order to learn. (pp. 337–338; objective 1)
2. **individual education plan (IEP):** A legal document that specifies a set of educational goals for a child with special needs. (p. 345; objectives 1 & 5)
3. **developmental psychopathology:** The field that applies the insights from studies of normal development to the study and treatment of childhood disorders. (p. 337; video lesson, introduction; objective 1)
4. **autism spectrum disorder:** Any of several disorders characterized by inadequate social skills, impaired communication, and unusual play. (p. 342; objective 2)
5. **autism:** A developmental disorder marked by an inability to relate to other people normally, extreme self-absorption, and an inability to acquire normal speech. (p. 342; video lesson, segment 1; objective 2)
6. **learning disability:** A difficulty in a particular cognitive skill that is not attributable to overall intellectual slowness, a physical handicap, a severely stressful living condition, or a lack of basic education. (p. 341; objective 3)
7. **dyslexia:** A learning disability in reading. (p. 341; objective 3)
8. **comorbidity:** The presence of more than one disorder in a person at the same time. (p. 338; objectives 1 & 3)
9. **ADHD (attention-deficit/hyperactivity disorder):** A behavior problem in which the individual has great difficulty concentrating, is often excessively excitable and impulsive, and is sometimes aggressive. (p. 338; objective 4)
10. **least restrictive environment (LRE):** A legally required school setting that allows children with special needs to benefit from the instruction available to other children, often in a mainstreamed classroom. (p. 344; objective 5)
11. **tuberous sclerosis:** A genetic disorder in which lesions develop on the brain, often triggering seizures and autistic behaviors. (video lesson, segment 1; objective 2)
12. **behavior modification:** The goal of operant conditioning that focuses on eliminating undesirable behaviors and establishing new, desirable ones, through the use of reinforcement, time outs, and other environmental consequences. (video lesson, segment 1; objective 2)

13. **social story:** A mental script that children with special needs can practice to prepare for and deal with new and difficult events and situations. (video lesson, segment 1; objectives 2 & 5)
14. **Picture Exchange Communication System (PECS):** A visual tool that helps autistic children develop speech and language. (video lesson, segment 1; objectives 2 & 5)
15. **epilepsy:** A neurological disorder in which a synchronized discharge of electricity in one part or all of the brain makes it malfunction for the duration of the seizure. (video lesson, segment 2; objective 2)
16. **Braille:** A system of tactile or touch reading for people who are blind which used a series of embossed dots arranged in quadrangular letter spaces or cells. (video lesson, segment 3; objective 5)

Summary

For the most part, childhood and adolescence are a time of relatively smooth development. For many children, however, the growth of new motor skills, social relationships, and ways of thinking is encumbered by a physical or mental disability. This lesson pays special attention to the causes, effects and treatments of disorders and disabilities such as **autism**, **epilepsy**, and blindness.

The field of **developmental psychopathology** applies insights from studies of normal development to the origins and treatment of childhood disorders, and vice versa. The *Diagnostic and Statistical Manual of Mental Disorders* (DSM-IV-TR) recognizes that each child's cultural frame of reference needs to be understood before any disorder can be diagnosed.

Autism is known as a *pervasive developmental disorder* because it can produce a range of different effects across the biosocial, cognitive and psychosocial domains. Autism is also known as a *spectrum disorder*, because its effects can range from mild to severe. Autistic children are unable, unwilling, or uninterested in communicating with or understanding others; they are often mute; they do not engage in imaginative play; and they typically score in the mentally retarded range of intellectual performance. On the other end of the autism spectrum is Asperger syndrome, a disorder in which a person has unusual difficulty with social perceptions and skills but has near normal communication skills and typically average to above-average intelligence.

Autism is typically detected very early in life, when deficiencies in communication abilities, social skills, and imaginative play first appear. Unaffected by the opinions of others, autistic children usually lack *emotional regulation*. The social disinterest of autistic children has caused some researchers to speculate that autistic children lack a *theory of mind*—that is, the awareness that psychological processes exist in other people. Twin studies make it clear that genetic factors play a role in autism. However, genes are not the whole story. In all likelihood, a genetic vulnerability in combination with either prenatal or early postnatal damage leads to autism. The most successful treatment for autism usually combines long-term behavior therapy with individual attention.

As you learned in Lesson 16, specific **learning disabilities** are said to exist when a child has no apparent physical problem, is not intellectually slow, does not live in severely stressful conditions, and does not lack basic education, but nevertheless has difficulty mastering academic skills such as reading (**dyslexia**), math (dyscalculia), spelling, or writing. The criteria for diagnosing a learning disability include disparity between expected performance on a given skill and actual performance and exclusion of other possible explanations, such as abuse, biological disability, or poor teaching.

One of the most puzzling childhood problems is **attention-deficit/hyperactivity disorder (ADHD)** in which the child has great difficulty concentrating for more than a few moments at a time and is almost always in motion. A child with ADHD is unusually impulsive, distractible, and sometimes aggressive. ADHD children seem to have a neurological difficulty in paying attention. Estimates of the prevalence of ADHD vary from 1 to 5 percent, in part because the diagnostic criteria vary from nation to nation. Four times as many boys as girls have this disorder.

Answer Key

Practice Questions I

Multiple-Choice Questions

1. b. is the correct answer. (objective 3)

   a., c., & d. are incorrect. The textbook does not give labels for learning disabilities in math, writing, or speaking.
2. d. is the correct answer. (video lesson, introduction; objective 1)
3. b. is the correct answer. (objective 4)
4. a. is the correct answer. (objectives 1 & 3)
5. c. is the correct answer. (video lesson, segment 1; objective 2)
6. d. is the correct answer. (objective 4)
7. d. is the correct answer. (video lesson, segment 1; objective 2)
8. a. is the correct answer. (video lesson, segment 1; objectives 1 & 2)
9. a. is the correct answer. (video lesson, segment 1; objective 2)

   c. & d. are incorrect. These risk factors were not linked to autism in the lesson.
10. a. is the correct answer. (video lesson, segment 2; objective 2)

    b. is incorrect. Although this disorder is linked to developmental deficits in every domain, it is not characterized by electrical discharges in the brain.
11. a. is the correct answer (video lesson, segment 1; objectives 2 & 5)

    b. & d. are incorrect. These terms not used in the lesson.

    c. is incorrect. Discrete trial training is a technique for systematically teaching children with special needs.

True or False Items

12. F With the proper assistance, many children with learning disabilities develop into adults who are virtually indistinguishable from other adults in their educational and occupational achievements. (objectives 3 & 5)
13. T (objective 3)
14. T (objective 4)
15. T (objective 5)
16. F Parents and other caregivers play a major role in the developmental progress of children with special needs. (video lesson, segments 1, 2, & 3; objectives 1, 2, & 5)

Practice Questions II

Multiple-Choice Questions

1. a. is the correct answer. (objective 2)
2. a. is the correct answer. (objective 3)

   b. & c. are incorrect. ADHD is a general learning disability that usually does not manifest itself in specific subject areas. Hyperactivity is a facet of this disorder.

   d. is incorrect. Dyscalculia is a learning disability in math only.
3. d. is the correct answer. (objective 4)
4. c. is the correct answer. (video lesson, segment 1; objective 2)
5. a. is the correct answer. (objective 3)
6. c. is the correct answer. (objective 5)

   a. is incorrect. Many general education teachers are unable to cope with the special needs of some children.

   b. & d. are incorrect. These approaches undermine the social integration of children with special needs.
7. b. is the correct answer. (objective 2)
8. a. is the correct answer. Adolescence and adulthood can make disabilities better or worse. (objective 4)
9. b. is the correct answer. (video lesson, segment 1; objective 2)

   a. is incorrect. Epilepsy is characterized by seizures.

   c. is incorrect. Although many children with tuberous sclerosis become autistic, some do not, and therefore do not develop these symptoms of autism.

   d. is incorrect. This disorder was not discussed.
10. c. is the correct answer. (video lesson, segment 1; objectives 2 & 5)
11. b. is the correct answer. (video lesson, segment 1; objectives 2 & 5)

Matching Items

12. k (objective 3)
13. h (video lesson, segment 2; objective 3)
14. c (objectives 1 & 3)

15. g (objective 4)
16. i (video lesson, introduction; objective 1)
17. e (video lesson, segment 1; objective 2)
18. f (video lesson, segment 1; objective 5)
19. b (objective 5)
20. j (objective 3)
21. d (objective 5)

Applying Your Knowledge

1. b. is the correct answer. (video lesson, introduction; objective 1)
2. d. is the correct answer. (objective 4)

   a. & b. are incorrect. Jack's difficulty is in concentrating, not in reading (dyslexia) or the result of seizures (epilepsy).

   c. is incorrect. Autism is characterized by a lack of communication skills.
3. d. is the correct answer. (objective 4)
4. d. is the correct answer. (objective 3)
5. c. is the correct answer. (objective 4)
6. a. is the correct answer. (video lesson, segment 2; objective 2)
7. c. is the correct answer. Medication alone cannot ameliorate all the problems of ADHD. (objective 4)
8. d. is the correct answer. (video lesson, segment 1; objectives 2 & 5)
9. d. is the correct answer. (video lesson, segment 1; objective 5)

   a. is incorrect. Discrete trial training is a form of behavior therapy.

Lesson Review

Lesson 26

Closing
Developmental Psychopathologies

Please Note: Use this matrix to guide your study and achieve the learning objectives of this lesson. It will also help you to view the video, which defines and demonstrates important concepts and skills as they relate to everyday life.

Learning Objective	Textbook	Course Student Guide	Video Lesson
1. Explain the developmental psychopathology perspective, and discuss its value in treating children with special needs.	pp. 337–338	Key Terms: 1, 2, 3, 8; Practice Questions I: 2, 4, 8, 16; Practice Questions II: 16; Applying Your Knowledge: 1.	Introduction all segments
2. Identify the symptoms of tuberous sclerosis, autism, autism spectrum disorder, Asperger syndrome, and epilepsy, and describe the most effective treatment for these disorders.	pp. 342–344	Key Terms: 4, 5, 11, 12, 13, 14, 15; Practice Questions I: 5, 7, 8, 9, 10, 11, 16; Practice Questions II: 1, 4, 7, 9, 10, 11, 17; Applying Your Knowledge: 6, 8.	Segment 1: *Timmy* Segment 2: *Jonathan* Segment 3: *Amelia*
3. Discuss the characteristics of learning disabilities.	pp. 341–342	Key Terms: 6, 7, 8; Practice Questions I: 1, 4, 12, 13; Practice Questions II: 2, 5, 12, 13, 14, 20; Applying Your Knowledge: 4.	
4. Describe the symptoms and possible causes of ADHD (attention-deficit/hyperactivity disorder) and summarize the various treatments available for children with this disorder.	pp. 338–341	Key Terms: 9; Practice Questions I: 3, 6, 14; Practice Questions II: 3, 8, 15; Applying Your Knowledge: 2, 3, 5, 7.	
5. Describe techniques that have been tried in efforts to educate children with special needs.	pp. 344–347	Key Terms: 2, 10, 13, 14, 16; Practice Questions I: 11, 12, 15, 16; Practice Questions II: 6, 10, 11, 18, 19, 21; Applying Your Knowledge: 8, 9.	Segment 1: *Timmy* Segment 2: *Jonathan* Segment 3: *Amelia*